Successful Group Care

Successful Group Care

Explorations in the Powerful Environment

edited by
MARTIN WOLINS
University of California, Berkeley

ALDINE PUBLISHING COMPANY, Chicago

About the Editor

Martin Wolins is Professor in the School of Social Welfare, University of California at Berkeley. He received his B.A. in Psychology and his M.S.W. at the University of California, Berkeley, and his D.S.W. at Columbia University. Previously he was Visiting Professor at Tel Aviv University and Hebrew University, and Director of the University of California Study Center in Jerusalem. He is author of numerous articles on child care and group care. Among his books are *Selecting Foster Parents: The Ideal and the Reality, Institution or Foster Family: A Century of Debate* (with Irving Piliavin), and *Group Care: An Israeli Approach* (edited with Meir Gottesmann).

Copyright © 1974 by Aldine Publishing Company

First published 1974 by
Aldine Publishing Company
529 South Wabash Avenue
Chicago, Illinois 60605

ISBN 0-202-36017-2
Library of Congress Catalog Number 73-75709

Printed in the United States of America

Contents

III. YOUNG CHILDREN IN GROUP CARE

IV. ADOLESCENTS IN GROUP CARE

V. MELIORATIVE ENVIRONMENTS

VI. TWO CHALLENGING PROPOSALS

Contributors

Rivka Arad is Research Associate, Szold Institute for Research in the Behavioral Sciences, Jerusalem.

Scott Briar is Dean, School of Social Work, University of Washington, Seattle.

Urie Bronfenbrenner is Professor of Psychology and of Human Development and Family Studies, Cornell University.

Reuven Feuerstein is Director, Youth Aliyah Child Guidance Clinic, Jerusalem.

Nicholas Hobbs is Provost, Vanderbilt University.

Trova Hutchins is Assistant Professor, School of Social Work, University of Washington, Seattle.

Abram Kardiner is in the Department of Psychiatry, Emory University.

Jeffrey Keefe is Professor of Pastoral Counselling, St. Anthony-on-Hudson, Rensselaer, New York.

David Krasilowski is Director, Psychiatric Services *Kupat Holim* (National Sick Fund), Tel Aviv.

Henry S. Maas is Professor of Social Work, University of British Columbia, Vancouver.

Riley Price is Assistant Professor, School of Social Work, Ohio State University, Columbus.

Chanan Rapaport is Director, Szold Institute for Research in the Behavioral Sciences, Jerusalem.

Richard H. Seiden is Associate Professor of Behavioral Science in Residence, School of Public Health, University of California, Berkeley.

Harold M. Skeels was a Director in the Community Service Branch, National Institutes of Mental Health.

Rene A. Spitz, M.D., is at the University of Colorado Medical Center, Denver.

Elias L. Trotzkey was Executive Director, Marks Nathan Jewish Orphan Home, Chicago.

Albert L. Weeks is Professor of Continuing Education, New York University.

Martin Wolins is Professor of Social Welfare, University of California, Berkeley.

Successful Group Care

Preface

Mention an institution, a group care program, and the image evoked is negative. Erving Goffman's *Asylum,* the horror stories of *Snake Pit,* the pitiful behavior of normal human beings under the stress of prison life—all these and many other carefully documented, regrettable consequences of constricted group life always stand before us. This kind of human community has great power, and it is seen generally as the power to coerce, to deprive the individual of initiative and direction, to instill in him a sense of slavery and mechanical obedience.

Are there no successful socalizing experiences—the positive outcomes of such group environments where the power of a small community is turned to the promotion of a capacity to "love and work"? The present volume attempts to assemble descriptions of such settings, to provide a positive answer to the very crucial question: Can group care be constructive? Obviously it can—sometimes beyond expectations. Some of the conceptions, practices, evidence, and conclusions are here. Hopefully they will provide some balance to what has been such a one-sided view.

MARTIN WOLINS

Introduction

An American professional faced with planning responsibilities for culturally disadvantaged, economically and emotionally impoverished, disturbed and delinquent children has relatively few alternatives for action open to him. He is constrained, inevitably, by financial limitations, existing facilties and programs, theoretical dicta, and, by no means least, his perception of the possible as it is practiced elsewhere. Theoretical and cultural predispositions direct him first toward solving the problem of such children within the context of the family. A professional will claim that every avenue of financial and clinical assistance is to be exhausted before recourse is made to substitution. When compelled to remove the child from his home, he tries to substitute one family for another. Rarely are other settings considered either practical or desirable for such a child.

Over the years the full- and part-time group care programs that have existed in this country have fallen into disuse—an occurrence that most professionals, who saw little good and much evil in their impact on children, greeted with considerable satisfaction. As professionals withdrew their approbation the programs deteriorated; innovation ceased, and cycles of prediction of bad results, and their fulfillment, spiraled the programs downward. With decay the range of alternative settings open to consideration as possibly competent to care for the needy, neglected, or culturally deprived —but not the delinquent or emotionally disturbed—child narrowed to nearly exclude day care and, more totally, institutions of any kind. American thinking on the group care of normal children seems to have frozen with the writings of Homer Folks, who in the late 1880s summarized the prevalent views on institutions versus families that may still be cited as contemporary without much fear of their seeming irrelevant or inappropriate. If a final af-

1

firmation was needed about the rightness of these views, it came from John Bowlby. Group care of normal children was, for all intents and purposes, off the professional's agenda either as a solution to some types of problems or even as a theoretical concern. Like Lamarckian genetics or the demon theory of mental illness, it had been laid to rest.

For several reasons, though, the corpse refused to lie still. There were the "always troublesome Russians" and their fellow communists of East Europe who ran all kinds of group care programs, and claimed successes. Then there were all those group-reared children of the kibbutz who, in the third generation of reproduction and adjusted productivity, appeared to contradict Western theoretical positions. And elsewhere also there were new group care developments that, produced by necessity or fostered by conviction, usually generated controversy and noise faintly audible to the American child care community.

In all likelihood group care controversies and claims on the eastern side of a broad Atlantic would have been ignored here were it not for a leavening of the American position by two types of events: reconsideration of the theoretical and methodological soundness and all-embracing implications of John Bowlby's historic WHO monograph, and the new look at America's deprived and poor. The first opened up this child care issue to theoretical review; the second compelled the conclusion that although ongoing programs may have been meeting some immediate needs they failed to disrupt the hereditary aspects of poverty or deprivation.

As the spirit of Bowlby's work on maternal care and mental health had spread upon the land, and as group care programs were questioned and abandoned, families (natural and foster) could not fully cope with the children who needed care. Rising employment of women, decreasing capability of nuclear, geographically mobile family units to cope with child care in the face of illness, income loss, or other psychosocial debility, and the insufficient supply of family-type substitutes to absorb children who require part- or full-time extrafamilial care has had the obvious effect—reconsideration. A reexamination of premises that led to the abandonment of group care programs was in the cards anyway, since much of the empirical evidence for that move was methodologically and perhaps even theoretically shaky. Now such material came.

Beginning in the late fifties and rapidly accelerating in the sixties, the literature on maternal deprivation increasingly reflected a questioning of the Bowlbian view. Evidence that began to accumulate showed that not separation from parents nor multiple mothering nor even long-term residence in group settings was *necessarily* harmful in the development of children. Reinforcing these limited field studies in the Western world were large social experiments in group care of children in Israel, in certain predominantly Catholic countries, and in some communist societies. Children in the Israeli kibbutz, the Soviet boarding school, the Austrian Kinderdorf were observed and even tested by Western scholars and found, despite theoretical expectations to the contrary, sound in body and mind and strongly identified with the values of their setting.

And so group care of children is returning to America, it seems. After a half-century of persistent decline, the number of children cared for in groups (in day centers, boarding schools, and institutions) is again rising and is taking on considerable respectability as a supplemental or substitutive service to the depleted family. The expanding day care programs, the rapidly expanding group home service, the serious talk about youth villages, and even some radical young people's efforts at communal living are other indicators of a trend. In part the mood is determined by a pendular swing away from the extreme familial position postulated in Freudian psychiatry and its empirical successors, the publications of Spitz, Goldfarb, and, of course, above all Bowlby. Partly it is affected by the group care programs of Israel and East Europe.

What solutions are accepted certainly will be a function of the spirit of this society and the theories it chooses to adopt and implement. However, a new openness appears to exist for the latter generation of group care thinking. To present some of the newer materials in group care is the function of this book, which opens with a review of some thoughts on successful group care. An attempt is made to draw on materials in the book in order to present the possibilities, both theoretical and applied, that group care has to offer. The argument is based on a hypothesis, reasonably well supported by empirical evidence, that effective group care exists when the setting is used as an instrument rather than as a vessel (a container within which professional intervention can conveniently take place). Professional roles are thus upgraded as well as downgraded. They include the planning and management of the effective milieu and the assumption of a partial, often minor role within it.

Part II presents some historical and philosophical issues in group care. It may come as a surprise to many readers that the argument "group care—friend or foe?" which began in the 19th century and became sharp (almost shrill) during the first White House Conference on Children of 1909, led rather rapidly to serious research, as exemplified in the excerpts (Chap. 2) from Trotzkey's *Institutional Care and Placing Out*. His book, though, is also an excellent reminder of the minimal impact that data (whose time has not come?) make on the professionals and theoreticians involved.

In fact, neither Trotzkey's data nor those of some others are in any way reflected in Kardiner's polemic (Chap. 5) against group care. Why the polemics, the passion, and the severe resistance to group care? Possibly these responses are an outgrowth of a value stance that goes counter to what are often assumed to be inevitable companions of group care—batch living, binary structure, and authoritarianism. Depriving the child or adolescent of his familial environment and possibly exposing him to the depersonalization of an institution where he is a subject (even an object) and others are the masters is clearly abhorrent to the Western mind, although supporters of group care in other societies claim that ideological commitment, social circumstance, and carefully planned programs can protect the group-reared child from such negative possibilities. They intend, instead, to create positive opportunities for children and to show society's responsiveness to the inevitable insufficiencies of contemporary, industrial-era nuclear families.

Several research papers included in Part III analyze the negative and positive effects of group care for young children. The emphasis is on the salutary effects because they reflect the intended tone of this book and, more importantly, because they result from imaginatively developed, growth-promotion settings. Clearly, as theoreticians, teachers, practitioners, and researchers we have the choice of chronicling the failures or the successes and a "passive acceptance" or an "active modification" approach.

Several teen-age group environments and their consequences are discussed in Part IV. In the younger age-groups, emphasis has been on issues of separation, mothering, and cognitive development, but the youth settings emphasize their peer effect on values and moral character. Here we should be concerned not only with the possibility of creating a powerful environment that promotes the values desired in the several settings described, but also with the compatibility of such a milieu with the values to be imbued.

Because group care of the disturbed, seriously problematic child is more familiar and more acceptable to him, the Western reader may possibly find Part V closest to his interests. Emphasis here is on the use of relatively nonprofessionalized, low-key, low-cost settings for the melioration of culturally deprived and emotionally disturbed preadolescents and adolescents.

Finally, in Part VI we attempt to look for patterns, to present some dreams and proposals that hopefully will affect group care thinking. In the opinions of some proponents, research evidence and theoretical formulations in group care are now equal to the critical task—the formulation and documentation of constructive alternative forms of childrearing that suit the needs of families in the later years of the 20th century and serve to benefit the child and society. The models presented are a reflection of this confidence, but they are also a collection of hypotheses to be tested in the years to come.

I

Group Care: A General and Affirmative View

Some Theoretical Observations on Group Care

MARTIN WOLINS

A break in the established order is never the work of chance. It is the outcome of a man's resolve to turn life to account.

ANDRE MALRAUX in Man's Fate

Group Programs Can Be Useful

The primary function of benign group settings is to protect and properly
host their members. Asylum, infamous though the term may now be, derives
from the Greek *asylos*, meaning protection from seizure. Indeed, as the various types of asylums are examined, from exclusive boarding schools and
elitist monasteries to the back wards of mental hospitals and dungeons of
prisons, most if not all claim to be doing just that. Other than those with
specifically destructive purposes (e.g., concentration camps, political prisons, certain prisoner-of-war installations), they are intent, at least in their public declarations, on protecting and promoting the special physical and spiritual needs of those segregated within them. That some of them try to save
the soul by killing the body and others succeed in preserving only the body
is not the point. The fact is that they aim for and perhaps can achieve much
more.

Physical survival and growth and the acceptance of socially lauded, at
least socially tolerable, behavior is the aim. While warehousing (of infirm or
grossly and permanently incompetent) or restraint (of disruptive or conta-

Reprinted from Donnell M. Pappenfort, Dee Morgan Kilpatrick, and Robert W.
Roberts, editors, *Child Caring: Social Policy and the Institution* (Chicago: Aldine Publishing Company); copyright © 1973 by Aldine Publishing Company. Reprinted by
permission of the author and publisher.

gious) may and in some instances even must occur, and biological continuity must be asserted, the main goal of asylums is socialization. Most institutions, just like the institutionalized family, claim and indeed do more or less successfully assume responsibility for

> the moralization of the individual into the society into which he is born as an amoral and egoistic infant. . . . [Though they may have to begin or even become institutionally fixated at one of the] successive stages, each of which must be traversed by every individual before he can attain the next higher: (1) the stage in which the operation of the instinctive impulses is modified by the influence of rewards and punishments, (2) the stage in which conduct is controlled in the main by anticipation of social praise and blame, (3) the highest stage in which conduct is regulated by an ideal that enables a man to act in the way that seems to him right regardless of the praise or blame of his immediate social environment [McDougall 1908].

Along with such learning of some level of morality is the acquisition of knowledge and skill in role performance. Asylums, like families, teach a member to be a somebody rather than remain a something. To be sure, in the most extreme cases of neglect and abuse the distinction between person and thing is blurred almost beyond recognition, but these represent the grotesque negative extreme of the institutional spectrum (see, for example, Spitz's description of hospitalism, 1945–46, or Solzhenitsyn's labor camp, 1963). While they may be found both in familial (see, for example, Gil 1968) and nonfamilial environments, the nonfamilial are more visible and more powerful, and their evils are more readily dramatized. It is not surprising, then, to find a whole *literature of dysfunction* which, as the apparent inventor of this term has rightly suggested, "has tended to confuse the elements in criticism by treating the institutional situation as a whole" (K. Jones 1967, p. 14; see, for example, Morris and Morris 1963, and Goffman 1961). Assuming that both the family and the asylums, which have perhaps as wide a geographic and temporal universality, are slated to persist, a *literature of function* (K. Jones 1967, p. 15) is sorely needed.

Actually, family and asylum function in inevitable interrelationship. Familial incapacity and asylum success serve to unlock the usually well-guarded gates of the other member. Both family and asylum must therefore be responsive to the needs of members in every stage of their development and provide the conditions in which they are met. The conditions are by and large not food and shelter (though these are critical in minimally adequate amounts) but people.

> The burden and the benefit come from the same source: life, and reality, is other people . . . [who are essential] not only for facts and beliefs about the nature of the world, but also for what he [man] has learned to want, to value, to consider right and good, to worship. The actions and reactions of others are not only his primary source of information, but they determine his primary

goals beyond those physical things he requires for survival [Berelson and Steiner 1964, p. 665].

As the process of the individual's development unfolds, the circle of participants expands and so does their influence. Yet at the core stands the family, bolstered by tradition, faith, and often a lack of tolerable alternatives. With childbearing and rearing as its primary and most satisfying function, and with the gradual but inexorable loss of others, the family and the social systems surrounding it are continually affirmed when a new, helpless, and useless member comes into the world and is reared to capability and social usefulness. Similar affirmation takes place when the sick are healed or the wayward aligned. Proponents of alternative modes, particularly when anxious to justify their rights to child care, find themselves in the unenviable position of praising and imitating or plotting the assassination of the king.

This phenomenon is most obvious in child care: every attempt to legitimate group care of children contains elements of imitation of or assault on the family. Gmeiner (1960b), arguing the good qualities of his *Kinderdörfer,* expounds on their similarity to normal families (see also Chap. 14). So, by the way, did the whole American cottage movement, which spread across the country in the early 1900s (see Wolins and Piliavin 1964). By contrast, the more outspoken ideological purists of Soviet communism or of the Israeli kibbutz movement deride the innate childrearing capabilities of the family. As recently as 1960 Soviet academician Strumilin advocated group care of infants and children by claiming that "the collective of children, especially if they are guided without pressure by the experienced hand of a pedagogue, can contribute much more of the best social habits to the rearing of a child than the most kindly and loving mothers." While the argument has strong ideological grounding in what was believed to be Marxian theory and was propounded long before Strumilin by such famous thinkers as Kollontai, Bukharin, and even Trotsky, the middle-level-oriented Soviet leadership of the 1960s chose to haul it down (see, for example, Kolbanovski 1961).

Group care for young children and infants especially was, like eating garlic, just not right in a self-respecting society. And like garlic consumption, the dictum failed to take effect at either extreme of the social scale. In the midst of all the adulation of motherhood and familiness, nannies and boarding schools reared children of the rich and orphanages housed the poor in Western Europe and America. East was like West. While most residents of Soviet boarding schools seem to have come from poor and disrupted families, some were also homes for children of a highly mobile military and diplomatic elite (Ambler 1961; Weeks, Chap. 4, this book).

Against this background, it is of no little interest, though not surprising, that evidence generally supports the success of families and the failure of asylums. In due course the definitive word was ready to be spoken. Bowlby, citing some dozen and a half papers of his own and other American writers "insulated from communication . . . by the Atlantic Ocean . . ." (Bowlby 1950 [1952 ed.], p. 32), pointed to the "monotonous regularity [with which] each put his finger on the child's inability to make relationships . . . and on the history of institutionalization . . . as being its cause" (p. 31).

Looked at in most simplistic terms, such a statement must be based on a fourfold comparison table. Ideally, the calculation would take into account children reared in good and inadequate families and those from competent and incompetent institutions. But such is not the case. Comparisons are typically like Goldfarb's (1943a and b), where controls lived from infancy in selected foster homes (presumably good) and the institution group came from a setting that "lacked the elementary essentials of mental hygiene" (Bowlby 1950 [1952 ed.], pp. 36–37). While another of the four cells— bad families—is filled in some studies (e.g., Simonsen 1947, or Theis 1924), Bowlby's argument that they are comparing with good institutions (pp. 68–69) is difficult to accept, particularly in the light of Skeels's (1938, 1942) contrary evidence on outcome which was apparently ignored in the rush to affirm familial infallibility by dusting off and saluting the motto: "Be it ever so humble, there's no place like home."

While the ease with which some children have been separated from vulnerable and unorthodox households may be lamentable, the popular generalized slogan against such action seems just as harmful. Some homes are so humble they are no place.[1] Whether this is true relative to certain limited tasks—e.g., formal education, treatment of nephrosis or a broken arm—or as a generalized environment, whether for short term or long, an alternative to the family is at times inevitable. It can also be constructive. The American woman whose bill of equal rights contains a demand for all-day child care, and the British nobility who sent their young sons to public schools as a first step to governing the Empire, surely do not suffer from the usual misapprehensions. Should they? Should society? Are not the deplorable conditions of many children who live in AFDC households (e.g., Burgess and Price 1963), the revolving-door rotation of those in foster homes (Maas and Engler 1959; Jeter 1963) a serious challenge to the noble slogan? Perhaps an asylum should not be rejected out of hand after all.

Personal and Environmental Stages

Entering a society and being moralized into its ways requires the orchestration of familial, peer-group, and broader societal environments. While the degrees of inclusiveness and involuntariness of these three developmental contexts are clearly unequal, each is inescapable. True, hegemony of the family, or peers, or of the broader society vary with age, condition, social context, and other attributes of the person and his milieu, but the permutations of growth-promoting arrangements are without any doubt much larger than Western tradition and Freudian psychology have accepted. Although, as Eisenstadt (1956) has pointed out, every society has "a broad definition of human potentialities and obligations at a given stage of life" (p. 22), the social contexts for their expression vary remarkably. Only a deliberate misreading of history and ethnography to suit theoretical and ideological preconceptions can lead to a conclusion that one arrangement is usually constructive and others disastrous. Yet the person's condition obviously imposes limitations and offers opportunities.

In the past half-century or so developmental-stage thinking has proliferated. Fundamentally a natural idea, it recognizes in gross form a progression from abject dependency to capability and exchange. On one end of this continuum is the totally dependent, completely self-focused infant whose world is no larger than he and his needs. On the other is the mature, quite self-sufficient adult who determines his own life while recognizing and promoting the welfare of others. Applied quite understandably to the growth processes of a healthy child-youth in a fairly competent familial environment, the schema has not yet been made to encompass an explanation of abnormal person and unusual setting. Infants in nurseries, sick adults in hospitals, recruits in army barracks, adolescents in boarding schools, aged in nursing homes—these cases require elaborations of and extrapolations from the age-stage theoretical statements if their conditions are to be comprehended. The mere recitation of types involved shows not only their great variability but also some threads of a pattern relating personal capacity and setting. Although related to age but not inevitably so, one consideration possibly governing all others is the condition of the person for whom a group program is intended.

DEPENDENCY

In early life or in severe illness, extreme social disgrace, or ideological surrender, a person is dependent. All theory and a substantial portion of the research on dependency implies a reliance on constant, adult-like, competent figures through whom the very substance of life flows. The singular, critical importance of such a near-umbilical attachment is that it requires constant reassurances to allay the persistent fear that the cord will be severed. Needs of the utterly dependent are quasi-physical, with a nearly total self-referent. If it is true, as Aristotle once wrote, that pleasure and nobility supply the motives for all actions, then dependency epitomizes the pleasure principle of evaluation. Such a motivation is largely instinctive and amoral. It concerns itself little or not at all with the needs of the other.

Dependency of such magnitude has quite simple social requirements—willing others. For the small child this other usually is the mother, and some have disputed the efficacy of substitutes. Some authorities (e.g., Bowlby

1950 [1952 ed.]; Ainsworth 1962), strongly supported by attitudes and values of lay publics in various political systems, have held rather firmly to the "natural mother at nearly all costs" position. Others have shown that constancy was of significance (Rheingold 1960) or not (Gardner et al., 1961), capability important (Spitz, 1945) or not (Skeels, 1966). While it should be conceded that a healthy, regularly available, and not intolerably possessive mother best exemplifies the willing other of this condition, alternatives for infants and other dependents are essential and far from impossible.

Regardless of setting, the danger lies in the relationship that dependency fosters. So great an inequality between donor and recipient, whether the pair is infant–mother, patient–physician, or prisoner–warden, implies a hierarchical, authoritarian arrangement in which all or most power to satisfy, act, and mediate lies in one member of the pair. He chooses whether and how to allow intrusion, and in doing so he may undernourish (Pavenstedt, 1967) or overwhelm (Levy, 1943) the dependent. Because the arrangement is so total, its consequences are profound, and the exclusionist character generally precludes the intervention of deliberate or even random factors that would tend to act as modifiers on a probability basis alone. Here may well lie the distinction in ultimate effect between the incompetent, inadequate, or even hostile family and the bad institution;[2] the first rarely can manage the exclusiveness of the second. In either case, though, the only assurance of a positive exchange is in the affect of the adults. In short, dependency requires love, but, as Levy found, it must be tempered with restraint to be constructive. When love and restraint are absent, this stage of care becomes a system of reciprocal tyranny. The dependent employs his helplessness and the caretaker his absolute power, each to manipulate the other.

NOMOCRACY

A condition less vulnerable than dependency, though often represented in asylums, is nomocracy. Such a law-and-order relationship, though heavily weighted in favor of the lawgivers, nevertheless contains some protection for the clients. Because the rules must be explicated, the amount of exclusivity and capricious behavior can be reduced by the occasional intrusion of outsiders. Whether these are the board of governors of an institution, the courts, or new and dissenting members, they exercise a measure of control over the rules and their observance.[3] Psychodynamically the rules that govern the keepers–kept relationship in such a system can be quite constructive; restraints they impose on the keepers reduce the capriciousness and hence increase the predictability of the system. By limiting the excesses of the inmates, rules aid in the definition of self and other, leading to reduction of behavior that is defined as unacceptable. However, the extent of internalization can be very limited in such an arrangement. An act is good if by the rules it leads to receipt of awards or avoidance of punishment: "My mother told me to . . ." of the young or restricted child; "We have rules here for . . ." of the custodially oriented delinquency-institution director (Street et al. 1966); "I carried out higher orders" of an Eichmann.

The implications of such an arrangement, whether in familial or group setting, are clear. Human referents that diverge from the rules are diffuse and uncertain; internalized criteria are weak or absent. In any event, questioning and, even more so, breaking of rules can hardly be tolerated in such an environment. Self-reference of behavior is even more precarious, for by what criteria can the person decide he is right when the rules say otherwise? Hence the most reasonable position is to accept rules even when they lead to outrageous consequences (e.g., Bettelheim 1960). In such a system of nomocracy the salient conditions of Erikson's (1950 [1963 ed.]) second and third stages of development are clearly observable. Cooperation is matched by willfulness, freedom of self-expression by its suppression, higher goals by determined instrumentalism as the person fights for self-assertion and growth and continually confronts his own limitations (often the reason for his being in care) and the restrictions of the setting.

A system where behavior is evaluated by its proximity to rules requires obedient others who will provide stability and acceptance. Since the structure is based on the assumed legitimacy of keepers and their right to promulgate criteria for evaluation, questioning a rule is to some degree subversive. To the extent that such questioning cannot be carried on openly it leads to several negative consequences: conservatism, evasion, and clandestine parallel authority. Rules stay fixed in part because the system remains uninformed. New conditions that are fully, often painfully clear to the inmates simply may not come to the consciousness of keepers, and since in any event change is trouble, new circumstances are better ignored. To the extent that an institution has the power, it may suppress any demands to change rules, but it can hardly avoid some evasion. Rendering unto Ceasar what is his is commonly found in severely autocratic families (Adorno, 1950; Peck, Havighurst et al. 1960), in jails, prisons (Sykes 1958), mental hospitals (Stanton and Schwartz 1954; Goffman 1961), and any other rule-dominated minimum participation system. In its extreme form the subversion of rules becomes a clandestine parallel authority more intimate and hence often more powerful than the legitimate one (Polsky 1962 [1967 ed.]).

Rules, like dependency, thus are filled with danger. Their overindulgence can be stifling, stunting the growth of those in care, leading them to clandestine avoidance or to what is perhaps the healthiest expression, open revolt. Again, as with dependency, the asylum sails precariously. It must navigate between the Scylla of suppression and the Charybdis of laissez-faire. The demoralizing capabilities of laissez-faire are perhaps not so great as those of authoritarian rule but hardly an alternative of choice (White and Lippitt 1960; Peck, Havighurst et al. 1960). For a person on the nomocracy level participation in rule making is usually constrained since the authority belongs to others on the assumption that he is incapable. This is hardly conducive to ego development (NICHD 1968, pp. 32-33). Greater participation demands more maturity—a real dilemma.

The positive medium of exchange in such conditions is respect. Janusz Korczak (1967), Polish-Jewish master of the benevolent orphanage with 30 years of childrearing to his credit, demanded:

> Respect for the mysteries and fluctuations of growth.
> Respect for the present moment.
> Respect for failure and tears.
> Respect for ignorance.

> [Essay "The Right to Respect"]

In his institution children made rules and changed them even under the stress of Warsaw ghetto conditions, but *Pandoktor* (Mister Doctor) remained the authority.

OTHER-ORIENTATION

An arrangement that requires more personal competence and permits greater self-determination by allowing, instead of autocratic or nomocratic rule, some form of group decision making is commonly found in benevolent settings for more mature children and trustworthy adults. Other-orientation guides such a system. While the other is usually a peer group (Sherif and Sherif 1965) that often includes the self, modeling of the successful adult and even of a rejecting reference group are possible. The aim is acceptance. In a group setting such an arrangement may have all the trappings and, in ideal conditions, even the reality of democratic self-determination: a kibbutz class decides what subjects to study (Spiro 1958); the ward discusses and agrees who is ready for outside employment (Fairweather 1964). Whether a person abides by the decision must be evaluated by the membership group and the reference group. When the two are coterminous adjustment should be easy with little anticipated subsequent change. When they diverge, as they must if growth is to take place, strain and change should follow. In either case behavior will be assessed and status determined vis-à-vis membership or reference group. Star, participant, isolate, or total reject, a person's crown of gold or thorns is in the hands of the group. It alone can bestow or remove a status and its privileges.

Several difficulties lie at the core of such an arrangement. First, in various asylums designed for treatment in particular, is the matter of expertise. Democratic rule and self-determination may be acceptable in principle, but how well informed can the decisions be in technically complex issues? Put another way the question is more penetrating: Can inmates be trusted to use knowledge in advancing their own welfare? In relation to recuperating mental hospital patients, for example, this includes such decisions as the ability to hold a job, live in the community, manage one's resources, and the like (see Fairweather 1964 for an extensive discussion of such an arrangement).

A second issue is the ideological or value trustworthiness of the incare group. As Polsky (1962 [1967 ed.]) has shown, not only the decision but also the process itself can be subverted, reverting to nomocracy or authoritarianism imposed by a group leadership. If the leadership is not in sympathy with the formal aims of the setting it may use the decision-making processes to subvert them and institute its own objectives.

Ways of coping with both of the above difficulties are available, but they inevitably modify the other-orientation arrangement by introducing external controls. One such restraint may be formal boundaries that set the limits for process and outcome. These boundaries may give a group leader (nonmember) or a technical specialist such a strong say in decision making that he exercises veto power—a not uncommon function of adults in institutional children's courts, where penalties are often more severe than the formal structure is willing to impose. Another limitation may be in the form of a preexisting and indisputable ideology. Thus the Soviet system of education uses peer pressure—"the collective will of peers"—to manage behavior in classroom and boarding school. In operation the procedure (as Bronfenbrenner 1962 describes it) moves the children from adult authority to rules to peer orientation. Bronfenbrenner illustrates this point regarding intergroup (though *not* interpersonal) competition.

> If measures arousing the spirit of competition are systematically *applied by experienced teachers* in the primary classes, then gradually *the children themselves* begin to monitor the behavior of their comrades and remind those of them who forget about the standards and *rules set by the teacher* [p. 552; italics added].

Children have no say about the kind of competition, if any, they want to explore. This comes down from party ideologists. What the group may decide is *how* it will promote the ideal and not *whether* to promote it. But even such constrained democracy appears to have the attributes recently stated in a review of American literature: "The more social participation, the more rapid the development of a mature moral ideology, one based on identification with the social order and with principles of justice" [NICHD 1968, p. 33; see also Bronfenbrenner 1967, 1970).

Faddism is a third problem of an other-orientation arrangement. This might be thought of as voluntary submission to authoritarian rule of stars. Since a group that has some constancy will develop a leadership with considerable persuasive power (Lippitt et al. 1958), and the leaders in an isolated system may feel relatively unconstrained by the traditions of the outside, they will innovate frequently and be followed massively. Such a situation will produce rapid shifts in attitude and behavior within the group setting, which can demoralize not only the inmates but also the caretakers. Whether the swing is produced by stars or by some other group condition, it can be drastic (see for example, Sherif 1961), and its direction need not be in line with objective evidence (Sherif 1936; Asch 1952; Berenda 1950).

Equality and reciprocity, when they govern the group, can preclude massive deviations, provided they are augmented by the interpenetration of other systems. In isolation a group composed of members on the level of other-orientation, unlike a rule- or authority-bound one, may defend itself successfully against the keepers but may not give members enough defenses against the power of peers. (The capacity of groups to produce conformity is well illustrated in Sherif and Sherif 1965.) The capacity of doubters and deviants to assert themselves will be enhanced by penetration of outside forces and the operation of principles of equality and reciprocity among members. Deviants and dissenters are the best device such settings have for producing socially constructive change. The more egalitarian the arrangement, the greater is the access to decision-making mechanisms and the more likely that unusual views—which at times represent the only voice of realism and morality—can at least be heard.

Other-directed systems are based on the assumption of members' considerable competence. Their competence also implies that the outside world need not be mediated through authority or rules but may impinge directly on individuals and their group. Education, work, and family can play important roles in affecting the membership and operations of such a system. All build on the assumption of present and even greater subsequent capability. A member of a group care program operated on the principles of other-orientation is considered competent to be part of a family, an educational and work unit. While his capacity in all or any one of these may be temporarily impaired by reason of age or disability, the impairment is considered limited in *degree* as well as time. Members are therefore expected to study, work, and continue their familial roles as sons, daughters, fathers, mothers. Such demands have both a present and a future aim. The present aim is reality-inducing—that is, compelling the inmate to confront lifelike situations of family, school, and job, although the level of risk may be lessened by the protective setting (see Moore and Anderson 1969). But the major power of these external intrusions is their future utility and its pull.

As indicated, other-directed settings are extrafamilial, and their members are quite competent. Their very competence makes it possible to separate the people (children or adults) in care from their familial ties. That this arouses anxieties in the families and needs special rationale has been noted earlier. However, there are other justifications for maintaining familial ties. In the main they provide an opportunity for modeling in situations that may be devoid of it. Contrary to much popular opinion, parents still appear to be the major models and judges in normal populations of adolescents (Douvan and Adelson 1966; Rosen 1955; Epperson 1964). What is even more important, some studies find high correlations between peer activities and good parent–child relations (C. L. Stone 1960). And the modeling may be in terms of roles to be assumed in the future against an unprotected social background. The realities of present and future family life are thus intruded into the group program, mitigating against maximal conformity (since outside conditions that confront each member are more varied than those inside) and an institutional outlook. Such an outlook, often referred to as an institutionalization syndrome, is part unreality, part immobilization, and part conformity, said to result from the sheltered life in such a setting.

Another source of independent expectation is the world of work. Like the peer group inside and the family outside, a work setting also has roles to bestow and rewards to give or withhold. Outside work settings (e.g., Soviet boarding-school children taking on certain factory jobs, or kibbutz youth group members working in the kibbutz) have more reality-testing possibilities to offer, but even those in the institution can make constructive contributions. They do so mainly because the criteria for evaluation of product or service are imported, and work force relationships must be guided at least in some measure by objectively determined productivity. Being mainly instrumental in character, the work setting—whether in the cold outside or the partly protected inside—generates its own models and values to counterpose the expressive-consumatory character that inevitably characterizes an environment of partially incapacitated persons.

EXCHANGE

It may be a matter of some wonderment that a discussion of the next level of group living should be included in this description of benevolent asylums based on differential membership capabilities. The idea of asylum implies incapacity of some kind and its requisite shelter. To say, then, that persons who operate on the highest level of psychosocial development may be found in exclusive environments seems like a contradiction. Yet the inclusion is necessary for both theoretical and practical reasons. Regardless of their existence in reality, certain self-contained settings comprised of self-sufficient, egalitarian, exhange-oriented members are at least a Platonic ideal, existing as a theoretical possibility—if not implemented then at least feasible of comprehension. Although the ideal Skinner expounded in his *Walden II* (1960) may be just that—the idea in the mind—certain approximations of it are indeed a part of man's experience. One need only read the descriptions of existing communal-egalitarian societies (see Viteles, 1967) to note the remarkable similarity with Skinner's ideal type. But if a social system is composed of such very mature persons, why the isolation? Why must it have the characteristics of an asylum? Apparently for self-defense, as in the previously discussed arrangements, but protection of the system and not of the person. An egalitarian setting (institution, community, small society such as a kibbutz) is vulnerable to the blandishments of less mature environments. In moments of stress, tiredness, boredom, or dissention, an exchange setting tends to succumb to the attractions of dependency, rules, and other-oriented submission, seemingly falling prey to a Gresham's law of institutions.

Composed of competent, mature members, this kind of setting cannot achieve much isolation from the world around it, no matter how much it tries. Participants insist on drawing from and giving to the larger human environment. Since rules and the evaluation of others are secondary to self-evaluation or to the clear conscience of the moral person as criteria for behavior, such individuals will define their sphere of rights and responsibilities outside as well as inside their setting. In doing so they will be guided and urged on by the considerable capacity for love and work *(Lieben und Arbeiten),* which Freud defined as the ultimate marks of maturity. But they will go beyond the requirements of the outside and the structured demands of the inside. In Kohlberg's (1969) terms such mature persons will be guided by

> moral internalization [not] as behavioral conformity to the cultural code, but rather as the development of a morality of principle which is above actual conformity to cultural expectations. . . . It seems likely that there are culturally universal or near-universal values suggested by the words "love," "work" and "morality," and that these values recognize natural developmental trends and progressions. The development of moral capacities (as well as capacities to work and to love) involves an orientation to internal norms, but this development cannot be defined as a direct internalization of external cultural norms [p. 413].

Members of such a setting are thus of the place and beyond it, of the surrounding community and also beyond it.

An optimal environment for such highly moral and competent persons is one governed by the truly revolutionary among Marx's bag of slogans: From each according to his ability, to each according to his need. Operated on egalitarian principles, evaluated by ideological, rational-altruistic standards, internalized by every member, such a system needs a minimum of rules and formal leadership. Indeed, the available examples (say, the kibbutzim) ascribe the most negative values to authoritarianism, bureaucracy, legalism, and even group conformity, although they have some real difficulties with conformity. (Distinction of a commonly agreed on course of action taken by virtue of its moral and generally beneficial nature from an other-directed group decision is no simple matter!) In its gross characteristics, though, this is the epitome of a learning society where the learning of specific skills, rules, and even attitudes is secondary to the "acquisition of a flexible set of highly abstract conceptual tools" (Moore and Anderson 1969, pp. 583–84) pertaining to morals, love, and work.

Egalitarian interaction being the prime requirement for the existence of an exchange system and for the development of persons capable of participating in it, how does it fit in a child-caring scheme? Or in systems that care for incapacitated adults? Clearly by limitation and partial emulation. But the issue is also what is meant by a child. Is it a preschooler of 5 or an adolescent of 15? They require different assumptions of capability not only by virtue of age-related development but, particularly in the older child, the previously experienced expectations, opportunities, and restraints. The influence of different setting types on behavior has been illustrated in the short term (White and Lippitt 1960) and the long term (Peck, Havighurst et al. 1960). Whether it was the temporary, artificially structured little task group, as in the first instance, or the long-term actions of the family in the second, higher order expectations (and opportunities) produced greater capability. As Levy (1943) showed long ago, a child can be swaddled into permanent incompetence,[4] or as Peck, Havighurst et al. (1960) found, he may be frozen into rule or group conformity by parental ineptness, hostility, or unconcern. But he may also be given the opportunity and encouragement to participate in an exchange system with the abilities and needs appropriate to him. For surely egalitarian principles do not mean that everyone has an equal say in all matters regardless of competence and proximity to the problem but, rather, that each person will be heard and his views considered in exchange for his extending the same right to others.

While such an arrangement is probably less strenuous among persons of small diversity in ability and need, it is achievable in other conditions. Peck, Havighurst et al. (1960) illustrate such an arrangement in describing the familial backgrounds of three rational-altruistic (i.e., morally mature) children.

> [In such families there is] more common participation among the members of the family than in the home of any other character type. . . .
> [The child is] more likely to share confidences with his parents. . . .
> [Parents are] more approving of peer activities. . . .
> Parents are *trusting of the child*, and the general tone of the . . . home is a *democratic one*. . . .
> [The child has a] share in family decisions [pp. 115-117; italics in original].

A child from such a home was not treated as an equal; yet he learned equality and participation by progressive approximations of the egalitarian setting.

Ontogenetic Rules

If group care has any objectives other than simple, more or less benign warehousing of persons, these objectives are on the continuum from prostrate dependency to productivity and egalitarian participation. A 12-year-old in a mental hospital whose daily routine consists of sleeping, being fed, and

TABLE 1.1. *Benevolent asylum: inmates and environments*

Levels of Functioning*

	dependency	nomocracy	other-orientation	exchange
Needs	Quasi-physical; id-oriented	Avoidance of the unknown	Approval-acceptance	Clear conscience
Evaluation	Instinctive, premoral	Rule-referred	Reference group	Ideological principled, rational-altruistic
Social requirement	Constant, nourishing "mother"	Rule-following others; authoritarian interpreter	Cue-sending others	Mature, giving-getting others
Relationship	Hierarchical authoritarianism	Legitimate subordination	Undifferentiated egalitarianism	Individualized egalitarianism
Danger	Tyranny of either member	Pursuit of meaningless or outrageous rules	Faddism; instability; anarchic populism	Unprincipled others
Antidote (a higher level opening)	Love, compassion, rules	Respect for persons; encroachment of new situations	Equality and exchange	moral duty (withdrawal in case of failure)
Peer functions	Minimal or none	Modest	Massive	Reduced by self-reference
Societal intrusion	Minimal and indirect	Caretaker-guided	Marked and direct, but demands are conditional	Very substantial except in cases of withdrawal to avoid contamination

* These levels are roughly similar to Kohlberg's (1969) stages of moral character development. Dependency being similar to Kohlberg's Stage I, nomocracy to Stages II and III, other-orientation to Stage IV, and exchange to Stages V and VI. However, the emphasis in the present discussion is not on the attributes of individuals but on the expectations and opportunities of the environment.

watching television should and in most instances could be pushed-pulled toward some rule recognition and observance. An 18-year-old in a correctional institution may be moved from responses to authority to some peer-group decisions about personal care, work, or even creativity. These changes in the behavior of persons are generated by qualities of the environment interacting with stages of human development. They seem to be governed by certain ontogenetic rules. Among them are: continuity and overlapping of both personal capabilities and setting demands and tolerance; the pull of higher stages in what seems to be a natural demand for growth; fixation at low levels of expectation and capacity; and the appearance of periods of personal and setting capability when fixation may be broken and growth accelerated.

One of the fundamental problems of extrafamilial care as contrasted with a healthy family environment is its unresponsiveness to varied personal capabilities of inmates. In large measure the difficulty arises from the near-certainty that diversity will exist even in the most selective setting. Not only will there be among inmates differences in the ability to meet demands on the dependency–exchange continuum, but even the single person in care will not have a regular, even capacity. He will be tired or rested, bored or excited, in the best of health or somewhat under the weather. The same demands for performance will therefore be unsuitable if they are universal within the setting and applied to all inmates at all times. Even the most callous, uninformed, and uncaring asylum is in some ways responsive to these differences in personal capability; surely an enlightened, professionally staffed group care program is developed with sensitivity to the problem. Difficulty arises, however, because an asylum, benevolent or not, must have greater functional specificity and more exclusion of outside influences than does the family.

Beginning with some definition of purposes, no matter how vague and well hidden these may be, a group program will acquire inmates, staff, rules, and, therefore, behavior considered appropriate to it. It will thus label itself, and the outside will recognize it as being the right place for certain types of persons who will be confronted there with a specific level of expectations. If it is a hidden geriatric ward in a mental hospital, the expectation will be terminal dependency and the inmates the incapable old. A juvenile hall will contain the aggressive young. Here, rule-obedient behavior will be generally expected by its inmates, staff, and community critics. A good boarding school acting in *loco parentis* will be suspended somewhere between rules to assuage the fears of parents and peer-monitored behavior to conform with the reality of a youth setting comprised of competent teenagers. Whatever the modal level of operation, it is most unlikely to fit all inmates and will certainly be inappropriate for some of them at some time.

The same is true of the family, of course. Some families insist on laissez-faire behavior that requires exchange-level maturity of a 10-year-old on the grounds that egalitarian participation (and parental irresponsibility?) must begin early. Others demand obedience and dependency from the healthy 18-year-old on the assumption that he must forever listen to his parents and seek their guidance. However, the family membership, age patterns, and external environment change more rapidly and are far less within its control than is true in an asylum. A family, even a rather insensitive one, is thus more likely to provide an environment where demand varies in accordance with personal, time-specific capacity.[5]

THE PROBLEM OF PROFESSIONALS

Rapid changes in expectations responsive to a person's needs for authority ("I am sick, tell me what to take"), for rules ("What is the law about. . .?"), for peer guidance ("How do people like us do it?), for mature exchange ("What is the right thing to do?") are an essential component of any asylum that aims for individualization and growth. It would appear that professional staffing is the way to assure such flexibility in demands; yet this is not necessarily so. By their mere presence certain types of professionals define the setting and its expectations. Physicians tend exclusively the sick in most societies, and, what is more, they are expected to prescribe and proscribe and not even to refer to any rules that govern *their* behavior. Teachers maintain discipline and tell students whether their answers are right or wrong.[6] Only social workers and psychiatrists (i.e., some special physicians) address the inmate in a nondirective manner, expecting a measure of mature capability; but it is generally assumed (and often quite correctly) that they do so because they have no personal authority or properly developed rules to impose. If the asylum is to promote peer orientation and exchange relationships, heavy investment in professional services is not likely to achieve it. The only way out is to open the setting to the effects of the outside, or bring the outside in—in brief, milieu therapy (see D. H. Clark 1965; M. Jones 1963; D. Martin 1962).[7]

As the best known proponent of this position has said, a therapeutic community must be both *focal*—i.e., maximizing the use of community and group influences and minimizing the interaction between inmate and professional—and *total*—i.e., applicable to every aspect of institutional environment (M. Jones 1963). Only by escaping the professional stamp and avoiding isolation from the influences of a healthy and demanding milieu can the group program achieve demand flexibility and growth-promoting capacity. Professionally staffed human warehouses may be more benign, but they will remain just storage operations as limited in their range of responses as those run by the untrained unless provision is made for environmental demand flexibility and escalation. Professionals can conceptualize, plan, and develop such an environment, but the less their presence is obvious, the better. This position is not intended to exclude professional expertise from direct influence on inmates. An asylum usually sets itself two tasks: socialization and technical modification of members. While the two are understandably intertwined, socialization appears to be most successful when direct professional intervention is minimized, particularly when the object of a program is adjustment. Technical modification requires much greater direct involvement of specialists, although even that is disputed by some recent work (Tharp and Wetzel 1969).

Professionals are a problem in yet another way. Any involvement with them implies incapacity. The sick need doctors, the ignorant need teachers, the lawless need judges and policemen. We, the healthy, the mature, the competent, care for ourselves, teach ourselves, police and evaluate our own behavior. White coats, black robes, shining buttons mean immaturity, inability in the person subjected to their ministrations. They imply "I will do it for you (or to you)" and advocate regression. But the healthy human condition is progressive growth—an expansion of capacity, need, and responsibility. A group care program that operates only on the level of current capability of inmates is thus by definition failing unless it caters to terminal cases; yet the promotion of independence and self-evaluated ability in a highly professionalized environment is uneconomic. What are the physicians and nurses to do if the patients say they are getting healthier and can care for themselves? What will be the teacher's role if the students learn from one another? What of the judge and policeman if justice and principled behavior are internalized? In a sense, then, the presence of professionals in the asylum also means that those who improve must leave and relinquish the expensive (professionally surrounded and served) environment to others who need it.

Such a cardinal cost-analysis principle for the investment of professional resources tends to concentrate the sick and incapable for maximal utilization of professional manpower. It makes some sense in the excision of infected appendixes and the immobilization of leg fractures. It makes little sense in group care. If growth in general and recovery from regressed (sick, retarded, antisocial) states is dependent on the pull of higher stages of operation—nomocracy pulling on dependency, peer evaluation on nomocracy, and the mature conscience on them all—then models and opportunities must permeate the asylum if it is to be benevolent.

MORE ON GROWTH

The inclination of human organisms toward growth and recovery is so strong that only very effective environmental measures manage to suppress it.[8] But many professionals and some parents are amazingly inventive. They boss too much, treat too much, or neglect too much, thereby preventing maturity or requiring its presence beyond the conceivable capacity of the inmates (see, for example, Levy 1943; Spitz 1945–46; or Peck, Havighurst et al. 1960). Growth is a ladder.

Stages of development are an accepted and well-supported conception. Piaget (1967), for example, has shown their presence in cognition; Kohlberg (1969) has observed it in the growth of moral character. Less has been said regarding the processes of regression and recovery and the pull of higher level stages on those beneath them. Discussing the development of moral judgment in children, Kohlberg (1969) showed that every child has a modal response and a statistically predictable range (patterned somewhat after the normal curve).

> On the average, 50 per cent of a child's moral judgments fit a single stage. The remainder are distributed around this mode in decreasing fashion as one moves successively farther on the ordinal scale from the modal stage. . . . While S's have difficulty comprehending stages above their own, and do not have difficulty with stages below their own, they prefer higher stages to the lower stages [pp. 386–87].

Having shown the stage consistency of persons and the pull of higher stages,[9] Kohlberg went further and claimed they represent "a hierarchical sequence quite independent of the fact that they correspond to trends of age-development [p. 388]". Such a theoretical formulation should encompass and produce evidence of regression (for 3 subjects out of 50 in Kramer's (1968) study, reform school and jail actually did have regressive effects) and of the pulling capability subsequent stages possess.[10]

This pulling capacity is of particular importance. If a benevolent asylum is intended to produce growth and recovery, then it must contain higher stages as models and as attainable expectations.[11] Attainability is in turn related to distance and help. How high can the child or lowered capacity adolescent or adult reach, and what kinds of boosts can the asylum provide? In terms of moral judgment, again, it seems that a person can comprehend all stages below his own, his current level of functioning, and a little above it. Kohlberg (1969) says: "Subjects can correctly recapitulate statements at all stages below or at their own level, correctly recapitulate statements at one stage above their own, and fail to correctly recapitulate statements two or more stages above their own [p. 386]." Since comprehension of the demands that each stage poses is a prerequisite (but not a guarantee!) of enactment, there is little use in providing environments that require a much higher level of competence (moral judgment or other) than the inmate has; it may even be disturbing or immobilizing. But he can grasp one stage above the level of his current functioning and prefers it to a lower level. This point is critical. The existence of such behavior in the asylum is therefore far more important for an inmate's development than is the presence of much higher levels of functioning that, given his condition, are unattainable to him. In more concrete terms, we may say that while the presence of professionals who function on an exchange level may lead to a positive general atmosphere in a group setting, their utility as models will be limited by the very distance in capability between them and the inmates. By contrast, models can be utilized if the setting contains a ladder of competence among inmates, some close to the level proper for initial entry (i.e., young, sick, asocial), others close to exchange capability, and others at numerous positions in between.[12]

A continuum of capability, which implies also a continuum of demand with emphasis on upward progression, provides not only a chain of continuously appropriate models but also the probability of self-evaluation. In such a setting the self may be measured against possible other selves that are within reach and against real or imagined behavior considered in terms of its painful or pleasant effect for self (in lower stages) and for self and various categories of others (in the higher stages). A major force for progression toward increased capability is thus an environment (asylum or other) that provides the proper models and evaluators as an inmate moves upward. The difficulty of providing such an environment outside the family (and sometimes within it; see, for example, Peck, Havighurst et al. 1960) is obvious. It hangs on producing a rationale for keeping recovering and fully healthy people in settings for the incapable in order to help the incapable, or, conversely, putting incapable into situations where most persons have greater and even very high capacity. In regard to childrearing as contrasted with treatment concerns, the difficulties are less. Various schemes for age mixing have evolved, though children's settings and in particular academically oriented establishments are predominantly and rather rigidly age graded. Since in childhood age and capability are rather highly correlated, separation based on age produces a narrow demand span in each group. Such an arrangment is in a more limited sense equivalent to exclusion of the able from a setting treating the disabled.

Narrowing the span of demands (only the sick are here) or offering a very broad span with wide internal gaps (psychotic children, guard-type attendants, and sympathetic social workers with egalitarian illusions) not only reduces the opportunities for self-definition through modeling and evaluation but also totally precludes feasible role playing. If only the sick are here then there is no room for someone who tries to help himself. Only those who cannot help themselves and those who can guard or treat others are acceptable in the system. Participation can therefore be either on the level of sickness or expertise, or not at all. In an orphanage as it is generally organized, participation may span two levels: dependency–authority and rule orientation. If children are kept in such an environment beyond the point where they should naturally move from one level of expectation to another, retardation is common (see Skeels, Chap. 10). Moving the child into a setting where role-taking opportunities increase (even vis-à-vis retarded youths and adults) leads to progression and growth (Skeels, Chap. 10); putting young people who function on the level of rule orientation into articulated peer groups within an exchange environment moves them toward exchange capability (Wolins, Chaps. 14 and 15).

THE CRUCIAL ROLE OF PEERS

That families provide no assurance of a continuous and appropriately demanding environment speaks to the fallacy of excluding nonfamilial settings as possibilities for the healthy but deprived child. Moreover, families alone are incapable of providing a continuum of expectations and the necessary opportunities for role taking and evaluation. It is within the peer group and eventually in the broader society that some of these must take place. While families can and many do provide possibilities for discussion of moral and other maturational competence and responsibility issues, the relationship between family patterns and child behavior accounts for only part of the differences in the children. Holstein (1968), for example, found that parents who were "taking a child's opinion seriously and discussing it" were considerably more likely (than parents who did not behave in this manner) to have 13-year-old mature children. Of the children in the first category 70 percent were in Kohlberg's moral stages 3 and 4, while only 40 percent of the others attained that level.

It appears that while discussing with the child implications of his own behavior may indeed be quite effective, particularly when the parent–child relationships are open and suffused with affection, the peer group may exert an even more powerful influence by providing egalitarian role opportunities. This is essentially Piaget's position in making the assertion that the hierarchical respect relationship of children to parents prevents role taking that involves egalitarian, mutual-respect evaluations.[13] Some recent research by Sherif and his co-workers has shown that "in making choices between their [the peers'] activities and standards and those of the family, church, or school, they frequently neglected the latter [Sherif and Sherif 1965, p. 279]."[14] While the powerful role of peers in promoting values divergent from those of parents appears to be taken for granted and supported by some evidence in the United States, the same does not appear to hold in some other societies. Neither Soviet teenagers nor those reared in the Israeli kibbutz have shown such a tendency. This absence may imply peer influence relatively lower than in the United States; however, researchers generally interpret it quite the opposite way—namely, as a convergence of adult and youth values in which the peer group with all the role playing, evaluation, and sanctioning repertoire at its disposal promotes the general values of the system (see Chap. 13; also Spiro 1958; Rabin 1965).[15]

Another possible explanation for the strength of peer groups in molding behavior is the probability that decisions there will not be unilateral. While many families are governed by authority and rules, peer behavior is mainly one of other-orientation and consensus. The generally egalitarian relationships in peer groups allow, and in fact for purposes of leadership require, discussion of alternatives. Standards of appropriate behavior are therefore produced in a group rather than privately. Evidence shows that group-formed standards are more persistent even in regard to relatively neutral stimuli (e.g., frequencies of auditory signals) than are those the person achieves on his own (Sherif and Sherif 1965, pp. 276–78). Further, the adherence to the norms developed is highest for stable groups—naturally produced in group care—least for individual decisions, and about halfway between these for ad hoc groupings.

Participation, then, is a critical matter in any social system that intends to promote growth, propel members in the direction of common values, and have its norms win out after a change in setting. Since an authoritarian or imposed rule-governed asylum yields few opportuntities for participation, its norms are unlikely to persist when the inmate leaves, even if they are successfully implemented internally. Nor does a collectivity of inmates capable of functioning exclusively on these levels provide the staff with an incentive or opportunity to explain the possible reasonableness of the norms. The lawmakers (lawgivers, almost) and the subjects are just too far apart in power and competence. Not so if some more competent peers are present who may be entrusted with a share in rulemaking and if the anticipation of one's own involvement is realistic in the light of the involvement of not very much more competent others. An ability to participate within the asylum is likely to affect not only the persistence of norms established there but also one's perception of rule-governed aspects of society in general. Kohlberg (1969) cites as an example the powerless dependent–authoritarian view of a lower class child in contrast with the exchange reaction of a middle class one.

> Question: "Should someone obey a law if he doesn't think it is a good law?"
> Response of lower-class boy: "Yes, a law is a law and you can't do nothing about it. You have to obey it, you should. That's what it's there for."
> Response of upper-middle-class boy with same IQ: "The law's the law but I think people themselves can tell what's right or wrong. I suppose the laws are made by many different groups of people with different ideas. But if you don't believe in a law, you should try to get it changed, you shouldn't disobey it" [p. 401].

Both boys are prepared to obey the law, the first out of a sense of powerlessness, the second out of consideration for the divergent interests that have promoted the existing rules. However, beyond the present acceptance is the question of subsequent reaction to the admittedly unfair law. Will it be the frustration and aggression of the helpless or the movement toward change of the self-perceived competent (see Maier 1949)? In short, performance at some level in one dominant setting, such as an asylum or a social class, tends to be generalized to others. Low levels of functioning persist in spite of higher intellectual and other capability when the environment fails to offer the opportunities for the kind of hand-over-hand climb that solid development, one precluding regression, appears to require.

STABILITY OR CHANGE?

Lack of capacity in person or setting reduces the probability of continuing or maintaining growth. Settling for a low level of functioning may result from total satisfaction or satiation—e.g., the overprotected, lovingly sheltered child (Levy 1943)—from overwhelming demand—e.g., American prisoners of war in North Korea (Segal 1957)—from boredom—e.g., children in standard orphanages (Goldfarb 1947; Skeels 1938). It is quite likely that persons so deprived will find their way into extrafamilial care by virtue of their impaired capability. With advancing age their level of functioning will stabilize and the probability of modification decline. Peck, Havighurst et al. (1960) spoke to this issue when they referred to "a characteristic personality and character pattern which was laid down by age ten and changed little thereafter" (p. 157). Bloom (1964) drew similar conclusions from a much broader range of data, including physical characteristics, intelligence, interests, and attitudes. Kohlberg (1969) and his co-workers also reported stabilization, though more protracted.

> As children move into adulthood . . . those who remain primarily at Stages 1 and 2 crystalize into pure types, an extreme example being some delinquents with an explicit Stage 2 con-man ideology. Subjects moving into the higher stages (4, 5 and 6) stabilize more slowly . . ., but by the middle twenties have become the purest types of all [p. 389].[16]

Some of the more pessimistic theories of personality contain assumptions that little can be done to modify such fixations on subadult levels of functioning. This is a curious position, particularly if the theory underlies prescriptions for treatment. However, our concern here is not with the theoretical issue but rather with indications of personal and environmental conditions which may allow the asylum to become benevolent—that is, enter the business of growth rather than assume the inevitability of warehousing. On the personal side openings for increased competence seem to arise from disorganization. Normally the transition from one level of functioning to another is, in the words of Erikson (1950, 1963 ed.), "a crisis, more or less beset with fumbling and fear [p. 255]", which is followed by reintegration and a new level of competence. Fixated behavior is generally the safe haven in the stormy sea of life. The dangers of attempting to scale the next level have been assessed and rejected in fear. Only a massive effort can induce the failure to make another try. Exactly because of its isolation, an asylum can produce the conditions needed for such an attempt—namely, the safe environment in which to fail and the massive push to succeed. In fact, some efforts at promoting growth may even call for inducing initial regression in order to assure subsequent success. Feuerstein (1971) has experimented with such an approach in the initial phases of institutional care for low achievers, which is then followed by raised expectations and considerable advances (see also Rapaport and Arad, Chap. 16). A naturally induced regression ensues when teen-agers from traditional families living in urban Israeli slums are placed in egalitarian, high-expectation kibbutz groups. Here, too, considerable change has resulted (Wolins, Chap. 15).

While evidence to separate the condition of the inmate from the power of the environment is very meager and observed changes could conceivably be ascribed completely to environmental forces that press the person "from every angle toward a particular type of development or outcome" (Bloom 1964, p. 212), initial disorientation seems not only inevitable but necessary. Effective conversion of civilians into soldiers, for example, has the two qualities of powerful environment and disorientation of the recruit. "The basic training period [is] . . . not one of gradual inculcation of the army *mores*, but one of intensive shock treatment. The new recruit, a lone individual, is helplessly insecure in the bewildering newness and complexity of his environment [Stouffer et al. 1949, I, p. 411]." However, as the disorientation is reduced and self-confidence grows, the ability to resist environmental pressures increases vis-à-vis the same army setting.

An asylum that aspires to more than warehousing functions must deal with the problem of treatment. Available treatment is by no means a pure blessing. For one thing, it carries the implication of abnormality in those being treated and the invidious distinctions between them and others in the setting. In addition, authoritarian disposition is usually an unwelcome concomitant of professional treatment. However, this may be a necessary price to pay for the advantages gained from expertise. The question is, if in a benevolent asylum the environment (i.e., the relevant others) is perceived as the medium of therapeutic intervention in which the professional expert is in the background, when should he stand up and be seen? Mainly, it would seem, when the intervention is radical, when it requires maximal expertise, and when it will lead to greater capability in person or setting shortly thereafter.

A healthy, competent environment is likely to make a mark *eventually* on any but terminal cases. Few inmates of asylums are in this category. The difficulty is that many more are so abrasive in their deviance that the environment either ejects them or reinforces their aberration. In order to avoid either of these outcomes, quick intervention is needed. On the one hand, the tolerance of the setting must be sustained; on the other, the disturbing behavior must be eliminated or reduced, and quickly. In these straits behavior modification—specific, rather rapid, and involving short-term professional intervention (see Chap. 19; Ullman and Krasner 1965; Ullman 1969)—promises to be more useful than clinical development of insight (see Paul 1966).[17]

An alternative to rapid intervention within the setting is the use of outside treatment facilities that permit long-term professional attention for those who need it without interpenetrating the institutional environment. Not only does such a procedure reduce the probability of regressing the whole program to a level compatible with substantial professional intervention (authority and rules again!), it also does not carry even the same connotations for the treated person. There is a great deal of difference between seeing the "headshrinker" or probation officer once a week while meeting more or less normal peer expectations the rest of the time as contrasted with being confined to a hospital, treatment center, or "hall" full time.

Occasional, limited intervention of professionals may probably be had without the further danger of separating the expressive from the instrumental aspects of life and focusing totally on the instrumental. Efficiency required for optimal use of expensive and scarce professional resources dictates heavy emphasis on the instrumental. An extreme example is a surgical ward, where the sick, the gadgets, the timing, the exclusion of outsiders and extraneous activity are all part of an efficient social structure for cutting out appendixes, or grafting skin, or transplanting kidneys. But exactly these conditions preclude any kind of expressive behavior on the part of patients, family visitors, and staff. Since in asylums many of the growth-promoting conditions are based on the tie between expressive and instrumental behaviors that a small community provides (Redfield 1941; Caudill 1958), infringements on expressive behavior can be most serious.

The professional, then, is a friend, but he must not come in as a dinner guest and turn into the host. Warily, though, the benevolent asylum can offer him opportunities not only to treat but also to do so more effectively than with persons not confined. First, the asylum can mobilize other forces in the direction of professional intervention, whether for the eradication of ticks or cleptomania or the development of a higher level of morality. Additionally, the asylum can be a safe environment where failure at newly attempted tasks is less serious than outside. That such safety is an important condition of growth is illustrated in a familial childrearing setting (e.g., Peck, Havighurst et al. 1960) as well as in experimental learning situations. As the formulators of these learning experiments put it, the formation of new patterns must be "cut off, in some suitable sense, from the more serious sides of the society's activity, that is to say . . . from immediate problems of welfare and survival" (Moore and Anderson 1969, p. 575). Since some therapeutic intervention requires risking new behavior, the asylum can provide the as-if world where it may be tried out for its social consequences without serious risk to welfare and survival.

Is the Asylum Really so Good?

Having spoken about the possibility of good asylums, we should not fail to point out some persistent difficulties that tend to plague them. Descriptions of institutional care of the young, the mentally ill, the aged, and the delinquent read like the Book of Lamentations,[18] and they should, since asylums, isolated from outside scrutiny and largely immune to the counter-power of inmates, may indeed be that way. Many are in fact snake pits, special hells, social systems of captives.

Goffman (1961), who has done an outstanding job of analyzing asylums, lists five types of such "total institutions": (1) for the incapable and harmless, such as the blind, aged, orphaned, and indigent; (2) for the incapable but dangerous, such as carriers of contagious disease, the mentally deranged; (3) for the capable dangerous, such as criminals, revolutionaries, dissenters; (4) for those who can best be improved through centralization in order to "pursue a worklike task"—for example, army recruits, boarding-school pupils, work camp members; (5) for those seeking escape—for example, monks.

All of these settings, according to Goffman, suffer from three fundamental difficulties: they generate batch living, a binary character, and authoritarianism. A rationalized, integrated, fully visible, and inescapable environment in which every act must be carried out is no doubt hard to take. There is no avoiding the setting capable of a total "assault on the self." An inmate may become a manipulated toy of the system, with no power to defend himself and no means of escape; in short, the environment is very strong and can lead to disaster. But it also has the built-in capacity to produce positive change if the batch living is mobilized, not for punishment, detention, or staff convenience, but for inmate growth. Young people in a kibbutz youth group are likely to be just as isolated and the stage of their activity as geographically constricted as orphans in an orphanage, but they do not stagnate, nor do they by and large seek to crawl down the cracks of their social structure.[19]

Perhaps the distinction arises from the other two of Goffman's negative absolutes. In an institution for the sick, the helpless, the outcast, it is not surprising that staff tend to separate themselves from inmates and create a binary structure—for the able and worthy, for the unable and unworthy. But this structure can occur only if the capability of inmates is kept continually low by exclusion and dismissal of the more able. Distance between staff and inmates is therefore a function not of isolation and totality but of the expectation and evidence of the inmates' increased capability. In the kibbutz youth group and the Austrian *Kinderdorf,* this evidence exists in former inmates who are now members of the productive adult group, whether kibbutz *chaverim* or child-care workers in the village.

Finally, there is the inevitable authoritarianism of an asylum, which leads inmates to withdraw, fight, show outward signs of submission (colonization), or accept the institutional values. The probability of authoritarian behavior in a setting for the incapable who may need to or be compelled to function on a dependency or rule-obedient level is undoubtedly high; it flows from the same sources as the binary structure and is subject to similar amelioration. Even ideological countervention is possible. An egalitarian kibbutz precludes the use of titles and honorifics; everyone, including the group leader of a new batch of slum kids, is called by his first name. An SOS *Kinderdorf* in Austria is built on the mother–child principle; so what is a more natural name, than *Mutti* for the lady in charge of a household and *Tante* for her relief?

Of Goffman's three major defects in institutional care, two have been overcome and the third, batch living, may be a positive force known in other contexts as a "powerful environment" (Bloom 1964). Other difficulties are even more stubborn than those he lists, but they become salient only when the focus of an asylum moves from confinement to growth of capability. A closed setting is by its very character deficient in occupational and familial models and the role-playing choices that precede the inmate's actual move into or return to the status of child or parent, worker or housewife. An asylum is a first-rate place for imitating sickness and having incapable behavior reinforced by inmates and staff.[20] It is a place the healthy avoid for fear of contagion, defamation, or abuse. It is a place where low levels of expectation produce low levels of functioning, which are then justification for the low expectations. To be sure, an asylum usually is that way, but it need not be and is not when the spiral is reversed by the forces of trust and risk. A benevolent asylum is not intended to be solely a haven to protect the inmate and the community but rather a base from which stakes are wagered in the always hazardous game of life.

NOTES

1. As Malone (in Pavenstedt, 1967) points out in a study of children from disorganized lower class families, many of the characteristics common to institutionalized children are also found among those reared in such families. They include: "delayed intellectual and language development, shallow nonspecific relationships, reduced investment in and enjoyment of themselves, diminished initiative and docile behavior (despite poor capacity to control and modulate impulses) [p. 111]."

2. The argument may also be made in the opposite direction. Bettelheim (1969) considers as a virtue the dispersion of parental functions in the kibbutz. He argues that in those instances when the parents are uncaring, incapable, or emotionally disturbed a social arrangement that permits (or, better yet, requires) regular penetration of the family and shared responsibility for child care is a clear asset.

3. In the broader society this level of functioning often is forced on low power groups. Thus, for example, the blacks in the United States or the Jews in the Soviet Union are compelled to appeal to the constitutional guarantees in their respective

countries in order to acquire rights that are legally assured and in actuality unavailable to them. The role of outsiders (a critical press, U.N. debates, statements by famous personages) is clearly important in such cases.

4. Alfred Adler (1964) describes this condition exquisitely:

> Whenever the mother abounds all too evidently with excessive affection and behavior, thought, and action, and even speech, superfluous for the child, then he will be more readily inclined to develop as a parasite (exploiter) and look to other persons for everything he wants. He will . . . seek to have everyone at his beck and call. He will . . . regard it as his right . . . *to take and not to give* [pp. 149–150; italics in original].

5. Baumrind (1970), after an exhaustive review of pertinent literature and a carefully designed longitudinal study of children in several types of familial environments, concludes that a laissez-faire parental position is not the most growth-promoting. Her data and those of others point to the superiority of the authoritative over the authoritarian or totally egalitarian familial arrangement. Baumrind's (1968) description of the authoritative parent–child relationship merits an extensive quotation. (Note that in the quotation "she" refers to a parent of either sex and "he" to a child of either sex.)

> [The authoritative parent attempts] to direct the child's activities but in a rational, issue-oriented manner. She encourages verbal give and take, and shares with the child the reasoning behind her policy. She values both expressive and instrumental attributes, both autonomous self-will and disciplined conformity. Therefore she exerts firm control at points of parent-child divergence, but does not hem the child in with restrictions. . . . The authoritative parent affirms the child's present qualities, but also sets standards for future conduct. She uses reason as well as power to achieve her objectives. She does not base her decisions on group consensus or the individual child's desires; but also, does not regard herself as infallible or divinely inspired [p. 261].

The authoritative parent's orientation is toward exchange behavior. Such a parent can tolerate occasional laissez faire, values the experientially attained norms embodied in the legal code, is cognizant of the group and its predispositions, but above all else presses toward an inner-directed integration of these pressures in accord with moral principles. In this respect the authoritative parent is a good model for the benevolent asylum.

Peck, Havighurst et al. (1960, p. 111) illustrate a relationship between the laissez-faire family and the child of "expedient" moral character. They describe such a person as

> primarily self-centered, . . . consider[ing] other people's welfare and reactions only in order to gain his personal ends. He tends to get what he wants with a minimum of giving in return. He behaves in ways his society defines as moral, only so long as it suits his purpose [p. 5].

In terms of our levels of functioning, this is dependency-nomocracy.

6. By acting in their professional roles and treating the inmates in accordance with the low level of competency into which they have been defined, the professionals aggravate the inmates' condition. They contribute to an "unprogrammed reinforcement of patients' behavior" (Gelfand et al. 1967).

7. While Maxwell Jones and his colleagues recognized some time ago the possibly optimal utilization of professionals as lying in indirect influences on institutional environments, it is the behavior modification adherents who have done the most telling

work on this subject (see, for example, Tharp and Wetzel 1969). Clearly the more specific the goal, the more precise and replicable the means the easier they are to communicate and hence to delegate to less trained members of the environment, be they inmates or staff. The application of such principles is discussed in some detail in Chap. 19.

8. Up to a point societal needs are also served by personal growth. Where the optimal point lies from a societal point of view is somewhat problematic. Clearly only the leper colony (or another society of the damned or doomed) can tolerate long-term dependency-level behavior. Authoritarian societies encourage growth at the very least to the nomocracy level. Unfortunately for them, any excursion into massive advanced education and extensive cognitive growth, needed to foster an industrial society, has a fallout of some small proportion of moral, exchange-level giants. Thus, Hitler had his Niemoellers, Kosygin et al. have their Sakharovs, and we have had our Martin Luther Kings. Each is an indication of the range of human potential, a witness to the failures of society around him and a persistent thorn in the communal flesh.

9. Why and how the higher levels exert such a pull is by no means clear. Surely it does not suffice to say that there is a natural tendency to grow. If the pull to higher levels of functioning exists as Erikson, Piaget, Kohlberg, and others claim and demonstrate, then the causal ingredients of this pull should become a basic component of institutional care. In the meantime, we must be satisfied with conjecture (see Wolins 1969).

10. A question may well be raised about the propriety of shifting from the dimension of general development to stages of moral judgment—a cognitive issue. Both Piaget and Kohlberg provide the justification in the evidence of marked correlations between cognitive and affective development, which gives grounds for assuming a common environmental base for both.

11. The role of models in child development is a major research area with a very substantial literature, mostly in Russian and English. (See, for example, Zaporozhets 1960; Bandura and Walters 1963.)

12. The importance of progression is illustrated in Turiel's (1966) research, which shows the ability of sixth-grade children to increase their moral judgments (on a six-stage continuum) when given advice one stage above their own, but no effect when the advice was two stages above. Blatt (1969), following the same rationale, was successful in raising some children's moral thinking two stages by presenting the highest only after the one below had been incorporated.

13. A child is capable of exercising behavior control with peers in a way prevented by parental fate control over him in the familial home (Thibaut and Kelley 1959).

14. There is a particularly interesting difference in the appraisal of parental versus peer skills. In a simple eye–hand coordination test when children are asked to judge the performance of their fathers and a friend, the younger overestimate father's performance, the older (adolescents) overestimate the friend's performance (Sherif and Sherif 1965, p. 280).

15. An analysis of adolescent value positions in kibbutz youth groups vis-à-vis the expectations of adult group leaders shows that the divergence that does occur is one of overzealousness—a push toward a holier-than-thou position on some issues (see Alterman et al. 1966, chap. iv).

16. Early stabilization of cognitive styles is demonstrated by Witkin (1969) and others who have also shown its relation to socialization patterns.

17. Bandura (1969) offers an extensive statement of behavior modification procedures. For the purposes of the present paper several subjects Bandura discusses are of particular interest. These include the specification (i.e., clear delimitation) of objectives, modeling, positive and aversive control, and the ethical implications of such control.

While the principles of behavior modification are recommended in this paper specifically for the purpose of dealing with single, rather delimited behavioral entities, they have also been used to affect the operation of a whole institution (see Ayllon and Azrin 1968). This work appears to show the possibility of ultimately combining the instrumental requirements of a goal-oriented institution with the great expressive demands made on any group-living environment without undue damage to either. Since sole emphasis on instrumental requirements is the basis for the batch-living attributes that Goffman decries and total concern with expressive demands a source of laissez-faire demoralization, neither is in itself an adequate condition for a *benevolent* asylum.

18. Even the titles are fearful: "A Special Hell for Children," *Snake Pit, The Society of Captives, The Last Refuge.*

19. Wolins (Chap. 15) has described some remarkable growth that occurs among young people in a particularly successful kibbutz youth group. Here the wards did not experience any sense of total visibility, though they were in a setting that exerts tremendous pressure. The countervailing forces in such a benevolent environment appear to be the affective stance the kibbutz assumes as foster mother and the high moral principles the *madrichim* (leaders) teach and practice.

20. This kind of setting, without substantial and prestigious models of health, is so disfunctional in treatment that some writers suggest the need to "insulate the individual from the larger group (the delinquent neighborhood or the social circles the alcoholic frequents) in order to reduce the efficacy of forces that maintain the individual's level of behavior [Riecken and Homans 1954, p. 827]."

II

History, Ideology, Politics, and Other Relevancies

2

Institutional Care and Placing-Out: The Place of Each in the Care of Dependent Children

ELIAS L. TROTZKEY

The issue of group care and the childrearing deficits it produces as compared with families has a considerable history. Early in this century opponents and proponents paraded their arguments and on some (rare) occasions supported them with evidence. Trotzkey's report is probably the most thoughtful and best documented of these formulations. That it is also obscure reflects more on American child care professionals than on its own relevance when written or now.

The "Institution vs Placing-out" Controversy

The closing years of the past and the opening years of the present century were marked by great progress in the field of dependent child care. Gradually and increasingly emphasis was properly placed where it really belongs, on conserving the child's natural home for which, it is generally recognized, there is no substitute, however well the dependent child may be cared for elsewhere. The question remained, however, where the child should be placed whose family could not be kept intact or for whose best interest it was to be detached from the natural home. With the general attitude centered on the home, it was natural that placement under conditions approximating as

In the early months of 1929, the Executive Board of the Marks Nathan Jewish Orphan Home requested the Executive Director, Elias L. Trotzkey, to prepare a memorandum on the subject of the institutional care of children with particular reference to the claims put forth on behalf of boarding-out. The Board desired information that would make possible an appraisal of the relative merits of both types of care, also an opinion on community organization with respect to child care. Chicago, Illinois, February 10, 1930.

closely as possible normal family life and not in institutions should be favored and urged.

There have always been varied views held regarding the respective merits of institutional care and placement in private family homes. Divergent expressions of opinion on the subject were heard from time to time for the past 50 years or more. It was only during the past three decades, however, that this controversy took on a more vigorous form and became even acrimonious in character. The advocates of private family care, or placing-out, were not satisfied with merely pointing out the advantages to the child they contended were to be found in placement in private homes, and with giving their best efforts to the perfecting of this mode of care, but became uncompromising in their insistence that the institution must go into the discard and be replaced entirely by the placing-out plan. Varying somewhat the Shakespearean slogan, "The play's the thing," the cry among social workers and lay communal leaders, who regarded themselves as advanced and enlightened in their views, became "The home's the thing" for the dependent child, the "home," not the "Home." If we may be pardoned the play on words, capital was made of this distinction by the more zealous advocates of placing-out in discrediting the institutional type of care with its more than two and a quarter centuries of continuous effort and expansion and its hold on the sympathies and support of a substantial public following.

In the heated discussions that took place from time to time, the institution bore the brunt of unsparing condemnation. In their highly meritorious zeal to secure for the child what they consider is for his best interests, the protagonists of private family care have not hesitated to condemn all children's institutions, efficient and progressive as well as inefficient and unworthy. It has been made to appear that the institution in itself is bad and cannot be made to function to the child's advantage, and must therefore go.

The fullest and frankest formulation of the sweeping attitude of the opponents of institutional care is that of a well-known and highly respected child welfare worker, Dr. R. R. Reeder [1925], a former superintendent of an institution for children, who declared:

> As a permanent home or care-taking proposition for normal children, the orphan asylum should go out of business; its day is past; it is not a real childhood home, and cannot by any courtesy of speech claim to be such [p. 313].

The effect of the agitation to do away with institutions and place children instead in private family homes, with complete disregard of what institutions of the better type have been and are doing and are further capable of doing, could have but one result. Two hostile camps were set up, at odds and at war with each other, both set in their respective views, each out to "get" the other and, if possible, put him out of business. To the less discriminating and less tolerant of the institutional-minded, the "home-finders" became increasingly objectionable, and relations with them reached the breaking point. Instead of co-workers in a common cause, they were viewed as trouble-makers and wreckers of institutions with venerable traditions and on the whole praiseworthy records of service to the dependent child. The crusading evangels of placing-out, on the other hand, regarded institutional workers as harpies from whose evil clutches they must rescue suffering childhood. Under such circumstances, reason, sane and informed discussion, friendly interchange of views, were out of the question. Sentimentality instead of sober study shaped attitudes and steeled determination. Dispassionate treatment of the matter was made impossible by the surge of feelings aroused, particularly among those in the anti-institutional placing-out camp who at times seemed more bent on discrediting institutions than protecting children and placing them under ideal conditions maintained by adequate supervision. It was a big job, indeed, that the determined proponents of placing-out had assumed, a job in itself sufficient to tax their energies without making unceasing and inconsiderate attacks on institutional care, but so constantly and uncompromisingly was this campaign against institutions carried on that the latter were placed on the defensive. It was natural for the institutions to "hit back" or at least defend themselves from the unjust attacks made upon them, but they were at a disadvantage, because of the growing wave of hostile sentiment that had systematically been stirred against them.

Fair-minded witnesses of the controversy outside the ranks of professional institutional workers felt it necessary from time to time to intervene. Thus Dr. Charles H. Johnson, secretary of the New York Board of Charities, was moved to say:

> The thousands of earnest people in this State who are giving their lives to institutional service, taking the place of the fathers and mothers who have neglected or deserted their children . . ., have little support from the public whenever anyone wishes to attack their respective institutions. The truth is that the institutions today are, as a rule, conducted on a high plane of human interest and that the standards of individual care are being constantly raised [U.S. Children's Bureau 1929, p. 34].

Edmund J. Butler, executive secretary of the Catholic Home Bureau for Dependent Children, New York City, while speaking favorably on placing-out and legal adoption, also deplored the attacks on institutions, saying:

> During a period of more than 40 years in which the writer has been in personal contact with directors of institutions he has never met one who did not hold that a normal family home is the best place for a dependent child. In view of the general attitude with respect to these methods of child-caring, it is surprising that any of their advocates should find it necessary to resort to abuse of well-regulated institutions [U.S. Children's Bureau 1929, p. 34].

Fortunately, there are evidences today of a more enlightened spirit. There are indications that the intolerance that ran riot during the past quarter of a century has spent its force. The realization is growing among child-care workers, able to emancipate themselves from one-sidedness, that all virtue does not inhere in any one type of care, that all types have advantages as well as disadvantages, that the time has come to weigh the relative advantages of each impartially, free from all prepossessions and prejudices, open-minded enough to recognize merit where it exists, animated solely by the consideration of what is best for the child when account is taken of the circumstances surrounding each child. Shortcomings in any type of care must be recognized and avoided; advantages in any type of care, old or new, should be considered and incorporated in that ideal and complete form of care to which as child-care workers worthy of the name we must aspire and as completely as possible and as soon as possible achieve.

Dr. C. C. Carstens, director of the Child Welfare League of America, in his Annual Report for the year 1922–23, encouragingly reveals the newer spirit when he says:

> There is a strong tendency and one wholly to be welcomed for both child-placing agencies and children's institutions to come into helpful relations with each other. . . . The spirit of competition in social work is discredited among honest and intelligent workers. The needs of the child are given more consideration. Cooperation is no longer practised merely as lip service, but is acted upon. To this the development of councils of social agencies and chests has contributed.

Dr. W. H. Slingerland [1919] adds his voice to the growing chorus of those who realize the need of more harmonious relations and more tolerant views among child-care workers. Sturdy and steadfast as he is in his advocacy of placing-out or boarding-out in which he is by virtue of his scholarly treatment of the matter a recognized authority, he yet declares:

> The child-placer and the institution officer need not feel that they represent two opposite poles of work, but rather that they are laboring in adjacent zones of service, whose boundaries are undefined and whose tasks intermingle. Let each do his best to give full proof of his ministry. At present, in most of the states, there is work for all. . . . The fair-minded advocate of child-placing now says to the advocate of institutions: "Let us cooperate. The world is full of needy children. Gather some of them in your institutions and do your best for their welfare. We will go ahead with our home-finding, eagerly welcoming all improved methods and facilities for doing good work" [p. 193].

One thing all ought to be fair and frank enough to realize and admit. We never will or can get very far when our viewpoint is colored by unreasoning bias against or hatred or distrust of any type of child care. We must, above all, have a higher and more excusable motive and objective than putting the other fellow out of business. Devotion to the child demands that we make possible for him the utmost fullness of life which alone gives meaning and value to any particular plan or program of child care. Let us therefore, as reasonable and honest child-care workers, conscious of our shortcomings as well as devoted to our ideals and convictions, be of service to one another as well as to the child. Only by so doing can we hope to be of the greatest service to the child.

Had this spirit been shown a quarter of a century ago, much of the heated controversy that all must regret would have been avoided and perhaps more progress would have been made in child care. The mistakes that have been made are not, however, without their value. In human affairs it is wholesome to criticize and even challenge and combat. Honest differences of opinion frankly and even vigorously expressed are essential to progress. Forced to face their relentless foes, institutions have been compelled to cast aside a self-satisfied attitude and put their houses in order. Improved methods have been adopted, and the "orphan asylum" has given way to the "orphan home." Objectionable features, which earnest and advanced institutional workers have never condoned, have been eliminated. Placing-out, too, has gone through a sobering process and now is ready to view the placement of children in a more competent manner and less intolerant spirit. Time has relegated the rabid in the ranks of opposition and resistance to institutional care to the rear, and prepared the way for a thoroughgoing study of the entire question of dependent child care, which can have but one result, the working out sooner or later of a comprehensive program which shall conserve the values and bring out the further possibilities of institutional custodianship and gain for child life the promise of good placement. The trend of thought and practice fortunately with respect to types of child care is away from antithetical exclusiveness and toward supplementary and complementary inclusiveness.

The Development of Institutional Care
and Placing-out

In order to have an intelligent insight into the problem of dependent child care, it is essential that we apply good casework methods that will give us the proper background of the growth of this phase of social service and a knowledge of how the problem has been viewed and treated in the past.

The dependent child is not a product or phenomenon of our own time or recent times. He is as old as human society. Victim of the vicissitudes of life in time of peace no less than war, it has been necessary since time immemorial to make special provision for his care.

The first humane views and legal enactments on record in behalf of dependent children are those to be found in the Pentateuch (especially Deuteronomy 14:28, 29; 24:21; 26:12, 13). It is perhaps more than an historical coincidence that the first champion of the cause of the dependent child should have been the infant who was "placed-out" hazardously among the bulrushes along the Nile and eventually in the luxurious home of Paraoh's daughter, and who was thus deprived of the privilege of being brought up in his natural home. Whatever may have been the practice in pre-Pentateuchal times, since this inspired code began its blessed task of elevating human life, the "fatherless" have been assured of as considerate treatment as successive generations have interpreted and applied its express injunctions, steadily supplemented by a growing body of child-protecting and -conserving legislation in the codes of the various nations of subsequent days.

No purpose is served by elaborating on historical and antiquarian details to establish the fact that either type of care antedates the other. Both types of care go back to earliest times. Institutional care and placing-out are as old as the Church and the synagogal traditions upon which it was established. In the earliest days, the type of care used was determined by conditions, not by a recognition of the superior claims of one form over the other. When institutional care was firmly established with the creation of Societies or Orders of the Church founded to care for dependent children as early as the second century of the civil era [Ulhorn 1883], it took and continued to be accorded precedence over other types of care down to modern times.

The modern period of child-welfare may be said to have begun with the founding in France in the year 1633, by St. Vincent de Paul, of the Sisters of Charity, which has ever since devoted its main energies to the care of needy and unfortunate children [McKenna 1907]. The little-known orphanage of the Spanish and Portuguese Jews was established in Amsterdam in 1648. What is usually considered as the first modern orphanage is that established by August Hermann Francke in Germany in 1695. Thus, for convenience we may say that organized institutional care dates from the middle of the 17th century, since which time alone it is necessary to study carefully its growth and development. The first modern placing-out work done on a large scale began when, under the Napoleonic decree of 1811, children in France were boarded out at national expense.

Since our interest is primarily in the development of various types of child-care in our own country, we may disregard European developments and begin our inquiry with colonial times and the years immediately preceding in the mother country.

We must be prepared for some very unpleasant revelations, but these are important, for they enable us to appreciate the conditions with respect to dependent child care that once obtained and the efforts at betterment that have been made from time to time until our own day.

Placing-out in our own land may be said to have begun in 1619 when the Mayor of London sent out to the Virginia country 100 children "to be placed with honest good masters." The crude and semibarbarous character of the placing-out of those days is well described by Dr. Slingerland [1919], as follows.

A precursor of some of the meretricious modern methods of exploitation was the old English child-placing for profit. Four hundred years ago, our English forbears were accustomed practically to enslave well-grown dependent children for work in factories and industrial service, using a system of indentures that later crossed the ocean with our ancestors, and was repeated in the early colonies of America. In 1562, national sanction was given by the English government to an apprentice system amounting to child slavery, an evil that it never fully corrected until less than a century ago. Meanwhile the indenture system came over to the colonies, and although it is now happily almost extinct in its original form, it placed its imprint upon all child-placing of partly grown children in the entire nation [p. 31].

Our national beginnings, therefore, did not open very promisingly for the dependent child. Child-placing certainly was not a term to conjure with in its early application on our shores. Slow indeed was the growth in the community at large of an enlightened and human attitude toward the dependent child now regarded as having special claims, but then considered by the severe and narrow morality of the time as a sacrificial offering for "the sins of the fathers." Even down to a relatively late date in our history, the dependent child was expected to be cringingly grateful for whatever consideration, however scant and gruff, was shown him. Anything was good enough for him. In some quarters this feeling unfortunately still prevails but it is happily now the exception, shamed by the nobler and more equitable prevailing attitude and practice of our day, and bidding fair, at least let us so hope, in the words of Abraham Lincoln, to be "in the course of ultimate extinction." Long and hard indeed was the road that had to be traveled by those true apostles of human betterment in both camps, institutional and noninstitutional, who cast all aside to answer to the call to conserve child life, before the advanced ground on which we stand today could be taken and held.

Institutional care in our country dates from 1729 when the Ursuline Convent in New Orleans made provision to shelter children orphaned through the Indian massacres. In 1740, Rev. George Whitefield founded the Bethesda Orphan House at Savannah, Ga., as a school for needy boys. These and other earlier children's institutions (established in the face of public indifference) were founded primarily to provide religious training and educational advantages not otherwise available to their charges [U.S. Children's Bureau 1927]. The lot of the children they took under their kindly if somewhat stern charge was in marked contrast with that of the mass of dependent children for whom the usual provision was the public poorhouse where they were "incarcerated" without segregation from the other older unfortunates.

The earliest reaction to callous care of children in the United States was against the almhouses, and an agitation began to place as many children as possible instead in private institutions.

"Up to the beginning of the nineteenth century," says Edmond J. Butler, "the prevailing method in this country of dealing with orphans and the children of shiftless, poverty-stricken, deserting, sick or unworthy parents, whose relatives were either unwilling or unable to care for them, was to turn them over to the custodial care of poorhouses, poor farms, or similar places of incarceration. As public institutions these so-called homes for the poor were administered by officials appointed for political reasons. For the most part, they were lacking in the qualifications necessary for adequate service to their poor charges, and their principal claim for a continuance in office was based upon a record of economical management. The evil conditions resulting from this method of child-caring grew to such proportions as to induce high-minded citizens to establish private orphanages and homes for children as a means of providing for them in a more humane way. The movement was slow in its development. It required thirty or more years to create the general interest necessary to produce a response commensurate with the needs of the work. From that time on, the private institutions grew rapidly. Opposition to the old system grew apace and developed a public opinion which during the latter part of the century forced the passage in many States of laws prohibiting the commitment of children to poorhouses or similar institutions. Thereafter public institutions entered the field to share the task of child-caring with those maintained by private agencies [U.S. Children's Bureau 1929, p. 33].

Massachusetts was the first State to rescue its dependent children from almshouse influences. In 1866, it established the first State institution for destitute children in the United States (Folks 1907).

The first private placing-out organization not only in our country but in the world was the Children's Aid Society of the City of New York, founded in 1853 by Charles Loring Brace, antedating by 13 years the earliest organization of a similar nature in England, Dr. Barnardo's Homes. This pioneer of its kind of child-care agency was formed not to make possible for dependent children the benefits of placement in private families as distinguished from mass rearing in institutions, private or public, but to send homeless city children to distant country homes. The contrast was between the country and the city as the proper place to raise children of a certain type, not between institutions and private homes.

In 1868, Massachusetts initiated the first efforts in our country to place children in private families at public expense, presumably because provision could not be made in the state's institution for dependent children for all cases needing care. This type of care soon became popular. Private organizations grew in number, and the work of placing-out increasingly expanded. "The Civil War's aftermath of orphaned and needy children" gave impetus to the establishment both of institutions and placing-out agencies, each type of care developing in its own way. As late as 1890, antagonism between different types of care had not yet developed, at least not in appreciable or organized form. That there was much to be desired in all types of care is not to the discredit of their sponsors and managers. The problem of the dependent child had not yet received the amount and the degree of public attention that later was to be devoted to it, nor—and this is most important—did child-care workers then view the problem in the same way they have since learned to view it. Little or no consideration was given by any type of care to the causes of child dependency or to anything beyond the child himself and his physical and moral needs, and even that in a very limited way. The viewpoint was still negative, to protect the child against ill-treatment and neglect, not positive, how to bring out the best in the child. The work then done was of the nature of child-rescuing rather than child conservation, which later was rightfully visioned not as a problem in itself but as a phase of family conservation. Neither child-placing nor institutional workers appreciated the basic importance of preserving and conserving the dependent child's natural home. Both took for granted that the natural home had been broken up by parental incompetence or obliquity, and it was therefore necessary to provide for the child elsewhere. Neither thought of making efforts to keep the natural home intact. Acting on the crude and cruel theory, as child-care agencies of all kinds, following the legal view of the matter, then did, that when the public stepped in, the parent had to step out, the way was closed to family rehabilitation. The mistake both forms of care made was in viewing the child as a unit apart from the family from which it was originally taken. Less important therefore than the shortcomings, theoretical and practical, of any type of care was the faulty social thinking of the time. Children were recklessly taken from their families by noninstitutional as well as institutional workers neither of whom made or recognized the need of making proper social investigation before placement in a foster home or an institution. Child care then concerned itself with caring for dependent children in increasing numbers with scant thought given to the possible lessening of the number of those needing care outside their own families or the finer practice of what has become a highly skilled and specialized branch of social service. Child care as understood today was not even in its infancy; it wasn't born.

The greatest growth of institutional care in the United States was during 1890–1903. This period coincides with the beginning of the greatest influx of immigration to our shores. During those years alone over 400 orphanages were established.

Placing-out also was extended during this period and after and began to be viewed as opposed to institutional care. Institutions, however, it must be borne in mind, have always to some extent engaged in placing-out.

"Placing-out by child care institutions," says Catherine P. Hewins, general secretary of the Church Home Society of Boston, "is no new thing. It is practically as old as the institution itself, in spite of a popular notion to the contrary. The very phrase 'placing-out' probably originated as connoting the opposite of 'placing-in.' In spite of much hesitancy in the formal acceptance of the methods and of very great difference in procedure, it is none the less true, if the term is used in the broadest and most inclusive sense, that placing-out has been resorted to by all orphanages. That this has not always been done under the banner of placing out or according to the most accepted modern standards does not alter the fact that many children have been put into family homes, often for adoption or by indenture and more rarely with the payment of board. The whole history of placing-out is so interwoven with that of institutional development that it is difficult to determine which began first" [U.S. Children's Bureau 1929, p. 97].

Institutional placing-out, however, was of a limited nature. It was not visioned as an ideal of care for average dependent children, nor did it assume the character of a policy capable of extension. It was practiced only under special circumstances, being regarded and used primarily and exclusively as a means for handling overflow or "problem" cases and very young children who could not consistently be cared for in the institution proper. That is as far as institutions went or felt it necessary to go with regard to placing-out. They viewed the latter as more or less of an experiment at best or a fad and hobby of sentimental enthusiasts. To them institutional care was firmly established and in no need of replacement. It was sanctified by time and above all by a deep religious spirit of which it was the product. Institutional workers of the older type could not conceive of caring for dependent children without religious motivation. It was a specialized activity of the Church, and only the Church could be relied upon to shelter and shield the dependent child and rear him properly. Placing-out workers, too, down to a late day were imbued with an earnest religious spirit. Child care was viewed and pursued by all primarily as "ministerial" and missionary in character. Religion was given the chief place in their program. Difficulty in finding not merely "good homes," in the meaning of the term as understood today, but religious homes of the same faith as the child, caused Catholic and Jewish orphanages to limit themselves in their placing-out work. Unsatisfactory and unfortunate experiences in their placing-out work, too, played their part in making institutional workers reluctant to accept this type of care as a cure-all for the general problem of dependent child care.

Placing-out viewed as the *preferential type of care* dates from 1899, when it was officially approved by the National Conference of Charities and Corrections in a report presented by Thomas M. Mulrey in behalf of a special committee of eminent child-care workers appointed to study child dependency and make recommendations. From that time on, placing-out began to play an increasingly more important part, and soon antagonism developed to institutional care as inimical to the child's best interests. At the historic Conference of 1899, however, although its deliberations and conclusions were attuned to the theme "there's no place like home" for the dependent child, the drawbacks of placing-out and the advantages of good institutional care were pointed out and recognized. Thus Edward A. Hall

[1900], a volunteer placement worker, with no illusions or delusions in the matter, said with sober common sense and commendable fairness of spirit:

> Those who have seen much of the placing of children in homes as it is generally done will agree that there is great room for improvement in the work of looking after children living in families. The beautiful, lovable homes that we read about, where people live who are lying awake nights, ready to take to their hearts the undesirable children of society for the dear children's sake, are few and far between; and the beauties often fade like a fairy vision when tested by practical experience. . . . [The choice in placing children is not] between the institution and a private home but between the institution and the street or worse. . . . I have personally tried the experiment of placing children in the towns of Massachusetts, Connecticut and Vermont; and wherever children were placed in families, directly or recently from their own homes, they were almost invariably returned as unsuitable and undesirable, whereas fully 90% of the children, boys and girls, who had been inmates of institutions for a year or more were placed in the same families and gave general satisfaction.

Here is a frank realization of the difficulty of placing-out children properly and an admirable recognition of the interrelations of both types of care, of how each can serve the other and both best serve the child.

This sane attitude, unfortunately, failed to secure the recognition it deserved. Inspired with a crusading zeal for placing children in private families instead of institutions and blinded by partisanship that did not recognize the reciprocal character of both types of care, a growing number in the home-finding field kept up an aggressive propaganda for their type of care to the exclusion of the other. The drift had set in for caring for children in private families, and it was inevitable that it should run its full course, with institutional care increasingly on the defensive.

Ten years later, at the epoch-making White House Conference held January 25–26, 1909, the pendulum had swung even beyond placement in private families. Then, for the first time, the problem of dependent child care was seen in its entirety. The foster home and the institution were both subordinated to keeping the child's own family life intact, thus making it unnecessary to care for the child elsewhere. Agitation for placement in private families in preference to institutional care, therefore, unwittingly rendered a great service. It directed attention to the child's own home and the need of preventing, if possible, its breakup. The White House Conference went to the very roots of the problem of child dependency when it announced as its first finding:

> Home life is the highest and finest product of civilization. . . . Children should not be deprived of it except for urgent and compelling reasons. Children of parents of worthy character suffering from temporary misfortune, and children of reasonably efficient and deserving mothers who are without the support of the normal bread-winner should, as a rule, be kept with their parents,

such aid being given as may be necessary to maintain homes for the rearing of the children. . . . *Except in unusual circumstances, the home should not be broken up for reasons of poverty, but only for consideration of inefficiency and immorality* [1909].

The White House Conference thus laid down a basic principle which all child-care agencies are in duty bound to respect and uphold. The child's own home comes first in any sound and justifiable program of dependent child care.

With regard to children "who for sufficient reasons must be removed from their homes, or who have no homes," the White House Conference recommended placing-out in preference to institutional care, primarily because of its family features, but not without important reservations. It declared:

It is desirable that if normal in mind and body and not requiring special training, they should be cared for in families *whenever practicable*. The carefully selected foster home is for the normal child the best substitute for the natural home. Such homes should be selected by the most careful process of investigation, carried on by skilled agents through personal investigations and with due regard to the religious faith of the child. After children are placed in homes, adequate visitation with careful consideration of the physical, mental, moral and spiritual training and development of each child on the part of the responsible home-finding agency, is essential. It is recognized that for many children foster homes without payment for board are not practicable immediately after the children become dependent, and that for children requiring temporary care only, the free home is not available. For the temporary, or more or less permanent care of such children, different methods are in use, notably the plan of placing them in families, paying for their board, and the plan of institutional care. Contact with family life is preferable for these children as well as for other normal children. It is necessary however that a large number of carefully selected boarding homes be found if these children are to be cared for in families. *Unless and until such homes are found the use of institutions is necessary* [1909].

The White House Conference saw no need to froth at the mouth with regard to institutions. Committed to the conviction that family life offers more to the child than institutional care, it of necessity inclined to the family type of care but it was sane enough to realize that "unless and until such homes are found" institutions have their place in caring for dependent children. It was mass handling of children which the Conference sought to do away with, the universal practice of institutions of those days. It therefore recommend that

so far as may be found necessary temporarily or permanently to care for children in institutions, these institutions should be conducted on the cottage plan, in order that routine and impersonal care may not unduly suppress individuality and initiative. The cottage unit should not be larger than will permit effective personal relations between the adult care-taker or care-takers of each cottage and each child therein. . . . . Existing congregate institutions should so classify their inmates and segregate them into groups as to secure as many of the benefits of the cottage system as possible, and should look forward to the adoption of the cottage type when new buildings are considered [1909].

The attitude of the White House Conference with respect to institutional care, it is apparent, was not positive but negative. It did not attempt to make a careful study of the actual workings of institutions, nor for that matter of placing-out, nor did it consider benefits accruing to the child from institutional care. It was concerned only and sought to do away with the drawbacks of congregate institutional care as seen from the angle of the utmost of personal attention to each child.

The spirit and essence of the notable conclusions of the White House Conference are well expressed in the following summary of its position.

That the particular conditions and needs of each child should be carefully studied and that he should receive the care and treatment which his individual needs require and which should be as nearly as possible like the life of other children in the community [1909].

It in no way, let it be made clear, took the position that "the worst private home is better than the best institution," as some placing-out enthusiasts insist. It did not file a brief or grant a charter to any type of care nor sign the death warrant of any other type of care per se. It concerned itself primarily not with types of care but with the best interests of the child and the fullest development of his personality.

The White House Conference truly inaugurated an era in dependent child care. Its clear formulation of the problem and the best way to cope with it have been responsible for much of the constructive child welfare thought and effort during the past 20 years. The immediate result of the White House Conference was the creation of the Federal Children's Bureau, the setting up of some state supervision in the field of dependent child-care-placing-out as well as institutional, the enactment of progressive child welfare legislation, federal and state, including mothers' assistance funds, children's codes, and child labor and other enactments that made possible the development of vocational training and initiated the great playground movement.

Beginning with the famous Baltimore Conference of the National Conference of Charities and Correction held in 1915, a period of critical surveys and analyses was ushered in, and attention began to be given to methods and standards of care. Each type of care started to take stock of its own work in unsparing terms. The shortcomings of both types of care were frankly pointed out and the need of honesty emphasized. One of the papers presented at the Baltimore Conference, "A Study of Results of a Child-Placing Society," whose authors were Ruth W. Lawton, Research Worker, and

J. Prentice Murphy, General Secretary, of the Boston Children's Aid Society [1915], stated at the very outset that it was written

"partly as a protest against the tendency of social agencies to under-state the great fallibility of their work. If social work is ever to develop into a profession, searching analysis and criticism of methods and results, no matter what the consequences may be, become prime essentials [p. 164].

The paper then proceeded to handle the question of placement of children in private families, as then practiced, without gloves. Similar treatment was accorded institutional care by William J. Doherty, Second Deputy Commissioner of the Department of Public Charities, New York [1915], who presented a paper at the same conference on "A Study of Results of Institutional Care" which he prefaced by saying:

I shall be compelled to inflict pain upon the finer sensibilities of a large number of devoted men and women who, animated by deeply conscientious motives, have given generously and unselfishly of their time and means to the advancement of the interests of the institutional care of children. . . .
I am actuated solely . . . with an impelling ambition to associate myself with any movement which will eventuate in the adoption of better and more progressive standards in our public and private child-caring institutions [pp. 174–75].

In 1917, we find Dr. Hastings H. Hart, eminent as an authority in child-care work and a pioneer in the field of placing-out, paying his respects to faulty child-placing in these words.

The faithful watch-care of the child in foster homes is seen to be the essential corollary of the child-placing method. We recognize the guilt of the father, perhaps out of work, who deserts the family, and of the mother who abandons her baby; but what shall be said of the conduct of a voluntary association which having put a child into the home of strangers, leaves it for one or two or three years without once trying to learn whether it is well-treated and the foster parents are doing their duty? Yet there are scores of placing-out agencies which grossly neglect to meet their imperative trust [Introduction to Slingerland 1919, pp. 21–22].

With regard to the casework then done, he had this to say.

"It is probably fair to say that of about 1500 institutions and agencies in the United States which place children in family homes, not 25 are doing such case work as would be recognized as adequate by any well-trained worker. There are many agencies, institutional and individual, who dispose of children, body and soul, with little more thought or conscience than they would give to the disposal of surplus kittens or puppies [Introduction to Slingerland 1919, pp. 21–22].

These sharp and stinging criticisms had a wholesome effect. They resulted in the formulation of minimum standards, those for institutional care drafted by Drs. Reeder and Bernstein and Mr. Doherty and adopted with but few modifications by most State departments of child welfare all over the country and in Europe, and the famous "Minimum Standards for Child Welfare" adopted at the Second Washington Conference, called by President Wilson and held May 5–8, 1919.

From the Wilson Conference another era may be said to date which during the past decade has been most fruitful in child-care effort, including the establishment of the National Child Welfare League of America which ever since its inception under the brilliant leadership of Dr. Carstens has given a mighty impetus to the movement for advanced child care, the introduction of psychometric and psychiatric work, and the undertaking of many important surveys by the Russell Sage Foundation dealing with all types of child care. The past decade has been featured as well by many important conferences such as those of Carson and Ellis Colleges in Philadelphia, and the development of numerous children's clearing bureaus, state and local, the more intensive development of aftercare work, the closer cooperation of institutions and placement agencies, and efforts at coordination of the two child-caring methods based on the more or less implied acceptance of the idea of the dual form of child care which has featured thought and practice during the past 10 years.

When we consider that all this remarkable development that has taken place in the field of child care came about as a result of the historic original White House Conference which established a precedent for the Second White House Conference held in 1919, and for the Third White House Conference to be called by President Hoover which is now in process of preparation and which, from all indications, "will be more inclusive than the two preceding conferences," the first White House Conference which President Roosevelt had the vision to summon may in truth be called the Magna Charta of Child Care.

The slogan in dependent child care ever since the first White House Conference has been, "Save the Home and you save the Child. The way to Child Conservation is through Family Conservation." With emphasis placed upon family life, greater importance of necessity attaches to the family agency. Here, let it be observed in passing, a new and all-important question presents itself. In the increasing emphasis that has been placed on the family agency with a corresponding subordination of the child-care agency, it is proper to ask if the pendulum has not swung too far and if in actual operation we have not become almost fanatical in our zeal for family conservation. Is the family agency to assume child-care functions? Can it? And if it does, what can we expect it to do for the child? The family agency is primarily concerned with adjusting family life to community conditions. It adapts itself to community standards; it does not try to change them; it cannot change the social order of things. Its task is to protect the family from economic hazards which might overwhelm and disrupt it, but "keeping the family together" does not of itself mean that the best interests of the child will at all times be safeguarded. On the contrary, there is danger that the welfare of the child will be unduly subordinated to the general welfare of the family. In so far as the child may be subordinated to the family, both institutional and placing-out workers must ever be on guard, lest the child suffer. Child-care workers accept the dictum "the natural home for the child at all costs," providing it does not become "the natural home at all costs of the child." They are concerned that the child shall ever receive the fullest measure of consideration for his individual needs to which he is entitled. They are not deterred by adverse community standards but "carry on" for the child's welfare until the community raises its standards for all children. That in fact is the function of child workers—community recognition of the rights of childhood. Can the work of both the family and child-care agencies be correlated, and if so, how? That is the outstanding practical problem that confronts child welfare workers with the readjustment of attitude with respect to the child's natural home brought about by the White House Conference.

The conclusions of the White House Conference have on the whole been accepted as the working principles of advanced child-care workers. One conclusion, however, has been and still is seriously challenged, namely, that "the carefully selected foster home is for the *normal child* the best substitute for the natural home." This conclusion, it must be borne in mind, was based on sentiment, not on a careful comparison of the results of placing-out and institutional care. For this the White House Conference is not to be blamed. No figures or criteria were then available as they have since become in the two decades that have passed. With due allowance for the soundness of the fundamental doctrine enunciated by the White House Conference that the best place for the child is his own natural home, it is still necessary to test in a way that was not possible before the validity of its finding that placing-out is better for the dependent child than institutional care, and this not as a question of theory but rather and mainly on the basis of the *actual work done by both.*

Our general outline and review of the development of the two outstanding types of child care in our country shows that great progress has been made in both, particularly in more recent years. Both loom large in the public eye in work done and resources at their command. In spite of unceasing opposition, the number of institutions in 1925 was in excess of 1,400, caring for over 150,000 children, with a total capital investment of more than $200 million, and an annual budget approximating $60 million [Reeder 1925]. But more important than this physical extension of institutional activity, is the inner transformation institutions have undergone. Forced to keep pace with the advanced thought and methods of the time, institutional care has revealed its possibilities. We can no longer regard the institution today as it was thought of when the White House Conference met. Placing-out, too, has expanded in volume by leaps and bounds and developed its technique. In 1923 there were over 400 child-placing agencies operating throughout the length and breadth of the land. We are now in a position, as the White House Conference was not, where we can and must weigh the relative merits of the two types of care on the basis of their respective positive effects on child-life in all its essential aspects and needs.

What Comparative Figures and Other Data Show on Institutional Care and Placing-out

In order to determine, as a general proposition, which is better for a dependent child, institutional or private family care, we must have direct evidence bearing on the growth and all-around development of the child under both types of care. Unfortunately, on none of the practical and fundamental considerations in the care of children has satisfactory material been assembled to establish beyond question the superiority of one type of care over the other. A number of studies, it is true, have been made here and there of the work of various child-caring organizations, but these are far from being well integrated. Whatever material there is, is fragmentary and unrelated to many essential factors in the problem and cannot by itself be used for judging definitely the comparative efficacy of the two types of care.

The completest studies that have been made, in the opinion of the writer, are those of the Bureau of Jewish Social Research of New York City which under the able leadership of its Director Samuel A. Goldsmith has for a number of years been engaged in making surveys of the social work of leading Jewish communities in the United States. In these elaborate surveys child care has received careful attention, and a conscious effort has been made to analyze the actual workings of institutional and placing-out effort on a casework and comparative basis. The most recent and important of these studies are those made of the Chicago Jewish community in 1925–26 and the Jewish community of Greater New York in 1926–28. In both there is to be found an abundance of valuable material bearing on dependent child care that enables us to approach the problem with some measure of scientific appraisal. It must be pointed out that carefully made as these studies were, even they must be taken with necessary reservations. After making due allowance, however, for fallible factors, human and otherwise, the factual material contained therein in the form of figures and tables is the most complete and reliable so far assembled, at least to the writer's knowledge, and will therefore be used as the basis of a comparative study of the actual workings of institutional care and placing-out.

Before proceeding with an analysis of what the figures in these studies show, it is necessary to make clear what they represent. The figures for Chicago cover in detail the work of two congregate institutions and one placing-out agency. Those for New York in the original Survey cover a variety of child-caring organizations, including infants' homes and others, but only the figures of six major organizations are used by us—three institutions conducted on the congregate and one on the cottage plan, and two placing-out agencies. The institutions studied in both cities are representative of the better type of child-care institutions in the country; so are the placing-out agencies. The placing-out agencies in New York, while operating as such in the fullest sense of the word, are affiliated with two institutions included in the study to the extent of having a central administration, which makes the present inquiry into both types of care all the more valuable, because it permits of a comparison of results where the same ideals prevail. The number of children involved is 2,523 under institutional care and 1,214 under placing-out, a total of 3,737 children. The names of the organizations and their designations in abbreviated form which will be used by us are as follows.

1. New York Hebrew Orphan Asylum, NYHOA, congregate institution, New York City, New York.
2. Brooklyn Hebrew Orphan Asylum, BHOA, congregate institution, Brooklyn, New York.
3. Hebrew Sheltering Guardian Society, HSGS, cottage plan institution Pleasantville, New York.
4. Hebrew National Orphan Asylum, NHOA, congregate institution, New York.
5. Marks Nathan Jewish Orphan Home, MNJOH, congregate institution, Chicago, Ill.
6. Chicago Home for Jewish Orphans, CHJO, congregate institution, Chicago, Ill.
7. Home Bureau, HB, boarding-out department of the HSGS, New York City, New York.
8. Hebrew Orphan Asylum Boarding-out Department, HOABD, the boarding-out department of the HOA, New York City, New York.
9. Jewish Home Finding Society, JHFS, boarding-out agency, Chicago, Ill.

Since the grand totals of the Child-Welfare Study of Greater New York cover more organizations than used by us, it was necessary to have some of the figures recast. The writer assumes full responsibility for the correctness of the figures given, in so far of course as their original source is concerned.

With this preliminary explanation, let us now endeavor to take institutional care and private family placement out of the intangible realm of noble but irresponsible sentiment and impressions and subject both to the acid-test of sober and inflexible reality. Let us as far as possible summon both to give an accounting of their stewardship and ask for a bill of particulars as to what they are actually doing for and with dependent childhood. With the object of determining which type of care surpasses the other, let us direct our comparative inquiry to the basic considerations in the care of children, namely:

1. Physical development and adjustment of health problems.
2. Mental development and educational achievement and opportunities.
3. Emotional development and character building.

PHYSICAL DEVELOPMENT AND ADJUSTMENT OF HEALTH PROBLEMS

With regard to physical development of children, pediatricians are in general agreement that a normal increase in weight for a given age and height usually indicates normal physical development. The exceptions to this standard, such as individual instances of a rapid increase in height during the adolescent period without a corresponding increase in weight, are comparatively so few that they do not influence to any appreciable extent the general results when fairly large groups are studied. For groups of children, therefore, a good basis of judgment as to whether or not the children are receiving good physical care and are developing physically at least to a normal degree is found in the progress which they make as to weights as compared with the general condition of other children in the community at large. The Wood–Baldwin Table of Age–Height–Weight relationship is generally used as a standard for the norm of physical development of children of preschool and school ages. This table was prepared on the basis of the findings of heights and weights of about 50,000 children with good heredity and environmental advantages and who are representative of well-developed types for normal standards. A child whose weight is 7 or more percent below the table weight for his age and height is considered a marked underweight, with a physical development below par. Thus a child who according to table weight should weigh, say, 100 pounds is considered an underweight if he weighs only 93 pounds or less. It is generally figured that the number of underweight children in the community at large is between 25 and 30 percent. The deviation of a group from the norm is regarded as a fairly accurate index of the physical development of the group.

Since the weight of a child is generally affected by the condition of his health, it is necessary, when comparing groups, to divide them into two classes, namely, those who present major health problems and those who do not with the possible exception of underweight.

Tables 2.1, 2.2 below indicate analyses of weights of the children of the various groups studied at the time of the first weighing on or after admission and at the time of study, also the progress made during the intervals between weighings. Only children who were weighed and measured twice are included in these tables, which will account for the discrepancies between the number of children given on admission and the time of study as well as between the totals at time of study and those of the population.

TABLE 2.1. *Physical development as determined by age-height-weight relationships institutional group—normal as to health*

Organization	NYHOA	BHOA	HSGS	HNOH	MNOH	CHJO	Total
Number of children							
At admission	700	447	229	204	94	98	1772
At time of study	660	416	229	204	94	98	1701
Number of underweights							
At admission	135	108	37	29	9	15	333
At time of study	33	107	34	14	7	19	214
Percentage of underweights							
At admission	19.2%	24.2%	16.2%	14.2%	9.6%	15.3%	18.8%
At time of study	5.0%	25.7%	14.8%	6.8%	7.4%	19.4%	12.6%
Percentage of underweights							
Increase (+)		+1.5%				+4.1%	
Decrease (−)	−14.2%		−1.4%	−7.4%	−2.2%		−6.2%

Bureau of Jewish Social Research of New York: New York Study, 1926–28, Child-care Section—Institutional, Table 17A-3, p. 155, also pages 54–59; Chicago Study, 1925–26, M. N. J. O. H. Section, Table 19A, also pages 8–11; C. H. J. O. Section, Table 19A, also pages 8–11.

Table 2.1 indicates that in the institutional group, as a whole, out of a total number of 1,772 children normal as to health at the time of admission there were 333 children or 18.8 percent underweights, while at the time of study out of a total of 1,701 children, 214 or 12.6 percent were underweight, a decrease of 6.2 percent in the number of underweights when the relative periods of admission and time of study are compared.

Table 2.2 indicates that in the placed-out group, as a whole, at the time of admission there were 123 children out of a total number of 752 normal as to health, or 16.4 percent underweights, while at the time of study the number of underweights was 84 out of a total number of 683 children or 12.3 percent, a decrease of 4.1 percent in the number of underweights from the time of admission to the time of study.

Particular attention is drawn to the fact that while the average improvement in the decrease of number of underweights as indicated by Tables 2.1 and 2.2, was 6.2 percent for the institutional group and 4.1 percent for the boarding-out group, relatively only a slight difference in favor of institutional care, the maximum results obtained by the institutional group as represented by the NYHOA were a decrease of 14.2 percent as against only 5.4 percent, the best results in the boarding-out reached by the Home Bureau, a

TABLE 2.2. *Physical development as determined by age-height-weight relationships boarding-out group—normal as to health*

Organization	Home Bureau HSGS	Boarding-out Dept NYHOH	JHFS Chicago	Total
Number of children				
At Admission	391	278	83	752
At time of study	391	209	83	683
Number of underweights				
At Admission	64	41	18	123
At time of study	44	24	16	84
Percentage of underweights				
At admission	16.4%	14.8%	21.7%	16.4%
At time of study	11.0%	11.5%	19.3%	12.3%
Percentage of underweights				
Increase (+)				
Decrease (−)	−5.4%	−3.3%	−2.4%	−4.1%

Bureau of Jewish Social Research of New York: New York Study, 1926–28, Child-care Section—Boarding-out, Table 10-A, page 196, also pages 45–47; Chicago Study, 1925–26, J. H. F. S. Section, Table 21A, also pages 6–7–8.

tremendous difference in favor of institutional care. Since our concern is not mediocrity but primarily the achievable goal, this fact is, we believe, of great significance.

Similar results are obtained in height–weight relationships. In the institutional group, as a whole, out of a total number of 2,308 children, at the time of admission, there were 479 children or 20.8 percent underweights, while at the time of study out of total of 2,223 children, 338 or 15.2 percent were underweights, a decrease of 5.6 percent in the number of underweights when the relative periods of admission and time of study are compared.

In the placed-out group, as a whole, at the time of admission there were 207 children out of a total number of 1,017 children or 20.4 percent, while at the time of study the number of underweights was 158 out of a total number of 934 children or 16.9 percent, a decrease of 3.5 percent in the number of underweights from the time of admission to the time of study.

It will be observed that in the case of the total of all the children, too, the maximum results show better possibilities for the institution than the boarding-out plan. The best results obtained were an improvement of 14.9 percent in the NYHOA as against that of only 6.4 percent in the Home Bureau.

The conclusions to be drawn from the data in the above tables are as follows.

1. That, contrary to the general impression, in the case of both groups, the institutional and the boarding-out, the physical development of de-

pendent children as determined by the age–height–weight relationship at the time of admission, is about the same as that of the average child in the community at large.

2. That under both types of care, institutional and boarding-out, children show a marked physical, development with an advantage in favor of institutional care and that, when best results obtainable are taken into consideration, this advantage of institutional care is overwhelming.

3. That at the time of the study the physical development of these children was appreciably better than that of the average child in the community.

4. That there is an appreciable number of children under both types of care who remain underweight, or physically under-developed, and whose health problems do not result in successful treatment, and that these children should be referred by both types of care for specialized care for which the community should make adequate provision.

5. That the great variations among individual organizations with respect to the number of underweights at the time of study as well as in the matter of the increase or decrease of the number of underweights during the relative intervals between admission and time of study would seem to indicate that as far as the physical development of the child is concerned, it is not so much the type of care as the standard of care that really counts.

MENTAL DEVELOPMENT AND EDUCATIONAL PROGRESS AND OPPORTUNITIES

It is obvious that any type of dependent child care is inadequate unless it promotes the mental development and educational progress of the child. Fine mentality is the apex of fine physique. The "healthy mind in the healthy body" is the objective that the child-care worker visions and shares with the educator. How do institutional care and placing-out compare in this respect? In the practical workings of both types of care, has either an advantage over the other?

Unfortunately, much remains to be done to make adequate comparison possible in the matter of mental development and educational progress. The available data do not permit of conclusions that could be regarded as final. Only after the most searching study of results obtained under both types of care would it be possible to claim superiority for either. Until then, we shall discuss the considerations that have to be taken into account and analyze the figures that are available where studies have been made.

Mental capacity, generally speaking, determines educational progress. Late enrollment in school, absence from school, illness and other factors may, of course, account for school retardation of bright children, and on the other hand special application and close supervision may account for dull children doing good school work up to a certain stage. In general, however, a definite correlation exists between educational progress and innate mental ability. Furthermore, what is a poor showing for a bright child may be a good showing for a dull child. In order therefore to judge the educational progress of a group of children, it is necessary first to ascertain the average mentality of the group on the basis of the distribution of the intelligence of the members comprising the group. Since dependent children come to child-care organizations with a definite mental equipment and it is not the organization's fault that it may happen to have a large number of dull and deficient children to deal with, it is to be understood that the facts with regard to the distribution of intelligence have no particular bearing on the degree of efficiency of the organization per se.

The mental capacity of a child is determined by means of various standardized psychological tests and expressed, according to the rating, in terms of mental age. This mental age is then compared with the chronological or life age, and the relationship thus found denotes the intelligence quotient, the IQ, of the child. Thus, if the mental age of a child corresponds with his life age, the resulting IQ is 1.00 or 100; if the mental age is above the life age, the IQ is 1.00 or 100 plus; if the mental age is below the life age, the IQ is below 1.00 or 100.

The usual psychological classifications of children according to their IQ's are as follows:

| | Mentality |
IQ	Classification
Below 70	Deficient
Between 70 and 79	Borderline
Between 80 and 89	Dull
Between 90 and 109	Average
110 and more	Superior

Since the educational progress of a given group of children can be decided only on the basis of comparison with the educational progress of children in the community at large, it is important to know how the mental levels of the dependent children studied compare with those of the general school population. There are no figures readily available of the intelligence of the children of the public schools of the city of Chicago. The Board of Education of the city of New York, however, has administered intelligence tests on pupils of 10 elementary schools located in Manhattan, Bronx and Queens, in December 1925, and the results of these tests will be used by us for comparative purposes. It must be borne in mind that the IQ's for the New York City school population as well as the Chicago child-care organizations were determined on the basis of group tests, while those for the New York child-care organizations were ascertained by means of individual mental examinations. In view of the fact, however, that a fairly high correlation prevails between results obtained from group tests and those secured from individual tests, it is fairly safe to compare the mental levels of groups regardless of whether group or individual tests were used, particularly when fairly large groups are compared.

With this preliminary explanation let us now see how the mental capacity of the various groups of dependent children studied compares with that of the children of the public schools of the city of New York. Table 2.3 presents the mental status of the children studied as determined by the distribution of the IQ's of the various groups.

TABLE 2.3. *Mental status of children as determined by the distribution of IQ's*

Organization	Total Tested	Average I.Q.	De-ficient below 70	Border-line 70–79	Dull 80–89	Average 90–109	Superior 110 and over
New York City			%	%	%	%	%
Public schools	9512	103.4	12.4		14.9	36.7	36
Institutions							
NYHOA	847	94	3.5	11.	24.5	47.5	13.5
BHOA	483	94	6.	10.	23.	46.	15.
HSGS	286	97	2.	9.5	22.5	48.5	17.5
HNOH (not tested)	....	....	....	....	....	....	....
Total	1616	....	3.8	10.6	23.7	47.4	14.5
Boarding-Out							
Home Bureau	} 612	93	4.	11.	27.5	44.5	13.
HOABO		93	6.	15.	18.	50.	11.
Total	612	93	5.	13.3	22.2	47.7	11.8
Chicago *Institutions*							
MNJOH	274	100	1.2	7.7	20.	44.5	26.6
CHJO	209	102	1.	2.4	14.3	56.3	26.
Total	483	....	1.	5.4	17.6	49.7	26.3
Boarding-Out							
JHFS	152	95	7.2	9.2	19.1	46.7	17.8

Bureau of Jewish Social Research of New York: New York Study, 1926–28, Child-care Section—Institutional, Tables 19, 20, 21, pages 164, 165, 166, also pages 67–69; Boarding-out, Ch. VI, pages 52–53, Table 12, page 202, also Tables 15–4–5–6, pages 208, 209, 210; Chicago Study, 1925–26, M. N. J. O. H. Section, Table 22, also pages 11, 12, 13; C. H. J. O. Section, Table 22, also pages 13–14; J. H. F. S. Section, Table 23; Summary, Table 24A.

A comparison of the above figures plainly indicates that the New York organizations, both institutions and placing-out agencies, and the placing-out agency of Chicago have under care a larger percentage of mentally deficient children and a smaller percentage of superior children, in other words, that they are handling groups of children who as such are inferior mentally to the average school population of the city of New York, while the Chicago institutions have a group of children whose mentality compares favorably with the average.

Having ascertained the mental equipment of the dependent children studied, we can now proceed with our study of the relative educational progress of the various groups under the two types of care. In view of the variations in educational methods and standards which generally obtain in different cities, it is necessary to compare the educational progress of the dependent children with that of the public school population of their respective cities.

Table 2.4 indicates the educational status at the time of study of the chil-

TABLE 2.4. *Educational progress as determined by school acceleration and retardation of children*

Organization	Total Studied	Normally Graded Percentage	Accelerated 1 Year or More Percentage	Retarded 1 Year or More Percentage
New York City				
Public schools	....	43.3	25.5	31.2
Institutions				
NYHOA	818	39.9	13.2	46.9
BHOH	610	44.3	14.6	41.1
HSGS	289	36.4	15.2	48.4
HNOH	234	39.7	22.7	37.6
Total	1951	40.7	15.1	44.2
Boarding-Out				
HB	464	47.6	15.1	37.3
NYHOABO	297	48.5	16.2	35.3
Total	761	48	15.5	36.5
Chicago				
Public schools	....	47.6	15.8	36.6
Institutions				
MNJOH	292	59.	19.	22.
CJOH	221	63.	8.	29.
Total	513	60.6	14.4	25.
Boarding-Out				
J.H.F.S.	202	51.5	9.	39.5

Bureau of Jewish Social Research of New York: New York Study, 1926–28, Child-care Section—Institutional, Table 22, page 167 also pages 71, 72, 73, 74; Boarding-out Section, Table 14, page 204, also pages 55–56; Chicago Study, 1925–26, M.N.J.O.H. Section, Table 24, also page 13; C.H.J.O. Section, Table 23, also pages 14–15; J.H.F.S. Section, Table 22, also pages 8–9; Summary, Table 25.

dren of the various agencies on the basis of their school gradation with respect to retardation and acceleration of one year and over.

It will be observed that in the case of both the institutions and the boarding-out agencies in New York, the percentage of acceleration is below and the percentage of retardation above that of the general school population; in other words, from the point of view of educational standing, the children of both groups are decidedly inferior. "This," to quote the words of the Bureau of Jewish Social Research of New York, "is of course to be expected in view of the fact that the organizations had under their care children who were, generally speaking, of a lower mental level as compared with the New York City school group."

A comparison of the educational standing of the children of the various organizations of the same type in New York indicates no marked difference. A comparison of the two types of care in New York shows that with about the same average IQ, the boarding-out agencies have among their children a smaller percentage of retardation and a correspondingly higher percentage of acceleration. The latter does not, however, necessarily mean that the children under the boarding-out care fared better educationally than the children in the institutions. In correlations of this kind many factors enter into consideration. In reply to our inquiry as to the probable cause of the marked difference in the educational standard of the two groups, Dr. Robert Axel, of the Bureau of Jewish Social Research, draws our attention to two important factors, namely, first, the age distribution of the two groups, and, second, the length of stay under care. The children of the boarding-out agencies were in general a much younger group and under the agencies' care for a much shorter period of time than those in the institutions and had, therefore, less opportunity to become retarded than the institutional group. It should be noted that this would apply particularly to the mentally retarded children, for it is a well known fact that they become more and more educationally retarded as they continue in school. After giving details of both groups in these regards, Dr. Axel concludes by saying:

> In view of the above we would say that merely because there is an apparent difference in the educational status of the children in institutions and foster homes, it does not necessarily follow that the foster home group has made better progress in school than the institutional group. It is quite possible that, if the educational progress of the children under both types of care were further analyzed in terms of age, there may not be that difference which apparently exists.

In this connection it is pertinent to point out another important consideration. If the figures given for the children under boarding-out care in New York contained the distribution of IQ's for all children in school and the grade records of all children under care, we would be in a position to compare the educational standing and progress of the children under both types of care. Unfortunately, however, these data are lacking. Of the total number of 761 children for whom school records are given only 612 were tested mentally which means that we have not the average IQ for the entire school group. As for school gradation, of the total number of 940 under care, 64 are below school age. Of the 876 children of school age records are available for only 761, leaving 115 of school age unaccounted for. Are all these 115 children attending school or were all or some dropped out because of retardation as is usually the case with the school population in general in the community but not in institutions? With this information lacking, it is obvious that no comparisons can be made between the two types of care in New York City with regard to educational standing and progress.

In view, however, of the fact that for Chicago we have records for all children of school age under both types of care and practically all have received mental tests, and particularly because the average IQ of Chicago children is about the same as that of the general school population, an ideal opportunity is given to compare both types of care. The figures for Chicago make clear that the boarded-out children, considering their mental equipment, make a fairly good showing, while the institutional children show unusual school achievement.

This is of course what one would expect of a group of average children under institutional care, for while there is no reason why a child should not make normal school progress in the average good private family home, it is obvious that an institution can and does have a closer and more efficient supervision of and a greater urge on the child with respect to school work than the average private family. Educators are agreed that the best results in schoolwork follow when school and home combine in the earlier education of the child. Institutions have long been setting an example to private homes of full and intelligent cooperation with school authorities. Retardation and acceleration, thus, in the case of the average child, come not as a result of any magic to be found in any type of care but from follow-up of school work and holding the child constantly up to a high standard.

In the matter of educational opportunities, another most important consideration must not be overlooked. Education means much more than formal schooling. Schooling consumes but 6 hours a day, 200 days in the year, while the total education of a child is accomplished through its experience all day long and every day in the year. From the point of view of the broader conception of education covering moral, religious, ethical, social, health, and many other phases of general education, there can be no two opinions as to where and under which type of care the child is getting more opportunities and better educational stimulus. The institution is unique and supreme in this respect.

We will now summarize what would seem to be warranted in the way of inferences with regard to effects of institutional care and boarding-out on mental development and educational progress and opportunities, as follows.

1. As far as educational progress is concerned, dependent normal children seem to do well under both types of care, exceptionally well under institutional care.

2. So far as educational opportunities and influences in general, such as mental, religious, moral, ethical, health, etc., are concerned, it is obvious that educationally conceived institutions have a decided advantage.

3. In the matter of the influence of environment on intelligence, although in individual cases in private families the environment may be even better than that possible in the best institutions, yet as a general proposition the most stimulating environment can be and is more easily assured for the child in an institution whose management and policies are under the control of an enlightened professional personnel and board of directors.

EMOTIONAL DEVELOPMENT AND CHARACTER BUILDING

In no phase of dependent child care is it claimed that there is a wider disparity and a greater fundamental inherent difference between institutional care and placing-out than in that which concerns the emotional needs and development of the child. The impression widely prevails that in this regard placing-out is so markedly and overwhelmingly superior as to leave no room for argument. It is largely because of this alleged superiority that preferential consideration is claimed for private-family placement.

The position taken by opponents of institutional care, as we understand it, and which is held by them to be unassailable, is briefly as follows: in the group life of institutions the child is lost in the shuffle; the whole regime of institutions is one of mass dealing; the restrictive and repressive nature of mass dealing cannot but affect the child adversely, starve him emotionally and dwarf the development of his personality, stamping upon him through life the impress of submissiveness, mediocrity, and an inferiority complex; all this, besides robbing the child of his right to be happy, handicaps him at the very outset in the battle of life; the institutional product therefore is generally much inferior to that turned out under private family care where the child receives more individual and sympathetic attention.

If this claim can be substantiated, if institutions actually function in the mechanical manner charged and turn out an emotionally anemic and attenuated type of child, then of course institutional care is wrong from the very start.

This matter is too important to be disposed of in an arbitrary fashion. It is necessary here more even than in other respects to reserve judgment until a proper and adequate comparison has been made between the two types of care. For a final determination of this issue, it is necessary to make a most searching psychological study of the actual emotional effects upon the child of institutional care and placing-out respectively. It is not our intention to approach it in this way at this time for several reasons. In the first place, the

scientific criteria and data are as yet lacking; and secondly, a purely speculative and abstract discussion would necessarily become too technical for the
lay and even the average professional child-care worker. We will not therefore plunge into technical psychological discussions, although it is evident
that only when the matter receives such attention and treatment, can it be
considered as authoritatively dealt with. We shall deal with this subject on
the basis of plain common sense, giving attention to the major and more obvious factors and considerations involved.

We combine character building and emotional development because,
broadly considered, one is part and parcel of the other. The emotional development of the child embraces his feelings and desires which must and do
react on his conduct and character. Emotional expression that makes possible the freest play of personality with due regard for the need of emotional
control and direction is the objective not only of good child care but of human society. This is a major consideration of either type of child care, and
as it promotes or retards this development in the child, is it to be commend-
ed or condemned.

If institutional care is, as is so often asserted, emotionally harmful to the
child, in what respects is it so? What is there in an institution of the better
type nowadays that militates against the wholesome development of the
child's emotional life as compared with boarding-out in a private family?
Wherein does institutional life of the better type differ in essentials from
well-regulated foster family life? It is contended that in the foster family the
child receives individual attention, while in an institution no consideration is
or can be given to his individuality which is sacrificed to group considerations and is "lost in the shuffle." No one can question the importance of giving attention to individual emotional needs particularly in the case of
dependent children. While dependent children are in no way different in essentials from other children more normally reared, yet it must be realized
that what they have lived through, their very removal from the influences of
a natural home, produces certain emotional scars and grooves that affect
their minds and lives. The dependent child therefore is peculiarly in need of
individual attention wherever he is cared for. Where can he and where does
he actually receive this needed individual attention?

The foster family, as a matter of fact, when not blissfully ignorant of the
importance of child study, is not equipped for it and has not the means to
make it possible. Institutions, however, can give each child the most thoroughgoing individual study and are actually doing so, as foster homes are
not. With this emphasis on the individual needs of each child, which is fast
becoming the outstanding feature of progressive institutional care at present,
what is left of institutional regulations, "institutionalism," over and above
what is absolutely essential for the maintenance of a semblance of order?
Doesn't a well-regulated private family have to have about the same meas-

ure of order and discipline, if you please, in its own home? Is the child in the private family allowed to do as he pleases with no restriction whatever? Does psychology or any other science that has a bearing on child care lay down the dictum that wholesome emotional development of the child implies uncontrolled freedom? Does not all competent authority rather stress the necessity of directing the child's emotional life as well as of shaping its character by regularity of habits? Wherein does institutional care fundamentally differ in this respect from good boarding-out care?

So much for "individual needs" rationally considered which institutions as a matter of fact do not overlook. The institutional child is by no means lost in the shuffle. In fact, institutional people claim, and perhaps not without warrant, that he gets a good deal.

Now let us analyze the claim that institutional care deadens and destroys self-assertion and initiative. Children are undoubtedly cowed by the consciousness of their inadequate strength when dealing with adults, and this makes them naturally "submissive" under all circumstances. In general it is not desirable that children should be too self-assertive with adults except in unusual cases as when they are treated unjustly or too severely. The child has sufficient outlet for self-assertion with his comrades and children of approximately his own age. Who can deny that the opportunities in this respect are greater in institutional life than elsewhere? The very group life for which institutions are censured and condemned is probably the most important factor in shaping the personality and character of the child. Group life day in and day out alone makes it possible for children to receive the approbation of their peers and of older children whom they attempt to imitate. Group life gives opportunity for hero worship on a large scale, a tremendous incentive to growth of character and personality. It also presents constant and innumerable opportunities for the older children to serve the younger, thus developing the altruistic sentiments and interests. The challenge and competition, too, of group life put the child on his mettle, "on his own"; he learns at an early age how to take care of himself and how to conduct himself with others. Virility and womanhood are fundamentally group products. The children who find group life too stimulating are obviously not average and need special provision. Self-assertion and self-expression, therefore, instead of being deadened and destroyed by institutional life are awakened and developed, and the child is thus adequately prepared for the broader social world that lies ahead.

It is evident that many more factors than those we have mentioned and treated have to be taken into account in dealing with the basic matter of the development of the child's character. We will not attempt a detailed analysis of these factors, since it is not our intention to write a manual on the subject. All we desire to point out is that in these regards, such as regularity of habits, good surroundings, religious training, moral, intellectual, and cultural influences, stimulating and inspiring adult associations, recreational opportunities and athletic development, and civic and economic training there can be no question that greater attention can be and actually is given to these in institutions than is possible under boarding-out care. Group life, of course, like everything else that is human is not 100 per cent perfect in beneficial influence; it has its disadvantages and drawbacks, and these have to be taken into account, but we believe that after these have been weighed and the matter has been considered relatively, as all matters must be, the good far outshadows the bad. From the point of view of character-building and all that goes to making the child socially fit, therefore, there is certainly no reason why the institutional product should be inferior to the average in the community, nor is there proof that it is.

At bottom, the whole question of where the average dependent child is better off from the point of view of emotional development, hinges on the personal equation. More important than *where* the child is cared for is *who* is attending to his care and *how*. If cared for under conditions where there is broad vision and a proper understanding of the needs and the soul of the child, it will grow and develop in a normal and wholesome way. Where these are lacking, the child will not get what is coming to it wherever it be. Neither type of care is warranted in assuming a unique endowment of vision, understanding, and sympathetic interest in the child.

3

Political Orientation, Social Reality, and Child Welfare

MARTIN WOLINS

Various forces predispose a society toward specific child-care arrangements. Developmental theories are clearly one of them, and, as Seiden (Chap. 6) argues, these are not clearly and totally on the side of familial care in every instance. An argument may well be made (Wolins and Piliavin, 1964), though, that decisions about the preferred location for the deprived child are based on other factors—specifically, ideology, economics, the role of women in society, and certain historical, traditional considerations—rather than child development data. So it has been in the United States; so it is also abroad. Wolins reviews these issues in the context of several East European countries and Israel, and outlines broadly the type of group care programs that have developed there and the consequences they have for the children in care. The paper was originally prepared in the early 1960s. Since then the extreme pro group care views cited have been considerably toned down, but these were and continue to be viable positions—points on the pendular trajectory of favored child care arrangements.

The whole need-meeting apparatus of any society is, in the final analysis, founded on a reciprocal relationship between the individual's production and consumption and the social system's effective mediation between these two. To accomplish such mediating functions effectively and with a fair amount of efficiency requires considerable patterning and flexibility on the part of both the person and the system. When major philosophical and oper-

The material for this paper was gathered in a project supported by the National Institute of Mental Health (Grant #MH 1430) and by the Ford Foundation. It is a revised version of Martin Wolins. "Political Orientation, Social Reality, and Child Welfare." *Social Service Review* 38 (4): 429–42. Copyright 1964 by the University of Chicago.

ational changes occur in a society, its various systems must adapt. One of these systems is the family, which, although it has universality and relative functional similarity attributed to it,[1] is clearly compelled to modify its activities in order to fit the social requirements of its time, place, and political setting.

In the past few decades we have been witness to massive social changes as a result of continuing industrial and political revolutions. Family life, too, has changed. In some instances it has failed to cope with its traditional functions and has gradually lost some of them to other systems of society. Loss has been particularly pronounced in the educational sphere, in which, even in those societies that place high value upon the acculturative capabilities of the family, functions have been moving to the school, the youth group, and the club. Similarly, but to a much lesser extent, economic responsibilities of family life have been devolving upon the broader society. Thus, each failure of the family has brought with it social welfare measures which, over time, have been institutionalized as new "legal organizations of society."

But the way in which the initial failure is perceived, the type of remedial measures that are considered desirable, and the institutional format into which they are finally consolidated vary, to some extent by accident but also by political orientation and social reality. These latter two forces and their consequences for child welfare programs in several countries will be the major concern of this paper, which will address itself to the values of several societies, their consequent preferences for child welfare programs, the restraints of social reality, and the anticipated and obtained results. The societies considered will be the Soviet, the Israeli *kibbutz*,[2] and, to a lesser extent, Poland and Yugoslavia.

Childrearing Goals

It may be taken for granted that in the educational process all of these societies strive for mental health and the fullest development of individual potential. None values neurotic or psychotic personalities. None wishes to suppress or squander the innate capabilities of its young. The societal values they espouse, however, are somewhat different from each other and markedly unlike our own.

When a Russian describes the *stroitel' kommunisma* (builder of Communism) he includes, among his other attributes, love of labor, concern for public wealth, comradely mutual assistance, friendship and equality among people, simplicity, modesty, and asceticism in public and private life.[3] When a pedagogue writes about the goals of the whole educational program in producing the "new Soviet man," his categories of attributes to be instilled in the young pupils are almost the same: self-reliance and independence, respect and a sense of duty toward fellow man, love of labor, respect toward collective property, ambition and creativity for the betterment of society as a whole, will power and self-control, and discipline. All in all, he envisages an equalitarian, activist person with a strong sense of social responsibility and future orientation.

The major ideologist of childrearing and education in the socialist *kibbutz* expresses himself in somewhat similar terms. The ideals of collective education are fulfilled when the child grows up to be a good *kibbutz* member, which includes being a good worker; a good *Mapam* (left-wing socialist) party member; a socially active, independent person developing high moral standards and collective consciousness (Golan 1961; Spiro 1956). The ideal *kibbutz* member, then, is also an equalitarian person but with less emphasis on instrumentalism. Comparing the two sets of values, one finds considerable similarity and yet some basic differences, which seem to center largely around the instrumental or the consummatory axis. The Soviet ideal is, it appears, far more than the ideal socialist *kibbutznik,* instrumentally focused. The present is mere prologue to a glorious future, and, while satisfaction can be garnered from both the given and the anticipated, the major rewards are yet to come. The emphasis, clearly, is on the builders *(stroiteli)* of Communism, not on those who simply exist in it *(obyvateli)*.

Description of the childrearing values (or this particular distillation of political ideology) in Poland and Yugoslavia is more difficult. The values in the Soviet Union and the socialist *kibbutz* seem to have substantial clarity and quite wide acceptance.[4] In Poland and Yugoslavia the socialist regimes are newer. The ravages of war were relatively even more severe; contrary ideological forces have continued to operate.[5] However, even in these countries the emphasis on equalitarianism and collectivism is strong, personal aggrandizement is frowned on, labor and the virtues of the socialist future are exalted. There is probably a less clear view of the official values and a greater discrepancy between them and the private values of the citizenry. Yet the ideology, which is reasonably clear, offers childrearing goals whose attainment is assessable.

In spite of the considerable differences in ideology between the Soviet, · Polish, Yugoslav, and *kibbutz* childrearing settings, sufficient similarity exists between them to permit a contrast with the United States. We, too, live in a future-oriented and largely instrumental society. Our values on that dimension would fall close to those of the Communist countries. We emphasize productivity, action, manipulation of the environment, and postponement of gratification. On another crucial dimension, however, we diverge markedly. While the Communist ideology emphasizes equalitarianism and specifically such virtues as cooperation, communality, nondifferentiation of the sexes, and strong commitment to the *kollectiv,* American ideology, in spite of some spectacular recent exceptions, is more oriented toward differentiation, status variability, and private, personal achievement. The divergence in goals is perhaps best reflected in the attribute for which each socie-ty has the greatest distrust. Authoritarianism in the *kibbutz*, parasitism[6] in the Soviet Union, and dependency in the United States seems to be the most suspect characteristics.

Given the respective ideological foundations and problems in the family requiring outside intervention in its economic and educational processes, what orientation should child welfare programs be expected to take? It is clear that every society will strive to achieve what one writer (Bloch 1955) on the *kibbutz* has called an "ideological collectivism"—a common vision that will reduce intergenerational strife.[7] Yet there can be no freezing of norms in a developing society. Hence, all these settings hold a tendency to-ward group care of children. This permits ideological consistency and, at the same time, the introduction of change in a collective environment with strong inner forces.

Group Care Programs

In the Soviet Union there has therefore been a flowering of boarding schools *(shkoly-internaty)*, and Khrushchev (1958) urged that they be greatly devel-oped as "a major form of rearing the growing generation."[8] The Israeli *kib-butz* has not only reared its own children in group settings but has, over the past 30 years, accepted for acculturation tens of thousands of immigrant children. Also, certain institutions for children have been founded on as-pects of *kibbutz* ideology with present or past members as personnel. Poland and Yugoslavia, with the development of ideological clarity, have been shift-ing toward group care, although foster-family programs are available and mothers' allowances are on the law books.[9] None of the arrangements has been perceived as wholly and unambiguously good, and pros and cons still persist.

The modern version of the Soviet boarding school was first introduced in 1956. Every effort was to be made toward building up a strong *kollectiv* (group structure), which would persist over time. In discussions about par-ental, educators', and pupils' roles, the educators have been clear.

> So that the collective will be closely-knit, it is necessary to take pupils into the boarding school and dismiss them from it in accordance with parents' wishes, but at strictly appointed times—only before the school year begins and after it ends. . . . Two to three weeks may be allotted for their [summer] stay at home. . . . [Such organization] permits the continuation of the school's educational influence on the children [Petrikeev and Dubkovski 1956].

Parents were approving but expressed some questions and doubts.

> When I first heard that boarding schools would be established [says a facto-ry worker], I immediately thought I would enter my children. Let them re-ceive a real education and upbringing, as in the military school. But then some

doubts occurred. A mother has no greater joy than to do things for her child. To refrain from this and not see her children for months is difficult. . . . Reunions with parents must not be limited to Sunday. Parents must have an opportunity to take a large part in the life of the school. We must bring up our young together (Mayakova 1956).

Subsequent to this and other discussions, policy on rearing the child was confirmed. In the first issue of 1964, the ideological journal of the Communist party quoted Senator Hubert Humphrey as saying "with obvious envy" that "millions of Russian children receive the opportunity for education and intellectual development such as only a few receive in the United States." It then added, as if to confirm the statement, that 1.2 million children were studying in boarding schools in 1961–62, at a cost of approximately 700 rubles ($770 at the official rate of exchange) each per year, of which parents paid not more than 10 percent *(Kommunist* 1964, p. 7).

The boarding school is thus developing as a major childrearing resource of Soviet society. It is seen as "at the same time an educational institution and a distinctive family" or "a school of organized, Communist life." Moreover, the intention is "to establish sufficient boarding schools to enable all parents who so desire to bring up their children in them [Knizheva 1960, pp. 61–62]."

Similarly, clarity but some doubt exists in the *kibbutz.* Pointing with considerable pride to her own background, a 12th-grade girl writes:

> Here there is no question of betraying the parents and leaving them. Here the children continue the work of their fathers; we change, renew, correct, fight evil, but the establishment as such is the same. Here there is no clash of ideals. . . . Here love for the parents expresses itself through identification with a common cause, a common struggle [Vardi 1956].

But the tie of ideology and parental love, the affection for parents as an expression of continuing their political and social outlook into the "second day of the revolution," is not without its concerns. The same adolescents who show such strong ideological commitment also have some concerns. Vardi (1956) writes:

> It may be said that the bourgeois tradition is still noticeable in all aspects of life in the *kibbutz* and also in education. . . . In spite of the fact that during the last years in the institution contact with the family is very limited, its influence is obvious, *and not exactly in the more favorable sense* [italics added].[10]

The source of concern is not limited solely to relationships with parents. Personality development is also brought into question. Vardi (1956) asks:

> Does our society create a synthetic personality, or does it produce a person who is cultured on the one hand and deprived on the other? Or, perhaps,

which is worse, a person who, by trying to encompass too much, emerges superficial?

On balance, and after much discussion, the decision of the *kibbutz* is also to continue group care.

> To the obvious criticism that children should not be separated from their mothers as they are in the *kibbutz,* there are two convincing answers. Firstly . . . no bad effects have been observed, while, on the contrary, many good ones have come about. Secondly, the well-to-do mother [outside] hands over her children . . . from the earliest age and usually sees them only at prearranged periods when she and they are at leisure; this is precisely what happens in the *kibbutz* [Ben-Yosef 1963, p. 65].

For several reasons the progressive children's institution in Israel is closely related to the *kibbutz*. First, institutional directors often have a common background of "concern for the land." Thus, one writer lauds the merits of an institution which, among other things, stands for a back-to-the-land philosophy and whose graduates have founded 20 new agricultural settlements and provided the nucleus for 27 others. Second, the institution, like the *kibbutz,* places heavy emphasis on the acculturative powers of the group. It is a place "without fear and without punishment, save what the children themselves, with the advice of the elders, award to a delinquent [Bentwich n.d., p. 46]." Third, because of the congeniality between their philosophies, these institutions often serve as recruitment settings for *kibbutzim,* particularly if the latter have members on the institution's staff as group leaders.

Given the political ideology of the several settings, there should be little reason for surprise that group care of children is favored either in general or, at least, when family units are unable to care for them. As one writer on this subject has said, collective education is not an answer to some lack—economic, social, or other—but a positive educational, political, social, ideological theory. The children's institution in the *kibbutz* is an integral part of the *kibbutz* at large, as a democratic society with a collective ideology and Freudian principles of education (Golan 1961, p. 14). There is, however, a most interesting and understandable limitation. Some of the technical aspects of the educational institution are the result of technical and/or financial possibilities of the *kibbutz* in its different stages of development. For example:

> The first child that made his appearance in Deganiya [the oldest group, established in 1912] caused considerable embarrassment; he ·confronted the group members with problems they had not thought of, not foreseen. The work and social status of women, the character of the family as a whole, were put to severe test. Actual educational problems arose later, when it appeared that the traditional way of family education did not suit the communal life-pattern. And thus, stage by stage, amid gropings, retreats and painful struggles, the great educational venture of the *kibbutz* movement took form [Golan 1961, p. 28].

Social reality enters and modifies ideological requirements. This reality consists in some measure of conditions that make group care desirable because of what it can offer, or unavoidable because of deficiencies in family life. Briefly, these come down to issues of acculturation and familial economics.

If there is indeed a gap between the society that is and the one that is desired, then group care offers a valuable setting. If the "first day of the revolution" carried through by the parents needs continual reaffirmation, then collective education may be very utilitarian. If children of immigrants have to be converted to a new ideology, new values, new modes of life, then the modern institution may be able to serve better than the family. These have, in fact, been the forces that added reality pressures to ideological desires. In addition, each of the settings has, by virtue of its mode of division of labor and housing conditions, either precluded or made difficult childrearing in the family (See Wolins 1963a).

Under these circumstances group care has developed without the stigma usually attached to it in the United States. As is obvious from the foregoing, no responsible member of the countries involved would consider as rational a statement once made by an American clinician that "children growing up in a large group of other children . . . carry their childish egoism and cruelty into adulthood [Peller 1943, p. 296]." On the contrary, Soviet pedagogues argue that the tremendous opportunities afforded by boarding schools are most convincingly manifest in the creation of closely knit children's collectives, capable of influencing the formation of the pupil's personality (Yabolokov and Kustkov 1959). Polish and Yugoslav educators would accept such a statement. Leaders of the *kibbutz* and the progressive children's institutions in Israel also agree, although with some qualifications.

Several types of group care programs have developed in these countries. Space does not allow a detailed description of each of them. Only a brief statement can be made about each of the variants noted.

The pseudofamily.   This type of institution assembles children of various ages into a single, relatively self-contained unit. Several such units, each with its own "mother," may be grouped together. The children are usually involved in the household and participate in the education programs of the community along with children who live with their own families. This type of program is found in Yugoslavia (one well-known institution in Belgrade is organized in this way) and in the *Kinderdörfer* organized by Hermann Gmeiner.[11]

The open, age-graded institution.   This type of institution has the children assembled in age groupings (sexes usually mixed). Children go into the regular school system, but formal study periods are observed for them in their institutions as well. Since crowded educational facilities necessitate double sessions, the formal study periods within the institutions are quite extensive. This type of program is found in Yugoslavia and Poland and, to some extent, in Israel.

The self-contained collective.   Children and unrelated adults are housed in a setting combining residential and educational functions. The groups are age-graded, and heavy emphasis is placed on self-government and group control of members' behavior. The Soviet boarding school and the liberal Israeli institutions described here are of this type.

"Kibbutz" programs.   There are two types of youth program in the *kibbutz*. One is for children of the *kibbutz* who are reared collectively and in separate quarters but with frequent parental contact. The other is for groups of immigrant and deprived youth who are placed in special groups in the *kibbutz* setting. The latter have infrequent contact with parents, who reside away from the *kibbutz,* often even abroad. Both programs are self-contained, and both combine residential and educational functions. Both are led by *kibbutz* personnel, and both place heavy emphasis on group controls.

Appraisal of Programs

How are these programs working out? This question of effectiveness is, of course, a most appropriate and crucial one. Unfortunately, it is not simple, nor is it easily answered. It is not always clear what is meant by effectiveness: How well do these children grow up to fit their own system? How would they fit into ours? How adjusted are they in terms of some kind of universal measure? Any of these questions may be asked; the last seems indefensible. No matter how much universalist theoreticians have strained, they have not sounded convincing. Certain personality traits that are functional in the *kibbutz* (e.g., noncompetitiveness) are dysfunctional in the American high school or business office. The children's ability to function in our society seems relevant only to the extent that we may value the attributes that are valued by the settings from which they come. For the children to meet expectations of their own environment is, of course, of paramount importance. These they appear to fulfil to a considerable extent. The evidence from three sources is not incontrovertible, nor is it always completely one-sided, but on the whole it seems positive. Outside and inside observers and scattered bits of empirical research provide what data there are.

OUTSIDE OBSERVERS

Evidence of outside observers is most pertinent to the *kibbutz*. On the whole, these observers agree with Golan (the major *kibbutz* ideologist of collective education) that the young people in the *kibbutz* are healthy in mind and body and are satisfied to continue the way of life in which they were reared (for example, see Darin-Drabkin 1961). But some problems also exist. According to one report, these young people are "everything their parents wanted them to be," but their parents also say that they "miss the idealistic thinking, the interest in spiritual matters, and the philosophic bent [Caplan 1954]." Another outside investigator finds that, although able and willing to live in a group of this kind, children reared in the *kibbutz* tend to stay there only "because that is where they were born [Spiro 1958]."

INSIDE OBSERVERS

The many observations by insiders on the outcome of work with children's groups are usually but not always favorable. It is, of course, hard to know the nature and extent of bias involved in the observations.

Little has been written about the pseudofamily type of institutional arrangement. Certainly this type of care merits further exploration. Settings for study are available in Yugoslavia, in Austria, and, to a limited extent perhaps, in the United States.[12] There is substantial literature on the other three forms of group care listed earlier, but mostly the evidence pertains to the self-contained institution and to the *kibbutz*.

Russian and Israeli observations include those of present and former wards looking back on their experiences. A girl reared in a Leningrad boarding school and now working in a factory writes:

> Don't worry about us, dear teachers. You gave us all that is necessary for life: We are trying to work well, we engage in sports and take part in amateur performances. I was elected a member of the dormitory council. As before, I am interested in living conditions. Our earnings are good—we are not in need of anything [Afanasenko and Kairov 1961, p. 23].

Similarly, the children placed by Youth Aliyah in Israeli institutions show good adjustment and report quite favorably on their institutional experiences [Nadad and Achiram 1962].

Young adults reared in *kibbutzim* report many satisfactions. Here is an excerpt from the diary of a young girl in a *kibbutz*.

> I feel that I have grown. I feel great satisfaction with my studies, my social activities, and my work in the group. This has been a good year, full of efforts —and many obstacles. But I have experienced the joy of creating, the formation of a new social body, united and strong from within. This is not negligible . . . we have created this year the basic quality and character of our society and group and I have laid the foundation upon which to erect the great building of my life [Tamar 1958, p. 330].

Adults involved in these programs also seem largely pleased. The director of a Russian boarding school writes: "Reports of our pupils are most favorable. They love their work, are disciplined, respect the opinion of the group, are active, cheerful, and not afraid of difficulties [Afanasenko and Kairov 1961, p. 24]." Another director of a school in Kazakhstan reports the comments of the community. "All our pupils, individually and as a group, distinguish themselves noticeably from pupils of general schools. We often hear, 'What good children you have!' and therein lies the great merit of the children's collective [Afanasenko and Kairov 1961, p. 286]."

The following excerpts show that adult writers from within the *kibbutz* also evidence pride in their childrearing accomplishments.

> The average *kibbutz* teenager will easily hold his own in comparison with his outside counterpart in general knowledge of world literature and affairs, an acquaintance with the history of art and music, a fair idea of social, political, and economic theory [Ben-Yosef 1963, p. 72].

> *Kibbutz* children come home from schools and army service and assume their places in the adult community in a most natural way. . . . . Our children are bound to this life and in love with it not less than we, the first generation, and with them everything is simpler and easier [Chazan 1956, p. 385].

This general attitude of satisfaction does not preclude a concern with the many unsolved problems that confront these childrearing systems. Thus, Soviet pedagogues working with children in boarding schools, while pointing to success in developing political consciousness, are concerned about those children who fail to achieve it. A Soviet educator writes:

> One student, after graduating from a boarding school, went to a theological school. When asked how this step could be compatible with his answers in class about the Marxist view on religion, he said: "They asked me about the views of Marx, and I answered; but nobody ever asked me about my personal views on religion" [Levshin 1963, p. 18].

Moreover, not all students appear to understand the meaning of *kollektiv*. It is not, as they assume, any group that works together, but only that which is bound to Communist ideology (Pyzhko 1963, p. 31). And not everyone is concerned about social property as he should be. Thus Soviet educators are concerned that "where children are entirely supported by the state, the development of a parasitical and merely consumer's outlook on life is a real danger [Afanasenko and Kairov 1961, p. 17]."

But these and other problems apparently have not changed the overall position on the boarding school from what it was at its inception—a worthwhile investment of social resources for the rearing of the new generation. The extreme view is that "unconditionally preferring public forms of upbringing to all others, we will expand them at such a rate that within fifteen to twenty years they will be general for the whole population, from the cradle to the graduation certificate [Strumilin 1960, p. 208]." While there is disagreement with the above position that children will be contented with "vitamins of love," i.e., the unrelated professionals who care for them instead of affection from the "lavish hearts of their parents," there is no disputing the continuation of the boarding school (Kolbanovski 1961).

Young people in the *kibbutz* and their educators also point to some concerns. An adolescent writes about the inescapability of certain status positions: "From an early age some kind of group hierarchy is established. . . . . This distinction is so clear-cut and public opinion so stable and fanatic that it is nearly impossible to change [Vardi 1956, p. 271]." Work status is often different from that desired. Many more people are developed who wish to be employed in agriculture than the system can absorb, and many more (particularly girls) end up in service tasks than desire to do so (Collective 1962).

Other young people write with feeling and beauty about their searchings in the group. At one school, students wrote about solitude, loneliness, and beauty, as follows.

> We strive to bring up a person able to fight for a new society, for the man of tomorrow. Is this a higher ideal than the social person? But for this, exactly for this, we need some solitude.

> Why am I always lonely? In my sleepless nights loneliness lies beside my bed. Others will groan in their sleep—warm bodies so near and yet so strange. Perhaps they are also awake? Why am I always so lonely?

> How much better would it be if we would try to understand one another and could express our love for each other. . . . The real change in our life-style would come when we know how to educate ourselves. Only then will our life be really beautiful [Collective 1948, pp. 502–7].

In general, though, the doubts are overbalanced by perceptions of achievement. Moreover, while some technical changes have taken place, the form of care is accepted in all *kibbutz* institutions (Golan 1961). Members of the *kibbutz,* young and old, generally view collective education as the only type possible, given their conditions and the personality characteristics to which they aspire (Spiro 1956).

EMPIRICAL EVIDENCE

There is a decided scarcity of available data on all of the settings—one volume on Yugoslav institutions, a peripheral study on Soviet boarding-school children, a few studies on the *kibbutz*. With the exception of the Yugoslav work, these studies are not intended to measure effectiveness in any all-embracing sense, and the Yugoslav material reflects postwar institutional conditions that have undoubtedly changed for the better. On the whole, the Yugoslav findings are negative. The graduates reflect the isolation to which they were subject (even though they went out to school). After leaving the institutions they experienced social and economic problems which they attribute to their upbringing. While the author gives many details, only his most telling summary can be cited here. It is embodied in the words of one former ward: "The home taught me how to live and find my way in a certain community, but deprived me of the knowledge of everyday life, which I now feel I lack [Nedeljković 1960, p. 84]."

Pertinent studies in the *kibbutz* are mostly those of Rabin, who has compared children reared there with those in other types of rural settlements in

Israel. His observations and those of others can be reported in brief as follows. (1) In comparison with other children studied, more children from the *kibbutzim* showed accurate perception of reality (on Rorschach), more breadth of interest and cultural background, better emotional control, and greater overall maturity (Rabin 1957). (2) Internalization of moral behavior seems to be higher among *kibbutz* than non-*kibbutz* children, as measured by the incidence of confessions in response to incomplete stories involving transgressions (Luria, Goldwasser, and Goldwasser 1963). (3) *Kibbutz* children show less oedipal intensity and sibling rivalry than the controls. (Blacky test was used as instrument.) (4) Adolescent *kibbutz* boys and girls show less severe guilt responses than their controls from city schools (Rabin 1965). (5) *Kibbutz* infants and toddlers show a higher incidence of thumbsucking, temper tantrums, and enuresis than similar-age children in Jerusalem. Although toddlers look like deprived children, the adolescents and young adults are sociable, have excellent interpersonal relationships, and are rather extroverted. They are prepared to make sacrifices for the group and are "everything the original settlers wanted their children to be [Caplan 1954, pp. 98–99]."

Summary

What then may we conclude on the basis of this broad survey? What are the origins of group care and what are its consequences?

Clearly, political ideology and social reality predetermine societies toward individual versus group care. Increasingly, the tendency is to provide institutional programs for children wherever the familial structure fails to care for them. Ideology is modified and, in some instances, reinforced by social reality. Scarcities of housing, shortages of time resulting from modifications in the status of women, family economics—all accelerate the change.

When group care is implemented it may take a number of forms, more or less familial, more or less peer centered, more or less community integrated, or independent from its milieu. Here again, ideology and societal possibilities come into play, structuring and molding a program typically native to its setting. Such predetermining factors naturally create variety. The institution's role in its society varies, as do the positions and functions of adults and children within it. Expected results are quite different, and perhaps most crucial, the meaning of group care ranges from the highly desirable to the nearly unacceptable.

The present paper deals with group care in several settings in which by virtue of ideological and reality circumstances it is deemed a good way or the best way to rear a child. From what evidence there is, the outcome merits a guarded optimism, although not for all types of settings. Interestingly, the children reared in the greatest isolation from their families or from the impact of the outside environment seem to reflect personality structure most closely approximating that desired. The impact of a strong collective seems to be best expressed in the self-contained schools and in the children of the *kibbutz*.

While empirical work is still very sparse, what does exist points to the possibility of achieving favorable results. Children reared in certain settings appear to grow to healthy maturity and to fit into their societies as responsible, constructive adults. But the evidence is by no means conclusive. There are flaws and problems in all settings, and group care, like childrearing in the family, is certainly not automatically good or successful. Yet it is an important and in some instances apparently a very effective way to solve certain social problems.

NOTES

1. For example, George P. Murdock (1949) finds that the family is universally responsible for at least four functions: sexual, reproductive, economic, and educational.

2. The *kibbutz* movement to be discussed is Hakibbutz Haartzi, the most socialist on the continuum of all *kibbutz* movements.

3. Abstracted and selected from the 1961 rules of the Communist party of the Soviet Union.

4. There is some dispute about the degree of convergence between official and private values in the Soviet Union; some authors believe that a substantial gulf exists between them, and others that they are drawing together. See Geiger (1964), for the first view and Werth (1962) for the second.

5. Concern for clarity in childrearing ideology is evident in Polish literature, for example. One author says: "To the question: Do we have a clear and single-minded formulation of an ideal toward which we rear, the answer is positive *if* we accept the educational upbringing ideal as socialism [Kasiuk 1962, italics added]."

6. Some interesting evidence of this concern in the Soviet Union has recently appeared in the form of a debate on combining the work record with the internal passport of every citizen, so that the meting-out of reward and approbation will be related to participation in the productive endeavor of society (*Izvestia* 1964; *Pravda* 1964; *New York Times* 1964.)

7. Bloch begins with the assumption that ideology will not be inherited but must be inculcated, and that the sruggle of the "second day of the revolution"—i.e., guarding what has been achieved—is no less important and certainly more difficult than the "first day" of conquest.

8. See also Ambler 1961.

9. The allowances, however, are far below the cost of childrearing. Institutional costs in Yugoslavia, for example, were about five to seven times the allowance per child. In Poland, the allowance for 1 child is 65 zlotys; for 5 children, 595 zlotys; and for every child above 5, 150 zlotys per month. Cost of institutional care is about 1,000–1,300 zlotys per month or, as in Yugoslavia, many times greater than the allowance. (See Yugoslav National Board 1956; Szczurzewski 1962.) Note that data are for 1956 and 1962. Since then both costs and allowances have risen.

10. One should add that the kind of self-criticism shown by the writer of this material is in itself evidence of the kind of personality development the *kibbutz* desires.

11. See Chap. 11 for a brief description.

12. Since this paper was originally published, new data have become available. They are presented in several subsequent chapters.

4

Boarding Schools in the U.S.S.R.

ALBERT L. WEEKS

As noted in Chapter 3, socialist societies generally are far better disposed toward group care than Western communities have been. The ideological foundations for such care were laid by Marx and the first Soviet feminist, Aleksandra Kollontai. Considerable stresses of war, rapid industrialization, and severe housing shortages in urban areas also have predisposed East European societies and the families that comprise them toward a more friendly view of group care. It is thus not surprising that in the Soviet Union some 20–30 percent of preschool children are in day centers and several hundred thousand in boarding schools. The actual number of children in this program cannot be determined with any degree of certainty, and in any event it has fluctuated considerably over the last two decades, but day care capacity clearly is increasing. Boarding schools have had a more mercurial history. In a comprehensive treatment of the subject Weeks traces the life history of the shkola-internat (boarding school).

> Do you charge us with wanting to stop the exploitation of children by their parents? To this crime we plead guilty. But you will say, we destroy the most hallowed of social relations when we replace home education with social. . . . The bourgeois clap-trap about the family and education, about the hallowed relationship between parent and child, becomes all the more disgusting as all family ties among proletarians become increasingly torn asunder by the action of modern industry. . . .
>
> Marx and Engels, *The Communist Manifesto* (1848).

This is an updated and somewhat revised version of "The Boarding School," *Survey* 56 (1965): 81–94.

The first condition for the liberation of the wife is to bring the whole of the female sex back into national industry . . . and this, in fact, means the abolition of the monogamous family as the economic unit of society. . . . Private housekeeping will be transformed into a social industry. The care and education of children will become a public affair.

> Engels, *The Origin of Family, Private*
> *Property and the State* (1884)

In place of the individualistic and egoistic house-groups, there will arise a great universal family.

> Alexandra Kollontai, *Communism and the Family* (1920).

Children's collectives are incomparably better suited to giving the most thorough inculcation of the best social habits in a child than the most loving or attentive mother . . . [with] the egoistic attachment of mothers to their children.

> Stanislav G. Strumilin, "The Daily Life of the
> Worker Under Communism," *Novy Mir*, July 1960.

These quotations cover 100 years of Communist teaching on the family. To these one could add many other Communist pronouncements of equal vintage and extravagance about future plans for the state (which is to wither away), for the economy (which is to satisfy fully everyone's basic and "reasonable" needs), for society (whose members will voluntarily obey all the rules of social living without recourse to legal sanctions). But there have been other programmatic goals which, it should never be forgotten, were either partially or wholly carried out in practice: the dictatorship of the proletariat, or as the Kronstadt Communists complained and Zinoviev boasted, dictatorship of the Party over the proletariat; state economic planning; nationalization of the land; inroads on bourgeois productive relations in the village; centralization of the means of communication and transportation; polytechnization of schools; and many others.

Realism toward Communist theory is a commendable attitude on the part of foreign observers of the Soviet scene, so long as the baby is not thrown out with the wash. Even those goals which seem at best only remotely realizable may, in a sense, exert an influence (something like Kant's "regulative" ideas) on the course of present-day Soviet policy and practice.

The difficult theory-versus-practice problem is related to the whole question as to what part of Soviet theory is mere window dressing or ritual, and what part is feasible and in earnest. Putting it another way; how can one distinguish those theories which are likely to see the light of practice from those which may only be attractive advertising?

An answer to this question cannot be given within the framework of this modest essay, but with regard to the program for the *family* and the post-1956 institution of the Soviet boarding school (shkola-internat), it seems likely that this goal—the socialization of the family and public rearing of children—may indeed belong to the first category, a goal whose realization is already partly under way. Inroads have already been made on the private family through the boarding school reform. Soviet leaders appear to be putting into action what political philosophers of the past (most notably Plato) dared not call more than an ideal laid up in heaven.

The Soviet Communist Party has embarked on the third revolution in Soviet history. The first was, of course, political: the seizure of power in November 1917. The second, the economic revolution, saw the carrying out of Stalin's five-year plans, collectivization, and laid the foundations of the socialist economy and its corresponding state institutions.

The third revolution, initiated under Stalin but rededicated and refined in theory if not in practice by Khrushchev, is social and spiritual and tied directly to the "concerted building of a fully communist society," the present officially stated basic aim of the Soviet domestic program.

This last and crucial revolution was first outlined, although rather sketchily, at the Party Congress in 1956. It was subsequently delineated more fully at the 21st Congress in 1959. Finally, with the 1961 50,000-word Program of the Communist Party (still in effect in 1971), the third epoch was further elaborated and made the basis for the Party's general line for the next two decades.

In the key year of 1956, notable more for its reappraisal than for any reformation or reaffirmation of basic communism, Khrushchev told the Party and the masses that the U.S.S.R. was about to enter an entirely new revolutionary epoch, an epoch which would demand maximum effort and sacrifice for the future, "the concerted transition from socialist to communist society . . . the broad outlines of which are now plainly visible." At the 1956 Congress, the First Secretary introduced what appeared to be one of the most characteristic institutions of the new epoch of spiritual reformation: the shkola-internat, or polytechnical boarding school.

Khrushchev dwelt on the importance and future prospects of this new institution: "It will rear and educate the new Communist Man. . . . Its teachers will be the engineers of the souls of the rising generation. . . . No funds or effort will be spared; the boarding schools will return the expenditures a hundredfold. . . . It is impossible to overemphasize the enormous importance of this type of education."

At the 21st congress in 1959, or 3 years after the new schools were founded, the First Secretary spoke of them in still broader terms: "The possibility of educating *all children* [my emphasis—ALW] in the boarding schools will be opened up in the future and will solve the problem of giving a communist upbringing to the rising generation. At the same time, millions of women will be released from the household chores of childrearing and fill productive jobs in the construction of communist society."

The intention of eventually enrolling all children in these schools has been cited down through the years, although with little additional comment in the Soviet press and pedagogical journals, especially in the boarding school monthly journal, *Shkola-Internat.* The speed and determination the Party and the Government showed in establishing the boarding schools illustrate the practical importance the Soviet leaders attached to them. Starting from scratch in 1956, the number of children housed and reared in the polytechnical boarding schools in 1961 was 700,000; in 1962, 1 million; and in 1963, around 1.2 million[1] in some 3,000 schools. Figures *(Pravda,* 24 January 1964) showed 2.4 million pupils at boarding schools and extended-day schools, or 360,000 above the 1962 school year. According to the current 7-year plan (1959–65), the number of boarding school pupils was to reach 2.5 million by 1965. This would have represented around 10 percent of the total elementary and secondary school-age population. By the end of "the second decade of building full communism," or by 1980, roughly a third of the Soviet youth from the age of 7 to 18 could dwell and be trained through 11 grades in these schools, judging from statements made by Soviet educators. At the seven-year-plan rate of expansion, the bulk of the children of the peasant and industrial working classes could by the 1980s be living and matriculating in these institutions.

The large-scale building of these new Communist schools prompts a number of questions. What advantages are the schools supposed to have in the building of pure Communism? What kind of curriculum and regimen has already been set up in them to realize their purpose? What means is the regime using to attract hundreds of thousands of Soviet children into the new schools, and what is the parents' attitude to the program? Last, and perhaps most important, what is the social and political rationale of the polytechnical boarding schools?

The veteran economist, former Gosplan executive and Lenin Prize winner (1958), 87-year-old Stanislav G. Strumilin, now deceased, was one of the U.S.S.R.'s leading authorities on the institutions to be established in the allegedly not-so-remote Communist society. His articles appeared in any number of journals and newspapers, including *Red Star.* In his long and important article in *Novy Mir* (July 1960), "The Daily Life of the Worker under Communism," Strumilin dwelt at length on the third revolution and the boarding schools.

> Upon emerging from the hospital—he writes—every Soviet citizen will be assigned to a nursery, then to a kindergarten maintained day and night, and then to a boarding school from which he will enter independent life. . . . It is our task to extend the public forms of upbringing in the next few years at a tempo that will eventually make them accessible to all, from the cradle to the diploma, within the next fifteen to twenty years.

Strumilin contrasts the "often egoistic attachment of mothers to their children" with the more rational, altruistic, and genuinely "comradely" relationship between children in the environment of the boarding school public family: "Children's collectives [of the boarding school type] are incomparably better suited to giving the most thorough inculcation of the best social habits in a child than the most loving and attentive mother. The advantages of public upbringing are so great that they will justify whatever public expense may be necessary to accommodate all children of the country."[2]

The Communist man of the future must be taught from the cradle on to regard himself merely as an "organic part" of the great collectivized commune, one voice in the gigantic communal chorus. As Khrushchev has said, individualism must give way to the Communist ethos of sacrifice for the group, of the "good of all as the condition for the good of each." And at the 21st Party Congress he said: "Man is a social animal. His life is unthinkable and indeed impossible outside the collective."

The boarding schools are also conceived as an institutionalized form of what may be called "social Pavlóvism." As Strumilin writes:

Egoistic inclinations in the child will be "snuffed out in the cradle." In place of them, all inborn social instincts and sympathies will be emphasized and brought out as the result of *newly conditioned reflexes* formed in the process of daily comradely interrelationships [my emphasis—ALW].

Pure communism, he goes on, will be practiced in the school.

Private ownership of toys, skates, bicycles, etc., is not recognized here. All gifts, edible or not, enter the common pool for all. All children, from the youngest to the oldest, are guided by the rule that all must be comrades, that the older children must help the younger, and that no one is allowed to be greedy. . . . Order and discipline must prevail at all times and in all things.

The Minister of Education of the RSFSR, Afanasenko, at the time an alternate CPSU member of the Central Committee, wrote in *Izvestia* (7 March 1961):

We are moving toward the day when the doors of all homes will be thrown open wide so that children will know about locks only from reading about them in books. We must throw open the doors of all schoolrooms and lockers. Libraries must have no librarians in them. Only in this way will genuine honesty be implanted.

The curriculum and regimen in the boarding schools are intended to serve as the model for the regular elementary and secondary schools, which will continue to exist until they are gradually enveloped by the expanding 11-year boarding schools.

The principal curricular *motif* of the boarding schools is polytechnism. It was the boarding schools which in 1956 and after pioneered the present program for installing universal polytechnical education in the U.S.S.R. Polytechnism was not begun in the regular schools until 1959 and has not been completed even now. The successful 3-year experience with the pilot polytechnical boarding schools, most of which are on an 11-year curriculum, convinced educational authorities and Party leaders of the feasibility of total polytechnization of the educational system.

Considerable opposition to this program was put up by certain education-alists who maintained that the intellectual quality of education would suffer and the continuity of a student's education be interrupted by the intermittent time-consuming training in factories required of polytechnical students dur-ing their actual time of study. One of the most eminent opponents of the poly-technization program in 1958–59 was Professor Nesmeyanov, then presi-dent of the U.S.S.R. Academy of Sciences, who criticized it publicly. (Soon after, he resigned as president of the academy.)

The necessity of the polytechnization program was spelled out in some-what strident tones by Mr. Khrushchev in September 1958.

> A number of 10-year secondary school graduates unwillingly go to work in factories, mills, collective farms, state farms, and some of them even consider it beneath their dignity. . . . This lordly, scornful, and erroneous attitude to-ward physical labor can also be found in a number of families. If a boy or girl does not study well, the parents and the people around him frighten the child by saying that if he does not study hard or fails to get a gold or silver medal, he will not be able to get into a university and will therefore have to work in a factory as a common laborer. . . . Such views are insulting to the toiling masses of socialist society.

He continued by pointing out that the schools, as then constituted, were "di-vorced from life, the chief and basic fault of our schools." Lenin's famous dictum on education, he said, had been forgotten: "Education must be com-bined with socially useful labor."

The 11-year polytechnical boarding schools have led and are leading the way in the expanding polytechnization program throughout the whole Soviet educational system. Professor Brickman, former New York University spe-cialist on Soviet education, was among a traveling team of 70 American ed-ucators who closely studied Soviet schools, including dozens of boarding schools, in 1958. He told the present writer that in an Alma-Ata boarding school, boys 16 to 18 years of age were working during school time in a nearby automobile factory. Boys and girls at the school worked away from school for 8 to 10 hours a week for several weeks. At the end of the on-the-job training, an examination was held and the results entered in each student's *dnevnik,* which, together with the Certificate of Skill, is, of course, a vital component of a boarding school graduate's dossier. At another boarding school a large group of its teen-aged girls was dispatched to a nearby "patron" factory having close ties with the "apprentice" boarding school. At the plant the girls were receiving on-the-job training in garment-making.

Productive labor is sometimes performed on the premises of the boarding school itself. For example, Leningrad Boarding School No. 2 recently put both its younger and older pupils to work assembling cardboard boxes for packing the shoes manufactured at a nearby patron shoe factory. The box-assembly brigades, which included children as young as eight or nine years, worked in afternoon shifts before supper, customarily a time reserved for supervised study. Boarding school administrators were pleased when the children joined eagerly in a schoolwide "socialist competition" for high quantity and quality output of assembled boxes.

Students at another boarding school earned 150,000 rubles in a single year of woodworking production on the premises. Money earned in this fashion goes into the communal fund of the school.

Beyond the purely polytechnical training in the boarding school curriculum, pupils are reared in the expectation that they will become model Communist toilers, in the moral and labor-discipline sense.

Discipline in the schools is rigid and intense, which is attested to by both Soviet and American commentators. There is more than a suspicion that some of the staff in the schools have had police experience; such personnel were in demand particularly in the first year or so of the schools' foundation, when a large part of the student body was made up of delinquents. The pupils move everywhere in strict double file—to meals, from class to class, and from activity to activity. The revamped "Stalin Code" of classroom behavior is strictly followed, more so in the boarding schools than in the regular schools. As in the regular schools, students snap to attention when the teacher enters the room. Boarding school students stand and recite at attention or march to the head of the class making smart, right-angle turns on the way to and from their two-student desks. The schools enforce a military-like regime consisting of early-morning rise, calisthenics, personal and dormitory cleanup and inspection, and supervised study in the evening. Classes generally meet from 9 a.m. to 2 p.m. From 2 to 4 p.m. the pupils have lunch and, for the younger ones, rest hour. From 4 to 6 p.m. they have supervised study or labor training, as the case may be.

One of the few breaks in the day comes from 6 to 8 p.m. At this time the pupil is free to participate in hobby clubs, watch TV in the Pioneer Room, play chess or checkers, dance (ballroom style only), or take part in other work or study activities in the various *kruzhki*.

Speaking of dancing, the boarding schools are universally coeducational. Boarding school officials often voice the hope that happy marital unions will result from friendships formed between the boys and girls in the boarding schools. In some schools, boys and girls are separated by floors in the dormitories, in other schools they dwell on opposite sides of the hall on the same floors.

Discipline is sometimes carried too far, as Soviet educators and administrators have pointed out. For example, B. E. Shirvindt, director of Moscow

B.S. No. 15, pointed out in *Sovetskaya Pedagogika* (December 1960) that the discipline enforced in some of the larger boarding schools[3] was "extremely oppressive and fatiguing for the children." The RSFSR Minister of Education Afanasenko gave the example of a boarding school in Kemerovo where the children were, he said, literally never allowed outdoors (the cold being no legitimate excuse) and as a consequence looked pale and fatigued from strict regimentation indoors. Educators have also complained of the leveling effect of some types of discipline and group punishment. Gifted boarding school children, they say, are simply being lumped together with the "problem children," large numbers of whom are among the residents in the schools; they are generally orphans, neglected children of large families, or simply "children of the streets."

From an ideological point of view, the boarding school setup offers excellent possibilities for thorough indoctrination of the rising generation on a 12-hour-a-day, 7-day-a-week basis.[4] In general, the curriculum is supposed to impart "love for the motherland and the cause of communism, hate for the enemies of communism"; "joyful, comradely communion"; the duty to "work, study, and live in a communist manner"; elimination of "egoistic and individualistic private-ownership psychology"; voluntary obedience and adherence to the Communist moral code, without recourse to overt punishment beyond "the force of public opinion of the communards themselves."

Sovetskaya Pedagogika and *Shkola-Internat* have reported that many boarding schools are trying out the technique of "Children's Courts" in which children who refuse to obey voluntarily are given various sentences by their young peers. (One of the worst forms of punishment is depriving the child of any activity whatsoever, a penalty whose impact is much greater than traditional penalties.) The American educators who visited schools with this type of court felt that the children tended to mete out more severe punishment to fellow offenders than school officials would have done.

As a thoroughly indoctrinated Communist Man, the boarding school graduate is presumed fully equipped to take his place in Communist society. He is supposedly willing actively to cooperate in stamping out the remnants of the acquisitive bourgeois spirit and to help bring about the withering away of punitive law and the state in the Communist millennium. What is not discussed, however, is the shock the young graduate will experience upon leaving the utopian, communal atmosphere of the boarding school and entering the highly competitive and atomistic Soviet society lying outside its walls.

In the Party's methods of attracting new pupils into the schools, American educators and other observers have so far reported no violation of the principle of voluntary consent of the parents. No cases of forcible enrollment of children are known to exist, with one major exception. However, cases are known of children who have been directed into these schools by the People's

Courts (and perhaps also by the other, paralegal courts) because their parents were allegedly unable or unwilling to give them an adequate material or spiritual environment or upbringing.[5] A recent issue of the Soviet legal journal *Sovetskoe Gosudarstvo i Pravo* cited examples of the application of this type of court order to juvenile delinquents. Presumably, the Party reserves the right to introduce whatever elasticity it wishes into the law on these matters, if voluntary admission does not support the planned pace of boarding school enrollments.

Instead of outright compulsion, the regime appears to be employing at present economic incentives to induce parents to send their children to the reasonably priced boarding schools. Under the nearly marginal economic conditions of the average Soviet family, monetary inducements evidently act strongly on the parents, or at least have done so up to now. Tuition payments are graded, from a low base, so that poorer families pay nothing while moderately well-off families pay from 30 to 40 rubles a month.[6] This also covers the boys' bluish-grey uniforms and the girls' brown dresses and blue aprons. Medical care is also included. Parents with large families, low incomes, and crowded living conditions are particularly attracted by the schools.

By means of the boarding school program, moreover, the Party plans to include millions of additional women, released from housework and child-rearing, in productive labor at a time when the Soviet Union is feeling the manpower pinch as the result of the low birth rate during the war. The figure of from 5 to 6 million women workers to be added to the labor force is fixed in the goals of the current 7-year plan. Part of this increment is supposed to result from the fact that millions of mothers will no longer be tied down at home by "unproductive" childrearing. The connection between public upbringing and the release of women for productive labor was indicated long ago, not only by Marx and Engels and other classical Communists, but by Mme. Kollontai, author of *Communism and the Family,* Lenin, and countless others in the Soviet period.

Western visitors to the U.S.S.R. have noted that home conditions for many of the children now in the boarding schools were so inadequate, the apartments so cramped, that the poorer children seem to relish the neat dormitories (which they clean and maintain themselves), the gay dining rooms (in which they serve as waiters and which, it is reported, are noisy in the extreme), recreation rooms (some have TV), gymnasiums where these are provided, and the other inducements in the boarding schools. Homesickness is a difficult problem, and *Shkola-Internat* published numerous complaints and much advice on this matter. To foreign observers, it has seemed that the children often miss their parents less than the parents miss them after the children have spent some time in the schools.

Complaints by boarding school officials of "maternal egoism" crop up

now and then, and there are other problems. Parents are known and reported to have complained about the all-too-brief and infrequent encounters
with their children which are permitted by the tight boarding school schedules. Children are generally allowed to go home on holidays and on several
weekends throughout the year. Trips home are often difficult, however, because the boarding schools are far away from the pupil's hometown or village.

As to the underlying political purpose served by the boarding schools, a
number of answers come to mind. Soviet spokesmen are especially reticent
about discussing this aspect of the boarding school program. Visiting educators have detected a reluctance on their part even to broach the subject. The
program nevertheless does suggest a number of political motivations on the
part of the regime.

First, the schools are necessarily intended mainly for the children of the
working class and peasantry, at least at the present time. It is estimated that
these two groups compose around 90 percent of the pupils in the schools.
When the new schools become nearly universal, only a small minority of
children will presumably be able to avoid being institutionalized in the ordinary boarding schools,[7] by virtue of their economic, social, and political influence. The regime is concerned above all with training and disciplining
new youthful reserves to work in the factories and farms, and loyally to support the regime in any trials that may lie ahead.

The link between the Party and the masses becomes particularly crucial
as the promised "self-administration" supposedly comes into operation during the transition to Communism, and impersonal automation spreads
throughout the economy, while at the same time "bourgeois influence from
abroad" and various strains of revisionism may become increasingly dangerous in the eyes of the one-party regime. There has been a "Worker's Opposition," before.

In 1957, a few months after the revolts of the workers in Poland and
Hungary, Mao Tse-tung publicly identified the party–masses relationship as
the key, recurring problem of Communist polities. Mao's shortlived tactic of
"let-a-hundred-flowers-bloom," a safety valve for releasing and detecting
pent-up grievances among the masses, was his alleged solution of the problem of what he called "the contradictions between ruler and ruled." Khrushchev and his associates, on the other hand, evidently reacted quite differently to the problem of worker disaffection, corrupting bourgeois influence,
and so on. They seem to have been thinking in more institutional terms than
Mao (their superior material base is an advantage in this regard). The Soviet answer to the contradictions problem evidently consisted of accelerating
the move toward what is called Communist society, which is the most highly
organized and disciplined society there is; in this context the polytechnical
boarding schools act as a typical institution of the new epoch.

The underlying political intent of this nearly total communization and collectivization of child upbringing is designed to cope with one aspect of the problem of political authority, its expression and its maintenance, peculiar to closed Communist societies. The legitimacy of their self-perpetuating oligarchies hangs delicately and precariously by the thread of theory and indoctrination. In fact, the Soviet state may be said, in a sense, to have "no roots . . . to hang in the air," as Tkachev said of the Tzarist state.[8] In pluralist democracies, on the other hand, political authority reaches upward and downward, from and to the grass roots, and is based on the periodic housecleaning carried out by free voters armed with multiple-list ballot papers.

In *Problems of Leninism,* still a valid manual on Communist statecraft, Stalin speaks of "the links of the Party with the masses by means of transmission belts" as the best answer to the contradictions problem. The education and organization of the youth, he pointed out, constitute the most important transmission belt between the Communist Party and the masses for ensuring that the many future demands made on those masses by the party-state would be met without protest.

The boarding school, which completely swallows up boys and girls from the age of 7 without letting them go into "independent life," as one Soviet authority put it, until they are 18 or so could forge a solid link between the broad masses and the ruling party.

The boarding schools also raise problems about social status and mobility. The elite status of the Soviet intelligentsia, in contrast to that of the graduates from the ordinary boarding schools, will clearly be enhanced. As more and more Soviet children are brought up in the polytechnical educational system, and the boarding schools in particular, only three tiny minority groups could avoid the schools and the accompanying stigma of being mere nonintellectual polytechnical cogs in the social and economic machine: the well-to-do with sufficient social and political influence to avoid attendance in the boarding schools; those boarding school graduates who will be permitted to go on to college and acquire the considerable status that attaches to a higher education in the U.S.S.R; and the graduates of the new Special Boarding Schools. The polytechnization of the schools, and of the boarding schools in particular, would seem to further entrench the Communist new class.

A characteristic of the immediate post-Khrushchev period (1965–66) was the criticism of some of the deposed First Secretary's pet projects—among them the cultivation of maize, five-story building construction, and the boarding schools. However, as the post-K period ripened, major pronouncements in the form of editorials began appearing in *Pravda,* stating the new regime's line on agriculture, foreign policy, science, the arts, education, et al.

The authoritative post-K editorial on education appeared in Pravda on 12 January 1965. It indicated that the boarding schools (now called *internaty pri shkolakh* or simply *internaty)* had received a strong vote of confidence from the new Soviet leaders. "The boarding schools," the editorial stated, "must be given constant attention. . . . Party and Soviet organs must undertake the continued expansion of the network of boarding schools."

A few days later, on 23 January, *Pravda* provided further evidence that the Brezhnev-Kosygin regime had endorsed the "schools of a new type," adding an endorsement of the "special" boarding school. One such "special physics and mathematics boarding school" is attached to Moscow State University. "This is an unusual school," the article continues. "Its students are winners of mathematics 'olympiads' held in 56 provinces of the country. Beginning with the ninth grade, these students matriculate in a special program under the guidance of some of the most outstanding mathematicians."

The close association of Special Boarding Schools with universities throughout the Soviet Union makes these schools radically different from the majority of "lower class" boarding schools. The latter, far from being attached to institutions of higher learning, are most often apprenticed to factories or farms, and tend to stress admission to "problem children," orphans, children of low-income families, and so on. They are intended to function as polytechnical training schools supplying young recruits for the Soviet labor force. The Special Boarding Schools, on the other hand, bear an elitist cast and seem to be intended to provide a source of talent for the new class of Soviet technocrats and possibly also for the party cadres.

Further developments during the Brezhnev-Kosygin regime bear on the Special (and ordinary) Boarding Schools.

First, the two party congresses, the 23rd and 24th in 1966 and 1971, saw a number of trends. A key boarding school proponent, RSFSR Minister of Education Afanasenko, was dropped (1966) from the Central Committee, of which he had been a Candidate Member. Nor was he reelected to the Committee at the 1971 Congress. The boarding school publication *Shkola-Internat* was discontinued after 1965, while other pedagogical journals occasionally ran items dealing with boarding school problems.

Second, both party congresses, and the second more than the first, sharply downgraded the importance of the future Communist society. Almost nothing was said at these authoritative party forums about broad outlines of the millenium-to-come. This pattern of deemphasis of pie-in-the-sky is presently matched by deemphasis of the 1961 Party Program, which is cited only very rarely today.

Third, as was mentioned in a footnote above, statistics on the number of boarding schools, whether Special or ordinary, are lacking in present-day Soviet materials. On a visit to the U.S.S.R. in 1966, the author was told in a semiofficial way that despite absent data boarding school expansion *has* been continued, but that the ordinary schools are just that—ordinary. Few better-off families are willing to send their children to them because they contain many "unsavory elements." But the author was also told that the schools provide important aid to children from poor or "broken" homes; such parents or stepparents relish the opportunity of sending their charges to these schools, which are free to the poorest families.

Fourth, the Special Boarding Schools seem to be getting a strong endorsement from the Brezhnev-Kosygin regime. One finds mention of them much more often in Soviet media than he does the ordinary boarding schools. This fact, together with various other changes in Soviet educational policy in the last five years, suggests that the regime is becoming self-consciously "elitist" in its boarding school policy of distinguishing a "higher" and "lower" type of school. Moreover, recent studies indicate that the Soviet "middle" and "upper" classes have become entrenched to a point where children of Party and Government officials (at all levels) obviously have a much better chance of getting good jobs, a university education, and higher incomes than does the Soviet common man and his children.

The regime in Moscow has shown awareness of the dangerous side of this inequality (as witnessed in Poland in December 1970, when workers struck and rioted against increased costs of living) by enacting special legislation that provides extra monetary help to disadvantaged families. This legislation, made into law early in 1971, is simply one more family-support measure, which, like the ordinary boarding school, seeks to close somewhat the very large gap that separates the lower classes in the U.S.S.R. from the middle and upper classes. The legislation, and the need for it, in both the political and the economic sense, suggests that the future of the Soviet boarding schools is secure.

NOTES

1. In recent years, Soviet statistics have given the number of boarding school pupils *plus* the extended-day school pupils as one. The extended-day schools, which discharge their pupils at the end of each day and at the end of the week for their return home, represent slightly less than half of the total boarding-school and extended-day student body. The lack of comprehensive statistics makes difficult a clear assessment of the *shkoly-internaty* during the Brezhnev-Kosygin period (about which see further in this essay).

2. *Kommunist* (No. 10, 1962) reviewed a book by N. Soloviev entitled *The Family in Soviet Society* (1962). According to the reviewer, Shakhnazarov, Soloviev is correct in criticizing "several authors" who maintain that eventually the family will be completely replaced by public familes of the boarding school type. Instead, writes Shakhnazarov, supporting Soloviev, the Party has in mind the "merging" (*sochetaniye*) of the family with public institutions. While this may be a proper reading of the present Party line on the family, it is interesting that Soloviev speaks not only of "several" authors who predict the utter destruction of the Soviet family but also of the "widespread" idea that this is the future of the family. That the Party crit-

icizes these authors may only mean that it would be imprudent to do otherwise, for then opposition to the boarding school idea might be generated precisely at the same time when the Party is relying on voluntary admission into the boarding schools.

3. *Pravda*, 30 April 1962, reported a 600-pupil boarding school in Tashkent.

4. Octobrist and Pioneer, not to mention Komsomol organizations, are extremely active in the boarding schools, embracing much larger percentages of the student body than their counterparts in the regular schools.

5. In this connection, a statement by Afanasenko appears somewhat ominous: "Many families are encountered, unfortunately, in which there are still strong remnants of the old life, private property-minded, and religious and nationalist prejudices. In addition to this, some parents are unsuccessful in the rearing of their children, at times influencing their behavior negatively [*Pravda*, 1 September 1963]."

6. Khrushchev indicated at the 22nd Congress and the Party Program promised that all pupils will eventually be nonpaying guests of the state. In explaining the program's references to the boarding schools, Khrushchev cautiously pointed out in 1961 that "people who take the position that the family is of dwindling importance in the transition to communism and that in time it will disappear altogether are quite mistaken; the influence of the family in the children's upbringing must be coupled with their public upbringing." While "disappearing altogether" may not be the fate of the Soviet family, it is surely destined to increased interference from the side of the state. Communist theoreticians have not, after all, predicted the end of wedlock and family parenthood; they do not envisage the communism of Plato's Guardians in *The Republic*. But they do favor a large encroachment by the state on what Mme. Kollontai called "egoistic house-groups" after the children are seven years old or so.

7. There is evidence of an emerging new type of "special boarding school" which has been referred to openly in the Soviet press and by Western correspondents. One such school, for "exceptional students," was reported in Novosibirsk (see *The New York Times*, 27 October 1963). These special schools are reported to operate from 9th to 11th grades and admit students with unusual abilities, especially in the sciences, on the basis of competitive examinations. In an era of advancing automation, these special schools seem designed to turn out men and women who will enjoy a special status in the technocracy.

8. Weeks (1968), p. 124.

5

When the State Brings
Up the Child

ABRAM KARDINER

Fundamental opposition to group care based on philosophical considerations and psychoanalytic theory is common in the United States. Kardiner, reviewing boastful Khruschevian proposals and kibbutz programs, points to the possible risks involved. To be sure, advocacy of massive group care in the Soviet Union was soon abandoned, leaving boarding schools considerably less well supported than Kardiner assumed they would be; nevertheless, the Soviet and kibbutz views on group care are far out, and Kardiner treats them as such. Interestingly, at about the same time another psychoanalyst (Bettelheim 1962) produced a ringing defense of communal education as practiced in the kibbutz.

The Soviet boarding school (described by Weeks in Chap. 4) aims at shaping behavior under the influence of group pressure. The purpose is to produce the "new Soviet man." These objectives may have a logic in relation to the Communist ideal. But the consequences for the children involved and for the community as a whole are not readily visible. It is possible that those who are responsible for this recommendation are ignorant of the potential feedback, first on the individual and ultimately on the society. The abandonment of the family as the basic unit of society is an undertaking filled with many unforeseeable dangers and some that are predictable. There is a vast amount of empirically verifiable material to support the conclusion that the family is a factor of high potency in the survival of man and in promoting his potential for social cohesiveness. When we tamper with the family, therefore, we tamper with the stuff of which social cohesion is made.

What is social cohesion? Is it an inborn quality? Or is it a cultivated or learned capacity, or one that appears under some conditions and not under others? The Russians seem to regard it in both ways. They speak of "inborn social instincts," and again of something that can be cultivated or "developed" by a pedagogue. There is no evidence to substantiate the position that "egoistic inclinations can be snuffed out in the cradle" by a social environment that, as we shall see, denudes the child of protective influences and augments the struggle for existence. This problem was all very simple when we assumed that there was a social or herd instinct that operated automatically. But the Russians have now oversimplified the matter with a naïve Pavlovianism that assumes that one can "condition" anyone to anything, without any feedback to the organism as a whole, either good or bad. We challenge this conclusion and suggest, moreover, that the Russian innovation bodes no good either for Russia or for the rest of the world.

In order to understand what the Russians are contemplating, and have already begun to implement, we must examine the family in relation to the entire society and to the individual that is its product.

There are several styles of family patterning. They vary in the number of spouses a male or female may have; that is, there may be monogamy, polyandry, or polygamy. The latter two are distinguished by the fact that the attention of the father or mother is dissipated away from the interests of the growing child. We do not know of a great culture that was polyandrous. Most of the great cultures, especially in the West, have been monogamous and patriarchally oriented. This is either a coincidence, or its survival is due to the fact that this type of family organization creates the most favorable climate for a child's development.

The family is not necessary for the propagation of the species. But what we call culture or civilization needs the family in order to insure effective forms of cooperation between its constituents, to maintain internal balance within the society, and to find effective means of mastering the external environment. We hold it to be the special merit of the monogamous family that it is best suited to the biological characteristics of man. The human infant has the longest period of helplessness and dependency. The compensation for this is that man has the widest range of adaptability known. But this adaptability is not inborn; it is acquired, learned, or integrated. The success with which effective adaptive devices are acquired depends in part on an inherited organic apparatus and predisposition, but it also depends on the effectiveness of the protection and the direction furnished by the culture and parent. In other words, neither growth nor instinct is responsible for the development of effective coping devices. The child is therefore at the mercy of the parents for physical survival and for emotional and intellectual development. It is precisely because the acquisition of adaptive tools is so slow and is contingent on experience that this period is filled with many hazards. The chief of these hazards is the possibility of defective, malformed, or ineffectual character traits.

Children will of course grow up under any kind of care. But character and emotional and intellectual potential will vary, depending upon whether the child is protected from being overwhelmed by stimuli it cannot master, or lives in a world that is interpreted in a directed manner and is hence made into a source of gratifications. Too much competition early in life strangles development; it does not, as is commonly believed, accelerate it. Under effective care there is a constant reciprocal relation between parent and child. Eventually the child comes to recognize the parents as the benevolent mediator between his weak self and what would otherwise be a hostile world. This leads, first, to the idealization of the parent and to an enhancement of his authority to impose discipline, and ultimately to the development of what we call conscience. Should this pattern fail to occur, the only remaining implement of social control is fear of punishment, which must rest either on institutional pressures or on the police. The absence of the usual attitudes toward the parent, for whatever reason, creates a child with an emotional deficiency that may well make him socially ineducable.

In short, the family is the conveyor of the cultural heritage and also the molder of character. Most of all, it is the breeding place of the social emotions: idealization of the parent, development of conscience, the ability to sympathize with and identify oneself with others and to have a healthy self-esteem, and the ability to know what goes on in the minds of other people. When these capacities develop they act as a powerful stimulus to the intelligence.

If the Russians believe that the "boarding schools" can take over the functions of the family, they would appear to be much deceived. Can they possibly believe visits by the parents "as often as the rules permit" can really be a substitute for the parental role? Or do they think that what is accomplished by the family can be accomplished by "daily comradely relationships"? I have heard of no extrafamilial educational organization that performs these functions. On the contrary, they effectively block the creation of the social emotions and in some instances block the growth of intelligence.

The Russians are, however, quite correct in their observation that the family tends to pull away from community interests toward itself. It is egocentric. All known efforts to destroy the egocentricity of the family have achieved their end only by creating a human being in whom these social emotions were defective.

In addition to these considerations, the family has a little-recognized function for the parents. The need to unite efforts toward the care of the young is a unifying force. In the contemplated Russian program, how will these childless parents—or, rather, childless communities—replace the co-operative incentive that comes from children? Parents will have the opportunity for the biological role of parenthood, but not the social one. One of the consequences we can safely predict, if the program is carried out on a large scale, is that it will have a demoralizing effect on the institution of marriage. In one community that made the care of children a public responsibility, the marital tie became less binding and the concept of paternity lost definition. When the state took over the care of the children, husbands tended to become little disturbed when their wives conceived children by other men. There is strong evidence that the entire fabric of the relation of family to society breaks down when children cease to be an integral part of it.

The evidence that the breakup of the family leads to disastrous effects on the child is varied and plentiful. We have seen the results that ensued from the evacuation of children from the cities of England during World War II; we have gained further evidence from the study of broken homes due to divorce; from studies of the inmates of orphan asylums; from the study of home conditions that prevail in cases of childhood schizophrenia and juvenile delinquency. These are all social patterns that accidentally interfered with parental care. In the case of orphan asylums, the results were so horrendous that they have been abandoned in all civilized communities. In the case of the juvenile delinquent, the significant role of the family in the genesis of this symdrome has recently been recognized.

But there are several types of family breakup that have been deliberately set in motion. In one illiterate society, for example, the absence of the mother for the greater part of the day, so that the child had to shift for itself, had disastrous effects on emotional development. Another variant of the same theme occurs where there is a rigid but loveless discipline with a high emphasis on obedience. This type of discipline is responsible for the creation of a defective form of adaptation known as the obsessional character. The conscience mechanisms become distorted, fail to develop the capacity for tender emotions, and tend to dispose of all human relations in terms of dominance and submission. Individuals thus afflicted have a lifelong battle with hostile impulses that are constantly threatening to get out of hand.

Relevant as these examples may be, however, they do not compare in aptness with recent experiments in social patterning which bear directly on the Russian undertaking. These are the Israeli kibbutzim. These societies were set up deliberately and with the expectation of certain social consequences.

When these cooperatives were established some 50 years ago, the pioneers discovered that the only form of social patterning that could lead to survival was the obliteration of private interests and complete cooperation toward a public goal. The family unit was, however, preserved. The kibbutzim then discovered that private interests could not be obliterated as long as the family was allowed to remain intact. Only after several failures did someone hit upon the idea of breaking up the family. Another reason for doing this was the need to have women join in the labor force. Work by women was necessary because of an extremely refractory environment and the limited number of people available. This type of organization seemed to work. When children came, the idea gradually took shape that one woman would be able to take care of six children. This practice became institutionalized, and the care, nurture, and character formation of the child was delegated to specially designated housemothers. With the child out of the family, the social environment of the child and the parents underwent an abrupt change. For the parents there could be no more *private* objectives; all were now in the public domain. For the children it was now an environment of competing peers with a supervisory housemother whose functions were to nourish, train, and discipline. The housemother was replaced every six months. The children's eating, sleeping, and playing were always done publicly and together. The parents visited at the beginning and end of the working day and on the Sabbath, the day of rest.

The earliest human contacts are therefore mostly peers and a housemother who has at least five others to look after. There is little time or incentive for coddling, play, and reciprocal stimulation. The upshot is that the child is thrown more on its own limited resources, tensions increase, and after 18 months of life the struggle for existence becomes very keen because the child must compete with his peers for the limited attention of the housemother. There is no room for individual needs; all systematic training must be started and completed as early as possible. For toddlers there are limited space and entertainment facilities. This means frequent fighting, which may stimulate pugnacity, but which also strangles all tender emotions. In this kind of emotional environment there must be a large proportion of defeated children. The blurring of the parental image caused by their sporadic presence in the midst of constantly changing housemothers must seriously interfere with the natural tendency of the child to idealize the parent as the source of all security and pleasure. Not only can such a parental image not be formed, but the child is, in infancy, robbed of the opportunity to feel omnipotent. This feeling is the natural result of effective maternal care; for the child under these conditions has a magical control over his environment. This is of importance only because this feeling of omnipotence is usually transferred to the parent. He or she becomes the magical agent, an idealization that lays the foundation for subsequent idealization of the deity, and also becomes an essential ingredient of healthy self-esteem. All these opportunities, if not completely crushed, are at least seriously impaired in the kibbutz. Individuality is sacrificed to standardization. And since each housemother has her own idea of what should be standard, the effect on the growing child can only be confusion. The tender emotions must suffer under this regimen, for high emphasis is placed on self-reliance although no basis for such development has been laid down. Dependency and the tendency to identify with a personal ideal are discouraged; idealization of the community is substituted.

We can now begin to see some serious incompatibilities in character formation under these influences. Self-centered interests are increased by the intense struggle for existence caused by too early conflict with peers. But these same peers are the very ones with whom the child is taught to share everything and with whom he is expected to cooperate. Since the social emotions are already blunted, the child's tendency is to share without generosity and to cooperate out of expediency. There are strong unconscious barriers against affection, cooperation, love, or interest in others, accompanied by strong conscious tendencies to cooperate out of coercion in the face of implacable and constant social necessity.

These conclusions are in a large measure borne out by the studies of a considerable number of native-born Israelis (sabras). The conspicuous feature of their personalities was shown to be an emotional isolation not commonly found in Western man, except in the case of severe pathology.

One of the most revealing of the experiences I had in connection with these studies was a series of interviews with one of the elders of a prominent kibbutz. After the first four interviews I noted something very unusual: there were no dramatis personae in his story; nothing but abstract ideas and situations were discussed. He had spent the first 19 years of his life in Poland and England, and I solicited some information about this part of his life. His story was filled with people and definitive characters. In all these interviews he had not even mentioned to me his martial status. I asked whether he was married. The laconic answer was "Yes"; but no further information was offered. I asked, "What is she like?" The answer was, "Very nice," and that was all. This is not the kind of reply one would get from a Westerner. On the other hand, he seemed a most intelligent and generous man. When I asked him to close his eyes and think of Israel he told me he saw a beautiful sunset and olive groves. There can be no doubt that the natives do not think so much in terms of people and their relations to them, as in terms of something much more abstract.

It must, however, be acknowledged that the kibbutz is, in its way, a very successful society. There is no crime, there are no police, the community is highly cooperative, and the enthusiasm for it is very high. But the emotional isolation of the individual in it is incredible. It is interesting to note that most marriages of the sabras are exogamic, that is, with mates from other communities. They cooperate with, but do not love each other.

The most urgent question concerning the relation of the kibbutz to the personality that emerges from it is whether this personality contributes to the goals of the society. The observable evidence is that it works out fairly well, judging from the kind of internal balance that is maintained. As the matter stands now, however, no case can be made for it one way or another for several reasons. The community which acts as host to these kibbutzim is not cooperatively organized; these cooperatives are permitted in a society that is organized as a democracy. Another reason is that these kibbutzim are subsidized by sources outside Israel. We must also note that the observations on which these conclusions are based were made about 12 years ago, and many of the institutions described have been radically altered.

The relevancy of these observations to the social changes contemplated in Russia is striking. It must be remembered that the Israeli experiments were on a very small scale, involving a few thousand people. In Russia a vast nation is involved. It is also possible, but unlikely, that the results of the Russian system will be very different. Judging from some of the studies of Russian national character by Inkeles and his associates, the proposed scheme of things would produce a personality that is very different from the one that now prevails. These students investigated a group of immigrant Russians who left the Soviet Union because of some special grievance, but who were born and educated there. It was therefore a dissident group. The investigators found that the Russian subjects had a strong need for affiliation, had a high potential for cooperation and affection, and laid great stress on achievement. On the other hand, they had no great need for approbation or for autonomy. They tended to need guidance and pressure from authority to control their impulses. Americans do not have this trait. The latter probably derives from living in a highly prescribed manner. In addition they are a very demonstrative people.

According to these investigators, the existing sociopolitical system already interferes with the free interplay of emotion between people, largely through its political surveillance and the tendency of the central government to break up local groups.

If the Soviet hierarchy sees fit to break up the most centripetal of all groups, it must be prepared for some of the consequences we observed in the kibbutzim. When the care of the child becomes the concern of the state, there develops a strong likelihood that this will start a chain reaction the limits of which cannot be foreseen. It is bound to affect the entire community.

These reflections on what is likely to happen in Russia are admittedly speculative and tentative. No analogy with what happens under one set of conditions is any basis for prediction of what will happen under another. Khrushchev says he expects 10 million youngsters under his control by 1970. This is indeed a great many, but it is not the entire child population of Russia. But if, as Strumilin states, all children are to be taken over by the state from infancy on, then we must expect drastic changes in the temperament of Russian youth. This new generation cannot have the warmth and richness of life that characterize it now. It must have less feeling, less empathy, less imagination.

If this turns out to be the case, how will the Russian state be able to carry out its corporate needs? This is one of the unmentioned but nevertheless great issues of our time. For if we now have trouble coming to terms with the Russian personality, we will have a lot more with the generation that follows. It will be not only a clash of personality type but also of the values that are functions and expressions of this personality. It is a certainty that the Russians to come will require not less but more pressure from the exoskeletal social structure, more and more coercion by the state. They will become less and less capable of inner direction. It is at this point that the most serious difference with the West will arise. The Russians will obliterate the concept of individuality, while in the West this concept has become emphasized to a degree that has become absurd. In the West this concept has become divorced from its orginal social function, to be the insignia of accomplishment. Now all the West has an individuality phobia. People want the name without the game, but in any case cheaply. In Russia this concept of individuality can be rendered meaningless, not by conditioning people out of it, but merely by making it socially irrelevant. Character becomes meaningless when it decides nothing in one's life.

We can only surmise that the Russian state wants the new regime because it believes, rightly or wrongly, that it can execute its corporate aims better with the kind of human unit it expects to get. Judging from the experience of the kibbutzim, we must agree that for short periods and for certain social emergencies, it is highly effective. But whether this effectiveness can be maintained over generations is another story. I am inclined to wager against it. Any society that sacrifices its youth to what looks momentarily like a desirable end must be prepared to pay a heavy price. The reason for my caution is that the plan goes counter to the trend of successful social evolution; it interferes with the very biological attributes of man. Those in Russia who maintain that indoctrination by a pedagogue from infancy on is superior to the best maternal care can have no knowledge of how the adaptive tools of man are created.

6

Salutary Effects of Maternal Separation

RICHARD H. SEIDEN

A fundamental argument against group care of children, accepted even by such proponents as Trotzkey (Chap. 2), is the inevitable separation from the mother. Yet even this seemingly universal constraint is not always applicable or justified. Clearly the orphaned or abandoned child has already been separated, and the constraints on separation do not apply to him, but in a far greater number of cases subtle judgments about the nurturing qualities of the maternal relationship must be made. Seiden argues that such a review may, and in some instances should, lead to the conclusion that separation would be beneficial, and perhaps not only to the child but also to the mother.

In the normal course of events no one would deliberately advocate the separation of a mother from her child. Yet there are some occasions when such action is necessary and, indeed, legally demanded—e.g., when a child cannot properly be cared for because of his mother's presumed emotional or physical disability. Social agencies approach the prospect of separation with great reluctance because they view it as psychologically harmful. Clinical observation tells us that this is not always the case, that for some children and parents separation may have benign, even therapeutic, effects. Such paradoxical effects either have been ignored or faintly praised in the literature on this subject. It is the purpose of this paper to determine what sup-

This investigation was supported by a traineeship from the National Institute of Mental Health, U.S. Public Health Service. Richard H. Seiden. "Salutary Effects of Maternal Separation." *Social Work* 10 (4): 25–29. Reprinted with permission of the National Association of Social Workers.

port can be marshaled for the position that separation of mother and child may yield salutary results and to question the prevailing notion that striving to keep mother and child together is necessarily indicated.

Interest in the consequences of mother–child separation is of recent historical origin. It appears coincident with the movement toward industrialization and urbanization. As industrialization has spread and more women have entered the labor force, concern has increased. Augmented by severe disruptions of family life during the two world wars, the problem was considered important enough to impel the Social Commission of the United Nations, in March 1948, to initiate a study of the needs of homeless children (UNESCO 1948). As part of this study, the World Health Organization made an investigation of the mental health aspects of the problem. One direct result of this investigation was publication of Bowlby's *Maternal Care and Mental Health* (1950, 1952 ed.), which reviews and analyzes the literature on separation of parents and children. Unfortunately Bowlby's findings that separation is psychologically harmful often have been accepted uncritically. This has led to the notion that any separation of a young child from his mother leads to serious emotional deprivation. The fallacy implicit in this argument is the equation of maternal separation with maternal deprivation. Bowlby (1958) replied to this criticism by acknowledging a valid distinction between separation and deprivation. He maintained, however, that both were adverse factors and that separation so affects the mother-child emotional attachments that a child should be separated from his mother only in exceptional circumstances. Even though the differences between separation and deprivation have been recognized, the consequence of this has been to minimize the damaging effects of separation without fully considering its possible positive effects.

Pertinent Studies

There have been few studies designed to illustrate the salutary effects of maternal separation and the evidence is often sketchy and incomplete. Nevertheless, the following material does seem pertinent.

BENIGN INSTITUTIONALIZATION

The work of Kanner (1943) indicates that home and mother may not always be the most favorable environment for a child. His studies of autistic children disclose numerous instances of cold, detached mothers who are unable, because of their own conflicts, to provide their children with the emotional warmth needed for adequate development. In such cases where the parent–child relationships are distorted and disturbed, removal from the home is necessary before any improvement can be expected. Along similar lines, it has been found that IQ gains made by mentally retarded patients during their institutionalization are frequently more substantial when the patients come from exceptionally adverse homes (Clarke and Clarke 1954). These observations suggest that home relationships prior to separation can be so poor that life in an institution may represent a real improvement. As Maenchen (1953) observed, "The child may never have been separated from its mother and yet have been deprived much more than if it had been placed in an institution with small groups under good nurses [p. 263]." Accordingly, Prugh and Harlow (1962), in their study of masked deprivation, state that "institutional placement may be the disposition of choice [p. 25]."

PEER GROUP INFLUENCE

Harlow's animal experiments appear to both challenge and support the position of salutary effects. A recent study reports that Bowlby's separation syndrome is found among monkeys as a basic instinctual response to maternal separation (Leay, Hansen, and Harlow 1962). The experiment, however, dealt with partial, contact separation (visual and auditory contact was maintained) and, more important, the mother–child relationship before separation presumably was normal. In contrast, studies of monkeys raised by "motherless mothers" (i.e., monkey mothers who had themselves been raised by wire or cloth surrogates) did not reveal close mother–child ties. Indeed, it was only through peer group experiences that the emotional development of these young monkeys was facilitated (Harlow and Harlow 1962). This finding is reminiscent of the work of Anna Freud and her associates (1942, 1951) with wartime groups of children separated from their mothers. These studies disclosed that there was a wealth of feeling and spontaneity and an absence of jealousy and rivalry unheard of in ordinary relations between young contemporaries. Of particular interest is the observation that attachments to a sole mother figure disturbed these positive peer relations. One is reminded of Margaret Mead's (1954) comment that "the assumed need for a single mother figure is not a universal belief and that adjustment is most facilitated if the child is cared for by many warm, friendly people [p. 477]. Certainly the *kibbutzim* of Israel that have a combination of nuclear and extended family practices are a direct application of this point of view.

RESIDENTIAL TREATMENT

A dramatic and vital illustration of the salutary effects of separation may be found in the work of the Children's Asthma Research Institute and Hospital, Denver, Colorado—a residential treatment center for intractably asthmatic children, who comprise about 10 percent of the childhood asthmatic population. During their two-year stay, their health improves so rapidly and significantly that hospitalization is often considered a lifesaving experience.

Finding the reasons for this therapeutic change can be a perplexing task. Can the change be owing to improved medical care? It does not seem likely since these children have received the best medical care available in their home communities. Can it be a result of tender loving care? Despite the usual psychiatric opinion concerning the families of asthmatic children, the parents are, in truth, no better or worse than parents in general and parents of seriously ill children in particular. Rather than villains, these parents are more often victims enmeshed with the child in a vicious cycle of emotional and physiological stress. Ruling out improvements in specific medical or psychological care, workers in this field have concluded that separation itself is the key factor in improvement. Peshkin (1930), the founder of the hospital and its medical consultant, considered it so vitally important that he termed this deliberate separation "parentectomy." When apprised of these particulars regarding beneficial separation, Bowlby then raised the critical question of duration of improvement. He wrote, "I do not doubt that separation is a wonderful therapy in the short run, I wonder how it works out in the long term?" (letter from J. Bowlby to author, July 16, 1963). There is no definitive answer to this question. Follow-up studies do show stabilized improvement after three years; however, the variable of increased biological maturity makes before-and-after comparisons misleading (Peshkin 1959). The consensus, however, is that the separation period allows for a "breathing spell" for both family and child during which time the cycle of attacks and emotional reaction may be broken.

"Smother-love"

What is the possible danger to the emotional maturity of a child when he cannot effect a separation from his mother? One of the major developmental tasks in our culture is the emancipation of a child from his family as a step toward his eventual independence. An overly strong maternal relationship with close, dependent bonds may impede this achievement. Clinical histories are replete with that type of smothering relationship described by Levy (1943) in which overprotective mothers have stifled their children's attempts at independence and maturity. This concern with "smother-love" is not unique to ourselves, as the cross-cultural study of Whiting, Kluckhohn, and Anthony (1958) indicates. They believe that a society with early childhood training practices that foster a close dependency between a mother and her young son must provide some drastic measures to break this bond and force the child to assume the male role. Although our society does not have the advantage of formalized puberty rites, less drastic measures such as boarding schools (particularly military schools), summer camps, and scouting serve a similar purpose. In a sense, the acceptance of these procedures admits that separation can be beneficial.

Working Mothers

Perhaps the most frequent conflict over separation occurs around the question of working mothers. Although employment of mothers outside the home is widely assumed to have harmful effects on children, Stolz (1960) discovered that almost anything can be said of employed mothers and the statement supported by some findings. There is no definite evidence that children are less happy, healthy, or adjusted merely because their mothers work. Though what, one wonders, is the effect of working on the mother's adjustment? Too often the focus is entirely on the child's status and overlooks the fact that separation has individual meaning for each participant in a relationship. Friedan (1963) elucidates this point when she discusses the deleterious effects of enforced motherhood on career-minded women who seemingly bury their own needs for personal recognition only to express them in a twisted, neurotic manner by vicariously living through their children. It may seem a difficult fact to accept, but many women do not view motherhood with unrivaled pleasure. Many women do not want to stay home with their children and resent being forced to. Mother–child interaction will not improve this situation. Are we to expect the relationship to improve magically simply by perpetuating the mother–child interaction? Rather, it would seem plausible that the effect of a mother's sacrifice would be far more devastating to her child's mental health than employment and self-satisfaction. It is possible that the hallowed view of mother–child togetherness is merely one instance of male propaganda in the continual war between the sexes—"a subtle form of antifeminism in which men, under the guise of exalting the importance of maternity, are tying women more tightly to their children [Mead 1954, p. 477]."

Social Ramifications

The value judgment that a child belongs with his mother is mirrored in many of our society's institutions. Examples are afforded by the law, social welfare policy, and child care programs.

LAW

The mother's right to her child in custody contests has become a doctrinaire, legal fiction by which custody is awarded routinely to the mother. This is done even when the father wants the child and is more capable of caring for him than is the mother. The trend is changing among more progressive jurists, but generally it is assumed that there is a biological mystique that endows all women with the ability to be good mothers.

WELFARE

Welfare policies regarding dependent children—the Aid to Families with Dependent Children program—are designed to keep mother and child together. Presumably this policy reflects the Depression-inspired concern that no child should be deprived of his home and mother for economic reasons alone. Despite its validity in the years of economic depression, such programs in present times often perpetuate instead of rehabilitate welfare recipient families. A logical alternative would be to promote incentives rewarding outside employment. At present, the closest incentive is to supplement individual earnings to match, not exceed, money the mother would receive had she stayed home and never sought or gained employment. In view of the political and religious concern with supplying birth control information to low-income families, the drop in fecundity of women in the childbearing years that could be anticipated by increasing their participation in the labor force offers an attractive alternate method of birth control.

CHILD CARE

Finally, the area of care for children of working mothers provides a more subtle example of the sacrosanct status of the mother–child relationship. Society provides meager resources for the mother who prefers to work outside the home in contrast, for example, to those societies that have factory crêches. Some low-cost facilities are provided, but they are limited to low-income mothers for whom working is a vital necessity. For the middle-class mother, work is often economically unfeasible because of the high cost of private nursery schools. Thus, employment has become a luxury for this group. These obstacles are further compounded by the lack of part-time jobs so that skilled, frequently college-educated, women are left to the dubious stimulation of suburban existence.

Conclusion

Quite clearly maternal separation should not be regarded as a singular concept to be studied and understood from a purely structural approach. Instead, investigation must concentrate on the dynamic qualities present in the interaction of mother and child. It becomes meaningless to ask whether separation is good or bad. What must be explored are the relevant intermediate variables. As a minimal requirement, the following areas call for careful examination in future research: (1) quality of previous maternal care, (2) the chronological, emotional, and physical maturity of the child, (3) emotional maturity of the mother, (4) nature of the mother–child relationship, (5) quality of substitute care to be provided, (6) length of separation, and (7) choice of child regarding separation.

While the nature of this paper has been to illustrate the possible salutary effects of separation, it should not be considered an apology for separation but rather a request for a more careful definition and exploration of the separation experience. Only with a more thorough awareness of the total situation, including relevant intermediate variables, can social workers be expected to temper social policy toward welfare planning, child custody, child care centers, and working mothers. Only with a thorough knowledge of these pertinent influences will social workers be able to realize their ultimate goal of predicting the harmful, neutral, or salutary effects of separation.

7

Group Care of Children:
The Problem of Legitimacy

MARTIN WOLINS

It is no simple matter to move away from tradition—more certainly so when the tradition is seen as psychodynamically and economicially functional. No childrearing arrangement has ever proven to be so massive, effective, and inexpensive as that comprised of a loving mother, providing father, and healthy child. To argue, as have founders of the kibbutz, that caring for a single child is prohibitively expensive or precludes the emancipation of women may be enough to carry the day but hardly settles the issue. To advance the "educators know best" position of Strumilin and other Soviet proponents of group care is also not enough. Nagging questions remain: What are the consequences for the child, the continued role of the family, and the relative positions of males and females in society?

In short, as Kardiner says issues related to the mere existence of group care as a normal phenomenon raise questions fundamental to the structure and functioning of a society. We should not be surprised, therefore, that group care is castigated yet accepted, or strongly opposed, or introduced blatantly as a new and better (revolutionary) approach to childrearing, or, barring all the above, disguised. By denigrating group care (it is for the sick, the helpless, the failures), or by accepting its utility for special groups (it is for the elite), the familial primacy is left secure. If the family is to be attacked (e.g., early postrevolutionary U.S.S.R. or early kibbutzim), group care can be legitimized by a frontal attack on familial capability. If neither

An earlier and somewhat different version of this paper appeared in Helen Fradkin, ed., *Organization of Services That Will Best Meet Needs of Children*, Arden House Conference, October 31–November 5, 1965, Harriman, New York. (New York: Columbia University School of Social Work, 1965). Reprinted by permission.

of these routes is suitable, then group care may be marketed as a familial derivative, even partaking of its terminology. Legitimizing group care is no simple matter, particularly in a society with strong familistic foundations.

Introduction

Any attempt to formulate child welfare policy must ultimately include the possibility and terms of substitution for the natural family. No matter how committed a society is to leaving a child with the natural parents, conditions beyond anyone's control may exclude this alternative in some cases. Hence substitutes for parental care are found in all modern societies, but their forms and preferences differ. The Western world, strongly influenced by laissez-faire philosophy and Freudian psychological thought, has in the past half-century leaned toward individual care in foster homes. Socialist kibbutzim (collective settlements) in Israel, predominantly Catholic countries of Europe and Latin America, and the Communist societies of Eastern Europe have preferred group care, because care in children's societies of the abandoned, neglected, and occasionally, orphaned fits their ideological stances as well as their economic conditions and manpower needs. Such symbiotic affinity between group care and other societal structures would seem to bode well for this form of childrearing; it should make it highly acceptable, lauded, and supported. In some measure this appears to be so, but insecurity, tension, and defensiveness also are found.

The problem of group care and its attempt to establish a place of acceptance and respect is best viewed in societies that are predisposed toward such care. When operating in an atmosphere of relatively friendly acceptance, group care proponents should be free of day-to-day rearguard action and may devote some of their energies to a consideration of basic programmatic issues. Such conditions are found relative to the youth group in the Israeli kibbutz, the Soviet *shkola-internat,* the Polish children's home, and the Austrian SOS *Kinderdorf* (Children's Village). Major differences of national milieu and internal organization characterize these four child-care settings; yet their modes of obtaining and maintaining acceptance—that is, legitimizing their status—are markedly similar.[1]

The Problem of Legitimacy

Considerable variability marks the settings described. The SOS *Kinderdorf* is familistic and Catholic and imbedded in a capitalist society. The programs in Communist Russia and Poland are communal. Israeli kibbutzim offer communal child care, but in a partly capitalist society ruled by a labor government and a welfare-state philosophy. All of the child-care programs described appear to have the respect and, in some instances, even the admiration of their publics. They give the impression of ideological clarity, economic stability and security, and approved purposefulness; yet underlying this assurance there seems to be an element of doubt and defensiveness. These settings, despite their apparent position of respect and even privilege, seem to feel threatened—appear to have some qualms about their legitimacy.

The problem of legitimizing a substitute is not new. At one point in their development schools had to be legitimized because they replaced education at the mother's knee; social security had to be legitimized because it replaced relative responsibility; adoption had to be legitimized because it replaced natural procreation in some families. However, the problem of legitimizing foster care, and in particular group care, is far more complicated. In the other programs the argument that a family is being supplemented may sound plausible, but foster care replaces the family or comes very close to it, and group care of children threatens the very assumption of universality that the family system lays claim to and is accorded (Murdock 1949).[2]

Against this most universal, most natural, most satisfying setting for childrearing, then, little argument is possible even when ideological conditions are conducive to it. That some families fail, of course, is not and cannot be stretched into an indictment of the family as a social structure, and yet when it does fail, children it cannot rear must be cared for in different settings, often outside the familial environment. Because the family is seen and acknowledged as *the* natural, as *the* proper locus for the socializing of children, others are obviously unnatural, improper, at best inadequate, and possibly unacceptable. Thus the extrafamilial structures for childrearing—the institutions, youth groups in kibbutzim, children's villages—find themselves in a most interesting, paradoxical situation: they are both essential and suspect. Need for them leads to their establishment; continual suspicion undermines their security by subjecting to question their very legitimacy.[3]

In order to function, the children's institution must establish its right as a social structure, which it may do by claiming exemption from many social requirements because of its deviancy or by asserting its superior utility and demonstrating it. American institutions usually have done the first, and the Russian, Polish, and Israeli group care settings have followed the second. A third and rather interesting approach has been that of the Austrian SOS *Kinderdörfer*. On the assumption that American children's institutions and their defense mechanisms are well known to U.S. readers, little space will be given them. The "we are superior places" approach found in Russia, Poland, and Israel and the special case of the *Kinderdörfer* will be discussed in some detail.

A simple way to deal with the legitimacy problem is refusal to claim it. American institutions perceive themselves and are in turn perceived by the society as deviant settings for childrearing. Like other settings of deviancy they are defined by the nature of their clientele (as dealing with custom, illness, or crime). As receptacles of problem children who result from custom they elicit a tolerant response. Note, for example, the good acceptance of southern institutions for dependent and neglected children (Maas and Engler 1959). When the institution receives mentally or emotionally disturbed children and defines them as such, it is perceived as a hospital that treats the ill; when it serves the delinquent it is a reform school or, more euphemistically, a training school. None of these settings claims acceptance by virtue of its superiority to certain natural families. They are seen and ask to be thought of as settings unfortunately needed for dealing with the problems of family and child breakdown, and their measures of achievement relate primarily to the successful return of the child to his familial environment. Not so for the specific childrearing institutions in the several earlier-named countries. They endeavor to acquire legitimacy as family substitutes, which in turn gives them a very special flavor. Legitimacy may be acquired in one or more of four ways: *"(a)* by tradition—a belief in the ligitimacy of what has always existed; *(b)* by virtue of affectual attitudes, especially emotional, legitimizing the validity of what is newly revealed or a model to imitate; *(c)* by virtue of a rational belief in its [the structure's or the rules's] absolute value *(Wertrational)* . . . ; *(d)* because it has been established in a manner recognized to be *legal* [Weber 1947, p. 130, italics in original]."

The child-care structures analyzed here seek legitimacy primarily by virtue of rational belief in their absolute value. On occasion—mostly in the SOS *Kinderdorf*—they resort to affectual and emotional attitudes and even to tradition, but usually they try to prove their worth or superiority through other alternatives. *The road to legitimacy appears to lead through differentiation. Its price seems to be the development of maturity, and its mark is demonstrated accomplishment.* Let us review these now in some detail.

Institution and Family Differentiation

In order to demonstrate its value a group care facility must have clear boundaries. The "we" in such a structure should be distinguished positively from the "they," who in most instances are the parents but at times also other adults in the outside world. The following states the requirement in Soviet Communist terminology and holds implications for other points to be noted subsequently.

> Pupils must have their own community and serve as the primary decisionmakers in it. "By acting as their own authorities, pupils will gain a profound understanding of the importance of their work, will be the organizers of their collective . . ." [Shirvindt et al. 1961, p. 85].

Such a pupil community, distinct and separable and with clear limits, will be enhanced and its boundaries strengthened by entry and exit rites. Certainly not everyone should be able to enter and leave as he chooses, or the system would be disrupted. Children, then, are permitted to visit parents at specified times only and to take short trips home during school vacation or at the end of the school year. And not everyone can get in. The program is good, and the demand for it is great; therefore, *"obviously, not everyone can be satisfied. Many must wait* until next year, when the number of shko-ly-internaty will have increased significantly [*Trud* 1956, p. 1; italics added]."

To delineate the structure more clearly and stress its desirability, entry and exit should have the character of a celebration, an achievement. Youth groups entering Israeli kibbutzim from the city are made to understand their accomplishment, and on exit the wholeness and separateness of the youth community is emphasized again. One of Poland's major writers in child care also underscores this point. Introduction to and separation from the system is an important matter that should receive careful attention from staff. "The completion of stay in an internat may take the character of a celebration, a summing up of the results of the graduates' work . . . [A. Lewin 1960, p. 19]."

It is generally recognized in these settings that evolution of a differentiated and substantially self-governing children's community has its special problems. One of these arises because parental authority is replaced by that of the leader and the group, and of parental discipline by group approval or disapproval. Another problem is that the children do not so easily take on responsibility for their own physical welfare and personal behavior. But these problems are claimed to be overcome by confidence in the leaders and acceptance of democratic self-rule (Tamari, 1960).

Clarity of "we" is accompanied by a definition of "they." "They" appear to be primarily the natural parents. In a kibbutz youth group whose parents are in or out of the kibbutz, in a Soviet boarding school *kolektiv,* or in a group of children who make up a *Kinderdorf* household, it is intended and considered desirable to differentiate the parents for various reasons. These include parental selfishness, intergenerational conflict, cultural backwardness or incapability, and a general category probably best labeled "the good of the child and/or the parents."

A conference on education for values in the kibbutz provides the general motif.

We do not wish [it is pointed out] to minimize the power of attraction of "home" and the parents. We are happy that our children are rooted in this home, this scenery, this way of life. *But we must not ignore the fact that no youth has ever determined his future mainly because of his ties with "home," scenery, and parents* [Alon 1961, p. 16; italics added]."

So no really serious effect results from loosening these ties somewhat; it may even be beneficial. In any event, more contact between parent and child may not be intended for the welfare of the child but may be a reflection of parental selfishness or an insistent overlooking of intergenerational conflict and the possible cultural incapability or backwardness of parents (Levin 1960).[4] Madrichim (group leaders) in the religious kibbutz point out that in their setting where "Honor thy father and thy mother" is an important value, young people feel handicapped in activating their measure of initiative unless they are separated, at least slightly, from their parents (Collective Authorship 1959). The atheists of the socialist kibbutz movement say amen to this statement but phrase it more floridly. "The integration of the second-generation kibbutz . . . ," they say, "will not be inherited from generation to generation." Ideological collectivism, a common vision, may soften the tension between the two generations, but the young must master their world by themselves (Bloch 1955).

Not only do the generations differ but also the parents are seen as lacking some vital qualities, skills, or desires. The children who come into care in the *Kinderdorf* are spoken of as *socialwaisen* (social orphans) (Gmeiner 1960b, p. 50) or even as *verwaiste kinder* (orphaned children) (p. 32), although most of the children do have parents living. A Soviet educator, the director of a boarding school in Kishinev, Moldavia, uses almost the same terminology when he describes his population as orphans and children of single mothers, of war invalids, of victims of industrial accidents, or from large families and not receiving proper care (Sulla 1957). Other backgrounds also present vexing problems. Some children who enter the Soviet boarding school come from undesirable religious families.

Anya K. [for example], was sent to fifth grade [Shkola-Internat No. 1 in Kaliningrad] from a family of fanatic sectarians. From early years her mother and father had hammered religious beliefs into her head and taken her to church services [Maksimova, 1961, p. 120].

Considerable similarity of these arguments exists, in and out of the Israeli kibbutz.

In many things I don't agree with my parents [writes a young man in a kibbutz]; therefore, I hardly ever consider their opinions. . . . In my opinion they do not fulfill the duty of a kibbutz member properly [from a questionnaire administered to youth, in Gerson 1957, p. 173].

Relative to an immigrant population, the argument sounds somewhat different.

The social structure imposes upon the family [of immigrants] during the period of their children's adolescence, important educational tasks which it is not capable of carrying out. Therefore, there is a great need to . . . take over these tasks from the family [Parnass-Honig 1958, pp. 127–128].

All of the arguments for separating children and parents are made in the negative manner described above, but separation is also seen as an outright value to the parents in freeing them for their adult activities while at the same time surrounding the child with a constructive developmental milieu (Gerson 1957; Collective, 1948; Mirkhaidarova 1963). However all of the arguments may prove unconvincing to the parents or to the social system within which the children's institution (of whatever kind) attempts to be recognized and accepted. The most telling evidence on this point appears in attempts to coopt the family model or the families themselves, a matter often discussed in kibbutz meetings and reflected in the literature of the kibbutz and of the Soviet boarding school. With all the defects in childrearing capability that the family seems to represent, it is nonetheless sought as an ally. If it accepts the primacy of the childrearing collective structure it can be an extremely useful partner; otherwise it is a potential source of competition for the child's allegiance (Talmon-Garber 1962). To gain strength from the family while at the same time substituting for it, the *Kinderdorf* coopts its model, the other settings solicit its support by claiming partnership.

Kinderdorf staff point out with considerable pride the independent households within the village, each with its own mother, its own budget, and to an extent its own family life. "There are only minor differences between the life of the *Kinderdorf* family and that of every other good, large family in the city or countryside," claims their founder (Gmeiner 1960*b*, p. 42). And while the *Kinderdorf* with 10, 20, or 30 such families in one location clearly has some features of an institution, it tries to disassociate itself from them by announcing that institutions are bad (Gmeiner 1960*b*, p. 55).

When the parents are effectively out of the picture (the *Kinderdorf* sees its children as *verwaiste* [orphaned]) it is safe to adopt the family model. But what if some families may be around the corner or in the next town and have strong legal and emotional holds on their children? Then the approach used in securing their cooperation is the one-sided partnership. While this approach is amply illustrated in the Israeli kibbutz, particularly with regard to families of outside youth, the Soviet literature provides the most quotable evidence. Two highly placed authorities in Soviet education write:

> Shkoly-internaty are not closed educational institutions which isolate children from the family. Children are placed there only at the wish of parents, they regularly rejoin their parents on days off, holidays, and during winter, spring, and summer vacations. The family's upbringing influence is thus not curtailed; but merely assumes different forms [Afanasenko and Kairov 1961, p. 34].

Or, expressed more simply, the pupil's character is claimed to be molded in the boarding school under the dual influence of the teachers and of the family (Manvelian 1961). Joint effort of this kind with apparently equal influence is, however, largely a lovely but unrealized dream that in fact may not even be desired. Some parents live far away; some children have no parents or, what is more problematic, have parents "who do not influence their children favorably [Mirkhaidarova 1963, p. 32]."

Maturity

Whatever their ties with the program, strong or flimsy, whether they represent models or scrutinizing society, the families of the children under care are on the outside. The boundary around the child-care system is reasonably closed. The "we" and "they" are fairly well identifiable, and the child-care system standing by itself must be legitimized. As mentioned earlier, the price of legitimacy appears to be a show of maturity. Evidence of maturity must be produced in order to enhance self-esteem and gain the approval of a not necessarily sympathetic outside world. The path to be traveled runs from *consumption to productivity, from dependence to independence and assistance to others, from selfishness to sacrifice, and from egocentrism to affiliation.*

With such expectations the children's society surely becomes, in the words of a kibbutz ideological statement, "an organic-education society," a frame of living and of educating—a means and an end in one. It involves a perpetual and uninterrupted creation in all fields—economic, social, educational, and the Movement (Collective 1948, p. 66). It is an interesting but by now not surprising coincidence that a very similar statement should be made by a Soviet chocolate factory worker writing to a teachers' newspaper.

> Our requirements of shkola-internat are not great. We desire only that children be occupied with socially useful creative work. . . . Every minute should be filled with obligation, intense striving, and small but noticeable collective achievements, so that the children live with expectation for tomorrow—a tomorrow of their own, made by their own hands, and not brought to them by good uncles in cellophane packages [Kakoi Dolzhna Byt 1965, p. 3. Note the occupational phraseology].

CONSUMPTION TO PRODUCTIVITY

Specifically, the emphasis seems to be first and foremost on work and particularly on what the Russians call socially useful work *(obshchestvenno poleznyi trud)*.[5] Work serves many purposes: it maintains the system; helps develop an appreciation for the toil of others; serves as a means to learning an occupation; and, along with all of these, legitimizes the system. In one Soviet boarding school children from the sixth through the ninth grades worked a certain number of hours each week in the sewing room, the dining room, the shoe shop, and the carpentry shop, and a record of their productivity was kept (Bel'gus 1959, pp. 165–68). In others they may undertake similar housekeeping tasks and even subcontract work from a nearby factory. The object is to prepare the young generation for work so that "for every young man and girl of the shkola-internat it becomes an organic need [Afanasenko and Kairov 1961, p. 17]."

In the kibbutzim, too, it is expected that every child from preadolescence, and even younger, at times will assume productive tasks. More than that, his successful internalization of work needs are judged to be a significant mark of the setting's achievement. A child prepares for adult life by learning to think of himself as a part of the "people of labor" and striving to "raise the standards of his work [S. Yitshaki 1956, pp. 381–82]."[6]

While acquiring a need to work one may, of course, learn an occupation, but, more important, one should learn to esteem one's own work *and* that of others. For this reason children in the Soviet boarding school often are involved in talks, discussions, and interviews about labor in general. They are encouraged to gain understanding and inspiration from talks with ". . . well-known potato farmers, with famous combine operators, with Heroes of Socialist Labor, and with decorated laborers, all of whom love to talk about their own work [Bel'gus 1959, p. 165]."

MUTUAL AID AND SACRIFICE

No matter how productive it is, work does not in itself constitute a sufficient mark of an acceptable social unit. It should be accompanied by evidence of mutual help and sacrifice. In the SOS *Kinderdorf* "the child learns to be responsible for his 'siblings,' particularly the younger ones [Gmeiner 1960b, p. 59]." A Soviet boarding school may let the younger children select upperclass patrons (shefy) who help them in studies, read to them, and encourage their good behavior and ". . . defend them from anyone who wants to hurt them. . . . [Yabolokov and Kustkov 1959, p. 94]." A description of group care in Israel rings a nearly identical note. One group, " . . . after a discussion of their studies . . . decided to help their more backward comrades. A number of children volunteered for the task. . . . The feeling of satisfaction engendered was common both to those extending and to those benefiting from it [Ettinger 1958, p. 20]."

AFFILIATION

Development of a strong internal structure underpinned with labor, mutual assistance, and sacrifice and marked by solidarity poses the danger of isolation, a circumstance that cannot be and is not allowed to happen. While the group care structure claims to be a community in its own right, it must feed directly into a societal mainline in order to avoid being perceived as deviant. Many educators stress the importance of the institution's participation in the community and of society's involvement in the institution. Contact with these settings and review of the literature by and about them provide ample evidence that linkage is taken seriously. One commonly and frequently hears that "the shkola-internat is not a closed institution of education and upbringing. It must put itself in the very thick of life. Its pupils must be active participants in our great task of construction . . . [Afanasenko and Kairov 1961, p. 18]."

Perhaps the most telling way of affiliating with the broader social system is in joining its code of values, learning how to be self-critical in relation to them, showing loyalty and leadership for them. The kibbutz claims to teach the child that the general interest comes first, that individual opinion must make place for public opinion, that "carrying out one's duty in service to society is what makes the person [R. Cohen 1958, p. 444]." Such a weaning away from egocentric qualities takes on for most children in institutions the character of culture change. The process and its difficulties are easily noted in youth groups formed to help in the acculturation of Israeli immigrants.

Of course, the values considered desirable, those of the broader society, differ substantially from Israel to Austria to the Communist countries of Eastern Europe. Kibbutz rearing attempts to produce a person " . . . with a scientific view on life, loyal to his country, identifying with the ideas of the workers' movement in the country and in the world, and looking upon the kibbutz group as the most natural and best setting in which to live [Darin-Drabkin 1961, p. 189]." Ideally, such a person would not only accept the values of the wider society but would also join a major political-social movement through which his value orientation would express itself. Thus, youth reared in the Kibbutz-Artzi (the most Marxist of the kibbutzim) will strive for admission into its movement. Children and adolescents in the religious kibbutzim will hope to join their youth organization and through it tie in with the kibbutz membership as a whole. Phrased very simply by one group leader of a religious kibbutz, "The aim of a youth group living in a collective settlement is the education of its members toward the social, religious, and ethical values of the settlement [Tamari 1960, p. 41]."

SOS *Kinderdörfer* similarly obligate themselves to the major values of *their* society and express it through *their* most appropriate movement—the Catholic Church. Children in the *Kinderdörfer* are, of course, taught ethical behavior and responsibility along with cultural values in the framework of Christian traditions, and in order to shield children from conflicts of creed *(Konfesionsproblematik)*, villages are planned to be exclusively Catholic or Protestant (Gmeiner 1960*b*, p. 26).

Statements from Soviet institutions, while stressing different values and another movement, have nonetheless a similar ring. "Upbringing and instruction in shkoly-internaty, the Draft Program of the Twenty-Second Party Congress points out, must form roundly developed members of communist society . . . [Kol'makova 1961, p. 12]." The boarding school is, ". . . in the full sense of the word a school of organized, Communist life [Knizheva 1960, p. 62]." Values emphasized are: collectivism; mutual assistance (one for all, and all for one); respect between individuals (man to man, a friend, a comrade, and a brother); honesty, simplicity, and modesty in social and private life (Manvelian 1961). In this context, too, and in contrast with the *Kinderdorf,* one negative value—scientific-atheistic work with both pupils and parents so that they may "understand once and for all the harm which religion causes people [Maksimova, 1961, p. 121]."

Continuous review of the extent to which the values are held and made operative is maintained in all these settings. Self-criticism, demonstrations of loyalty, and the assumption of leadership in promulgating such values are the major tests. Self-criticism is best illustrated in several examples of the children's writings. A young girl in a kibbutz youth group: "I must understand that there is no individual who is not dependent upon the whole. . . . I must understand the harmony between the individual and the group, in order to find my place in the group [Tamar 1958, p. 360]." It is a mark of the honesty of such self-criticism that it reveals not only the ascendancy of group norms and values of the larger society and the movement but also the conflict between them and personal strivings. Tamar writes: "I have always nursed this individualistic dream of a corner of my own . . . where I could be alone with myself to my heart's content. This is something of a reaction to the sometimes exaggerated social education in the institution." She then adds charmingly and most appropriately for a romantic, adolescent girl, "and now this 'I' has been expanded to engulf another beloved person [p. 401]."

Polish and Soviet group care structures also rely heavily on the self-criticism principle to keep the system attuned to the outside values. That writings reveal not only positive but also negative content attests to the reality of this effort. A staff member of a Soviet boarding school describes the diary of an older pupil who complains about the boredom, lack of privacy, and "grandmother's" work, such as cleaning and bedmaking, in the internat. Such a pupil, we are told, must be led to better understand the values. He must understand that life is good and interesting when it is sensible, when grand prospects for contributing to the society are ahead (Rat'kova 1961, pp. 180–81).

Loyalty to the movement, to the party, to the church—to a system of values dominant or central in the interests of the legitimizing structure—is stressed in the program, and attempts are made to demonstrate it. For the kibbutz youth group, proof lies in the loyalty to the "movement and the home kibbutz," readiness for a "life of labor," for "fighting and building the kibbutz collective [S. Yitshaki (1956), pp. 381–82]." Elsewhere the objects of demonstration are different, but it is required no less.

Beyond the loyalty is the possibility of leadership. The Israeli kibbutz child is trained to lead in kibbutz life or to help form new kibbutzim. He is intended as a model in his movement. He will see the young adults, only a few years his seniors, going off on important political, organizational, and military missions, and he will dream of being like them; the kibbutz teaches him to be like them. In training the children of new immigrants in the kibbutz or institution, one of the goals may well be to help them to leadership positions that supersede those of their elders (Parnass-Honig 1959).

Some Soviet boarding schools also conduct classes to prepare leaders. One school in Moscow reports that after a few years of such training it is possible to speak with optimism about the success of its experimental leadership classes. They anticipate that this program will yield not only leaders but also future boarding school staff (Shirvindt et al. 1961).

PROVING ACCOMPLISHMENT

So much for the price of legitimacy. Work, mutual help, sacrifice, and affiliation are the attributes that appear to be needed ingredients in a "respectable" group care setting that accepts reasonably normal children and wants to claim for itself the right to rear them away from their parents. But paying the price is not necessarily followed by getting the product. Hence if a system chooses to seek legitimacy on the grounds that it is successful, being acknowledged superior in operation is not enough; it must also show good results. The final mark of legitimacy is, then, not in the content of a program but in the achievements of the graduates and of the organization. A childcare unit that seeks legitimacy by virtue of its obvious superiority to mother's milk must prove itself. It will seek research evidence, testimonials, or whatever it can get to support its claims.

On the very lowest level of such assertions is the structure's utility as a parental substitute in the absence of other alternatives. Often invoked is a statement of the type "If it had not been for this setting I could never have made it."

> Some of our boys who have already finished military training and learned an occupation and who now stand with both feet firmly in [adult] life declare briefly and clearly that without the care of the SOS Kinderdorf during their crucial years, they probably would have quit [Gmeiner 1960b, p. 74].

Since the SOS *Kinderdorf* uses the traditional model of family as its source of legitimacy, it can allow itself to be satisfied with such a modest claim.

Next in order appears to be the assertion that the graduates have become very good citizens within the going society. "In 1960 thirty pupils completed the Sudzianski shkola-internat in Kursk province. Seventeen of them are studying at higher schools and technikums; eight left for the construction of a new mine . . . [Afanasenko and Kairov 1961, p. 24]." Or the kibbutz version: 30 percent of the present religious kibbutz membership came from the immigrant youth groups who came into "group foster care." In one religious kibbutz 90 percent of the members come from among these groups sent there for *hakhshara* (training) (Tamari 1960).

Higher in the order of claims appears to be acculturation—that is, instances in which the setting has served to adjust the child to new cultural demands. This, of course, is one of the major duties of all Israeli Youth Aliyah facilities as well as of the shkoly-internaty in the Soviet Union, but evidence of culture change is not readily available even though assumptions and assertions abound. One Soviet author, who announces by the title of his article that a good future lies ahead of the boarding school, claims that it is the answer to producing the "new man" of the Soviet Union. "Graduates" have a much better chance of fitting into the new society (Petrov 1961, p. 6).

Finally, claims of leadership are supported whenever possible by evidence. Kibbutz literature is apt to point to the high rate of kibbutz-reared youth in the officer class of the Israel Defense Forces. Educators and others cite with pride a well-known scientist's findings that the young adults reared in the kibbutz are sociable, have good personal relationships, are prepared to make sacrifices for the group, are steadfast in battle, and *lead men well* (Caplan 1954).

An internat expression on the subject of leadership may be individual or collective. A student nearly ready to graduate writes "The group in my shop . . . has been awarded the order of a Collective of Communist Labor . . . Every worker tries to overfulfill the norm. . . [Gorshkova 1961, p. 261]." Individual citations and recognition of all kinds are carefully noted and reported. The graduate who is an outstanding worker, or is socially active, or is chosen to lead a group is mentioned as an example of "the fame that is achieved" by children from the boarding school (Gorshkova 1961, p. 267).

Conclusion

As one observes the child-care programs described here and reads the literature about them, several points appear to require special attention.

First is the obvious defensiveness that permeates the pronouncements and gives them a polemic quality. While defensiveness should not be surprising, considering the need for legitimization that the youth groups, villages, and boarding schools continually face, it does nonetheless predispose everyone to discount assertions and claims of achievement. It is, however, questionable whether these organizations really need to be so defensive considering the level of acceptance they appear to have within their own countries and the rather good impression their programs make on reasonably dispassionate outside observers.

Second is the *déjà vu*-like feeling one experiences in reading some of this material. It is tempting to note the similarities in some of these descriptions and claims, and even in some of the programs with those we have tried to abolish in the United States over the past half-century. The junior republic, the orphanage, the small child-care group in a convent all come to mind, but these analogies are only superficially applicable. All of the structures described here work hard at, and succeed in, integrating their populations into the mainstream of their societies, and they are in most instances proud and centrally located systems. Certainly this could not have been said about many of the United States' 19th-century group care structures with which they may be compared.

Third, the shortage of objective data about the functioning and consequences of these schools, villages, youth groups, and "families" permits distortion in many directions. Obviously this state of affairs allows proponents to make exaggerated claims of success and opponents to overemphasize likely shortcomings. Probably neither should be taken at face value, for we know as yet little about outcome here: What happens to the children who remain for long periods of time or to the dropouts who leave or are expelled? Who are the successes and who are the failures? What are the consequences of different structures and varying intake policies and populations? What is the impact of various staffing patterns and personnel qualifications? None of these questions has as yet been adequately answered.

Despite the criticisms that some independent, but not necessarily objective, outside observers have leveled at these programs, and the defensiveness they show, these modes of childrearing away from the natural family are remarkably well accepted in their own countries. Obviously, in order to gain such approval they must have a high commitment to the society in which they operate and must make heavy demands of their inmates. Apparently the children live up to the maturity expected of them, and on leaving the program they also seem to meet the societal requirements for young adults.

Considering the almost universal condemnation of such programs in the United States—condemnation seemingly grounded in long years of unsatisfactory experiences with them—and their acceptance, implementation, expansion, and reasonably successful legitimization elsewhere, questions arise about this divergence of views. Of course, each culture demands personality types suited to its needs. Certainly, historical, philosophical, and economic predispositions vary, but is there not also a possibility that the self-fulfilling prophecy manifests itself here? In the absence of adequate data and the continuing presence of much sentiment and emotion on this subject, is it possible that causality is made to run from acceptance to quality to success, and that failure is a natural consequence and not merely an antecedent of disapproval?

NOTES

1. Brief descriptions of these programs are also found in Chap. 3.

2. Much recent evidence shows that even in societies that are or have been disposed to aggrandizing to other institutions what traditionally have been familial functions the family has retained a high degree of vitality. Attempts to abandon or markedly modify the family as a childrearing system in the kibbutz or in the Soviet Union have failed (Timasheff 1960, and Spiro 1960). A Soviet academician's (Strumilin 1960) recent proposal that the family childrearing functions be markedly limited in the future produced a flurry of correspondence and an apologetic retreat acknowl-

edged by another academician who wrote that: "If one takes into consideration a significant increase in freedom from productive and domestic work, one can see that the family will have more opportunity to bring up their children. . . . Parents in the future will joyfully give their attention to children and their development. . . . The pedagogical illiteracy of parents which S. G. Strumilin describes can also be eradicated. A body of knowledge on childrearing must be included in the general education of each citizen and family man [Kolbanovski 1961, p. 282]."

3. In this respect an extrafamilial child-care structure—say, an institution—is similar to the adult education programs so common in American cities. Some authors view the absence of legitimacy as a difficulty, others as a blessing. For a view of the first see D. H. Clark (1965). "Without a firmly legitimized status the adult schools have little control over the conditions of their existence [p. 332]." London, Wenkert, and Hagstrom (1963) hold the opposite position: "Indeed, its [the adult education program's] lack of tradition and lack of substantial support as a legitimatized social institution in society provides a stimulus for greater creativity to deal with diverse problems [p. 141]."

4. And if the family raises objections there is an answer for it. "The family will be built and will build the kibbutz if its essence is not a refuge from the kibbutz but an identification with it and its special social values [Levin 1960, p. 97]."

5. Incidentally, the socially useful work concept is applied not only to the production of goods but also to creative activity and services, which may include walking smaller children in the park, cleaning up the town square, teaching a group to play harmonicas, or growing vegetables for the communal kitchen.

6. In a more restrained but nonetheless quite emphatic manner, the *Kinderdorf* also underscores work. Although it is labeled *Arbeitstherapie* it appears to be more socially and economically than psychologically motivated. But in using the family model for legitimization, the *Kinderdorf* is careful to note that the work is household help and that children have ample time to play and engage in artistic creativity (Gmeiner 1960*b*, p. 64).

ADDITIONAL READING FOR PART II

Brace, Charles L. *The Dangerous Classes of New York and Twenty Years' Work Among Them.* New York: Wynkoop and Hallenbeck, 1972.

Bronfenbrenner, Urie. *Two Worlds of Childhood: U.S. and U.S.S.R.* New York: Russell Sage Foundation, 1970.

Chilman, Catherine S. *Growing Up Poor.* Washington, D.C.: U.S. Department of Health, Education and Welfare, May 1968.

Folks, Homer. *The Care of Destitute, Neglected and Delinquent Children.* New York: MacMillan Co., 1902.

Korczak, Janusz. *Selected Works of Janusz Korczak.* Warsaw: Scientific Publications Foreign Cooperation Center, 1967. Available through the U.S. Department of Commerce and in Depository Libraries.

Neil, A.S. *Summerhill: A Radical Approach to Child Rearing.* New York: Hart Publishing Co., 1960.

Pringle, M. L. Kellmer. *Deprivation and Education.* London: Longmans, 1965.

Spiro, Melford E. *Kibbutz: Venture in Utopia.* Cambridge, Mass.: Harvard University Press, 1956.

Weinberg, Ian. *The English Public Schools: The Sociology of Elite Education.* New York: Atherton Press, 1967.

Wilson, Monica. *Good Company: A Study of Nyakyusa Age-Villages.* Boston: Beacon Press, 1951.

Wolins, Martin, and Piliavin, Irving. *Institution or Foster Family: A Century of Debate*. New York: Child Welfare League of America, 1964.
Wootton, Barbara. "A Social Scientist's Approach to Maternal Deprivation," in *Deprivation of Maternal Care*. Geneva: World Health Organization, 1962.

III

Young Children in Group Care

8

Hospitalism

RENÉ A. SPITZ, M. D.

No statement on group care of children can be complete without reference to the catastrophic consequences some institutions have had for very young children. Early in the 20th century the professional and public consciences were stirred by some well-documented reports that foundling homes of that period commonly lost through death about three-quarters of their infants. That these revelations had and should have had enormous shock quality goes without saying, but not until the appearance of Spitz's work in the 1940s did the full effect register, for Spitz added to the evidence in two important ways. First, he showed that high mortality was not the only negative consequence of certain institutional programs: cognitive and psychosocial retardation, though not as final as death, was nevertheless a probable outcome to be reckoned with. Second, Spitz produced some visual evidence (films) that linked the institutional environment in his study to obvious deterioration.

It seems safe to say that Spitz's detailed evidence, followed a few years later by Bowlby's (1950) WHO monographs, became a major deterrent to group care in the Western world. So profound was the impression, so compatible with childrearing attitudes generally held, that his work has withstood a considerable amount of modifying evidence—namely, that group care need not be destructive to the infant and young child providing, of course, it meticulously avoids the debilitating conditions an institution may offer. Spitz's findings and their profound impact are thus an obstacle and a

René A. Spitz, M.D. "Hospitalism: An Inquiry into the Genesis of Psychiatric Conditions in Early Childhood." *Psychoanalytic Study of the Child.* Vol. I (1945) and II (1946). The preliminary report (1945) and the follow-up material (1946) are combined in the present article. Reprinted by permission.

warning. The obstacle proponents of group care must overcome by contrary evidence; the warning is of the profound impact poor group care has on the young child.

A careful, honest scientist, Spitz contributed to the subject of group care even more than he is usually credited. The major paper on hospitalism reproduced here also contains evidence to deny its inevitability in institutional settings. To be sure, Spitz showed that institutions for infants can be mercilessly destructive, but he also showed (Table 8.2) that they need not necessarily be so—a bit of evidence most of his readers found conveniently forgettable. Thus if Spitz is given the attention he deserves, he shows not only what negative effects institutional care can produce but also the essential differences between stultifying and growth-promoting group environments.

"En la Casa de Ninos Expositos el nino se va poniendo triste y muchos de ellos mueren de tristeza."

(1760, *from the diary of a Spanish bishop*)

The Problem

The term *hospitalism* designates a vitiated condition of the body due to long confinement in a hospital, or the morbid condition of the atmosphere of a hospital. The term has been increasingly preempted to specify the evil effect of institutional care on infants, placed in institutions from an early age, particularly from the psychiatric point of view.[1] This study is especially concerned with the effect of continuous institutional care of infants under one year of age, for reasons other than sickness. The model of such institutions is the foundling home.

Medical men and administrators have long been aware of the shortcomings of such charitable institutions. At the beginning of our century one of the great foundling homes in Germany had a mortality rate of 71.5 percent in infants in the first year of life (Schlossman 1920). In 1915 Chapin (1915a) enumerated 10 asylums in the larger cities of the United States, mainly on the eastern seaboard, in which the death rates of infants admitted during their first year of life varied from 31.7 percent to 75 percent by the end of their second year. In a discussion in the same year before the American Pediatric Association (Chapin, 1915b), Dr. Knox of Baltimore stated that in the institutions of that city 90 percent of the infants died by the end of their first year. He believed that the remaining 10 percent probably were saved because they had been taken out of the institution in time. Dr. Shaw of Albany remarked in the same discussion that the mortality rate of Randalls Island Hospital was probably 100 percent.

Conditions have since greatly changed. At present the best American institutions, such as Bellevue Hospital, New York City, register a mortality rate of less than 10 percent (Bakwin 1942), which compares favorably with the mortality rate of the rest of the country. While these and similar results were being achieved both here and in Europe, physicians and administrators were soon faced with a new problem: they discovered that institutionalized children practically without exception developed subsequent psychiatric disturbances and became asocial, delinquent, feeble-minded, psychotic, or problem children. Probably the high mortality rate in the preceding period had obscured this consequence. Now that the children survived, the other draw-backs of institutionalization became apparent. They led in this country to the widespread substitution of institutional care by foster home care.

The first investigation of the factors involved in the psychiatric consequences of institutional care of infants in their first year was made in 1933 in Austria by H. Durfee and K. Wolf (1933). Further contributions to the problem were made by L. G. Lowrey (1940), L. Bender and H. Yarnell (1941), H. Bakwin (1942) and W. Goldfarb (1943a, 1944a, 1944b, Goldfarb and Klopfer 1944). The results of all these investigations are roughly similar. Bakwin found greatly increased susceptibility to infection in spite of high hygienic and nutritional standards. Durfee and Wolf found that children under three months show no demonstrable impairment in consequence of institutionalization; but that children who had been institutionalized for more than eight months during their first year show such severe psychiatric disturbances that they cannot be tested. Bender, Goldfarb, and Lowrey found that after three years of institutionalization the changes effected are irreversible. Lowrey found that whereas the impairment of children hospitalized during their first year seems irremediable, that of children hospitalized in the second or third year can be corrected.

Two factors, both already stressed by Durfee and Wolf, are made responsible by most of the authors for the psychological injury suffered by these children.

First; lack of stimulation. The worst offenders were the best equipped and most hygienic institutions, which succeeded in sterilizing the surroundings of the child from germs but which at the same time sterilized the child's psyche. Even the most destitute of homes offers more mental stimulation than the usual hospital ward.

Second; the presence or absence of the child's mother. Stimulation by the mother will always be more intensive than even that of the best trained nursery personnel (Ripin 1930). Those institutions in which the mothers were present had better results than those where only trained child nurses were employed. The presence of the mothers could compensate even for numerous other shortcomings.

We believe that further study is needed to isolate clearly the various factors operative in the deterioration subsequent to prolonged care in institutions. The number of infants studied by Bakwin, Durfee and Wolf, and Lowrey in single institutions is very small, and Bender and Yarnell and Goldfarb did not observe infants in the first 12 months of life. We are not questioning here whether institutions should be preferred to foster homes, a subject now hardly ever discussed—the decision can by implication be deduced from the results of the studies of the Iowa group in their extensive research on the "Nature Versus Nurture" controversy (Skeels 1938, 1940, et al. 1938; Skodak 1939; Stoddard 1940; Updegraff 1932). It may seem surprising that in the course of this controversy no investigation has covered the field of the first year of life in institutions.[2] All Iowa investigators studied either children in foster homes or children over one year of age, using their findings for retrospective interpretations.[3] They did not have at their disposal a method of investigation that would permit the evaluation and quantification of development, mental or otherwise, during the first year of life. Their only instrument is the IQ which is unreliable (Simpson 1939) and not applicable during the first year. However, the baby tests worked out by Hetzer and Wolf (1928) fill the gap, providing not only a quotient for intelligence but also quantifiable data for development as a whole, such as indication of Developmental Age and of a Developmental Quotient. They provide, furthermore, quantifiable data on six distinct sectors of personality, namely: development of perception, body mastery, social relations, memory, relations to inanimate objects, and intelligence (which in the first year is limited to understanding of relations between and insight into the functions of objects).

With the help of these data ("dimensions"), a profile (personality curve) is constructed from which relevant conclusions can be drawn and with the help of which children can be compared with one another. Averages of development in any one sector or in all of them can be established for given environments. Finally, the relevant progresses of one and the same child in the several sectors of its personality can be followed up. The profiles present a cross-section of infantile development at any given moment; but they also can be combined into longitudinal curves of the developmental progress of the child's total personality as well as of the various sectors of the personality.

The aim of my research is to isolate and investigate the pathogenic factors responsible for the favorable or unfavorable outcome of infantile development. A psychiatric approach might seem desirable; however, infant psychiatry is a discipline not yet existent: its advancement is one of the aims of the present study.

Material

With this purpose in mind a long-term study of 164 children was undertaken.[4,5] In view of the findings of previous investigations this study was largely limited to the first year of life, and confined to two institutions, in order to embrace the total population of both (130 infants). Since the two institutions were situated in different countries of the Western hemisphere, a basis of comparison was established by investigating noninstitutionalized children of the same age group in their parents' homes in both countries. A total of 34 of these were observed. We thus have four environments.

TABLE 8.1

Environment	Institution No. 1*	Corresponding Private Background†	Institution No. 2	Corresponding Private Background
Number of children	69	11	61	23

* Institution No. 1 will from here on be called "Nursery"; institution No. 2, "Foundling Home".

† The small number of children observed in this particular environment was justified by the fact that it has been previously studied extensively by other workers; our only aim was to correlate our results with theirs. However, during the course of one year each child was tested at least at regular monthly intervals.

Procedure

In each case an anamnesis was made which whenever possible included data on the child's mother; and in each case the Hetzer-Wolf baby tests were administered. Problems cropping up in the course of our investigations for which the test situation did not provide answers were subjected to special experiments elaborated for the purpose. Such problems referred, for instance, to attitude and behavior in response to stimuli offered by inanimate objects, by social situations, etc. All observations of unusual or unexpected behavior of a child were carefully protocoled and studied.

A large number of tests, all the experiments, and some of the special situations were filmed on 16/mm film. A total of 31,500 feet of film preserve the results of our investigation to date. In the analysis of the movies the following method was applied: Behavior was filmed at sound speed—i.e., 24 frames per second. This makes it possible to slow action down during projection to nearly one-third of the original speed so that it can be studied in slow motion. A projector with additional handdrive also permits study of the films frame by frame, if necessary, to reverse action and to repeat projection of every detail as often as required. Simultaneously the written protocols of the experiments are studied and the two observations compared.

Results

For the purpose of orientation we established the average of the Developmental Quotients for the first third of the first year of life for each of the environments investigated. We contrasted these averages with those for the last third of the first year. This comparison gives us a first hint of the significance of environmental influences for development.

TABLE 8.2

| Type of Environment | Cultural and Social Background | Developmental Quotients | |
		Average of first four months	Average of last four months
Parental home	Professional	133	131
	Village population	107	108
Institution	"Nursery"	101.5	105
	"Foundling home"	124	72

Children of the first category come from professional homes in a large city; their Developmental Quotient, high from the start, remains high in the course of development.

Children in the second category come from an isolated fishing village of 499 inhabitants, where conditions of nutrition, housing, hygienic and medical care are very poor indeed; their Developmental Quotient in the first four months is much lower and remains at a lower level than that of the previous category.

In the third category, "Nursery", the children were handicapped from birth by the circumstances of their origin, which will be discussed below. At the outset their Developmental Quotient is even somewhat lower than that of the village babies; in the course of their development they gain slightly.

In the fourth category, "Foundling Home", the children are of an unselected urban (Latin) background. Their Developmental Quotient on admission is below that of our best category but much higher than that of the other two. The picture changes completely by the end of the first year, when their Developmental Quotient sinks to the astonishingly low level of 72.

Thus the children in the first three environments were at the end of their first year on the whole well developed and normal, whether they were raised in their progressive middle class family homes (where obviously optimal circumstances prevailed and the children were well in advance of average development), or in an institution or a village home, where the development was not brilliant but still reached a perfectly normal and satisfactory average. The children in the fourth environment, though starting at almost as high a level as the best of the others, had spectacularly deteriorated.

The children in Foundling Home showed all the manifestations of hospi-

talism, both physical and mental. In spite of the fact that hygiene and pre-
cautions against contagion were impeccable, the children showed, from the
third month on, extreme susceptibility to infection and illness of any kind.
There was hardly a child in whose case history we did not find reference to
otitis media, or morbilli, or varicella, or eczema, or intestinal disease of one
kind or another. No figures could be elicited on general mortality; but during my stay an epidemic of measles swept the institution, with staggeringly
high mortality figures, notwithstanding liberal administration of convales-
cent serum and globulins, as well as excellent hygienic conditions. Of a total
of 88 children up to the age of 2½, 23 died. It is striking to compare the
mortality among the 45 children up to 1½ years, to that of the 43 children
ranging from 1½ to 2½ years: usually, the *incidence* of measles is low in
the younger age group, but among those infected the mortality is higher than
that in the older age group; since in the case of Foundling Home every child
was infected, the question of incidence does not enter; however, contrary to
expectation, the mortality was much higher in the older age group. In the
younger group, 6 died—i.e., approximately 13 percent. In the older group,
17 died—i.e., close to 40 percent. The significance of these figures becomes
apparent when we realize that the mortality from measles during the first
year of life in the community in question, outside the institution, was less
than 0.5 percent.

In view of the damage sustained in all personality sectors of the children
during their stay in this institution we believe it licit to assume that their vitality (whatever that may be), their resistance to disease, was also progressively sapped. In the ward of the children ranging from 18 months to 2½
years only 2 of the 26 surviving children speak a couple of words. The same
two are able to walk. A third child is beginning to walk. Hardly any of them
can eat alone. Cleanliness habits have not been acquired, and all are incon-
tinent.

In sharp contrast to this is the picture offered by the oldest inmates in
Nursery, ranging from 8 to 12 months. The problem here is not whether the
children walk or talk by the end of the first year; the problem with these
10-month-olds is how to tame the healthy toddlers' curiosity and enterprise.
They climb up the bars of the cots after the manner of South Sea Islanders
climbing palms. Special measures to guard them from harm have had to be
taken after one 10-month-old actually succeeded in diving right over the
more than 2-foot railing of the cot. They vocalize freely, and some of them
actually speak a word or two. And all of them understand the significance of
simple social gestures. When released from their cots, all walk with support
and a number walk without it.

What are the differences between the two institutions that result in the
one turning out normally acceptable children and the other showing such
appalling effects?

SIMILARITIES[6]

1. Background of the children. Nursery is a penal institution in which delinquent girls are sequestered. When, as is often the case, they are pregnant on admission, they are delivered in a neighboring maternity hospital and after the lying-in period their children are cared for in Nursery from birth to the end of their first year. The background of these children provides for a markedly negative selection since the mothers are mostly delinquent minors as a result of social maladjustment or feeblemindedness, or because they are psychically defective, psychopathic, or criminal. Psychic normalcy and adequate social adjustment is almost excluded.

The other institution is a foundling home pure and simple. A certain number of the children housed have a background not much better than that of the Nursery children; but a sufficiently relevant number come from socially well-adjusted, normal mothers whose only handicap is inability to support themselves and their children (which is no sign of maladjustment in women of Latin background). This is expressed in the average of the Developmental Quotients of the two institutions during the first four months, as shown in Table 8.2.

The background of the children in the two institutions does therefore not favor Nursery; on the contrary, it shows a very marked advantage for Foundling Home.

2. Housing Conditions. Both institutions are situated outside the city, in large spacious gardens. In both hygienic conditions are carefully maintained. In both infants at birth and during the first six weeks are segregated from the older babies in a special newborns' ward, to which admittance is permitted only in a freshly sterilized smock after hands are washed. In both institutions infants are transferred from the newborns' ward after two or three months to the older babies' wards, where they are placed in individual cubicles which in Nursery are completely glass enclosed, in Foundling Home glass enclosed on three sides and open at the end. In Foundling Home the children remain in their cubicles up to 15 to 18 months; in Nursery they are transferred after the sixth month to rooms containing four to five cots each.

One-half of the children in Foundling Home are located in a dimly lighted part of the ward; the other half, in the full light of large windows facing southeast, with plenty of sun coming in. In Nursery, all the children have well-lighted cubicles. In both institutions the walls are painted in a light neutral color, giving a white impression in Nursery, a gray-green impression in Foundling Home. In both, the children are placed in white painted cots. Nursery is financially the far better provided one: we usually find here a small metal table with the paraphernalia of child care, as well as a chair, in each cubicle; whereas in Foundling Home it is the exception if a low stool is to be found in the cubicles, which usually contain nothing but the child's cot.

3. Food. In both institutions adequate food is excellently prepared and varied according to the needs of the individual child at each age; bottles from which children are fed are sterilized. In both institutions a large percentage of the younger children are breast-fed. In Nursery this percentage is smaller, so that in most cases a formula is soon added, and in many cases weaning takes place early. In Foundling Home all children are breast-fed as a matter of principle as long as they are under three months unless disease makes a deviation from this rule necessary.

4. Clothing. Clothing is practically the same in both institutions. The children have adequate pastel-colored dresses and blankets. The temperature in the rooms is appropriate. We have not seen any shivering child in either setup.

5. Medical Care. Foundling Home is visited by the head physician and the medical staff at least once a day, often twice, and during these rounds the chart of each child is inspected as well as the child itself. For special ailments a laryngologist and other specialists are available; they also make daily rounds. In Nursery no daily rounds are made, as they are not necessary. The physician sees the children when called.

Up to this point it appears that there is very little significant difference between the children of the two institutions. Foundling Home shows, if anything, a slight advantage over Nursery in the matter of selection of admitted children, of breast-feeding and of medical care. It is in the items that now follow that fundamental differences become visible.

DIFFERENCES

1. Toys. In Nursery it is the exception when a child is without one or several toys. In Foundling Home my first impression was that not a single child had a toy. This impression was later corrected. In the course of time, possibly in reaction to our presence, more and more toys appeared, some of them quite intelligently fastened by a string above the baby's head so that he could reach it. By the time we left a large percentage of the children in Foundling Home had a toy.

2. Visual Radius. In Nursery the corridor running between the cubicles, though rigorously white and without particular adornment, gives a friendly impression of warmth. This is probably because trees, landscape and sky are visible from both sides and because a bustling activity of mothers carrying their children, tending them, feeding them, playing with them, chatting with each other with babies in their arms, is usually present. The cubicles of the children are enclosed, but the glass panes of the partitions reach low enough for every child to be able at any time to observe everything going on all around. He can see into the corridor as soon as he lifts himself on his elbows. He can look out of the windows, and can see babies in the other cubicles by just turning his head; witness the fact that whenever the experimenter plays with a baby in one of the cubicles the babies in the two adjoining cubicles look on fascinated, try to participate in the game, knock at the panes of the partition, and often begin to cry if no attention is paid to them. Most of the cots are provided with widely-spaced bars that are no obstacle to vision. After the age of six months, when the child is transferred to the wards of the older babies, the visual field is enriched as a number of babies are then together in the same room, and accordingly play with each other.

In Foundling Home the corridor into which the cubicles open, though full of light on one side at least, is bleak and deserted, except at feeding time when five to eight nurses file in and look after the children's needs. Most of the time nothing goes on to attract the babies' attention. A special routine of Foundling Home consists in hanging bed sheets over the foot and the side railing of each cot. The cot itself is approximately 18 inches high. The side railings are about 20 inches high; the foot and head railings are approximately 28 inches high. Thus, when bed sheets are hung over the railings, the child lying in the cot is effectively screened from the world. He is completely separated from the other cubicles, since the glass panes of the wooden partitions begin six to eight inches higher than even the head railing of the cot. The result of this system is that each baby lies in solitary confinement up to the time when he is able to stand up in his bed, and that the only object he can see is the ceiling.

3. *Radius of Locomotion.* In Nursery the radius of locomotion is circumscribed by the space available in the cot, which up to about 10 months provides a fairly satisfactory range.

Theoretically the same would apply to Foundling Home. But in practice this is not the case for, probably owing to the lack of stimulation, the babies lie supine in their cots for many months and a hollow is worn into their mattresses. By the time they reach the age when they might turn from back to side (approximately the seventh month) this hollow confines this activity to such a degree that they are effectively prevented from turning in any direction. As a result we find most babies, even at 10 and 12 months, lying on their backs and playing with the only object at their disposal, their own hands and feet.

4. *Personnel.* In Foundling Home there is a head nurse and 5 assistant nurses for a total of 45 babies. These nurses have the *entire* care of the chil-

dren on their hands, except for the babies so young that they are breast-fed. The latter are cared for to a certain extent by their own mothers or by wet-nurses; but after a few months they are removed to the single cubicles of the general ward, where they share with at least seven other children the minis-trations of *one* nurse. It is obvious that the amount of care one nurse can give to an individual child when she has eight children to manage is small indeed. These nurses are unusually motherly, baby-loving women; but of course the babies of Foundling Home nevertheless lack all human contact for most of the day.

Nursery is run by a head nurse and her three assistants, whose duties do not include the care of the children but consist mainly in teaching the chil-dren's mothers in child care, and in supervising them. The children are fed, nursed and cared for by their own mothers or, in those cases where the mother is separated from her child for any reason, by the mother of another child, or by a pregnant girl who in this way acquires the necessary experi-ence for the care of her own future baby. Thus in Nursery each child has the full-time care of his own mother, or at least that of the substitute which the very able head nurse tries to change about until she finds someone who really likes the child.

Discussion

To say that every child in Nursery has a full-time mother is an understate-ment, from a psychological point of view. However modern a penal institu-tion may be, and however constructive and permissive its reeducative policies, the deprivation it imposes upon delinquent girls is extensive. Their op-portunities for an outlet for their interests, ambitions, activity, are very much impoverished. The former sexual satisfactions as well as the satisfac-tions of competitive activity in the sexual field, are suddenly stopped: regu-lations prohibit flashy dresses, vivid nail polish, or extravagant hair-do's. The kind of social life in which the girls could show off has vanished. This is especially traumatic as these girls become delinquent because they have not been able to sublimate their sexual drives, to find substitute gratifica-tions, and therefore do not possess a pattern for relinquishing pleasure when frustrated. In addition, they do not have compensation in relations with family and friends, as formerly they had. These factors, combined with the loss of personal liberty, the deprivation of private property and the regimen-tation of the penal institution, all add up to a severe narcissistic trauma from the time of admission; and they continue to affect the narcissistic and libidi-nal sectors during the whole period of confinement.

Luckily there remain a few safety valves for their emotions: (1) the rela-tionship with wardens, matrons, and nurses; (2) with fellow prisoners; (3) with the child. In the relationship with the wardens, matrons, and nurses, who obviously represent parent figures, much of the prisoner's aggression and resentment is bound. Much of it finds an outlet in the love and hate relationship to fellow prisoners, where all the phenomena of sibling rivalry are revived.

The child, however, becomes for them the representative of their sexuality, a product created by them, an object they own, which they can dress up and adorn, on which they can lavish their tenderness and pride, and of whose accomplishments, performance, and appearance they can boast. This is manifested in the constant competition among them as to who has the better dressed, more adanced, more intelligent, better looking, the heavier, bigger, more active—in a word, the better baby.[7] For their own persons they have more or less given up the competition for love, but they are intensely jealous of the attention given to their children by the matrons, wardens, and fellow prisoners.

It would take an exacting experimenter to invent an experiment with conditions as diametrically opposed in regard to the mother–child relationship as they are in these two institutions. Nursery provides each child with a mother to the nth degree, a mother who gives the child everything a good mother does and, beyond that, everything else she has.[8] Foundling Home does not give the child a mother, nor even a substitute mother, but only an eighth of a nurse.

We are now in a position to approach more closely and with better understanding the results obtained by each of the two institutions. We have already cited a few: we mentioned that the Developmental Quotient of Nursery achieves a normal average of about 105 at the end of the first year, whereas that of the Foundling Home sinks to 72; and we mentioned the striking difference of the children in the two institutions at first sight. Let us first consider the point at which the developments in the two institutions deviate.

On admission the children of Foundling Home have a much better average than the children of Nursery; their hereditary equipment is better than that of the children of delinquent minors. But while Foundling Home shows a rapid fall of the developmental index, Nursery shows a steady rise. They cross between the fourth and fifth months, and from that point on the curve of the average Developmental Quotient of the Foundling Home drops downward with increasing rapidity, never again to rise (Curve I).

The point where the two curves cross is significant. The time when the children in Foundling Home are weaned is the beginning of the fourth month. The time lag of one month in the sinking of the index below normal is explained by the fact that the Quotient represents a cross-section including all sectors of development, and that attempts at compensation are made in some of the other sectors.

However, when we consider the sector of Body Mastery (Curve II) which according to Wolf is most indicative for the mother–child relation-ship, we find that the curves of the children in Nursery cross the Body Mastery curve of the Foundling Home children between the third and fourth month. The inference is obvious. As soon as the babies in Foundling Home are weaned the modest human contacts which they have had during nursing at the breast stop, and their development falls below normal.

One might be inclined to speculate as to whether the further deterioration of the children in Foundling Home is not due to other factors also, such as the perceptual and motor deprivations from which they suffer. It might be argued that the better achievement of the Nursery children is due to the fact

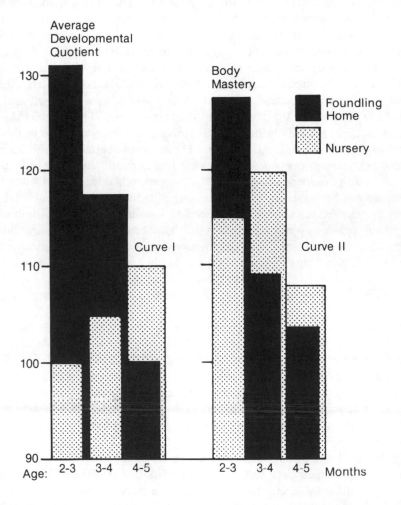

FIGURE 8.1 Comparison of development in nursery and foundling home during the first five months.

that they were better provided for in regard to toys and other perceptual stimuli. We shall therefore analyze somewhat more closely the nature of deprivations in perceptual and locomotor stimulation.

First of all it should be kept in mind that the nature of the inanimate perceptual stimulus, whether it is a toy or any other object, has only a very minor importance for a child under 12 months. At this age the child is not yet capable of distinguishing the real purpose of an object. He is only able to use it in a manner adequate to his own functional needs (C. Bühler 1931). Our thesis is that perception is a function of libidinal cathexis and therefore the result of the intervention of an emotion of one kind or another.[9] Emotions are provided for the child through the intervention of a human partner —i.e., by the mother or her substitute. A progressive development of emotional interchange with the mother provides the child with perceptive experiences of its environment. The child learns to grasp by nursing at the mother's breast and by combining the emotional satisfaction of that experience with tactile perceptions. He learns to distinguish animate objects from inanimate ones by the spectacle provided by his mother's face (Gesell and Ilg 1937) in situations fraught with emotional satisfaction. The interchange between mother and child is loaded with emotional factors, and it is in this interchange that the child learns to play. He becomes acquainted with his surroundings through the mother's carrying him around; through her help he learns security in locomotion as well as in every other respect. This security is reinforced by her being at his beck and call. In these emotional relations with the mother the child is introduced to learning, and later to imitation. We have previously mentioned that the motherless children in Foundling Home are unable to speak, to feed themselves, or to acquire habits of cleanliness: it is the security provided by the mother in the field of locomotion, the emotional bait offered by the mother calling her child, that "teaches" him to walk. When this is lacking, even children two to three years old cannot walk.

The children in Foundling Home have, theoretically, as much radius of locomotion as the children in Nursery. They did not at first have toys, but they could have exerted their grasping and tactile activity on the blankets, on their clothes, even on the bars of the cots. We have seen children in Nursery without toys; they are the exception—but the lack of material is not enough to hamper them in the acquisition of locomotor and grasping skills. The presence of a mother or her substitute is sufficient to compensate for all the other deprivations.

It is true that the children in Foundling Home are condemned to solitary confinement in their cots. But we do not think that it is the lack of perceptual stimulation in general that counts in their deprivation. We believe that they suffer because their perceptual world is emptied of human partners, that their isolation cuts them off from any stimulation by any persons who could signify mother-representatives for the child at this age. The result, as

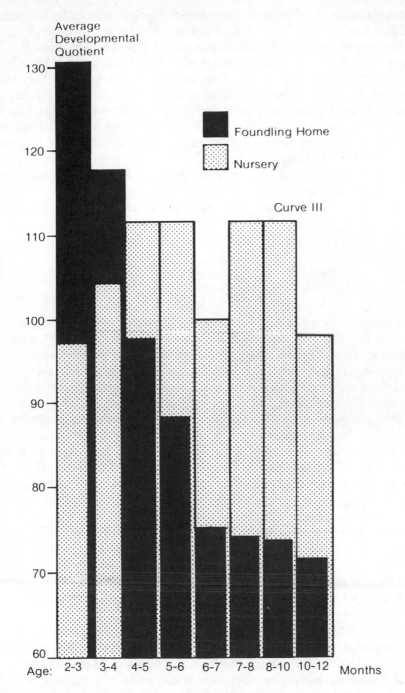

FIGURE 8.2   Comparison of development in nursery and foundling home.

Curve III shows, is a complete restriction of psychic capacity by the end of the first year.

This restriction of psychic capacity is not a temporary phenomenon. It is, as can be seen from the curve, a progressive process. How much this deterioration could have been arrested if the children were taken out of the institution at the end of the first year is an open question. The fact that they remain in Foundling Home probably furthers this progressive process. By the end of the second year the Developmental Quotient sinks to 45, which corresponds to a mental age of approximately 10 months, and would qualify these children as imbeciles.

The curve of the children in Nursery does not deviate significantly from the normal. The curve sinks at 2 points, between the 6th and 7th, and between the 10th and 12th months. These deviations are within the normal range; their significance will be discussed in a separate article. It has nothing to do with the influence of institutions, for the curve of the village group is nearly identical.

Provisional Conclusions

The contrasting pictures of these two institutions show the significance of the mother–child relationship for the development of the child during the first year. Deprivations in other fields, such as perceptual and locomotor radius, can all be compensated by adequate mother–child relations. "Adequate" is not here a vague general term. The examples chosen represent the two extremes of the scale.

The children in Foundling Home do have a mother—for a time, in the beginning—but they must share her immediately with at least one other child, and from three months on, with seven other children. The quantitative factor here is evident. There is a point under which the mother–child relations cannot be restricted during the child's first year without inflicting irreparable damage. On the other hand, the exaggerated mother–child relationship in Nursery introduces a different quantitative factor. To anyone familiar with the field it is surprising that Nursery should achieve such excellent results, for we know that institutional care is destructive for children during their first year; but in Nursery the destructive factors have been compensated by the increased intensity of the mother–child relationship.

These findings should not be construed as a recommendation for overprotection of children. In principle the libidinal situation of Nursery is almost as undesirable as the other extreme in Foundling Home. Neither in the nursery of a penal institution nor in a foundling home for parentless children can the normal libidinal situation that obtains in a family home be expected. The two institutions have here been chosen as experimental setups for the purpose of examining variations in libidinal factors ranging from extreme frustration to extreme gratification. That the extreme frustration practiced in Foundling Home has deplorable consequences has been shown; the extreme gratification in Nursery can be tolerated by the children housed there for two reasons.

1. The mothers have the benefit of the intelligent guidance of the head nurse and her assitants, and the worst exaggerations are thus corrected.

2. Children during their first year of life can stand the ill effects of such a situation much better than at a later age. In this respect Nursery has wisely limited the duration of the children's stay to the first 12 months. For children older than this we should consider a libidinal setup such as that in Nursery very dangerous indeed.

Further Problems

This is the first of a series of publications on the results of a research project on infancy that we are conducting. As such it is a preliminary report. It is not intended to show more than the most general outline of the results of early institutional care, giving at the same time a hint of the approach we use. The series of other problems on which this investigation has shed some light, as well as the formulation of those problems that could be recognized as such only in the course of the investigation, have not been touched upon in our present study and can only summarily be touched upon; they are headings, as it were, of the chapters of our future program of publication.

Apart from the severe developmental retardation, the most striking single factor observed in Foundling Home was the change in the pattern of the reaction to strangers in the last third of the first year (Gesell and Thompson 1934). The usual behavior was replaced by something that could vary from extreme friendliness to any human partner combined with anxious avoidance of inanimate objects, to a generalized anxiety expressed in blood-curdling screams which could go on indefinitely. It is evident that these deviant behavior patterns require a more thorough and extensive discussion than our present study would have permitted.

We also observed extraordinary deviations from the normal in the time of appearance and disappearance of familiar developmental patterns, and certain phenomena unknown in the normal child, such as bizarre stereotyped motor patterns distinctly reminiscent of the stereotype in catatonic motility. These and other phenomena observed in Foundling Home require an extensive discussion in order to determine which are to be classified as maturation phenomena (which appear even under the most unfavorable circumstances, and which appear with commensurate retardation when retardation is general); or which can be considered as the first symptoms of the development of serious psychiatric disturbances. In connection with this problem a more thorough discussion of the rapidity with which the Developmental Quotients recede in Foundling Home is intended.

Another study is to deal with the problems created by the enormous over-protection practiced in Nursery.

And finally the rationale of the one institutional routine as against that of the other will have to be discussed in greater detail. This study will offer the possibility of deciding how to compensate for unavoidable changes in the environment of children orphaned at an early age. It will also shed some light on the social consequences of the progressive disruption of home life caused by the increase of female labor and by the demands of war; we might state that we foresee in the course of events a corresponding increase in aso-ciality, in the number of problem and delinquent children, of mental defec-tives, and of psychotics.

It will be necessary to take into consideration in our institutions, in our charitable activities, in our social legislation, the overwhelming and unique importance of adequate and satisfactory mother–child relationship during the first year, if we want to decrease the unavoidable and irreparable psychi-atric consequences deriving from neglect during this period.

A Follow-up Report

I

The striking picture of the infants studied in Foundling Home encouraged us to make every effort to get whatever information we could on the further development of the individual children. Distance made it impossible for the author to attend to this personally. The investigator who assisted in the orig-inal study was therefore directed to ascertain, at regular intervals, certain objectively observable facts on all those infants who were still available. He visited Foundling Home during the two years following our own study, at four-monthly intervals. On these occasions, equipped with a questionnaire prepared by the author, he asked the nursing personnel a series of questions. He observed each child's general behavior, and tried to make contact with each. He took some motion pictures of them, and a set of stills at the end of the two years, Finally, some bodily measurements—namely, weight, height, and occipital circumference were taken.

The questions referred to three principal sectors of personality.

1. Bodily performance: the gross indicator used was whether the child could sit, stand, or walk.
2. Intellectual capacity to handle materials: the gross indicator used was whether the child was capable of eating food alone with the help of a spoon, and whether he could dress alone.

3. Social relations: these were explored by ascertaining the number of words spoken by each child, and by finding out whether he was toilet-trained.

We are only too well aware that the resulting information is inadequate for a thorough study. As will be seen, however, even this inadequate follow-up yields a number of instructive data.

As is usually the case in follow-up investigations, only a relatively small number of the children originally seen could be checked on. Two years ago, when we first visited the ward reserved for the children from birth to 1½ years, and the ward for children from 1½ to 3 years, a total of 91 children were present. In the course of the first year, 27 of these died of various causes, among which were an epidemic of measles, intercurrent sickness, and cachexia; by the end of the second year, another 7 of those originally seen had died; this represents a total mortality of over 37 percent in a period of 2 years.

Thirty-six children could not be learned about because: 23 had been taken back to their families; 7 had been adopted (mostly by their own illegitimate parents); 2 had been placed in children's institutions; and 4 could not be accounted for.

At the time of this writing (1946) 21 children of those originally seen are still at the institution. Of these the youngest is two years of age, the oldest four years and one month. The data on their development are as follows.

1. Bodily development:
   Incapable of any locomotion: 5
   Sit up unassisted (without walking):   3
   Walk assisted: 8
   Walk unassisted: 5

   Total   21

2. Handling materials:
   Cannot eat alone with spoon: 12
   Eat alone with spoon: 9

   Total   21

   Cannot dress alone: 20
   Dresses alone: 1

   Total   21

3. Adaptation to demands of environment:
   Not toilet-trained in any way: 6
   Toilet-trained, partially:[1]   15

   Total   21

4. Speech development:

Cannot talk at all:	6
Vocabulary: 2 words:	5
Vocabulary: 3 to 5 words:	8
Vocabulary: a dozen words:	1
Uses sentences:	1
Total	21

As seen from these data, the mental development of these 21 children is extraordinarily retarded, compared to that of normal children between the ages of two and four, who move, climb, and babble all day long, and who conform to or struggle against the educational demands of the environment. This retardation, which amounts to a deterioration, is borne out by the weights and heights of these children, as well as by their pictures.

Normal children by the end of the second year weigh, on the average, 26½ pounds, and the length is 33½ inches. At the time of this writing, 12 of the children in Foundling Home range in age between 2.4 and 2.8; 4, between 2.8 and 3.2; and 5 between 3.2 and 4.1. But of all of these children, only three fall into the weight range of a normal *two-year-old* child, and only two have attained the length of a normal child of that age. All others fall below the normal 2-year-level—in one case, as much as 45 percent in weight and 5 inches in length. In other words, the physical picture of these children impresses the casual observer as that of children half their age.

In our previous article on the subject (see first part of chapter) we ex-

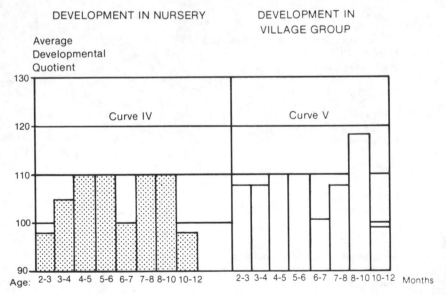

FIGURE 8.3.

pressed the suspicion that the damage inflicted on the infants in Foundling Home by their being deprived of maternal care, maternal stimulation, and maternal love, as well as by their being completely isolated, is irreparable. Our follow-up confirms this assumption. After their 15th month, these children were put into more favorable environmental conditions than before— i.e., in the ward for the older children. This is a large room, sunny, without the partitions which in the ward for the younger children isolated the infants from each other and from every environmental stimulus. Three to five nurses are constantly in the room, and they chat with each other and with the children. The children are also taken out of their cots and placed on the floor. Thus they have infinitely more active stimulation than they previously experienced in the ward for younger children. Notwithstanding this improvement in environmental conditions, the process of deterioration has proved to be progressive. It would seem that the developmental imbalance caused by the unfavorable environmental conditions during the children's first year produces a psychosomatic damage that cannot be repaired by normal measures. Whether it can be repaired by therapeutic measures remains to be investigated.

We have advisedly spoken of psychosomatic damage. From the figures given above it can be seen that quite apart from the inadequate psychic and physical development, all these children showed a seriously decreased resistance to disease, and an appalling mortality. Those who survived were all far below the age-adequate weight reached by normal children of comparable age.

II

In view of these findings we once again examined the data on Nursery, the institution compared to Foundling Home in our previous article. The organization of Nursery did not permit a follow-up extended to the fifth year, as did that of Foundling Home. As a rule children leave Nursery when they are a full year old. However, a certain number of exceptions are made in this rule, and in the course of our study of Nursery, which now covers a period of 3½ years, 29 children were found who stayed longer than a year. The age at which these left varied from the 13th to the 18th month (1.1 to 1.6). This means that the *oldest* of them was *half-a-year younger* than the youngest child in our follow-up in Foundling Home, and *two-and-a-half years younger than the oldest*. In spite of this enormous difference in age, the Nursery children all ran lustily around on the floor; some of them dressed and undressed themselves; they fed themselves with a spoon; nearly all spoke a few words; they understood commands and obeyed them; and the older ones showed a certain consciousness of toilet requirements. All of them played lively social games with each other and with the observers. The more advanced ones imitated the activities of the nurses, sweeping the floor, carrying and distributing diapers, etc. In all these children, tests showed that the developmental quotients which in the 11th and 12th months had receded somewhat, not only came up to the normal age level, but in most cases surpassed it by far.

But the gross physical picture alone, as expressed by the figures on morbidity and mortality of the children in Nursery, is sufficiently striking. During the 3½ years of our study of Nursery we had occasion to follow 122 infants, each for approximately a full year. During this time *not a single child died*. The institution was visited by no epidemic. Intercurrent sickness was limited, on the whole, to seasonal colds, which in a moderate number developed into mild respiratory involvement; there was comparatively little intestinal disturbance; the most disturbing illness was eczema. The unusually high level of health maintained in Nursery impelled us to look into its past record. We investigated the files of Nursery for 10 years prior to the beginning of our work there. We found that during the whole of the last 14 years a total of 3 children had died: 1 of pneumonia at the age of 3 months; and 2 of pyloric stenosis, the first at the age of 1 month, the second after several operations at the age of 9 months.

It is in the light of these findings, which show what can be achieved in an institution under favorable circumstances and adequate organization, that the consequences of the methods used in Foundling Home should be evaluated.

NOTES

1. *Hospitalism* tends to be confused with *hospitalization,* the temporary confinement of a seriously ill person to a hospital.

2. Woodworth (1941) in discussing the results of the Child Welfare Research Station of the State University of Iowa makes the following critical remarks (p. 71): "The causes of the inferior showing of orphanage children are obviously open to debate. . . . It would seem that a survey and comparative study of institutional homes for children would be instructive. . . ."

3. H. E. Jones (1940) takes exception to this method as follows: "It seems probable that we shall turn from retrospective surveys of conditions assumed to have had a prior influence, and shall prefer to deal with the current and cumulative effects of specific environmental factors. It may also be expected that our interest will shift to some extent from mass statistical studies . . . to investigations of the dynamics of the growth process in individuals."

4. It is interesting to note that independently of our approach to this problem (mapped out and begun in 1936) Woodworth (1941) recommends a research program on extremely similar lines as being desirable for the better understanding of the problem of heredity and environment.

Orphanages. Present belief based on a certain amount of evidence regards the orphanages as an unfavorable environment for the child but the causes are not well understood. Two general projects may be suggested.
(a) A survey of institutional homes for children with a view to discovering the

variations in their equipment and personnel and in their treatment of the children with some estimate of the results achieved.

(b) Experimental studies in selected orphanages which retain their children for a considerable time, with a view to testing out the effects of specific environmental factors. For example, the amount of contact of the child with adults could be increased for certain children for the purpose of seeing whether this factor is important in mental development. It is conceivable that an orphanage could be run so as to become a decidedly favorable environment for the growing child, but at present we do not know how this result could be accomplished.

5. I wish to thank K. Wolf, Ph.D., for her help in the experiments carried out in "Nursery" and in private homes, and for her collaboration in the statistical evaluation of the results.

6. Under this heading we enumerate not only actual similarities but also differences that are of no etiological significance for the deterioration in Foundling Home. These differences comprise two groups: differences of no importance whatever, and differences that actually favor the development of children in Foundling Home.

7. The psychoanalytically oriented reader, of course, realizes that for these girls in prison the child has become a hardly disguised phallic substitute. However, for the purposes of this article I have carefully avoided any extensive psychoanalytic interpretation, be it ever so tempting, and limited myself as closely as possible to results of direct observations of behavior. At numerous other points it would be not only possible but natural to apply analytic concepts; that is reserved for future publication.

8. For the nonpsychoanalytically oriented reader we note that this intense mother–child relationship is not equivalent to a relationship based on love of the child. The mere fact that the child is used as a phallic substitute implies what a large part unconscious hostility plays in the picture.

9. This is stating in psychoanalytic terms the conviction of most psychologists, beginning with Compayré (1893) and shared by such familiar authorities in child psychology as Stern (1930) and K. Bühler (1942), and in animal psychology, Tolman (1932).

10. These children are trained "to a certain extent." According to my observer many of the so-called toilet-trained children were found to soil in their beds; their training appears to be limited to their making use of the toilet when put on it.

9

The Young Adult Adjustment
of Twenty Wartime Residential
Nursery Children

HENRY S. MAAS

Societal reluctance to tamper with the dominant childrearing patterns is at times overcome by cataclysmic events. Early writers on the kibbutz (see Viteles 1967) thus found parents very much at a loss on how to care for children in their new social situation, since their own childhoods provided no examples. To be sure, ideological considerations predisposed them toward group care, but in retrospect it seems that harsh economic realities may well have exerted as much influence on the long-term childrearing patterns in the kibbutz as did the dedication to egalitarian principles, women's liberation, and early exposure to group decision making and social constraints.

In wartime (World War II) England all of the ideological pressures undoubtedly were arrayed against separating young children from their London parents to rear them in countryside nurseries a good distance away. Yet, ironically, the country that gave us the influential Bowlbian position against group care has also, under the stress of the time, yielded some natural experiments to test its general validity. Freud and her co-workers (1942, 1951) described the early development of children in these circumstances. Maas studied adult adjustment of wartime group care children.

This is a report, necessarily condensed, of a study[1] of 20 young adults who, as preschool children in London during World War II, were placed for their physical safety by their parents in British wartime residential nurseries for at least one year. The purpose of the study was to clarify some questions about

Henry S. Maas. "The Young Adult Adjustment of Twenty Wartime Residential Nursery Children." *Child Welfare* 42: 57–72. Copyright, Child Welfare League of America, Inc., 1963. Reproduced by permission.

a working assumption in child welfare practice—that the preschool child who is separated from his parents and placed in any group care residence suffers irreversible psychosocial damage.

The literature on the problem of "maternal deprivation" and, more specifically, on the separation of the young child from his natural family has grown to almost overwhelming proportions since the 1930s.[2] A systematic review of this literature is obviously impossible here. Regarding the substantive complexities of the separation problem, Mary D. Ainsworth and John Bowlby (1954) wrote, in one of the latter's most cogent if least accessible contributions:

> . . . it has become increasingly clear that "separation" is not a simple aetiological factor, and that the term refers to a wide range of events and an intricate complex of associated conditions, which in different constellations may have different effects on the course of development [p. 105].

Probably the clearest expression of child welfare's present working assumptions regarding separation and group care and their effects on the child is the review of research John Bowlby wrote for the World Health Organization over a decade ago (Bowlby 1950, 1951 ed.). While subsequent studies, including Bowlby's own investigations, have somewhat modified formulations found in the WHO publication, in essence the ideas of this report still echo through the halls of practice. It is here that we read:

> . . . the infant and young child should experience a warm, intimate, and continuous relationship with his mother (or permanent mother-substitute). . . . [If not, we may expect to find] anxiety, excessive need for love, powerful feelings of revenge, and, arising from these last, guilt and depression. In the second and third years of life, the emotional response to separation is . . . just as severe; . . . vulnerability between three and five is still serious, though much less so than earlier. Deprivation after the age of three or four . . . still results, however, in excessive desires for affection and excessive impulses for revenge, which cause acute internal conflict and unhappiness and very unfavorable social attitudes . . . sceptics may question whether the retardation is permanent and whether the symptoms of illness may not easily be overcome. The long-term after-effects . . . can sometimes be calamitous . . ., [with such results as] superficial relationships; no real feeling . . .; deceit and evasion, often pointless; stealing; lack of concentration at school. [To the professional world of child-care workers, the prescription is unequivocal:] To sum up, then, it may be said that group residential care is always to be avoided for those under about 6 years, that it is suitable for short-stay children between 6 and 12, and for both short-stay and some long-stay adolescents. It is also indispensable for many maladjusted children . . . [pp. 11, 12, 23, 26, 57, 15, 25, 31, 137.].

Bowlby drew these conclusions from a review of his own research and that of Goldfarb, Spitz, and others. Effects were seen as permanent, though

Bowlby (1950, 1951 ed.) noted in passing that ". . . the studies of Theis and of Beres & Obers show that many such children achieve a tolerable degree of social adaptation when adult [p. 39]."

Also warranting observation are certain problems in study design. In regard to such problems, a recent Social Science Research Council report states:

> Two animals—or children—exposed to the same stimulus probably will not respond in the same way because the sum of their experiences previous to the stimulus differ, as do experiences intervening between the observed stimulus and measurement of the desired response. This old dilemma in research is particularly troublesome in studies of the effects of deprivation, for the behavioral changes of greatest interest are those that are shown to be stable over time, and the greater the lapse of time, the greater the opportunity for different intervening experience. Mason [William A. Mason, conference participant] suggested that much parametric investigation is needed, on different ages at which separation occurs, the duration of the deprivation, and the reversibility of the apparent disorders developed [Palmer 1961, p. 16].

In the designs of the studies reviewed, some problems are common. First, while the question for investigation was the effects of separation, there was usually no control over the children's preseparation experiences. The children coming out of disintegrated family situations that necessitated their placement might have been damaged before they were separated from their parents. Could not one study children who were separated from intact families, free from gross pathology, so that preseparation experiences might be assumed to be noncontributory to whatever subsequent damage was found?

Second, the children studied had often been placed in what we would now agree were "bad" institutions, understaffed or staffed by persons influenced by the child care standards of their day and, consequently, more concerned with physical hygiene than with human feelings and responsiveness to the children. For others, as in the case of Bowlby's 60 former tuberculosis sanatorium children, the institutional experience involved much more than separation and residential group care, for these youngsters, under four years old, were "confined to cots for rest much of the time" and given gastric lavages, etc. (Bowlby et al. 1956 pp. 213, 215). (Clearly, studies of ill children using medical facilities are not studies of simply childhood separation and group care.) But might not one control for institutional effect be to study children from different *kinds* of parent-substitute institutions, run according to different specifiable principles of child care, and compare the results?[3]

Third, children studied in follow-up investigations were sometimes selected from the caseloads of clinics and social agencies. For example, the 38 persons between the ages of 16 and 26 studied by Beres and Obers were "all taken from the Youth Service Department," set up for young people who, after early years in an infant home, later years in foster care, and then perhaps a cottage school, required "additional care." Obers and Beres (1950) note the "factor of selectivity" in their study and that "the degree of pathology in our series of cases is greater than might have been found if all cases . . . had been followed. . . . [but] it would have been altogether impossible to trace these [pp. 214–15]." Perhaps one could do just this—trace children in the community after they had left institutional care. Though they might well be found to be clients of mental health or welfare agencies, at least they would not have been located through a source that, by their presence in an active caseload, marks them as troubled people or people in trouble.

Fourth, the study of persons whose placements were in many different living groups encompasses the effects of considerably more than merely separation and early group residential care. A multitude of changes in living groups for children has been found to be associated with confusion about identity.[4] In trying to assess damage incurred by separation and group residential care alone, one should plan to study persons who have undergone just that—separation and placement in a single children's center. And, as a corollary criterion, early separation should not be equated with permanent severance from own parents. One should thus focus the study on children who have lived in a single group residence and who subsequently returned during childhood to their own families.

Fifth, it seems clear that the child's age at placement is a significant variable in separation research since the meaning of the experience to the child theoretically depends upon his stage of development at its inception. It is obviously possible to select persons age-grouped by separation age for comparison of the effects.

Finally, most of the research has been on the short-term effects on children. Irreversibility of damage is assumed, although there are a few conflicting reports concerning long-term effects on adults. Using a battery of interviews and tests, and drawing other observations from home visits and agency records, one could examine the present adjustment of criteria-meeting young adults. The separation literature indicates what to assess—certain aspects of their feeling life, inner controls, relationship patterns, role performance, and intellectual functioning—if theory on irreversibility of damage is to be tested.

British Wartime Residential Nurseries

Some of the problems cited seemed manageable if one chose to study young adults who had been separated from intact families, apparently free of gross pathology, and returned to their families during their childhood years after a stay of at least one year in a British wartime residential nursery. (The civilian evacuation scheme in wartime Britain involved about 400 residential nurseries before the war's end.) Richard Titmuss and colleagues have described the problems in launching and operating this program (Titmuss 1950; Ferguson and Fitzgerald 1954). A reading of their publications and others on the evacuation of British children suggested to me that, in 1960 or 1961, one might study young adults who, as preschool children, had been separated from their parents, not because of the disintegration of their families, but as part of a large-scale movement to send children to places that were, hopefully, remote from enemy bomb targets.

The Ministry of Health assumed from the start that ". . . separation might involve greater risks than did air-raids [Ferguson and Fitzgerald 1954, p. 234]." Psychiatric clinicians at a 1941 Tavistock Clinic meeting predicted:

> There is in this situation a very real danger that the seeds of neurosis will be sown in an increasing number of children, and apart from the immediate distress and disability arising from this, there is the wider question of what these children will go through as adolescents and adults [*British Medical Journal*, 1941, p. 129].

But parents in London streets in 1939 were reading large black- and red-lettered London County Council posters announcing registration and meeting places for the evacuation of children. When war broke out in September 1939, there were plans for children's flight. Earlier than this, there had been a brief trial-run evacuation of school children, including some from day nurseries. Of the wartime scheme for children, Susan Isaacs (1941) remarked in the *Cambridge Evacuation Survey:* "The parents who parted from their children, far from having failed them, were acting from a sense of duty, often at great sacrifice [p. 14]." Here, then, was a "natural experiment" to study separation without the necessity of prior intrafamily trauma.

Young Children in Wartime and Infants without Families, by Anna Freud and Dorothy Burlingham (1942, 1944), made clear that within the British wartime residential nursery program there was at least one child-care center that differed radically from the literature's model of the understaffed and impersonal institution of prior separation research,[5] and finally, advance correspondence assured me that some, if not many, of the former residents of at least two quite different wartime nurseries might be found in London in 1960 and 1961. But not until my early field work in London was completed could I be sure of what was feasible.

In fact, three quite different wartime residential nurseries provided alumni for the group of 20 adults in this study. The three nurseries will be called Nursery N, Nursery E, and Nursery S. To characterize and compare them, three dimensions will be used. (It must be remembered, however, that nurseries, like the children in them, change over time, and only a capsule presentation can be made here. Fuller documentation of the bases for my inferences, drawn from both contemporaneous reports and interviews with staff, will appear in a fuller report on this study.) The three dimensions are: (1) numbers of children and staff, (2) children's relationships with their parents, and (3) staff orientation to the children.

In brief, Nursery N is the middle-sized one in terms of numbers of children, with the most generous supply of staff members to children. Each staff person had at least one child assigned to her. A common pattern among the three- to five-year-olds was the assignment of living groups of about five children to one staff helper. Parents could visit at any time and there were "strong contacts with parents."[6] In a time of gasoline shortage, the fact that Nursery N was physically closer to London than either of the other two nurseries is important. With the older children in Nursery N, "we talked about parents, wrote to them. We had pictures of parents. Sunday nights were always exciting. There was a bus every Sunday. Some were very sad when Mummy had gone. Perhaps we can write a letter. We didn't put any child to bed who was upset. We took them in our rooms and talked to them. They could talk about it." This was a key to the Nursery N approach to children—the expression of feelings was encouraged, guided by a depth of psychological understanding of young children that was not present in either of the other two nurseries.

The second nursery, E, was the smallest, able to accommodate only about 20 children. Its staff consisted of a professionally untrained woman, Mrs. E, and her physiotherapist daughter, Miss E, with occasional part-time domestic help from the nearby Welsh village. Thus, the ratio of staff to children was about 10 to 1. Deep in the Welsh countryside, Nursery E was the most inaccessible to the London parents whose children were routed to Mrs. E and her daughter through an East End settlement house. Interviews and the log book of Nursery E indicate that parents' visits were most infrequent. The alien nature of the East End culture to Mrs. E's stern Welsh world and her approach to the children are best suggested by her own words: "Those were very interesting days and I personally loved every one of them! Bedwetter, sleep walkers, lively heads, and sores. We got the better of the lot, and P was our only failure, and a doctor at the London hospital said he was incurable [as a bedwetter], poor lad. They were all fairly undisciplined—but very soon 'fell in' and we really were a very happy family—no friction anywhere." Nursery E was in marked contrast to the psychologically oriented Nursery N.

The third of the nurseries, S, was eventually the largest and had the highest ratio of children to staff. Nursery S had been a model day nursery school for the children of working mothers. Those who had been attending the school were evacuated as a unit like other school classes—starting out with 47 children who knew one another, their head teacher, and her three helpers. There was "no domestic help at first." Parents visited Nursery S at

Christmas or Easter time, in a bus they arranged for themselves, and a festive spread was miraculously provided by Lady X, in whose home Nursery S was billeted. Many anecdotes suggest the teachers' possessiveness regarding the children in their charge during their country's time of crisis. The teachers were trained nursery school educators, not psychologists, as the head teacher remarked, "with their psychological jargon, their observations, and their graphs." These teachers told their children that they had left London because the King had wanted them to. Children's songs and games, spiritual values, God and country, and the wonders of nature were central themes. The time that the busload of parents was getting ready to leave and the geese were let loose to distract the children was described with delight. In Nursery S, I was told, weeping at parting occurred among the parents, but not among the children. (The statement, not the fact, is important.)

In brief contrast, then, substitute parenting at Nursery N was open and expressive; at Nursery E somewhat firm, if not stern, and suppressive; and at Nursery S, with its faith in God, King, and denial, rather inspirational and repressive, and quite possessive.

The Young Adults for Study

In addition to comparisons by type of residential nurseries, the plan for this study was to compare young adults grouped by age at separation. I wanted 20 persons, 5 from each of 4 different age-at-separation groups: the Ones, separated in the first year of life; the Twos, separated at about 2 to 2½; the Threes, separated at about 3 to 3½, and the Four-pluses, separated between 4 and 5. For obvious reasons, I wanted each age group to be composed of representatives of all three nurseries and, thus, each nursery group to span the age groups. Finally, relatively equal numbers of men and women seemed desirable.

WHERE THE SUBJECTS WERE FOUND

Procedures for selecting the young adults for study were quite different for the three nurseries. For 23 young adults who had been residents for at least 1 year, Nursery N provided a roster of names and addresses, together with age at placement. The addresses derived from their own 1958 letter survey of former residents. Of the 23, 6 were eliminated as ineligible because they were illegitimate children, over age (well past fifth birthday) at placement, or from gross-pathology family situations, involving death or institutionalization of parent. Of the 17 letters I mailed, 6 were returned "not known at this address," 6 did not reply, and 5 replied agreeing to see me, but one was a British soldier stationed in Germany. The final group of seven Nursery N young adults in the study comprised four of the responders (one of the four being a young woman whose sister had written for her as well as for herself) and three of the six nonresponders. Because the ages at separation of these three fitted my design needs, I chose to make repeated home visits until I found them in. (The unchosen three of the six nonresponders were a sibship of three sisters, and I already had three pairs of sibs in the study.)

Nursery E gave me a roster of 20 names and the ages at placement of all children who had spent a year or more in Wales. There were London (East End) addresses, as of World War II, for 15 of them, and for 5 there were only names. Using the Register of Electors (dated 10 October 1959) for the Metropolitan Borough of Bethnal Green, I found two of these families still at the same address. One of them proved to be a major source of leads—which new housing estates others had moved into, whose brother ran which pub, who had boxed recently at a settlement house that would know his address. By sole-wearing footwork, I discovered the addresses of nine persons on the list. Had I needed them, I probably could have located all but three of the others. Two of these, however, would have been eliminated from the study. The seven I approached, selected first according to my design needs for age at separation and second for a relatively balanced sex distribution, all agreed to participate in the study; no one I visited refused.

Nursery S, the former day nursery school located in a stable working-class neighborhood, had had as its head teacher a woman who lived where she taught and who was still in casual contact with the parents of some of her former charges. Having obtained their addresses from their parents because she herself was eager to see them grown up, she invited eight of them, with their spouses, to a party at her house to meet me. Four came, and the other four telephoned or wrote apologies. Three of those who attended the party and two who did not constitute the Nursery S study group. The 20th young adult had been a resident of a nursery, called Nursery O, directed by a woman now affiliated with the psychotherapeutic group that ran Nursery N. Since no other adults who had been separated and placed during their first year of life were available to me from nurseries E and S, and I already had three in this age group from Nursery N, I included him.

DESCRIPTION OF THE YOUNG ADULTS

Since the findings of our study concern the adjustment of these 20 young adults, some data on their backgrounds should be reported. Of the 8 women and 12 men, aged 19 to 26 years, just half were 21 years old or less when they were studied in 1960–61 (Table 9.1). They grew up primarily in working-class families, nine of them in London's East End. About a third were in families headed by unskilled workers—e.g., a stoker, a dustman (garbage collector)—another third were the children of bus or lorry drivers or tailors, and the final third were in families another notch or two up the occupational ladder—a grocer who owned his shop, a clerk-salesman, a teacher.

TABLE 9.1. *The 20 cases, by separation age and residential nursery*

Age Group at Separation	Case	Nursery	Sex	Age at Interview (Years)
The Ones	A	N	m	19
	B	N	f	19
	C	S	f	21
	D	N	m	19
	F	O	m	20
The Twos	G	S	f	23
	H	N	m	21
	J	N	f	21
	K	E	f	21
	L	E	m	22
The Threes	M	E	f	20
	P	E	m	22
	Q	S	m	24
	R	N	f	23
	T	E	m	23
The Four-Pluses	V	N	m	23
	W	E	m	24
	X	E	m	21
	Y	S	m	26
	Z	S	f	26

There were three pairs of siblings—two sisters, two brothers, and a brother and a sister. My tabulation of numbers of siblings in their families and the ordinal position of the persons studied indicates a range from two only children to the third of nine children. The 20 occupy 13 different sibling statuses.[7] When interviewed, all but one of the subjects were living either with their parents or with their spouse and children. In 16 cases both parents were still alive, and 15 couples were still living together.

The subjects' ages at separation and placement ranged from 2 months to 61 months, clustered, by design, in the 4 age-at-separation groups previously described. Overall length of placement in the nurseries ranged from 12 months to 50 months, with just over 3 years as the midpoint. As might be expected, the younger the child at placement, the longer his stay was likely to be, though in a few cases this relationship was violated (e.g., a Two who stayed just 12 months and a Four-plus who stayed over 50 months).

While all of these young adults returned to their families during their growing-up years, two of the Ones and one Four-plus spent four or more years in a boarding school, a training school, or an institution for deprived children subsequent to their wartime placements, and one other Four-plus, before returning to her family, finished out the war years in a series of nonrelative family billets. In summary, three of the Ones, all of the Twos, all of the Threes, and three of the Four-pluses, that is, 16 of the 20, grew up with their families without interruption after their wartime nursery school stay.

REASONS FOR ABSENCE OF A CONTROL GROUP

Finally, I must comment on the absence of a control group in this study. A control group in an investigation of this type and size should, ideally, be matched with the persons being studied, like them on all relevant variables except the independent variable of early childhood separation and placement in a wartime residential nursery. But children who were not evacuated and stayed in London with their families were exposed for many years to the horrors of aerial attack upon London, and children who were evacuated with their mothers experienced the difficulties of being billeted in someone else's house, often as unwelcome guests, often with many changes of billet.

In addition to these two variations, there was another fundamental difference between possible "controls" and the persons studied. In the case of the nursery school children, the parents *had* decided—admittedly under the force of circumstances—to place their children in a nursery. Our earliest interviews with parents suggested that this fact possibly had multiple and dynamic implications reflecting on the parents as personalities and as members of a family group, and especially on their feelings about parental roles. Any control group would have had to have been matched on this criterion, too. Young adults in such a control group would have to have parents who had decided to place their children for their safety, but for some reason did not. Ignoring this variable would have meant that the children's growing-up years in their own families were spent with parents whose orientations to parental roles, at least in the children's preschool years, were probably different in crucial, although difficult to specify, ways.

We discovered one city where an evacuation nursery was planned and applications were filed, but the scheme was not realized. This seemed at first to answer our needs for a control group, but it became clear that growing up in this city after the war was not really similar to growing up in any of the London boroughs in which our 20 persons lived. At this point we abandoned the search for controls.

The plan for study, then, provided four comparison age-at-separation groups and three comparison nursery groups. It seemed to me that the basic questions we asked could be answered by rating against assumed norms for an urban population. Other controls, such as the blind analyses of some of the data, were built into our procedures for study.

Methods of Data Collection and Analysis

I used a direct approach with these 20 adults. I explained that I was a visiting American interested in the care of small children who had had to live away from their parents. Since, for their physical safety, they all had been evacuated during the war, I thought that some things could be learned about such early childhood care if I had a chance to talk with them, primarily about how they were getting along now. Many of them replied in essence that if their participation would help children, they would help us. There was only one exception, a Four-plus who was married and the mother of two children. She completed a first session with my interviewer colleague, Leslie Bell, of The London School of Economics, and then, ostensibly because she was moving and starting a new job, etc., could not arrange a second appointment with me. Confronted with our time limits, she readily agreed to our getting a substitute for her. Our substitute, a Four-plus mother of one child, six months pregnant with her second, was an alumna of the same nursery school. She and all the others kept every appointment, in one case as many as five.

The questions we asked about the adjustment of these young adults were formulated in the light of the literature on early childhood separation. This literature predicts that damage would be manifest in five areas: First, *feeling life* would suffer—apathy, inability to express feelings, narcissism, depression, and/or low self-esteem would be more apparent than their opposites on each continuum. Second, assessment of *inner controls* would reveal extremes of impulsiveness or overcontrol; lack of manifest anxiety or an excess of this; antisocial proclivities or overconforming rigidity; and/or extremes in orientations to pleasure, achievement, and short-term goals. Third, *relationships with people* would be characterized by lack of emotional attachment, social isolation, shallowness, short duration, receptive dependency, distrustfulness, noninitiating passivity, and/or sexual inappropriateness. Fourth, *performance in key social roles,* as, for example, son, daughter, husband, wife, parent, employee, friend, would be characterized by lack of involvement and/or inadequacy. Fifth, *intellectual functioning* would tend to be low and/or unstable. (Chart 9.1).

INTERVIEW METHODS

To provide data for rating each of the 20 adults on a 5-point scale for each of 24 items dealing with the 5 major variables, Leslie Bell and I interviewed and tested the young adults, interviewed their parents, and consulted collateral agency records. A case folder on each participant was then submitted for rating to James Robertson and his wife, of the Tavistock and Hampstead clinics, respectively.

───────────────(Case)   (Rater)───────────────

1. *Feelings* (Write X on one of 5 dashes, or circle ? for "Don't know")
   a. apathetic (lacking feelings)   ─ ─ ─ ─ ─ ? vital (alive)
   b. repressive (unable to express) ─ ─ ─ ─ ─ ? spontaneous (free)
   c. narcissistic (self-centered)   ─ ─ ─ ─ ─ ? altruistic (outgoing)
   d. pessimistic (depressive)   ─ ─ ─ ─ ─ ? optimistic (happy)
   e. low self-esteem   ─ ─ ─ ─ ─ ? high self-esteem

2. *Inner controls* (X one of 5 dashes, or circle ? "Don't know")

   a. impulsive, acting out   ─ ─ ─ ─ ─ ? overcontrolled
   b. no anxiety, guiltless   ─ ─ ─ ─ ─ ? anxiety laden, guilty
   c. antisocial   ─ ─ ─ ─ ─ ? over conforming
   d. low achievement orientation   ─ ─ ─ ─ ─ ? high achievement orientation
   e. high pleasure orientation   ─ ─ ─ ─ ─ ? low pleasure orientation
   f. short-term goals   ─ ─ ─ ─ ─ ? long-range goals

3. *Relationships with people.* (For relationship with mother, write *m;* father, *f;* sib, *s;* husband or fiance, *h;* wife or fiancee, *w;* child(ren), *c;* employer, *e;* friend, *f; other, o.* Write appropriate letter, wherever evidence permits.)
   a. emotionally unattached   ─ ─ ─ ─ ─ ? emotionally attached
   b. socially isolated   ─ ─ ─ ─ ─ ? socially belonging
   c. shallow   ─ ─ ─ ─ ─ ? deep
   d. short-term   ─ ─ ─ ─ ─ ? long-term
   e. receptive (dependent)   ─ ─ ─ ─ ─ ? giving
   f. hostile, distrustful   ─ ─ ─ ─ ─ ? friendly, trusting
   g. passive, non-initiating   ─ ─ ─ ─ ─ ? aggressive, initiating
   h. sexually inappropriate   ─ ─ ─ ─ ─ ? sexually appropriate

4. *Role performances* (For role of son, *s;* daughter, *d;* husband, *h;* wife, *w;* parent, *p;* employee, *e;* friend, *fr;* recreation time, *r;* citizen, *c.*)
   a. uninvolved, unmotivated   ─ ─ ─ ─ ─ ? involved, identified in
   b. sees self as inadequate in role ─ ─ ─ ─ ─ ? sees self as adequate
   c. seen as inadequate by others in
      role   ─ ─ ─ ─ ─ ? seen as adequate by others

5. *Intellectual functioning* (X one of 5, or circle ? as in 1 & 2 above.)
   a. low functioning (manifest)   ─ ─ ─ ─ ─ ? high level functioning
   b. uneven functioning   ─ ─ ─ ─ ─ ? stable functioning

CHART 9.1.   *Case rating sheet*

Using a minimum of structure for the interviews, we asked for certain face-sheet data and facts about the chronology of living arrangements, and then for material on work history, leisure-time interests, most recent school experience, and family life (both family of origin and marital family). We cut across these life areas with our questions about the areas of predicted failure listed above. In addition to the interview, each person was asked to tell stories in response to 14 Thematic Apperception Test (TAT) cards, and 10—5 men and 5 women—completed the California Psychological Inventory.[8] The number of interview sessions with each person, the hours for each session, and the informal situations in which we met varied considerably. We saw 14 subjects interacting with their own parents, 4 with spouses and own children or fiances. We had an informal dinner, tea, or a pub snack and bitters with about half of them. With 15, we walked from office to home or from either to the underground station. Observation as well as tests and interviews seemed important as sources of data.

We also arranged visits with the parents of all but 2 of the 20.[9] We hoped that their memories would provide us with useful data on the children's earliest days, their leavetaking, and homecoming, but these hopes were rarely fulfilled. Asked to tell what her son was like when he returned home, one harried East End mother of six replied, "He'd had a haircut," and nothing more could be evoked. A less pressed and better educated mother had more vivid recollections of her own reactions at her son's departure than of his. After the bus left, she said, "I went cycling all day long—not to be back in this empty house." Home visits to the parents did, however, provide independent evidence of the young adults' current adjustment. In addition, these were invaluable opportunities to observe family life and the behavior of parents and siblings together. But if any early damage had occurred, we got essentially no evidence from the parents to describe it.

A final source of information was the records of social and medical agencies and the nurseries themselves. Of the 20 adults, 9 grew up in the East End. The district office of the Children's Department that had full records on all dependent and delinquent children in its area screened the nine names provided and made folders available. These folders amplified details of the material previously given by the young adults and their parents, but in no case did they reveal any inaccuracies. Specifically, four of the nine had told me in the interviews of episodes that led me to believe the Children's Department would have a file on their family, but the other five described no such episodes. These five were unknown to the Children's Department. Records on the other four essentially corroborated what they had told me: in one case a bicycle theft at age 11, and in the other facts about the dependency or sexual or other delinquencies of siblings in their families. Records from another social agency and from two medical facilities similarly substantiated what our subjects or their parents had said. All this confirming evidence suggests the validity of the interview data. It seems that an American visiting for a year is a safe recipient of London secrets. Or, perhaps an opportunity to talk honestly about one's self in our times is still all too rare to miss.

ANALYSIS CONTROLS

As another control on the data and their analysis, each respondent's TAT stories were sent for blind analysis to George A. De Vos, a psychologist on the University of California faculty and a specialist in projective tests and in the fields of personality and culture, and delinquency. He was given no more information about each case than age and sex. Although he knew of the problem for investigation, he knew nothing about the sources of cases, their separation ages, or which might be "controls" or "experimental" cases.

Since ratings of case material may, of course, prove unstable even when made consensually, as the Robertsons worked, by corating, a table of random numbers was used to draw five cases for rerating. Norma Haan, of the Institute of Human Development, University of California, Berkeley, rerated them. There were two women and three men; one One, two Twos, one Three, and one Four-plus; one from Nursery N, two from Nursery E, and two from Nursery S. The analyses were examined for agreement in the same dichotomous intervals that were used as the basis for findings in this report, and the ratings agreed on a case-by-case basis in a range from 69 percent to over 90 percent. For the 5 variables, agreement was 76 percent on *feelings,* 75 percent on *inner controls,* 76 percent on *personal relationships,* 92 percent on *role performance,* and 80 percent on *intellectual functioning.*

One procedure for analyzing the ratings is to compare them with a typical metropolitan population. It was arbitrarily assumed that clinicians would rate a typical population on 5-point scales in a 5 percent–20 percent–50 percent–20 percent–5 percent distribution. Thus, references to this metropolitan population are to persons for whom 50 percent of the ratings fall in the central interval, with lower and upper quartiles below and above. We tested the observed rating frequencies against this expected distribution (Table 9.2). Our findings include comparisons of the four age-at-separation groups, on each of the five psychosocial variables studied, and contrasts of the three nursery groups.

Findings

We are now ready to consider some of the findings and to offer a few interpretations and some questions for further study. We found the following.

1. Although these 20 young adults may have been seriously damaged by their early childhood separation and residential nursery experiences, most of them give no evidence in young adulthood of any extreme aberrant reactions. There are no ratings at the extremes for 12 of the 20, and 15 have fewer than 10 percent of their total ratings at the extremes.[10] To this extent, the data support assumptions about the resiliency, plasticity, and modifiability of the human organism rather than those about the irreversibility of the effects of early experience.

2. Where there is evidence in individual cases of aberrancy in the adjustment of these young adults, in almost every case the data on their families seem sufficient to explain it. Although our design called for the inclusion only of persons from intact families without gross pathology, as the families

became better known, so did their disabilities. In the final section of this paper, the nature of some of these families, in relation to their surrender of preschool children, is described. At this point, however, it should be noted that, far from permitting the reversibility of early damage, growing up in some of these families might well have given reinforcement to it; and that, seen against their family and neighborhood backgrounds, a few of these young adults give vivid testimony to the strengths that are either inherent in them or were initially developed during years that included their nursery experiences.

3. The data do support the prediction that children placed in residential group care during the first year of life will show evidence of damage in their young adult years. Every test shows that this age group fared the worst of the four groups. (Details on the Ones appear later in this paper.) The family data, however, indicate parenting problems in this group that cannot be ignored in explanations of these young adults' adjustment.

4. None of the evidence from the Four-plus group supports the prediction that separation and group care starting at this period are followed by enduring damage that is evident in young adulthood.[11]

5. The Twos fared quite well, better than the Threes, differing from our metropolitan population on only one of the five psychosocial variables. Possible explanations for the difference between these two age-at-separation groups are offered later, since this fact raises questions about the assumed linear relationship between age at separation (and group residential care) and the extent of enduring damage. In other words, these findings do not support the assumption that the earlier the child is separated, the more permanent is the damage to the child.

With these basic findings as a background, some facts about work and love in the total group are relevant. When interviewed, 17 of the 20 were gainfully employed in the London labor market, 2 were married women and mothers who had good employment histories, and the 20th was a university student in her last year of training as a teacher. In four or five cases, at most, could job histories be characterized as unstable. Occupations for the men ranged from an industrial engineer, who was graduated from Oxford, to a dustman. Half of the 12 young men were employed at trades for which they had begun apprenticeships on leaving school at age 15, and 5 were employed in unskilled jobs. The unmarried women's jobs were file clerk, typist, switchboard operator, waitress, and tailor. Work seemed important to the young people, and it was an obvious source of satisfaction to most of them. It was manifestly a drain and merely a means of income for only four, and one of these had applied and been accepted at a university after three-and-a-half years of secretarial work, which she had found tedious. Out of a total of 43 ratings made by the Robertsons and Mrs. Haan on involvement and

TABLE 9.2. *Distribution of ratings on five-step scale, by psychosocial variable and age group*

Age Group	Five-Step Frequencies					Dichotomies for Testing*		Probability
	Variable 1: Feelings					*Low*	*Normal & Above*	*Probability*
I	20	—	5	—	—	20	5	p < .001
II	5	1	14	5	—	6	19	n.s.
III	15	—	8	1	—	15	9	p < .001
IV	2	—	17	5	—	2	22	n.s.
	Variable 2: Inner Controls (a)					*Low*	*Normal & Above*	*Probability*
I	15	—	5	5	1	15	11	p < .001
II	7	—	16	7	—	7	23	n.s.
III	5	—	11	10	—	5	21	n.s.
IV	6	—	21	3	—	6	24	n.s.
	Variable 2: Inner Controls (b)					*Normal & Below*	*High*	*Probability*
I	15	—	5	5	1	20	6	n.s.
II	7	—	16	7	—	23	7	n.s.
III	5	—	11	10	—	16	10	n.s. (p ≅ .10)
IV	6	—	21	3	—	27	3	n.s.
	Variable 3: Relationships					*Low*	*Normal & Above*	*Probability*
I	21	47	13	3	—	68	16	p < .001
II	7	37	75	9	—	44	84	p < .02
III	17	48	66	4	—	65	70	p < .001
IV	—	29	70	9	—	29	79	n.s.

Variable 4: Role Performance

						Low	Normal & Above	Probability
I	9	9	8	1	1	18	10	p< .001
II	—	12	21	9	—	12	30	n.s.
III	5	9	22	1	—	14	23	n.s.
IV	—	8	21	10	—	8	31	n.s.

Variable 5: Intellectual Functioning

						Low	Normal & Above	Probability
I	—	5	2	1	2	5	3	p< .02
II	—	1	5	1	—	1	8	n.s.
III	—	3	4	3	—	3	7	n.s.
IV	—	1	7	2	—	1	9	n.s.

* Tested against expected distributions of 5%, 20%, 50%, 20%, 5%, or, as dichotomized, 25% and 75%, with values smaller than those required for .05 level considered non-significant (n.s.).

feelings of adequacy at work, "normal and above" accounted for 35 ratings, or 81 percent. To this extent, the group made an occupational investment and a socially responsible contribution.

Love seems more difficult than work for a research person to assess (The data on *feeling life* and *relationships,* to be presented shortly, bear on this topic.) Two of the women and one of the men were enjoying marriage and had parented a total of seven children. Another 6 of the 20 had set dates for their marriages. Three had what American teenagers call "steadies." Only four seemed at the time of interviews to be "unattached" by plan, and four others were between attachments. In a country where, as of 1959, the average age at marriage for men was 25 years, and for women, 23 years,[12] this group of 19- to 26-year-olds seems well on schedule.

RATINGS ON VARIABLES BY AGE AT SEPARATION

Analysis of ratings on the five variables is, however, more revealing.

1. *Personal relationships* present some problems in three age groups, but not for the Four-pluses. That is, ratings on this variable differ significantly from the normal metropolitan population for the Ones, the Twos, and the Threes, but not ratings at the very bottom extreme for the Twos.

2. *Feeling life,* for the Ones and the Threes is less vital, spontaneous, and outgoing than it is for more normal groups, such as the Twos and the Fours.

3. The evidence that is available on *intellectual functioning* fails to indicate retardation or instability for any group but the Ones.

4. The *role performance* ratings indicate that all but the Ones are performing key social roles with involvement and feelings of adequacy that lie within the expected distribution.

5. Problems with *inner controls* fail to appear in the pattern predicted by the separation literature for any group but the Ones. The Twos and the Four-pluses are rated within a normal distribution for inner controls. The Ones alone present a group picture of somewhat greater impulsiveness. The Threes also show a group tendency to differ, approaching the .10 level of significance, but in the direction of above normal control and conformity.

In summary then, the ratings indicate that relationships are some problem for all but the Four-plus group. The other variables present a scattering of age-differentiated findings that principally involve the Ones, who emerge as the lowest rated group on all variables. The Four-pluses pass on all tests, and the Twos are a better adjusted group than the Threes.

RATINGS BY NURSERY

There are also findings on these young adults as alumni of the three quite different wartime nurseries. For this analysis, the Ones were eliminated because

Nursery E is unrepresented and Nursery N is overrepresented in this age group. This leaves only 15 cases, but there are 176 to 277 ratings for each nursery group (Table 9.3). Examination of these ratings by nursery group reveals that the graduates of the somewhat firm, if not stern, and suppressive small Welsh Nursery E appear as young adults to be essentially no better or worse adjusted than the graduates of the psychologically sophisticated and much larger Nursery N. The group that is clearly the best off is the one from the day nursery school evacuated as a unit—Nursery S, with its faith in God, King, and denial and its rather inspirational, repressive, and posses- sive approach to the children.

TABLE 9.3. *Comparison of three Nursery Groups by summated frequen- cies of ratings on five-step scale*

Nursery	Rating Frequencies					Total
N	11	54	78	31	2	176
4 cases	6%	31%	44%*	18%	1%	100%
E	19	116	126	16	—	277
7 cases	7%	42%	45%*	6%	—	100%
S	—	18	175	32	—	225†
4 cases	—	8%	78%*	14%	—	100%

* 50 percent of ratings expected in "normal" central step.

† There are a larger number of ratings per case for Nursery S than for other two nurseries because the three married adults in the study, all parents, were in this group. They thus had more "relationships" and "roles" to rate, and therefore more ratings.

Some Questions and Interpretations

A study of only 20 persons, though relatively intensive, cannot provide a sound base for contributions to agency program planning. Rather, such a study may help sharpen questions about assumptions that underlie practice. Therefore, I shall further examine three issues: the superior adjustment of Nursery S graduates, the better adjustment of the Twos than of the Threes, and the matter of family background, especially among the Ones.

SUPERIOR ADJUSTMENT OF NURSERY S GROUP

The procedure of group residential placement following a period of day care, where children come to know the other children involved and the adults in charge, is unusual. At a day care nursery school, teachers and working mothers meet to discuss childrearing and child-care problems, and some awareness of each others' values is communicated. Continuity in way of life and in personal relationships for the children between their day care and their residential group is provided for. "For the infant and young child," as Yarrow (1961) says, "changes result in a loss of environmental predictability. The degree of stress involved is likely to vary with the degree of unpredictability [p. 481]." The Nursery S placement plan seems to reduce the unpredictability of residential care. Whether this arrangement alone induces results such as the superior adjustment of Nursery S children would seem to warrant further study.

SUPERIOR ADJUSTMENT OF THE TWOS

Why should the Twos have fared better than the Threes? The range and average number of years they were separated are similar, midpoints of just under three years. In both age groups, coincidentally, there are three persons who had older siblings present at their residential nursery, and in each group there is one sibling who was the elder sibling at the nursery. During the study the data suggested that younger siblings fared well to the detriment of elder sibs, but later analysis failed to support this proposition any more than it supported the proposition that children placed as sibling units do better than children placed apart from their siblings. Development theory suggests that two-year-olds are closer to the autonomy phase, to use Erikson's (1950, pp. 222–26) term, than are three-year-olds, who are beginning to be more involved in Oedipal alignments with parents. The Threes also seem cognitively better equipped to understand—and misunderstand—the whys of separation than are the Twos. These developmental differences probably contributed significantly to the findings of this study, but we have no data available that help to indicate just how.[13]

Another plausible explanation, however, involves the manifest disturbances in three of the five families in each of these two age groups. Did earlier removal of the Twos than of the Threes give them a sounder base for coping with familial strife upon their return home? Since in the families of both age groups there are unevacuated younger siblings who seem more troubled than the once-separated persons in this study, questions about the families as causal agents are appropriate. The inference is that separation from such troubled families at age two may be preferable to separation at age three because by that time greater damage has been inflicted on the child. This proposition might be tested on sibling groups in institutional or foster family care.

HOME LIFE OF THE ONES

If the Twos fared better than the Threes because of earlier separation, why then did the Ones not fare better still? They were the earliest separated of all and from troubled parental situations in every case. As young adults, however, the Ones fared the worst of the four age groups. But here the issues of when the damage first occurred, its irreversibility, and its reinforcement seem hopelessly confounded. When did it first occur? Nursery N's longitudinal records, written while the children were in residence, describe three of the Ones. They tell vividly of A's slow motor, language, and social development (because of congenital defect, birth injury, or separation?); of B's growth from a peaked, birdlike two-month-old at arrival into a willful, active child; of D's excellent physical development and voracious eating, and other not unusual behavior. Except for A's retardation, which is of unknown origin, there is no evidence of gross pathology in any of these records. Only a nursery staff member's memories of F as a wild, unmanageable under-five foreshadow reports on his later markedly regressive behavior at about age eight. During the intervening years he had returned home to what is probably the most aberrant family situation among the 20 persons studied.

Why are the Ones the worst off as young adults? They were not only the earliest separated, but also, except for C, the earliest to return to their own parents. What can be said about the families in which the Ones grew up? I present just a few observations on four of the families to indicate why I question whether the Ones are the most damaged group by far because they were irreversibly scarred during early separation, or whether their multiple adjustment problems were induced or reinforced by their post-nursery school lives in their relationships with such parents as these.

A's mother, widowed since A was 12, lives in a tiny East End flat, sharing a bedroom with the boy, now 19, her only child. She had kept her husband waiting as a suitor for 12 years before they married, ostensibly because of her relationship with her own mother. She reminisced, "But from the moment we were married, it was wrong from the first time." The symbiotic bond between Mrs. A and her son today follows upon Nursery N's early descriptions of her regular weekend visits. But despite requests that she take him home because he was such a slow developer, she did not do so until Nursery N closed down. The role of mother to infant and preschool children seems to have been impossible for this simple, immature woman to have performed effectually, as was the role of wife. She could not engage in either of the differing kinds of mutuality required for each role.

For Mrs. A, her son in his infant and preschool years was a body to be fed and protected by someone else. A spoke of his growing-up years in terms of illnesses, outpatient visits to the hospital, and physical impediments to relationships with his peers. Mrs. A's attentions in those years were constantly focused on an unable body. Mrs. A still devotes herself to feeding and protecting this body, although A at 19 is a large 6-footer.

B grew up with her immediate family in a house owned and occupied by maternal grandparents. A brief excerpt from Nursery N's wartime records reads: "When Mrs. B arrived, B started to cry immediately. Her mother picked her up but B cried more and more. Perhaps the ill baby who vomitted so easily could not stand the mother's rocking; perhaps B felt her mother's anxiousness. B got restless each time her mother came to see her. . . . It was hard to feel the disappointment of the kind, shy woman who never complained."

Leslie Bell's impressions of Mrs. B, almost 20 years later, were that she was "very naïve and unintrospective in her observations of her children," and that her early difficulties in feeding B before she placed her in Nursery N at 2 months could not have been a matter merely of her being simple. Even though she is deeply indebted to Nursery N, Mrs. B still feels B became spoiled and willful there, and accounts for the difficulties in their relationship with this idea.

C's mother, an extremely intelligent woman, was outspokenly troubled by her inability to reach or understand her daughter from her birth to the present day. Mrs. C returned to work soon after C's birth and placed her in a wartime nursery at five months. In talking of C's undemonstrativeness, Mrs. C said that she had not had a mother herself and that, consequently, she found it difficult to show her feelings and to give physical affection. C was kept at boarding school until she was nine. Her father died when she was 11, but she remembers most vividly his scolding her for not getting better school reports. The distance from each other that characterizes the members of this family seems to be a model for C's own underlying remoteness from people.

D's parents, superficially warm, had three repeatedly delinquent children with approved school (correctional institution) histories. D, the youngest, seemed to have escaped such a career by acceding to his obese and hypochondriacal mother's demands and by avoiding a close relationship with his father. Mr. D emerged quite accurately in the blind analysis of D's TAT stories as "a rather passive individual who has borderline conformity to the law . . . a corrupter of the young." In the D family, one finds again parents interested in feeding the child's body but too preoccupied with themselves to be able to give much more than food. The fact that D does not more closely resemble Bowlby's (1946) descriptions of the "affectionless character" may be because he was in placement for 40 months so early in his life. His older siblings, who spent more of their earliest days with these same parents, have far more aberrant histories than D.

Are the shallowness and the restricted nature of the young adult relationships of these Ones and the flatness of their feeling lives an irreversible result of infant separation and early group care? Or have these parents contributed appreciably during the children's growing-up years to these conditions? The available facts provide no basis for conclusive answers.

They do, however, suggest that parents who voluntarily place a child away from home in the first year of life, albeit in a program sanctioned by society and in a time of national crisis, often have limited or distorted feeling lives and relationship capacities for caring for their children. Even in the families of some of the children separated at an older age, parental roles seem ego-alien. Therefore, the effects of separation cannot be considered apart from the family life from which the children were separated and, in the case of the group under study, to which they were returned.

Concluding Comments

With these facts in mind, the good adjustment made by many of these young adults—who grew up in a time of war and unsettling postwar years—is worth pondering. As a group, they attest to the plasticity of human personality and, perhaps, also reflect favorably on their early nursery parent substitutes. Finally, they assure us that, at least from about age two, early childhood separation and preschool residential care are not themselves *sufficient* antecedents to a seriously troubled or troublesome young adulthood.

NOTES

1. *Author's note:* This study was done with the help of a small grant from the Institute of Social Sciences, University of California, Berkeley. During the data-gathering phase, 1960–61, the writer was studying on a Special Research Fellowship from the National Institute of Mental Health, U.S. Public Health Service, as a Visiting Member, The London School of Economics and Political Science, University of London. His indebtedness to his sponsor, Professor R. M. Titmuss, and the many others in England who helped to make this study possible obviously cannot find adequate expression in this note.

2. During 1961, two critical reviews of this extensive literature were published—Yarrow (1961) and Casler (1961).

3. Heinicke's (1956) comparative study of six residential nursery children and seven day nursery children is of this order.

4. See Factor II–a, p. 128, and Factor III–b, p. 134 (Fanshel and Maas 1962).

5. Note, additionally, that in the mimeographed "aftercare" newsletters from the Hampstead Nurseries, circulated through Foster Parents' Plan for War Children, Inc., New York, one finds the following observation as reported "by Mrs. Hansi Kennedy, a former worker in the Hampstead Nurseries." "Bridget came to the Nursery in 1941, when she was 9 months old, and returned home shortly before her 5th birthday. . . . She . . . suffered acutely by Nursery life and the separation from her mother. . . . In Bridget's case, the absence of normal family-life in the first 5 years has so far shown no unfavorable after-effects; she has settled down well in her home surroundings and developed normally during the 6 years since her return home. It is however important to see whether this progress will be maintained during pre-adolescence and adolescence." *Hampstead Nurseries After-Care Ninth Half-Yearly Report, April, 1951* (New York: Foster Parents Plan for War Children, 1951), pp. 1 and 6.

6. All direct quotations regarding the nurseries are from interviews with the persons in charge.

7. As the sibling statuses and family size happen to be quite evenly represented among the four age-at-separation groups and the three nursery groups, so, I assume, are many other less readily describable family variables. Specifically, in reference to sibling status among the 20 persons, there are 2 only children (A,V); 3 who are the first of 2 (F,H,W); 4 who are the second of 2 (C,K,T,Z); 2 who are the fourth of 6 (G,J); and 1 each of the following: first of 3 (Q), second of 3 (B), third of 4 (M), fourth of 4 (Y), fifth of 5 (D), second of 6 (P) third of 6 (R), second of 9 (L), and third of 9 (X). Defining small families as one- or two-child units and large families as those having three or more children, we find that each age-at-separation group has two or three small and large families, except for the Threes, who split one and four. Nursery N splits three and four; Nursery E, three and four; Nursery S, two and three. Similarly, top, middle, and bottom statuses are quite evenly distributed among age and nursery groups.

There is, however, one aspect of family life not evenly distributed. All four parents who were widowed by 1960–61 were confined to the Ones. A's father died when he was 12, C's when she was 11, and B has no memory of her father, who died during the second year after her return home. B grew up with her mother and two siblings, however, in a house owned by the maternal grandparents, and the grandfather was described as an attentive and indulgent father surrogate. Also among the Ones is F, whose father's date of death is unknown. By the time of the interviews, his mother was remarried, with a "new family," and F was completely alienated from her.

8. The CPI's had not been analyzed when the case folders were submitted for rating. Therefore, the CPI data are not included in this report.

9. In F's case, he was the only one of the 20 alienated from his mother. For this reason we did not arrange an interview with her, but drew as extensively as possible upon medical and social agency collateral material. The other parents not interviewed were Z's, who was the late substitute for the Four-plus we "lost." We did, however, interview Z's husband, and obtained a picture of Z's relationships with her parents and sibling that was documented by recent photographs. Although Y's parents were separated (the father moved out when Y was about 17), they still saw each other and we interviewed them both.

10. More specifically, there were no ratings at the lowest extreme on *intellectual functioning* for any of the 20, no ratings at the extremes of *feelings* or *inner controls* for 19 cases, on *role performance* for 14 cases, on *relationships* for 12 cases. Compare Yarrow's (1961) summary statement of findings—albeit largely "clinical impressions"—on the social and personality disturbances of institutionalized children: ". . . characteristics described are usually at the extreme end of the scale, reflecting exaggerated pathology or a complete lack of capacity, rather than a relative deficiency [p. 468]."

11. This finding is not a function of shorter periods of separation from family for this age group, since V was in the nursery for 50 months, and 2 others, Z and X, had subsequent periods of separation from family of 5 and 7 years.

12. *The Registrar General's Statistical Review of England and Wales for the Year 1959,* Part II (London: Her Majesty's Stationary Office, 1960), Table L, p. 72.

13. Findings that the Threes included some of the most overcontrolled and overconforming of the young adults studied suggest that identifications occurred in the course of early development among these persons although the parent figures present were not their own parents. The extent to which these more rigid ego controls were patterned after nursery staff adults, or developed in response to the institutional children's groups with whom they spent their early years—from about three years until school age—is a nice question for study. Are children who begin residential group life at about age three, among age-mates with whom they pass through the Oedipal period, more likely to be overcontrolled and conforming than children who do not spend these years in group residential life or who begin it much earlier or much later?

10

Adult Status of Children with Contrasting Early Life Experiences

HAROLD M. SKEELS

A growth-promoting environment may be the result of planned and carefully contrived conditions. Caldwell and Richmond (1964), for example, describe the implementation of a specific conceptual model based on theoretical assumptions and a maximum of available research evidence; Gewirtz (1968) and others also have approached the issue of optimal environment from that direction. Obtaining a good environment for the young child in this manner is highly probable and economic providing the variables that underlie such a milieu are well defined, the optimal position on each and their interrelationships are known and are amenable to construction in a given society at a given time. Russian claims and actions notwithstanding (see Chauncey, 1969), many have asserted and some still would argue that such conditions do not yet obtain. In the circumstances the most likely route is variability and experimentation, which, given our very reasonable caution in regard to contrived social environments, will tend to exploit existing social situations that offer some (or most) of the milieu conditions known from research and/or clinical experience as exerting positive influence on the child. Skeels' work, a classic example of utilization of a naturally positive situation, is all the more instructive for having a serendipitous quality to it. While Skeels (in the 1930s) was surprised that placement in an institution with adult retardates should have promoted growth of children aged six months to four years, we ought not be if we compare the qualities of his program

with Caldwell's (1967b) "characteristics of growth-fostering environments."
Nor did Skeels remain puzzled after he examined what the institution for retardates offered the young children he placed there—despite its label and
despite his obvious and understandable reluctance to make use of this facility.

Introduction

The present study is a report on the status as adults of two groups of children originally encountered in the Iowa institutions. One group experienced
what was then regarded as the normal course of events in a child-caring institution, while the other experienced a specifically designed and implemented intervention program. Reports on the development of these children have
appeared in two previous publications. The first (Skeels and Dye 1939) described the original experimental period, and the second (Skeels 1942) reported a follow-up some two years later. The study was not planned nor the
data gathered in a way to form the basis for studies of personality structure
in depth. The findings reported here, therefore, are concerned with the question of whether and for how long a time mental development is affected by
major changes in early environment and, specifically, with the factors significantly associated with deflections in mental development. It is hoped that
these findings will contribute to the growing body of evidence on the effects
of deprivation and poverty on the young child's ability to learn.

The Original Study

All the children in this study had become wards of the orphanage through
established court procedures after no next of kin was found able to provide
either support or suitable guardianship. Of the 25 children, 20 were illegitimate and the remainder had been separated from their parents because of
evidence of severe neglect and/or abuse. Then as now, the courts were reluctant to sever the ties between child and parents and did so only when
clearly presented with no other alternative. All the children were white and
of north-European background.

The orphanage in which the children were placed occupied, with a few
exceptions, buildings that had first served as a hospital and barracks during
the Civil War. The institution was overcrowded and understaffed. By present standards, diet, sanitation, general care, and basic philosophy of operation were censurable. At the time of the study, however, the discrepancies
between conditions in the institution and in the general community were not
so great and were not always to the disadvantage of the institution. Over the
past 30 years, administrative and physical changes have occurred that reflect
the economic and social gains of our society. The description of conditions
in the institution in the 1930s, therefore, does not apply to the present.

At the time the original study was begun, infants up to the age of two years were housed in the hospital, then a relatively new building. Until about six months, they were cared for in the infant nursery. The babies were kept in standard hospital cribs that often had protective sheeting on the sides, thus effectively limiting visual stimulation; no toys or other objects were hung in the infants' line of vision. Human interactions were limited to busy nurses who, with the speed born of practice and necessity, changed diapers or bedding, bathed and medicated the infants, and fed them efficiently with propped bottles.

Older infants, from about 6 to 24 months, were moved into small dormitories containing two to five large cribs. This arrangement permitted the infants to move about a little and to interact somewhat with those in neighboring cribs. The children were cared for by 2 nurses with some assistance from 1 or 2 girls, 10 to 15 years old, who regarded the assignment as an unwelcome chore. The children had good physical and medical care, but little can be said beyond this. Interactions with adults were largely limited to feeding, dressing, and toilet details. Few play materials were available, and there was little time for the teaching of play techniques. Most of the children had a brief play period on the floor; a few toys were available at the beginning of such periods, but if any rolled out of reach there was no one to retrieve it. Except for short walks out of doors, the children were seldom out of the nursery room.

At two years of age these children were graduated to the cottages, which had been built around 1860. A rather complete description of "cottage" life is reported by Skeels et al. (1938) from which the following excerpts are taken.

> Overcrowding of living facilities was characteristic. Too many children had to be accommodated in the available space and there were too few adults to guide them. . . . Thirty to thirty-five children of the same sex under six years of age lived in a "cottage" in charge of one matron and three or four entirely untrained and often reluctant girls of thirteen to fifteen years of age. The waking and sleeping hours of these children were spent (except during meal times and a little time on a grass plot) in an average-sized room (approximately fifteen feet square), a sunporch of similar size, a cloakroom, . . . and a single dormitory. The latter was occupied only during sleeping hours. The meals for all children in the orphanage were served in a central building in a single large dining room. . . .
>
> The duties falling to the lot of the matron were not only those involved in the care of the children but those related to clothing and cottage maintenance, in other words, cleaning, mending, and so forth. . . . With so much responsibility centered in one adult the result was a necessary regimentation. The children sat down, stood up, and did many things in rows and in unison. They spent considerable time sitting on chairs, for in addition to the number of children and the matron's limited time there was the misfortune of inadequate equipment. . . .

No child had any property which belonged exclusively to him except, perhaps, his tooth brush. Even his clothing, including shoes, was selected and put
on him according to size [pp. 10–11].

After a child reached the age of six years, he began school. His associates
were his cottage mates and the children of the same age and opposite sex
who lived on the other side of the institution grounds. Although the curriculum was ostensibly the same as that in the local public school, it was generally agreed that the standards were adjusted to the capabilities of the orphanage children. Few of those who had their entire elementary-school
experience in the institution's school were able to make the transition to the
public junior high school.

The orphanage was designed for mentally normal children. It was perpet-
ually overcrowded, although every opportunity to relieve this pressure was
exploited. One such relief occurred periodically when new buildings were
opened at other institutions, such as at the schools for the mentally retarded.
It was not uncommon for a busload of children to be transferred on such occasions. A valued contribution of the psychologists was the maintenance of
lists of children who, on the basis of test scores and observable behavior,
were regarded as eligible for transfers.

The environmental conditions in the two state institutions for the mentally retarded were not identical but they had many things in common. Pa-
tient-inmates were grouped by sex, age, and general ability. Within any one
ward, the patients were highly similar. The youngest children tended to be
the most severely disabled and were frequently "hospital" patients. The older, more competent inmates had work assignments throughout the institution and constituted a somewhat self-conscious elite with recognized status.

Personnel at that time included no resident social workers or psychologists. Physicians were resident at the schools for the mentally retarded and
were on call at the orphanage. Administrative and matron and caretaking
staffs were essentially untrained and nonprofessional. Psychological services
were introduced in the orphanage in 1932 when the author, on the staff of
the Iowa Child Welfare Research Station, State University of Iowa, became
the first psychologist to be employed by the Iowa Board of Control of State
Institutions. Over the years this proved to be a happy marriage of service
and research related to the care of dependent children.

IDENTIFICATION OF CASES

Early in the service aspects of the program, two baby girls, neglected by
their feebleminded mothers, ignored by their inadequate relatives, malnour-
ished and frail, were legally committed to the orphanage. The youngsters
were pitiful little creatures. They were tearful, had runny noses, and sparse,
stringy, and colorless hair; they were emaciated, undersized, and lacked
muscle tonus or responsiveness. Sad and inactive, the two spent their days
rocking and whining.

The psychological examinations showed developmental levels of 6 and 7 months, respectively, for the two girls, although they were then 13 and 16 months old chronologically. This serious delay in mental growth was confirmed by observations of their behavior in the nursery and by reports of the superintendent of nurses, as well as by the pediatrician's examination. There was no evidence of physiological or organic defect, or of birth injury or glandular dysfunction.

The two children were considered unplaceable, and transfer to a school for the mentally retarded was recommended with a high degree of confidence. Accordingly, they were transferred to an institution for the mentally retarded at the next available vacancy, when they were aged 15 and 18 months, respectively.

In the meantime, the author's professional responsibilities had been increased to include itinerant psychological services to the two state institutions for the mentally retarded. Six months after the transfer of the two children, he was visiting the wards at an institution for the mentally retarded and noticed two outstanding little girls. They were alert, smiling, running about, responding to the playful attention of adults, and generally behaving and looking like any other toddlers. He scarcely recognized them as the two little girls with the hopeless prognosis, and thereupon tested them again. Although the results indicated that the two were approaching normal mental development for age, the author was skeptical of the validity or permanence of the improvement and no change was instituted in the lives of the children. Twelve months later they were reexamined, and then again when they were 40 and 43 months old. Each examination gave unmistakable evidence of mental development well within the normal range for age.

There was no question that the initial evaluations gave a true picture of the children's functioning level at the time they were tested. It appeared equally evident that later appraisals showed normal mental growth accompanied by parallel changes in social growth, emotional maturity, communication skills, and general behavior. In order to find a possible explanation for the changes that had occurred, the nature of the children's life space was reviewed.

The two girls had been placed on one of the wards of older, brighter girls and women, ranging in age from 18 to 50 years and in mental age from 5 to 9 years, where they were the only children of preschool age, except for a few hopeless bed patients with gross physical defects. An older girl on the ward had "adopted" each of the two girls, and other older girls served as adoring aunts. Attendants and nurses also showed affection to the two, spending time with them, taking them along on their days off for automobile rides and shopping excursions, and purchasing toys, picture books, and play materials for them in great abundance. The setting seemed to be a homelike one, abundant in affection, rich in wholesome and interesting experiences, and geared to a preschool level of development.

It was recognized that as the children grew older their developmental needs would be less adequately met in the institution for the mentally retarded. Furthermore, they were now normal and the need for care in such an institution no longer existed. Consequently, they were transferred back to the orphanage and shortly thereafter were placed in adoptive homes.

At this point, evidence on the effects of environment on intelligence had been accumulated from a number of studies. Skeels and Fillmore (1937) had found that older children who came from inadequate nonnurturant homes were mentally retarded or borderline but that their younger siblings were generally of normal ability, which suggested that longer residence in such homes had a cumulatively depressing effect on intelligence. Children also became retarded if they remained for long periods in an institution (1930-style) supposedly designed for normal children (Skeels 1940). However, if children were placed in adoptive homes as infants, or even as young preschoolers, their development surpassed expectations, and improvement continued for long periods following placement (Skodak 1939). In even more extreme cases, seriously retarded children were able to attain normal levels of functioning when placed in a setting officially designed for the mentally retarded (Skeels and Dye 1939). The consistent element seemed to be the existence of a one-to-one relationship with an adult who was generous with love and affection, together with an abundance of attention and experiential stimulation from many sources. Children who had little of these did not show progress; those who had a great deal, did.

Since study homes or temporary care homes were not available to the state agency at that time, the choice for children who were not suitable for immediate placement in adoptive homes was between, on the one hand, an unstimulating, large nursery with predictable mental retardation or, on the other hand, a radical, iconoclastic solution, that is, placement in institutions for the mentally retarded in a bold experiment to see whether retardation in infancy was reversible.

By the time these observations were organized into a meaningful whole and their implications were recognized, individual psychological tests were available for all children in the orphanage. As part of a continuing program of observation and evaluation, all infants over three months of age were given the then-available tests (Kuhlmann-Binet and Iowa Tests for Young Children), and were retested as often as changes seemed to occur. Retests at bimonthly intervals were not uncommon. Older preschoolers were reexamined at 6- to 12-month intervals; school-aged children, annually or biennially. Children who were showing marked delay in development were kept under special observation.

Children whose development was so delayed that adoptive placement was out of the question remained in the orphanage. The only foreseeable alternative for them was eventual transfer to an institution for the mentally retarded. In the light of the experiences with the two little girls, the possibility was raised that early transfer to such an institution might have therapeutic effects. If not all, then at least some of the children might be able to attain normal mental functioning. In the event they did not, no significant change in life pattern would have occurred, and the child would remain in the situation for which he would have been destined in any case.

This radical proposal was accepted with understandable misgivings by the administrators involved. It was finally agreed that, in order to avoid the stigma of commitment to a state school for the retarded, children would be accepted as "house guests" in such institutions but would remain on the official roster of the orphanage. Periodic reevaluations were built into the plan; if no improvement was observed in the child, commitment would follow. Insofar as possible, the children were to be placed on wards as "only" children.

In the course of time, in addition to the two little girls who have been described and another transferred to the second of the two institutions at about the same time, 10 more children became "house guests." The transfers were spaced over a year's span in groups of three, three, and four. All went to one institution for the mentally handicapped, the Glenwood State School. Unfortunately, the number of "house guests" exceeded the number of "elite" wards of older girls and necessitated the use of some environments that were less desirable. Consequently, in some wards there were more children, or fewer capable older girls, or less opportunity for extra stimulation, with a resulting variation in developmental patterns.

EXPERIMENTAL GROUP

The experimental group consisted of the 13 children who were transferred from an orphanage for mentally normal children to an institution for the mentally retarded, as "house guests." All were under three years of age at the time of transfer. Their development had been reliably established as seriously retarded by tests and observation before transfer was considered.

The identification and selection of the children who constituted the experimental group can perhaps be best explained by a description of the procedures that were normally followed. County or welfare agencies, faced with the problem of care for an illegitimate or ward-of-the-court child, applied to the Board of Control and/or the Iowa Soldiers' Orphans' Home, as it was then known. When accepted (rejections occurred rarely and only under most unusual circumstances, such as obvious multiple handicaps identifiable at birth), the child was brought to the institution and placed in the hospital for observation. During the first few days he was given routine medical examinations and was observed for abnormalities or infections, etc. Within two to four weeks after admission he was also given a psychological examination. The legal commitment, available social history, and other information were collated and at the monthly assignment conferences decisions were made regarding the child. These conferences were attended by the superintendent of the institution, the director of the Children's Division of the State Board of Control, and the psychologist. On call also was the head nurse or the pediatrician and any other staff member who could supply pertinent information. If no legal, medical, or developmental impediments to adoptive placement were found, the child was assigned to an adoptive home, largely on the basis of requested sex, coloring, and religious background.

Decisions on the children who were unplaceable for legal, medical, or developmental reasons were reviewed at each subsequent monthly conference until a resolution was attained. Consequently, the children who remained in the pool of unplaced infants or toddlers became very well known to the conference participants.

As the evidence from the research studies accumulated, concern about the future of these children increased and led to the decision that some radical measure was justified. Coincidentally, a change had occurred in the administration of the state institution for the mentally handicapped which created a favorable climate for social experimentation. Those children who happened to be in the infant to three-year-old age range, were not ineligible for placement for legal reasons, were not acutely ill, but who were mentally retarded, became members of the experimental group. The entire project covered a span of some three years and was terminated when a change in the administration of the state school reduced the tolerance for such untidy procedures as having "house guests" in an institution. The onset of World War II and the departure of the principal investigator for military service effectively closed the project.

A project such as this could not be replicated in later years because infants were no longer kept exclusively in the orphanage. Temporary boarding homes came to be utilized prior to adoptive placement or for long-term observation and care.

The experimental group consisted of 10 girls and 3 boys, none with gross physical handicaps. Prior to their placement as "house guests," the examinations were routinely administered to them without any indication that they would or would not be involved in the unusual experience.

At the time of transfer, the mean chronological age of the group was 19.4 months (SD 7.4) and the median was 17.1 months, with a range of from 7.1 to 35.9 months. The range of IQ's was from 35 to 89 with a mean of 64.3 (SD 16.4) and a median of 65.0. Additional tests were made of 11 of the 13 children shortly before or in conjunction with the pretransfer tests reported in Table 10.1, using the Kuhlmann-Binet again or the Iowa Test for Young Children, and the results corroborated the reported scores.

The children were considered unsuitable for adoption because of evident mental retardation. For example, in Case 1, although the IQ was 89, it was felt that actual retardation was much greater, as the child at 7 months could scarcely hold up his head without support and showed little general bodily activity in comparison with other infants of the same age. In Case 3, at 12 months, very little activity was observed, and the child was very unsteady when sitting up without support. She could not pull herself to a standing position and did not creep. Case 11 was not only retarded but showed perseverative patterns of behavior, particularly incessant rocking back and forth. Cases 5, 8, and 13 were classified at the imbecile level. In present-day terms, they would have been labeled "trainable mentally retarded children."

Table 10.1 lists for each child the pretransfer test findings and ages at time of transfer; also shown are posttransfer test results, length of experimental period, and changes in IQ from first to last test.

CONTRAST GROUP

Since the original purpose of the experiment was to rescue for normalcy, if possible, those children showing delayed or retarded development, no plans had been made for a control or comparison group. It was only after the data had been analyzed that it was found that such a contrast group was available because of the tests that were routinely given to all children in the orphanage. To select such a contrast group, therefore, records were scrutinized for children who met the following criteria:

1. Had been given intelligence tests under two years of age.
2. Were still in residence in the orphanage at approximately four years of age.
3. Were in the control group of the orphanage preschool study (Skeels et al. 1938).
4. Had not attended preschool.

The Skeels et al. (1938) study had included two groups of children matched in chronological age, mental age, IQ, and length of residence in the institution, of which one group had the advantages of the more stimulating environment of preschool attendance while the other group, the controls, experienced the less stimulating environment of cottage life. Since the purpose of the contrast group in the present study was to provide data on children in a relatively nonstimulating environment, those who had attended preschool were not included. Such limitations, however, did not constitute a selective factor as far as the characteristics of the children were concerned.

A total of 12 children were selected on the basis of the criteria and became the contrast group. The mean chronological age of the group at the time of first examination was 16.6 months (SD 2.9), with a median at 16.3 months. The range was from 11.9 to 21.8 months. The mean IQ of the group was 86.7 (SD 14.3) and the median IQ was 90. With the exception

TABLE 10.1. *Experimental group: mental development of children as measured by Kuhlmann-Binet Intelligence Tests before and after transfer*

Case Number*	Sex	Before Transfer test 1 chronological age, months	IQ	Chronological Age, Months, at Transfer	After Transfer Test 2 chronological age, months	IQ	Test 3 chronological age, months	IQ	last chronological age, months	IQ	Length of Experimental Period, Months	Change in IQ, First to Last Test
1	M	7.0	89	7.1	12.8	113	...	...	12.8	113	5.7	+24
2	F	12.7	57	13.1	20.5	94	29.4	83	36.8	77	23.7	+20
3	F	12.7	85	13.3	25.2	107	...	...	25.2	107	11.9	+22
4	F	14.7	73	15.0	23.1	100	...	...	23.1	100	8.1	+27
5	F	13.4	46	15.2	21.7	77	32.9	100	40.0	95†	24.8	+49
6	F	15.5	77	15.6	21.3	96	30.1	100	30.1	100	14.5	+23
7	F	16.6	65	17.1	27.5	104	...	...	27.5	104	10.4	+39
8	F	16.6	35	18.4	24.8	87	36.0	88	43.0	93	24.6	+58
9	F	21.8	61	22.0	34.3	80	...	...	34.3	80	12.3	+19
10	M	23.3	72	23.4	29.1	88	37.9	71	45.4	79	22.0	+7
11	M	25.7	75	27.4	42.5	78	51.0	82†	51.0	82†	23.6	+7
12	F	27.9	65	28.4	40.4	82	...	...	40.0	82	12.0	+17
13	F	30.0	36	35.9	51.7	70	81.0	74†	89.0	81†	52.1	+45

* Arranged according to age at time of transfer.
† Stanford-Binet IQ.
SOURCE: Adapted from H. M. Skeels and B. B. Dye (1939, Table 1).

TABLE 10.2. *Contrast group: mental development of children as measured by repeated Kuhlmann-Binet Intelligence Tests over an average experimental period of two-and-one-half years*

Case Number*	Sex	Test 1		Test 2		Test 3		last		Length of Experimental Period, Months	Change in IQ, First to Last Test
		chronological age, months	IQ	chronological age, months	IQ	chronological age, months	IQ	chronological age, months	IQ		
14	F	11.9	91	24.8	73	37.5	65	55.0	62	43.1	−29
15	F	13.0	92	20.1	54	38.3	56	38.3	56	25.3	−36
16	F	13.6	71	20.6	76	40.9	56	40.9	56	27.3	−15
17	M	13.8	96	37.2	58	53.2	54	53.2	54	39.4	−42
18	M	14.5	99	21.6	67	41.9	54	41.9	54	27.4	−45
19	M	15.2	87	22.5	80	35.5	74	44.5	67	29.3	−20
20	M	17.3	81	43.0	77	52.9	83†	52.9	83†	35.6	+ 2
21	M	17.5	103	26.8	72	38.0	63	50.3	60	32.8	−43
22	M	18.3	98	24.8	93	30.7	80	39.7	61	21.4	−37
23	F	20.2	89	27.0	71	39.4	66	48.4	71	28.2	−18
24	M	21.5	50	34.9	57	51.6	42	51.6	42	30.1	− 8
25	M	21.8	83	28.7	75	37.8	63	50.1	60	28.3	−23

* Arranged according to age at first test.

† Stanford-Binet IQ.

SOURCE: Adapted from H. M. Skeels and H. B. Dye (1939, Table 2).

of 2 cases (16 and 24) the children had IQ's ranging from 81 to 103; the
IQ's for the 2 exceptions were 71 and 50, respectively. When the children
were examined, it was not known that they were or would become members
of any study group. The reexaminations were merely routine retests that
were given to all children.

At the ages when adoptive placement usually occurred, nine of the children in the contrast group had been considered normal in mental development. All 12 were not placed, however, because of different circumstances:
5 were withheld from placement simply because of poor family histories, 2
because of improper commitments, 2 because of luetic conditions, 2 because
of other health problems, and 1 because of possible mental retardation.

The subsequent progress of the children in both the experimental and the
contrast groups were influenced by individual circumstances. The groups
were never identified as such in the resident institution; the members of each
group were considered together only in a statistical sense. A child in the experimental group remained in the institution for the mentally retarded until
it was felt that he had attained the maximum benefit from residence there.
At that point, he was placed directly into an adoptive home or returned to
the orphanage in transit to an adoptive home. If he did not attain a level of
intelligence that warranted adoptive plans, he remained in the institution for
the mentally retarded.

The contrast-group members remained in the orphanage until placement.
One was returned to relatives, but in most instances the children were eventually transferred to an institution for the mentally retarded as long-term
protected residents. A few of the contrast group had been briefly approved
for adoptive placement, and two had been placed for short periods. None
was successful, however, and the children's decline in mental level removed
them from the list of those eligible for adoption.

Table 10.2 lists the chronological ages and test findings for the children in
the contrast group over the experimental period and the changes in IQ that
occurred.

DESCRIPTION OF EXPERIMENTAL AND CONTRAST GROUPS

Birth Histories. The birth histories of the two groups were not significantly different. Prematurity was of particular interest in relation to the initial
tests of intelligence, as a somewhat slower rate of mental and motor development or possible brain damage or retardation may be associated with it.

The experimental group included three premature births (Cases 4, 7, and
9). Case 4 was, in addition, a breech delivery, although without observable
birth injury. An intelligence test given prior to the pretransfer examination
had resulted in the same numerical score. Case 7 was a seven-months' infant, and the only one to have spent some time in an incubator (two
months). Her first infant intelligence test at 14 months of age resulted in an

IQ of 82, followed by lower test findings at 16 months. The results of the latter test were used to determine transfer. Case 9 was also a seven-months' premature baby, although not given incubator care. Before the age of four months she had been hospitalized for poisoning, after her drunken parents had patched the nipple of her nursing bottle with tire cement. The mother had a 4+ Wassermann. The child received treatment for a luetic condition prior to admission to the children's home at four months of age, and received additional antiluetic treatment during the first year of life, which was followed by negative tests. No infant intelligence tests were available on her prior to those reported in the study.

The contrast group contained only one instance of prematurity (Case 23). Incubator care had not been required. She had also been a breech delivery, but no indications of birth injury were found. As an infant, she was considered suitable for placement in an adoptive home but was held for later placement with her mother who, at the time, was serving a sentence in the Women's Reformatory. At 20 months, the infant's IQ was 83, and there was a subsequent decline in mental growth.

There were two cases of Caesarean section, one in the experimental group (Case 11) and one in the contrast group (Case 18), but no effect on mental development was indicated in either case.

One boy in the contrast group (Case 17) was known to have had a birth injury resulting from a low-forceps delivery with intracranial hemorrhage. After birth, he had periods of cyanosis and generalized twitching, and took his feedings poorly. Subsequently, the cyanosis diminished and convulsions did not occur after the first week. At 15 days, his condition was considered to be normal, and there was no evidence of brain damage during his childhood. However, diagnoses as an adult again referred to the mechanical injury at birth.

In the experimental group, Case 13 was admitted to the children's home at 28 months with no information on birth history. On admission, she was rather emaciated with a relatively large head. Later development and observations, however, ruled out a diagnosis of hydrocephalus. One case in the contrast group (Case 24) was admitted at 15 months, also with no information on birth history. Pediatric examination revealed no indication of organic defect. Specific information on birth histories was lacking for Cases 1 and 8 in the experimental group, and 20, 21, and 25 in the contrast group, but when they were admitted to the orphanage in early infancy, pediatric examinations revealed no indications of birth injury. For all other cases, specific information indicating full-term normal delivery was available.

The absence of minor neurological dysfunction or central-nervous-system aberrations cannot be assumed on a basis of the general pediatric examinations, even when supplemented by psychological and nursing observations. With more precise neurological examinations and the administration of

EEG's, certain abnormalities might have been revealed. This possibility is strongly suggested by Kugel's (1963) study of young children from lower socioeconomic levels, who had at least one mentally retarded parent and who were in treatment through "environmental enrichment." He found evidence of minor neurological dysfunction in many of the children and abnormal EEG's in almost half. Had such measures been available at the beginning of the present study, in all probability such defects would have appeared with comparable frequencies in both the experimental and contrast groups.

Medical Histories. In evaluating the medical histories of both the experimental and contrast groups, little of significance was found in the relation between illnesses and rate of mental growth. In the experimental group, one child, Case 9, had congenital syphilis, but immediate antiluetic treatment following birth was adequate, and her serology was negative during the experimental period.

In the contrast group, two children, Cases 14 and 16, were luetic, but Case 16 responded to early antiluetic treatment, and all serology was negative during the period of the study. In Case 14, however, a question may be raised about the contributing effects of persistent syphilis. Although blood Wassermann and Kahn were negative in the child at 9 months of age, examination at 30 months revealed 4+ Wassermann and Kahn, and treatment was again instituted. At 46 months, both blood and spinal fluid serology were negative. Case 16, on admission to the orphanage, had enlarged spleen and liver, and a tentative diagnosis of Gaucher's disease was made. The activity of the child was not seriously affected during the course of the original study, however. The subject died at age 15 of a hemorrhage of the esophageal varices.

For the children in both groups, various upper respiratory infections, occasional contagious diseases, and mild eczema had been recorded. Both groups had had middle-ear infections and mastoid surgery to a degree that seems excessive in the light of present-day medical treatments.

Family Backgrounds. Social histories of the children revealed that all in both the experimental and contrast groups came from homes in which the social, economic, occupational, and intellectual levels were low. The family backgrounds are comparable to those reported by Skeels and Fillmore (1937), in their study of the mental development of children from underprivileged homes, and in Skodak's (1939) study of younger siblings placed in adoptive homes at ages two to five.

Mothers.   Information relating to education was available for 11 of the 13 mothers in the experimental group and for 10 of the 12 mothers in the contrast group. The mean grade completed by mothers of children in the experimental group was 7.8, with a median at grade 8. Only 2 had any high-school work; 1 completed grade 11 and one grade 10 (Cases 3 and 6). In one case, it was doubtful if the second grade had been completed (Case 8). Two (Cases 1 and 5) had dropped out of grade 8 at the age of 16.

In the contrast group, the mean grade completed was 7.3, with a median at 7.5. One mother (Case 19) had completed high school and one had an equivalent of ninth-grade education.

Occupational history of mothers, available on seven of the mothers of the experimental group and on nine of the mothers of the contrast group, included mainly housework, either in the homes of their parents or on jobs as domestics. In only one instance was there a higher level (Case 24 of the contrast group); the mother had been a telephone operator and general office worker.

Intelligence tests[1] had been obtained on five of the mothers in the experimental group and on nine of the mothers in the contrast group. The mean IQ for the 5 mothers of the experimental group was 70.4, with a median at 66. Four mothers had IQ's below 70, and 1 was classified as normal with an IQ of 100. One additional mother, although not tested, was considered feebleminded and had gone only as far as the second grade. Of the 9 mothers tested in the contrast group, only 2 had IQ's above 70: one, 79 and the other, 84. The other scores ranged from 36 to 66. The mean IQ was 63, with a median at 62.

Fathers.   Little information was available on the fathers, and in fact, in many cases paternity was doubtful. Ten of the children in each group were illegitimate. In the experimental group, information relating to education was available on only four fathers: two had completed the eighth grade, one had completed high school, and one had gone to high school, but how far was not known. Occupational status was indicated for only three of the fathers: one was a traveling salesman, one a printer, and one a farmhand.

In the contrast group, educational information was available for four fathers. One had completed high school and was considered talented in music (Case 24), two had completed eighth grade (Cases 15 and 18), and one, the sixth grade (Case 21). Occupational data were known for eight of the contrast-group fathers: three were day laborers, two were farmhands, one worked on the railroad section, one was a farm renter, and one was in a C.C.C. camp.

A qualitative analysis of social histories seems to justify the conclusion that within these educational and occupational classifications, the parents represented the lower levels in such groups. Most of the fathers and mothers had dropped out of school because they had reached the limits of achievement and were not, in any sense of the word, average for their grade placements. The same may be said about occupational status.

DESCRIPTION OF THE ENVIRONMENTS

Experimental Group. Children in the experimental group were transferred from the orphanage nursery to the Glenwood State School, an institution for mentally retarded, and were placed on wards with older, brighter inmate girls. The wards were in a large cottage that contained eight wards
with a matron and an assistant matron in charge and with one attendant for
each ward. Approximately 30 patients, girls ranging in age from 18 to 50
years, were on each ward. On 2 wards (2 and 3), the residents had mental
ages of from 9 to 12 years. On 2 other wards (4 and 5), the mental levels
were from 7 to 10 years, and on another (ward 7), the mental ages were
from 5 to 8 years. With the exception of ward 7, the wards housed few or
no younger children other than the experimental "house guests." It was
planned to place one, or at the most two, children from the experimental
group on a given ward.

As with the first two children, who, by chance, were the first participants
in the experiment, the attendants and the older girls became very fond of
the children placed on their wards and took great pride in them. In fact,
there was considerable competition among wards to see which one would
have its "baby" walking or talking first. Not only the girls, but the attendants spent a great deal of time with "their children," playing, talking, and
training them in every way. The children received constant attention and
were the recipients of gifts; they were taken on excursions and were exposed
to special opportunities of all kinds. For example, it was the policy of the
matron in charge of the girls' school division to single out certain children
who she felt were in need of special individualization and to permit them to
spend some time each day visiting her office. This furnished new experiences, such as being singled out, receiving special attention and affection,
new play materials, additional language stimulation, and meeting other office callers.

The spacious living rooms of the wards furnished ample space for indoor
play and activity. Whenever weather permitted, the children spent some
time each day on the playground under the supervision of one or more older
girls. Here they were able to interact with other children of similar ages.
Outdoor play equipment included tricycles, swings, slides, sand boxes, etc.
The children also began to attend the school kindergarten as soon as they
could walk. Toddlers remained for only half the morning and four- or five-
year olds, the entire morning. Activities carried on in the kindergarten resembled preschool rather than the more formal type of kindergarten.

As part of the school program, the children attended daily 15-minute exercises in the chapel, which included group singing and music by the orches-
tra. The children also attended the dances, school programs, moving pictures, and Sunday chapel services.

In considering this enriched environment from a dynamic point of view, it must be pointed out that in the case of almost every child, some one adult (older girl or attendant) became particularly attached to him and figuratively "adopted" him. As a consequence, an intense one-to-one adult–child relationship developed, which was supplemented by the less intense but frequent interactions with the other adults in the environment. Each child had some one person with whom he was identified and who was particularly interested in him and his achievements. This highly stimulating emotional impact was observed to be the unique characteristic and one of the main contributions of the experimental setting.

The meager, even desolate environment in the orphanage has been described. The contrast between the richly stimulating, individually oriented experience of the children in the experimental group and the depersonalizing, mass handling, and affectionless existence in the children's home can hardly be emphasized enough.

MENTAL DEVELOPMENT

The mental development of individual children in the experimental group from the beginning to the end of the experimental periods is presented in Table 10.1. The 1922 Kuhlmann Revision of the Binet was used as the standard measure of intelligence, except for two or three tests on children who were four years of age or more for whom Stanford-Binet (1916) was used. All examinations were made by trained and experienced psychologists. Test one was the measure of intelligence just prior to transfer. Tests two, three, and the last were given at varying intervals of time following transfer. The last test was given at the end of the experimental period and was the second, third, or fourth, depending on the number of tests available at representative time intervals for a given child. Similar data showing the mental growth of the individual children in the contrast group over the two-and-a-half-year period are presented in Table 10.2.

The comparisons of means, medians, and standard deviations for scores from first to last test for both groups are presented in Table 10.3. Using the *t* test, the difference for the experimental group between the means of first and last tests was statistically significant at the .001 level. Every child showed a gain of from 7 to 58 points. Three children made gains of 45 points or more, and all but 2 children gained more than 15 points (Table 10.1).

Length of the experimental period was from 5.7 months to 52.1 months. The period was not constant for all children as it depended upon the individual child's rate of development. As soon as a child showed normal mental development, as measured by intelligence tests and substantiated by qualitative observations, the experimental period was considered completed and the child's visit to the school for mentally retarded was terminated. Either he was placed in an adoptive home or returned to the orphanage.

These results are directly comparable with those reported by Kirk (1958) for his community experimental and contrast groups. After preschool experience, his experimental group made significant gains in IQ, whereas the contrast group did not.

The mental-growth pattern for children in the contrast group was quite opposite that of the experimental group. Using the *t* test, the difference between the means of first and last tests was statistically significant ($p <$ .001) but with the exception of 1 child who gained 2 points in IQ from first to last test, all children showed losses of from 9 to 45 points. Ten of the 12 children lost 15 or more points in IQ over the period of the study.

In the experimental group, children who were initially at the lower levels tended to make the greater gains. The three children classified at the imbecile level on the first examination made gains of 58, 49, and 45 IQ points. Also, the greatest losses in the contrast group were associated with the highest initial levels. Six children with original IQ's above 90 lost from 29 to 45 points in IQ. While this shift may be partially due to regression, there must have been other factors operating to bring about such a large and consistent change.

These results, although more marked, are comparable to the findings reported in the orphanage preschool study by Skeels et al. (1938). In that study, children of the preschool group who were initially at the lower levels made the greatest gains following a period of preschool attendance, and children in the control group who were originally at the higher levels showed the greatest losses.

Family History and Children's Mental Development. No clear relation between family-history information and the mental-growth pattern of the children could be identified. Since the number of cases was small, examination of the data, rather than statistical treatment, was advisable.

In the experimental group, children whose mothers were classified as mentally retarded showed gains as marked as those children whose mothers were at a higher mental level. The greatest gain in intelligence (58 points IQ) was made by Case 8, whose mother was known to be mentally retarded and had gone only as far as the second grade in school.

In the contrast group, the only child (Case 20) who failed to show loss in rate of mental growth from first to last test was the son of a mother with an IQ of 36. Case 24, the most retarded child in the group on first examination (IQ 50), had a rather flattering family history. His father had graduated from high school and was talented in music. His mother, an eighth-grade graduate, had gone to an evening business school and subsequently had been a telephone operator and general office worker.

That the gains in intelligence evidenced by the children of the experimental group were true gains and not the results of vagaries in testing, seems validated. Improvement was noted independently by members of the medical staff, attendants and matrons, and school teachers. Practice effects could not have been a contributing factor to these gains, as the children in the contrast group, who showed continual losses in IQ, actually had more frequent tests than the children in the experimental group.

Parent Surrogates and Children's Mental Development. A close bond of love and affection between a given child and one or two adults who assume a very personal parental role appears to be a dynamic factor of great importance. Nine of the 13 children in the experimental group were involved in such relationships. The four other children (Cases 2, 9, 10, and 11) tended to be less individualized on the wards; their relationships with adults were more general, less intense, and did not involve any individual adult. It is significant that the children who experienced the more intense personal relationships made greater gains than those who were limited to more general interactions. The 9 children in the "personal" group made gains in IQ ranging from 17 to 58 points, with an average gain of 33.8 points. The 4 children in the more "general" group made gains of from 7 to 20 points, with an average of 14.

Two children (Cases 10 and 11) showed little progress on ward 7 over a period of one and a half years. This ward differed significantly from the others in that it housed 8 to 12 children of younger ages (3 to 8 years), and the older girls were of a lower mental level. The attendant on the ward was especially fine with young children but was unable to give much individual attention because of the large number of young children. At one time it was feared that the two children would continue to be hopelessly retarded. However, they were subsequently placed as singletons on wards with brighter girls and, after a period of six months with the more individualized attention, showed marked gains in intelligence.

FIRST FOLLOW-UP

The experiment ended for each child in the experimental group when the decision was made that he had attained the maximum benefit from his "house-guest" experience. Of the 13, one remained in the institution until adulthood, 5 went directly into adoptive homes from the host institution, 6 had brief periods in the orphanage in transit to adoptive homes, and one was returned to the orphanage for some years and then was committed to the institution for the retarded.

As part of the preadoptive procedures and the planned follow-up evaluations, all the children were given individual intelligence tests approximately two and a half years after the close of the experimental period. Thus, the 11 adopted children were tested after approximately 2½ years of living in a family home, and the 2 children remaining in the institutions, after a similar

period of continuing residential care. The mean length of the postexperimental period was 33 months (SD 8.0) and the median 29.8 months, with a
range of 21 to 53 months.

The children in the contrast group were still wards of the state institutions
and were given routine reexaminations. Those tests that most nearly coin-
cided with the two-and-one-half-year-interval testing for the experimental
group were used for comparison purposes in this study.

For the contrast group, the mean interval between the follow-up test and
the last experimental-period test was 36.0 months (SD 12.2), with a median
of 34.2 months. The 1916 Stanford-Binet was used as the standard measure
of intelligence since all the children were past four years of age.

The IQ scores recorded after the follow-up tests for the individual children in the experimental and contrast groups are presented in Table 10.4,
with the means, medians, and standard deviations for each group.

Mental Development of the Experimental Group. The mean IQ of the 13
children in the experimental group on the follow-up examination was 95.9
(SD 16.3), and the median was 94.0. For the 11 children who had been
placed in adoptive homes after the experimental period, the mean IQ at the
time of the follow-up study was 101.4; the range of IQ's was from 90 to
118. Changes in IQ for the 11 children ranged from +16 points to −5
points. The greatest gain (16 points) was made by a child (Case 4) who
had been placed in a superior adoptive home; the child (Case 5) showing
the only loss was in a home considered to be far below the average of the
other adoptive homes.

Losses of 17 and 9 points, respectively, were shown by the 2 children
(Cases 9 and 2) who were not placed in adoptive homes. Case 9 had been
returned to the orphanage although it was felt that the move was
premature.[2] It was true that she became lost in the orphanage group and received very little, if any, individual attention, but whether her development
would have been influenced by a different environment is speculative. Case
2, whose IQ was 77 at the close of the experimental period, had remained in
the institution for the mentally retarded and, at the time of the follow-up,
was expected to require continuing residential care.

Mental Development of the Contrast Group. To facilitate comparisons
between the experimental and contrast groups, the time interval between the
examinations during the experimental period and the time of examinations
for follow-up purposes were kept as nearly the same as possible. For individual children, the test intervals ranged from 20.1 months to 57.6 months.
The mean IQ of the 12 children in the contrast group was 66.1 (SD 16.5),
a mean gain of 5.6 points over the last test of the experimental period. Despite this small average gain, 8 of the 12 children showed marked mental
deterioration between the initial test and the follow-up test. During the three

TABLE 10.3. *Experimental and contrast groups: mean, median, and standard deviation comparisons of mental growth from first to last tests*

Measure	Chrono-logical Age, Months	Mental Age, Months	IQ	Chrono-logical Age, Months	Chrono-logical Age, Months	Mental Age, Months	IQ	Length of Experi-mental Period, Months	Change in IQ First to Last Test
	Before transfer			Transfer	After transfer				
Experimental group (N = 13)									
Mean	18.3	11.4	64.3	19.4	38.4	33.9	91.8	18.9	+27.5
Standard deviation	6.6	4.2	16.4	7.4	17.6	13.0	11.5	11.6	15
Median	16.6	10.8	65.0	17.1	36.8	30.0	93.0	14.5	+28
	First test			Transfer	Last test				
Contrast group (N = 12)									
Mean	16.6	14.2	86.7		47.2	28.7	60.5	30.7	−26.2
Standard deviation	2.9	2.9	14.3		5.9	6.4	9.7	5.8	14.1
Median	16.3	13.6	90.0		49.3	29.3	60.0	28.8	−30.0

SOURCE: Adapted from H. M. Skeels and H. B. Dye (1939, Table 3).

TABLE 10.4. *Mental development of individual children as measured by repeated intelligence tests experimental group (N = 13)*

		Experimental Period							Follow-up Study				
		Before transfer			after transfer				follow-up test‡				
		initial test‡		chronological age, months, at transfer	last test‡		length of experimental period, months	change in IQ, initial to last test	chronological age, months	IQ	length of post-experimental period months	change in IQ during post-experimental period	total change in IQ from initial to follow-up test
Case Number*	Sex	chronological age, months	IQ		chronological age, months	IQ							
1	M	7.0	89	7.1	12.8	113	5.7	+24	56	118	43.2	+ 5	+29
2	F	12.7	57	13.1	36.8	77	23.7	+20	65	68	28.2	− 9	+11
3	F	12.7	85	13.3	25.2	107	11.9	+22	55	116	29.8	+ 9	+31
4	F	14.7	73	15.0	23.1	100	8.1	+27	55	116	31.9	+16	+43
5	F	13.4	46	15.2	40.0	95‡	24.8	+49	93	90	53.0	− 5	+44
6	F	15.5	77	15.6	30.1	100	14.5	+23	65	102	34.9	+ 2	+25
7	F	16.6	65	17.1	27.5	104	10.4	+39	68	109	40.5	+ 5	+44
8	F	16.6	35	18.4	43.0	93	24.6	+58	77	96	34.0	+ 3	+61
9	F	21.8	61	22.0	34.3	80	12.3	+19	63	63	28.7	−17	+ 2
10	M	23.3	72	23.4	45.4	79	22.0	+ 7	74	92	28.6	+13	+20
11	M	25.7	75	27.4	51.0	82‡	23.6	+ 7	72	92	21.0	+10	+17
12	F	27.9	65	28.4	40.4	82	12.0	+17	67	90	26.6	+ 8	+25
13	F	30.0	36	35.9	89.0	81‡	52.1	+45	118	94	29.0	+13	+58
Mean		18.3	64.3	19.4	38.4	91.8	18.9	+27.5	71.4	95.9	33.0	+ 4.1	+31.6
Standard deviation		6.6	16.4	7.4	17.6	11.5	11.6	15.0	16.7	16.3	8.0	9.1	17.0
Median		16.6	65.0	17.1	36.8	93.0	14.5	+28.0	67.0	94.0	29.8	+ 1.0	+29.0

TABLE 10.4. Continued
Contrast Group (N = 12)

| Case Num-ber* | Sex | Experimental Period | | | | | | | Follow-up Study | | | | |
| | | before transfer initial test† | | after transfer | | | | | follow-up test‡ | | | | |
		chrono-logical age, months	IQ	chrono-logical age, months, at transfer	last test† chrono-logical age, months	IQ	length of experi-mental period, months	change in IQ, initial to last test	chrono-logical age, months	IQ	length of post-experi-mental period, months	change in IQ during post-experi-mental period	total change in IQ from initial to follow-up test
14	F	11.9	91	....	55.0	62	43.1	−29	81	64	26.0	+ 2	−27
15	F	13.0	92	....	38.3	56	25.3	−36	81	52	42.7	− 4	−40
16	F	13.6	71	....	40.9	56	27.3	−15	75	80	34.1	+24	+ 9
17	M	13.8	96	....	53.2	54	39.4	−42	82	51	28.8	− 3	−45
18	M	14.5	99	....	41.9	54	27.4	−45	62	35†	20.1	−19	−64
19	M	15.2	87	....	44.5	67	29.3	−20	101	89	56.5	+22	+ 2
20	M	17.3	81	....	52.9	83‡	35.6	+ 2	77	91	24.1	+ 8	+10
21	M	17.5	103	....	50.3	60	32.8	−43	73	49	22.7	−11	−54
22	M	18.3	98	....	39.7	61	21.4	−37	74	78	34.3	+17	−20
23	F	20.2	89	....	48.4	71	28.2	−18	106	75	57.6	+ 4	−14
24	M	21.5	50	....	51.6	42	30.1	− 8	91	68	39.4	+26	+18
25	M	21.8	83	....	50.1	60	28.3	−23	96	61	45.9	+ 1	−22
Mean		16.6	86.7		47.2	60.5	30.7	−26.2	83.3	66.1	36.0	+ 5.6	−20.6
Standard deviation		3.2	13.9		5.6	9.7	5.8	14.1	12.3	16.5	12.2	13.8	25.6
Median		16.3	90.0		49.3	60.0	28.8	−30.0	81.0	66.0	34.2	+ 6.0	−24.0

* Arranged according to age at time of initial test.
† Kuhlmann-Binet (1922) IQ.
‡ Stanford-Binet (1916) IQ.

years following the close of the experimental period, a number of changes were made in the group's living situation. Two children (Cases 15 and 16) were transferred to the Glenwood State School, where they experienced essentially the same type of environment as that of the experimental group, but beginning at an older age. The 2 were 41 months of age at time of transfer. Thirty-four months following this transfer, Case 16 was examined and obtained an IQ of 80, showing a gain of 24 points. She was returned to the orphanage, therefore, as continued residence in the institution for mentally retarded seemed unwarranted. Case 15, on the other hand, failed to show any gain after 34 months. An examination 6 months later resulted in an IQ of 52, a 4-point loss.

Six of the contrast children were transferred to the Woodward State Hospital and School following the close of the experimental period. This transfer was made on a permanent basis, inasmuch as mental retardation and lack of development and adjustment made continued residence in the orphanage seem inadvisable. Four of the children (Cases 14, 17, 18, and 21) were transferred within 3 months after the close of the experimental period, and the other 2 (Cases 22 and 24) were transferred 16 months after the close of the experimental period.

The children sent to Woodward experienced a different environment from that of the experimental children who had been "house guests" at Glenwood. The children sent to Woodward were much older at the time of transfer and received, in general, less individual attention and had fewer interactions with adults. They interacted primarily with children of a similar or slightly older chronological age who were mentally more retarded.

Over a period ranging from 2 to 3 years, 2 of the 6 transferred children experienced further losses in IQ (Cases 18 and 21), 2 remained relatively constant (Cases 14 and 17), and 2 showed gains (Cases 22 and 24). None attained a level higher than that of borderline intelligence.

The two children who showed marked gains in intelligence had experienced enriched environments. Case 22 was quite the favorite from the time of his transfer. After a year he was placed in the primary group in school. His teacher was especially fond of him and took a great interest in his achievements. The psychologist reported, "Because he was a likable boy with possibilities for improvement under training, he has been given much special attention. His reports show that though he appears quiet and unassuming he has an active imagination and curiosity and often shows initiative." At six years of age he surpassed all members of his class in reading skills and in identifying flash cards.

Case 24 was the only one of this transfer group not placed in the nursery ward. He was placed on a ward with older, brighter boys, where his adjustment was consistently satisfactory. Since he was one of the younger boys on the ward, he received additional individual attention from attendants and older boys.

The three contrast children who remained in the orphanage after the close of the original study subsequently also experienced a change of environment. Case 20 did not attend preschool but entered kindergarten at 68 months of age, and he had just completed the year in kindergarten when the follow-up examination was given. Case 23 attended preschool one year, kindergarten one year, first grade one year (with a D average in grades), and, at the time of the follow-up examination, was nine years of age and in the second grade.

Of the three children who remained in the orphanage, Case 19 had the most enriched and varied experience during the follow-up period and showed by far the greatest gain (22 points) in IQ. Beginning at five years of age, he spent one year in preschool and one year in kindergarten. During the year in kindergarten, he was also included in a special mental-growth stimulation study, which was carried on by a research assistant from the State University of Iowa (Dawe 1942), that included an intensified, individualized program of experimental instruction and frequent trips away from the institution. He was the only child from the contrast group included in this special study.

The last of the contrast children to be accounted for (Case 25) was paroled to his grandparents immediately following the close of the experimental period. The home was a very marginal one, and the family had been on relief for years. At the time of the follow-up examination at eight years of age, the boy was still in the first grade, doing failing work, and was continually "picked on" by other children. A recommendation was made to transfer the boy to an institution for the mentally retarded.

The Follow-Up Study of Adult Achievement

STATEMENT OF THE PROBLEM

The purpose of this follow-up study was to obtain answers to a few very simple questions: What happened to the two groups of children when they became adults? How were the differences in mental growth in childhood reflected in adult achievement and adjustment? Were the two divergent pathways maintained or did they converge over the years? Were there significant changes indicating improvement or regression within and between groups? Was there a relation between adult status and such factors as social history, health history, or environmental experiences?

Reality considerations influenced the kind of information that could be secured. Since the study had not been originally planned as a lifetime follow-up research, certain details of information, predictions that might have been verified, and baseline data were not available. No provision had been made for subsequent visits and, as far as the subjects and the adopting parents were concerned, relationships with the agencies had long since been terminated. In addition, all the issues relating to privacy and confidentiality arose. In view of the small number of cases, it was essential not only to locate every single subject but to secure maximum and, if possible, uniform information for each. To jeopardize this goal by making excessive demands for time and details and by probing emotionally charged material did not seem justified. The earlier guidelines of a descriptive natural-history approach were accepted as the most appropriate. No attempt was made to convert the adult follow-up into a more penetrating and detailed assessment of dynamics. Hopefully, this needed aspect of research is being pursued by others.

The adult follow-up study began 20 years after the postexperimental follow-up (Skeels and Skodak 1965). The initial task was to locate and obtain information on every single case in the two groups. In a study based on such small numbers, the failure to locate even two or three cases could materially limit the conclusions or impressions. At first there were serious misgivings about whether it would be possible to locate some of the individuals. Of particular concern were those cases in which the adoptive parents might have died, or the adopted child was a girl who might have married and could be identified only under another name, or the family might have moved from the last known address shortly after the first follow-up.[3]

GENERAL OVERALL FINDINGS

Survival Data. All 13 subjects in the experimental group reached adulthood. Among the 11 adoptive homes in which subjects were placed as children, both adoptive parents were deceased in 2, and the adoptive parents were divorced in 1 but the adoptive mother had remarried and maintained a relationship with the subject.

In the contrast group, 11 of the 12 subjects were living; 1 (Case 16) died at the age of 15 while still a resident of the institution for the mentally retarded. None had been placed in adoptive homes.

Mobility. Among the adoptive parents, 2 of the 11 families had moved out of the state, 1 prior to the first follow-up study and the other later. Of the 13 subjects in the experimental group, 6, including the 2 not placed in adoptive homes, still lived in the state. Of the 7 who had moved out of the state, 2 were residing in Minnesota and 1 each in Arizona, Nebraska, California, Kansas, and Wisconsin.

In the contrast group, 9 of the 11 living subjects still resided within the state of Iowa. One (Case 23) was living in Nebraska, one (Case 22) was located in California (after tracing him from Florida), and he later moved to Montana.

Occupational Levels. The 13 subjects in the experimental group were all self-supporting and none were wards of any institution—public or private.

Two, a boy (Case 1) and a girl (Case 6), however, had spent some time in a state correctional school during adolescence. Nevertheless, no member of the group exhibited evidence of antisocial or delinquent behavior, economic dependency, or need for psychiatric or agency support.

Table 10.5 summarizes the occupational status of the experimental- and contrast-group subjects and their spouses. The women's vocational achievements cannot be compared directly with those of the men since women do not have equal opportunities for advancement, and early marriage influences their vocational patterns. In the present study, 8 of the 10 girls were married; 2 married shortly after leaving school and had no employment records (Cases 5 and 8). Case 7 took the examination and was accepted as a stewardess for an airline after graduation from high school, but married instead. She worked as a dining-room hostess for a short time after her marriage. The two cases (2 and 9) who had never been placed in adoptive homes worked as domestics.

The occupational status of the 11 living members of the contrast group was significantly different. The contributions to society of the four residents of state institutions were limited to the unskilled tasks assigned to ward patients. One (Case 25) had intermittent paroles to a grandmother; while with her he occasionally mowed lawns or shoveled walks.

One boy (Case 24) was an employee in the institution for the mentally retarded in which he had been a patient for many years. Upon reaching adulthood, it was felt that his retardation was not sufficient to justify his being kept on as a resident. Placement in a community was attempted but failed completely. He was then placed on the employees' payroll in the institution but continued to live on a patient ward; subsequently, he was made a regular employee and transferred to the employees' home. He had no interests other than his work and had no friends among either inmates or employees.

Of the seven who were employed and living in communities, one (Case 21), a male, was still a ward of an institution for the mentally retarded but out on a vocational-training assignment that eventuated in his discharge from the institution. As a dishwasher in a nursing home he earned $60 a month and board and room. Two others, one male (Case 17) and one female (Case 15), previously wards of a state institution for the mentally retarded, were discharged from state supervision and worked as dishwashers in small restaurants. One girl (Case 23) remained in the orphanage from infancy to 17 years and was then returned to her mother. She found employment in a cafeteria where her duties were folding napkins around silverware. On paydays, her mother called for her checks and deposited them in the bank for her.

One man (Case 20) had had brief periods of part-time work on a farm during his teens. He spent his childhood in the orphanage and his adolescence in a training school for delinquent boys. He escaped from the training

TABLE 10.5. *Experimental and contrast groups: occupations of subjects and spouses*

Case No.	Subject's Occupation	Spouse's Occupation	Female Subject's Occupation Previous to Marriage
Experimental Group:			
1*	Staff sergeant	Dental technician	....
2	Housewife	Laborer	Nurses' aide
3	Housewife	Mechanic	Elementary school teacher
4	Nursing instructor	Unemployed	Registered nurse
5	Housewife	Semiskilled laborer	No work history
6	Waitress	Mechanic, semi-skilled	Beauty operator
7	Housewife	Flight engineer	Dining room hostess
8	Housewife	Foreman, construc-tion	No work history
9	Domestic service	Unmarried	....
10*	Real estate sales	Housewife	....
11*	Vocational counselor	Advertising copy writer†	....
12	Gift shop sales‡	Unmarried	....
13	Housewife	Pressman-printer	Office-clerical
Contrast Group:			
14	Institutional inmate	Unmarried	....
15	Dishwasher	Unmarried	....
16	Deceased	....	....
17*	Dishwasher	Unmarried	....
18*	Institutional inmate	Unmarried	....
19*	Compositor and typesetter	Housewife	....
20*	Institutional inmate	Unmarried	....
21*	Dishwasher	Unmarried	....
22*	Floater	Divorced	....
23	Cafeteria (part-time)	Unmarried	....
24*	Institutional gar-dener's assistant	Unmarried	....
25*	Institutional inmate	Unmarried	....

* Male.
† B.A. degree.
‡ Previously had worked as a licensed practical nurse.

school, got to the West Coast, and within a few months was hospitalized following bizarre behavior and a severe depression. He was returned to his home state and has been hospitalized as mentally ill ever since.

Another boy (Case 22) was a "floater" whose travels had taken him from coast to coast. His vocational activities included plucking chickens in a produce house, washing dishes in a hospital kitchen, and doing the heavy packing for shipment in a stationery company. One trip to Iowa and two to the West Coast were made to locate him.

Still another, the last of the employed subjects in the contrast group to be accounted for was the man (Case 19) who stands out from the group in many ways. He became a compositor and typesetter for a newspaper in a city of 300,000, and his income easily equaled that of all the other employed contrast-group members combined.

COMPARISONS OF OCCUPATIONAL STATUS

In addition to the foregoing information on occupational achievement, an attempt was made to compare the two groups on a more objective and quantitative basis. The Warner Index of Status Characteristics (Warner, Meeker, and Eells 1960), and the U.S. Census Socioeconomic Status Score (U.S. Bureau of the Census 1963*a*) were used for the comparison.

The Warner Scale is made up of rating on occupation, source of income, house type, and dwelling area. Each classification is rated on a seven-point scale. The ratings are multiplied by weighted scores, the products are totaled to provide the Index of Socioeconomic Status, and the resulting scores are then related to social class equivalents; a rating of 12–17 represents upper class status and 70–84, lower lower class.

In the U.S. Census Scale, scores of socioeconomic status are computed by converting the data for occupation, education, and family income for the chief recipient into scores and by averaging the scores for the three components. Unlike the Warner Scale, higher scores on the U.S. Census Scale represent higher positions on the socioeconomic scale.

Occupational scales, at best, are approximations and are subject to errors from personal bias and from insufficient information. To offset this limitation as much as possible, the ratings reported here are averages based upon four independent ratings.[4]

There was a high degree of concurrence among the four raters. Had ratings by any one of the four been used instead of the average, the results would have been the same.

Warner Index of Status Characteristics for subjects in both the experimental and contrast groups are shown in Table 6 (This and the following tables appear in the original monograph. Since Skeels summarizes them, they were omitted in the interest of brevity. M.W.).

For the experimental group, a mean weighted total score of 54.5 and a median of 56.0 was obtained. For the contrast group, the comparable scores were 71.8 and 71.5, respectively. Using the *t* test, the difference between the means of the two groups was statistically significant at the .01 level.

Scores of socioeconomic status, based on the U.S. Census methodology are presented in Table 7 for both the experimental group and the contrast groups. The table shows grades completed and converted scores for both the experimental subjects and their spouses. However, in computing the overall average score, ratings on the husbands of females were used, except for Case 4 whose husband was temporarily out of work, and the household was supported by her. Mean and median scores for grades completed and occupations of household heads are comparable (in the 55–67 range); the mean and median scores for income are somewhat lower. The disparity is probably due to the fact that the subjects and their spouses are relatively young and the scale was standardized on adults of a much wider age range. It is expected that as the subjects grow older their incomes will increase.

The scores of socioeconomic status for subjects in the contrast group are also presented in Table 7. In all categories the scores indicate levels of achievement much lower than those of subjects in the experimental group, with the exception of one (Case 19), whose occupational achievement has already been described.

The percentage distribution of family heads by socioeconomic status in the north central region of the United States, 1960, is compared with the distribution of family heads of the experimental and contrast groups in Table 8. It is apparent that, for the contrast group, again with the consistent exception of Case 19, the subjects are concentrated in the two lowest socioeconomic status classifications. The experimental group, however, approximates the distribution of the total population.

Summary and Implications

In the original study, the 13 children in the experimental group, all mentally retarded at the beginning of the study, experienced the effects of early intervention, which consisted of a radical shift from one institutional environment to another. The major difference between the two institutions, as experienced by the children, was in the amount of developmental stimulation and the intensity of relationships between the children and mother-surrogates. Following a variable period in the second institution, 11 of the 13 children were placed in adoptive homes.

The contrast group of 12 children, initially higher in intelligence than the experimental group, were exposed to a relatively nonstimulating orphanage environment over a prolonged period of time.

Over a period of two years, the children in the experimental group showed a marked increase in rate of mental growth, whereas the children in the contrast group showed progressive mental retardation. The experimental group made an average gain of 28.5 IQ points; the contrast group showed an average loss of 26.2 IQ points.

The first follow-up study was made two and a half years after the termination of the original study. The 11 children in the experimental group that had been placed in adoptive homes had maintained and increased their earlier gains in intelligence, whereas the two not so placed had declined in rate of mental growth. Over the three-year postexperimental period, the children in the contrast group showed a slight mean gain in IQ but were still mentally retarded to a marked degree. In those children that showed gains in intelligence, the gains appeared to be associated with improved environmental experiences that occurred subsequent to the original study.

In the adult follow-up study, all cases were located and information obtained on them, after a lapse of 21 years.

The two groups had maintained their divergent patterns of competency into adulthood. All 13 children in the experimental group were self-supporting, and none was a ward of any institution, public or private. In the contrast group of 12 children, 1 had died in adolescence following continued residence in a state institution for the mentally retarded, and 4 were still wards of institutions, 1 in a mental hospital, and the other 3 in institutions for the mentally retarded.

In education, disparity between the two groups was striking. The contrast group completed a median of less than the third grade. The experimental group completed a median of the 12th grade. Four of the subjects had one or more years of college work, one received a B.A. degree and took some graduate training.

Marked differences in occupational levels were seen in the two groups. In the experimental group all were self-supporting or married and functioning as housewives. The range was from professional and business occupations to domestic service, the latter the occupations of two girls who had never been placed in adoptive homes. In the contrast group, four (36 percent) of the subjects were institutionalized and unemployed. Those who were employed, with one exception (Case 19), were characterized as "hewers of wood and drawers of water." Using the t test, the difference between the status means of the two groups (based on the Warner Index of Status Characteristics applied to heads of households) was statistically significant ($p < .01$).

Educational and occupational achievement and income for the 11 adopted subjects in the experimental group compared favorably with the 1960 U.S. Census figures for Iowa and for the United States in general. Their adult status was equivalent to what might have been expected of children living with natural parents in homes of comparable sociocultural levels. Those subjects that married had marriage partners of comparable sociocultural levels.

Eleven of the 13 children in the experimental group were married; 9 of the 11 had a total of 28 children, an average of 3 children per family. On intelligence tests, these second-generation children had IQ's ranging from 86 to 125, with a mean and median IQ of 104. In no instance was there any indication of mental retardation or demonstrable abnormality. Those of school age were in appropriate grades for age.

In the contrast group, only two of the subjects had married. One had one child and subsequently was divorced. Psychological examination of the child revealed marked mental retardation with indications of probable brain damage. Another male subject (Case 19) had a nice home and family of four children, all of average intelligence.

The cost to the state for the contrast group, for whom intervention was essentially limited to custodial care, was approximately five times that of the cost for the experimental group. It seems safe to predict that for at least four of the cases in the contrast group costs to the state will continue at a rate in excess of $200 per month each for another 20 to 40 years.

IMPLICATIONS OF STUDY

At the beginning of the study, the 11 children in the experimental group evidenced marked mental retardation. The developmental trend was reversed through planned intervention during the experimental period. The program of nurturance and cognitive stimulation was followed by placement in adoptive homes that provided love and affection and normal life experiences. The normal, average intellectual level attained by the subjects in early or middle childhood was maintained into adulthood.

It can be postulated that if the children in the contrast group had been placed in suitable adoptive homes or given some other appropriate equivalent in early infancy, most or all of them would have achieved within the normal range of development, as did the experimental subjects.

It seems obvious that under present-day conditions there are still countless infants born with sound biological constitutions and potentialities for development well within the normal range who will become mentally retarded and noncontributing members of society unless appropriate intervention occurs. It is suggested by the findings of this study and others published in the past 20 years that sufficient knowledge is available to design programs of intervention to counteract the devastating effects of poverty, sociocultural deprivation, and maternal deprivation.

Since the study was a pioneering and descriptive one involving only a small number of cases, it would be presumptuous to attempt to identify the specific influences that produced the changes observed. However, the contrasting outcome between children who experienced enriched environmental opportunities and close emotional relationships with affectionate adults, on the one hand, and those children who were in deprived, indifferent, and unresponsive environments, on the other, leaves little doubt that the area is a fruitful one for further study.

It has become increasingly evident that the prediction of later intelligence cannot be based on the child's first observed developmental status. Account must be taken of his experiences between test and retest. Hunt (1964, p. 212) has succinctly stated that,

> . . . In fact, trying to predict what the IQ of an individual child will be at age 18 from a D.Q. obtained during his first or second year is much like trying to predict how fast a feather might fall in a hurricane. The law of falling bodies holds only under the specified and controlled conditions of a vacuum. Similarly, any laws concerning the rate of intellectual growth must take into account the series of environmental encounters which constitute the conditions of that growth.

The divergence in mental-growth patterns between children in the experimental and contrast groups is a striking illustration of this concept.

The right of every child to be well born, well nurtured, well brought up, and well educated was enunciated in the Children's Charter of the 1930 White House Conference on Child Health and Protection (White House Conference 1931). Though society strives to insure this right, for many years to come there will be children to whom it has been denied and for whom society must provide both intervention and restitution. There is need for further research to determine the optimum modes of such intervention and the most appropriate ages and techniques for initiating them. The present study suggests, but by no means delimits, either the nature of the intervention or the degree of change that can be induced.

The planning of future studies should recognize that the child interacts with his environment and does not merely passively absorb its impact. More precise and significant information on the constitutional, emotional, and response-style characteristics of the child is needed so that those environmental experiences that are most pertinent to his needs can be identified and offered in optimum sequence.

The unanswered questions of this study could form the basis for many lifelong research projects. If the tragic fate of the 12 contrast-group children provokes even a single crucial study that will help prevent such a fate for others, their lives will not have been in vain.

NOTES

1. Stanford-Binet (1916) intelligence tests. Most of the tests were given by psychologists either at the Psychopathic Hospital or at the University Hospital of the State University of Iowa. Maximum chronological age used was 16 years.

2. The return followed a change in administration rather than psychological readiness.

3. Skeels' procedures for finding and interviewing the original subjects are described in considerable detail on pp. 28–31 of the monograph. It should be noted that he was extremely successful in locating the subjects in both the experimental and the contrast group. (M.W.)

4. For these ratings the author is indebted to Dr. Howard Davis, clinical psychologist; Dr. Thomas Gladwin, social science consultant, Community Research and Services Branch, National Institute of Mental Health; and Mr. Lowell Schenke, psychologist, Children's Division, Iowa Board of Control of State Institutions. (Apparently Skeels or someone in his project was the fourth rater. M.W.).

11

Young Children in Institutions: Some Additional Evidence

MARTIN WOLINS

The SOS Kinderdorf and the Yugoslav Djete Dom organized on the familial or semifamilial model are excellent places to test some of Skeels' conclusions. Both of these facilities accept relatively young children—some from reasonably normal and some from deprived backgrounds—and surround them with many caring persons. A small child entering the Kinderdorf finds a mutti and some older brothers and sisters. They nourish and support, set examples and challenge, praise and chastise. Similarly, the Yugoslav children's home gives the small child an instant human environment of near-peers and others much more mature and authoritative.

Though all the children who enter these programs at an early age must suffer severely from the traumas of separation, and though many of them have had very difficult early familial experiences, they function well as teenagers in the two institutions. In this paper the adolescent performance of 12 Kinderdorf and 13 Djete Dom children is described, and they are compared with children admitted to these facilities later in life and with those living with their parents.

Johann and Annemarie are both adolescents in an Austrian children's village (Kinderdorf) which they entered at an early age. Johann came when his family of "mama, papa, and four children" split up. He was only two

This study is based on materials from a project, Child Care in Cross-Cultural Perspective, supported by the National Institute of Mental Health, United States Public Health Service, Health, Education and Welfare (MH 01430), the Ford Foundation, and the Institute of International Studies, University of California, Berkeley. Martin Wolins. "Young Children in Institutions: Some Additional Evidence." *Developmental Psychology* 2 (1). Copyright 1969. American Psychological Association. Reproduced by permission.

years old then. Since that time he has lived in the Kinderdorf with his *Mutti* —"she is good to us"—and the *Dorfleiter* (village director)—"he is so smart." Indeed, the director who runs these 33 houses containing some 300 children and their "mothers" and "aunts" is insightful enough to know that Johann, who has lived in the Kinderdorf "family" for 12 years, is *problematisch*.

Johann and his tests confirm this impression. Reasonably bright (Raven Matrix Percentile 41), he nevertheless is failing in school. His *Mutti* says that he has serious psychological and social problems: "he can't fit into the family." Every Thematic Apperception Test (TAT) story confirms Johann's fear, distrust, and disinvolvement. The girl [Card 7GF] pays no attention to her mother. The boy [3BM] has not obeyed his mother. The man wants to leave his wife [4]. The man and woman [6BM] are quarreling. The older man tries to persuade the younger [7BM] to do something evil. Each item, every new piece of evidence fits the expectations Bowlby (1950, 1952, ed.) laid down in his World Health Organization monograph: Early separation, long-term institutionalization, and the expected impairment of ego and superego development are all here, and in a time sequence that implies causality and tempts again the conclusion of inevitability.

By contrast with Johann, staff impressions of Annemarie, who also came 12 years ago, are favorable on all counts. Apparently, Annemarie lived in a reasonably normal family until she was orphaned at the age of four. Now, at 16½ her TAT stories still convey the pain of that condition but also speak about her accomplishments at present and her hopes for a bright future: "The boy does not have a mother or father now. He is alone . . . [3BM]." "The boy will become an orphan. This will be terrible for such a young boy [8BM]." And on another card: "He thinks of the wedding, his future wife and the children they will have. He is certainly looking forward to it [14]." Annemarie's sentence completions are fairly shallow, though generally positive. Some good examples are: "I like you," "I worry about you," "groups can be a lot of fun." In spite of considerable intellectual capability (Raven Percentile 78), the girl is quite conforming, almost compulsively so, but she fits well in her environment and is evaluated by the staff as *sehr in Ordnung,* very much all right.

Annemarie does not quite fit Bowlby's (1950, 1952, ed.) conclusions. She more nearly conforms to the data from the work of Skeels (1966), Gardner, Hawkes, and Burchinal (1961), Gavrin and Sacks (1963), Pringle and Bossio (1958), and to the children seen in Soviet boarding schools, in Israeli kibbutzim, and the others here in the Kinderdorf. Her presence challenges the conclusion that a Johann is the inevitable outcome of early separation and subsequent institutional care. Even Johann provides some support for a more positive outlook. He tells a story of surgery (Card 8BM) and concludes with "they will take good care of him." Two sentences about groups and work with others he completes with "learning" and "happiness."

His world is not totally glum, and at times he is, to use his own words, "full of inspiration." Individually the stories of these two young people support and conflict with some long-held assumptions about early separation and institutional care. Fortunately, in a current study of group care in several countries (Wolins 1969), two institutions—Kinderdorf Wienerwald and a children's home in Belgrade—had among the adolescents a number (12 and 13, respectively) who had come in at an early age. Using 80 months as a cutoff point, it was possible to compare indicators of intelligence, personality maturity, and values of these early admissions (who of necessity had been in the institutions for many years), later admissions to these same programs, and children living at home.

Both the Austrian and Yugoslav institutions are familial, but their populations, structures, and objectives differ substantially. Kinderdorf Wienerwald, set in an affluent suburb of Vienna, admits relatively normal often out-of-wedlock children. Every effort is made to duplicate the familial structure by having a single-family dwelling for every nine children and mother, a mixture of boys and girls of various ages, a *pater familias* in the person of the director, and permanent separation from the natural family. The stated objective is integration into lower middle class, Catholic Austrian society.

The Yugoslav children, by contrast, have much more difficult past histories. They now live in a single large apartment house in Belgrade. "Families" consist of some 16–18 children and an "aunt" or "uncle" who often is older sister/older brother in age. Contact with natural families is maintained, although considerable misgivings are expressed about their negative genetic legacy. ("What can you expect from children of mental patients, prostitutes, and alcoholics?" is heard more often than one would anticipate.) The objective is to undo early damage to the child, to enhance development, and to instill a local version of socialist values which is by no means internally consistent and clear.

The children's current condition should be poor: Johann's case should appear many times over in the Austrian and Yugoslav settings. But this did no seem to be the case. Although there was much variability in the Raven Progressive Matrices (RPM) test scores, the Austrian children all appeared to have a mean age-adjusted position around the English median and the Yugoslavs around the third decile. Both groups did slightly less well than the comparison children reared at home, but the differences were quite small. Also, the seemingly better achievement of early over later admissions in Austria, and the normal IQ (104.0) on the Wechsler Intelligence Scale for Children (WISC) (Belgrade version and norms) for the early Yugoslav admissions provided further evidence that early entry was not associated with poor performance. This view was also supported by the lack of correlation between age of entry and RPM percentile scores of all Kinderdorf children for whom these data were available *(N = 66, r = .000)*.

TABLE 11.1. *Basic information on early admissions to the Austrian kinderdorf and the Yugoslav children's home*

| Case No. | Age at Entry (in mo.) | Age when Tested (in mo.) | Length of Stay (in mo.) | Intellectual Performance | | | Problems in Placement | | | |
				Raven percentile	WISC IQ*	Standing in school	medical	psychological	learning	social group
Austria Kinderdorf										
1012	57	216	159	84		3	M	N	N	N
1021	19	178	159	06		5	S	Mo	?	N
1031	23	163	140	41		4	N	S	Mo	S
1322	70	207	137	65		2	N	N	N	N
1332	49	198	149	78		3	N	N	N	N
1342	51	188	137	65		2	N	M	N	N
1351	64	180	116	37		4	N	N	S	N
1391	76	160	084	85		4	N	M	Mo	Mo
1442	69	153	084	12		3	N	Mo	M	N
2021	43	219	176	65		2	N	M	N	N
2161	52	206	154	40		2	N	M	N	N
2271	57	176	119	50		2	N	Mo	Mo	N
M	52.5	187	134.5	52.33						

Yugoslavia children's home

ID					IQ*					
1032	64	196	132	24	108	3	M	N	N	M
1061	28	160	132	37		4	Mo	S	S	S
1122	39	171	132	23		4	Mo	Mo	S	S
1161	77	173	096	14	109	3	N	N	M	N
1171	73	169	096	15	109	3	N	Mo	Mo	Mo
1182	49	179	130	10		3	N	N	Mo	M
1192	59	212	153	16	102	3	N	M	Mo	M
1202	38	158	120	16		3	N	N	Mo	Mo
1252	64	184	120	09	105	2	M	N	N	N
1262	77	197	120	50	98	3	M	M	Mo	N
1291	42	198	156	47	96	3	M	Mo	?	N
1321	68	164	096	04	105	3	N	N		Mo
1392	73	205	132	07		2			HA	Mo
M	57.8	182	124.2	20.9	104					

NOTE: N = none, M = mild, Mo = moderate, S = serious, ? = unknown, HA = high achievement; 1 = very good, 2 = good, 3 = average, 4 = unsatisfactory, 5 = poor for standing in school.

* Yugoslav form of Wechler-Bellevue intelligence scale. See note to Table 11.2.

Intelligence test performance may, however, be considered a more limited criterion for the assessment of intellectual functioning than is school achievement. Because the fulfillment of institutional expectations is better reflected in staff judgment than in grades, the supervisory personnel in each setting was asked to evaluate every child's school performance. Although there is no way of knowing the validity of these judgments—that is, the extent to which they reflected capacity for present institutional and, more significantly, future life adjustment—it is known that the staff was very close to these children and followed school performance with much interest and concern.

Again, the evidence failed to meet the prophecy. Early admissions did well in school or average or poorly with about the same frequency as the other children. Of the 25 cases represented by the combined Austrian and Yugoslav data, no child admitted before the age of 6 did very good work in school, and about a fourth did unsatisfactory or poor work, but most children (about 70 percent in each admission group) were judged as good or average students.

Intelligence and school achievement data are modified by other, more general information. Were the early institutional placement a marked handicap in the children's development it should be noticeable in the proportion of certain "problems in placement" reported for such children. There should be more physical illness and more difficulties in psychological and social adjustment. Here, consistent but very small differences did appear. Of the eight comparisons (medical, psychological, learning, and social problems viewed separately in the Austrian and Yugoslav samples), only one favored the early admissions. The incidence of learning and social problems for early and later admitted Austrians were identical, but the early admissions showed somewhat more often moderate or serious medical and psychological problems, and the "early" Yugoslavs had higher proportions of moderate or serious problems in all four categories. As noted in the preceding paragraph, the differences were quite small (and, given the small samples, individually insignificant), but their general direction probably makes them worthy of attention.

While considering the import of these differences in the incidence of problems, it must be remembered that staff judgments of children's problems in placement were not necessarily assessments of current functioning. In fact, the questions put to staff were intentionally slanted toward a retrospective view, since it seemed unlikely that staff would be able to isolate current difficulties from those experienced by each child over the period of his stay in the program. A similar processual view of each child's situation appears in his own projective materials. Repeatedly the children told about the boy (or girl) who has no parents or whose parents don't care for him: "A forlorn boy sitting in the street at a bench. He does not have his parents

TABLE 11.2. *Raven progressive matrices standings of early and later admissions to group care and of home-reared children*

Item	Austria: Kinderdorf			Yugoslavia: Children's Home		
	early (n = 12)	later (n = 54)	home (n = 67)	early (n = 13)	later (n = 23)	home (n = 72)
Mean age at entry (in yr.)	4.4	9.6	—	4.8	11.8	—
Mean age when tested (in yr.)	15.6	15.8	13.9	15.2	15.9	15.3
Mean length of stay (in yr.)	11.2	6.2	—	10.4	4.2	—
Mean RPM percentile score	52.3	44.2	54.1	20.9	29.3	37.3
IQ				104.0	104.8	105.3

NOTE: Because of the generally low scores on the Raven Progressive Matrices (RPM) test, most children were retested on a Yugoslav version of the Wechsler Intelligence Scale for Children (WISC) specially constructed for group administration. Belgrade norms were based on a sample of 3,768 children distributed over an age range of 14–18. The WISC has a mean of 100, $SD = 15$. The n was somewhat reduced ($n = 8$ for early entrants, $n = 14$ for later, $n = 26$ for home) because not all children in the original sample were available for retesting.

TABLE 11.3. *Standing in school of early and later admissions as judged by group care staff*

Standing in School	Austria: Kinderdorf		Yugoslavia: Children's Home	
	early (n=12)	later (n=60*)	early (n=13)	later (n=23)
Very good	0.0%	11.7%	0.0%	8.7%
Good	41.7	26.7	15.4	13.0
Average	25.0	40.0	69.2	56.5
Unsatisfactory	25.0	18.3	15.4	21.7
Very poor	8.3	3.3	0.0	0.0

* Includes six children for whom other test data were not available.

anymore. He is terribly hungry and tired [3BM]." Or "he lost his father and now mother died just a few hours ago. He cries incessantly—how will that go on?" And then the boy who wrote these TAT-inspired stories, like so many others in the institutions, graphically depicted his own plight: "There is no one who could help him, no grandparents, relatives, or friends. . . . He thinks of the future. Who will educate me? [3BM]."

Although the stories and sentence completions were of a troubled, often somewhat romanticized past ("Every family knows how nice it is when everyone is home—[7GF].") and an ambivalent, even psychologically uncertain institutional present (*I often feel that I am* . . . "sick," "abandoned," "dreaming," "no longer able to stand it," "have to run away"), there were strong wishes for future success, health, a beautiful and happy life, and considerable confidence, goal orientation, and maturity in the present. In completing the sentence *When alone* . . ., some children were "hiding things" and were "sometimes afraid," but more claimed to be "peaceful," "thinking of and planning for the future," "thinking of others." Even more revealing were many of the TAT outcomes. Despite sad, often miserable familial experiences, the Austrians persistently told about parents' concerns for children, husbands' for wives, and about unidentified others who "will take good care of him." Heroes plan and attain occupational goals, get married and have families.

No important differences denoting lack of personal security appeared between early admissions, later admissions, and children who had always lived with their parents. On the TAT protocols scored along the Erikson (1950, 1963) schema of developmental stages, the frequencies of negative tone for the three groups (Austrian children only) ranked as follows: Children living with their own parents were highest (53 per cent), all children in group care were lowest (about 40 per cent), and the early admissions fell between the two (49 per cent). (The frequency of negative tone found in a large number (727) of children in several countries is 43.6 per cent.)

Sentence-completion data also failed to single out the early admissions as particularly more troubled. No more often than otherwise comparable children did they respond with insecurity or dissatisfaction when continuing sentences like *I am often full of* . . . All children of this age, it appears, had a relatively high rate of negative reactions to such a beginning, concluding their sentences with "hate," "anger," "sadness," and similar responses, but the early placed children were not markedly different in this respect.

TABLE 11.4. *Problems during placement of early and later admissions to group care*

Problems	Austria: Kinderdorf		Yugoslavia: Children's Home	
	early (n=12)	later (n=60*)	early (n=13)	later (n=23)
Medical				
None or mild	91.6%	98.3%	84.6%	73.9%
Moderate or serious	8.4	1.7	15.4	26.1
Psychological				
None or mild	58.3	63.4	69.2	73.9
Moderate or serious	41.7	36.6	30.8	21.7
Learning				
None or mild†	66.7	66.7	30.8	52.1
Moderate or serious	33.3	33.3	61.6	43.5
Social group				
None or mild†	83.3	83.3	53.9	73.9
Moderate or serious	16.7	16.7	46.1	21.7

* Includes six children for whom other test data were not available.

† Includes several children who showed achievement or even distinction in learning and social relationships; their number was small in both the early and later placements.

Some hint of insecurity seemed to appear, though, around questions of competition, innovation, and the adherence to adult-made rules. The early admitted Austrian child may have been slightly more rejecting of "competing with others to find out who is best," and of the idea of being "himself even though others may not like him," and the early Yugoslav a trifle more accepting of the idea that "those smarter than he make the decisions." These attitudes were summarized in the somewhat greater rejection of Factor I_c (Self-Expression) by the early Austrian children and the *Mütter,* and the greater children as compared with later and home acceptance than the "mothers" wish of Factor IV_c (Deference). However, this slight hesitation to express oneself independently of others was not accompanied by any marked tendency to avoid Self-Assertion (Factor III_c), nor any reluctance to "make his own decisions" or to "decide for himself what is right and what is wrong."

TABLE 11.5. *Personality security and afflative responses of early and later admissions to group programs and of children living at home*

Sentence Completions	Austria: kinderdorf			Yugoslavia: children's Home		
	early (n=12)	later (n=54)	home (n=67)	early (n=13)	later (n=25)	home (n=72)
Personal security						
I am often full of . . . [negative feeling].	33.3%	38.9%	53.7%	53.9%	48.0%	40.3%
I often have the feeling that . . . [negative].	66.5	48.1	62.7	61.6	72.0	45.8
When I am alone I . . . [negative].	8.3	7.4	11.9	7.6	12.0	15.3
Social affiliation						
Working closely with others can be . . . [negative].	0.0	5.6	13.4	23.1	16.0	23.6
Working in groups can be . . . [negative].	0.0	1.9	11.9	0.0	0.0	0.0
I am most happy when . . . [social affiliation].	8.3	5.6	10.5	15.4	16.0	7.0
I am most happy when . . . [family].	41.7	25.9	28.4	0.0	4.0	2.8

As might be anticipated from the preceding paragraph, there was also no clear-cut difference among the groups in affiliative responses. Trying "to work with others whenever he can" was not often rejected by anyone in the Austrian and Yugoslav settings. Even more encouraging in the sentence completions was the Austrian children's spontaneous identification of the family as positive and happy. In view of the early placement of these children and their very extended institutional residence, this reference must be to the Kinderdorf family rather than to the natural one.

Sharing and helping, the other expressions of affiliative concerns, were also well thought of by the early placement children. "Willing to help anyone no matter how great the price" and "always ready to share what he has with others" were both embodied in Factor II$_C$ (Social Integration). The early Austrian placements were as positive on this factor as the other children in the institution and those living at home. The early Yugoslav placements were slightly less taken with the idea of helping others no matter how great the price, but they were more accepting of the sharing attitude and, hence, of the factor. In typical adolescent fashion, all the kids said "yes" with considerable gusto (mean position halfway between "definitely" and "I think so") to such altruistic statements as "wants to devote his life to helping other people" and "is always ready to share what he has with others." This concern for others appears to be, in part, a search for security, but when combined with the expressed readiness to seek out assistance, it indicates a balanced giving–getting associational pattern. Accordingly, the children showed no reluctance to shift focus from almost sacrificial sharing–helping to strong Self-Assertion (Factor III$_C$), consisting of an expressed desire to be alone, make one's own decisions, and decide for oneself on matters of right and wrong. Early placed Yugoslavs in particular responded more positively to self-orientation items than their institutional or home counterparts.

Self-orientation does not, however, indicate any lack of social sensitivity. *One should always* . . . and *One must never* . . . were more often than in the other categories answered with "understand others," "think of others even in the face of personal adversity," "avoid exploiting other people." But there was no great emphasis on moralizing or self-control. Responses of basic morality were equally or less frequent as compared with those of other children, and self-control endings, generally infrequent among all groups, were nearly absent among the Kinderdorf early placements. If one is to believe assertions that congregate institutions for children produce undifferentiated, authoritarian personalities automatically reeling off meaningless morality sermons, then evidence must have come from qualitatively different settings than these two in Yugoslavia and Austria.

In summary, the early admissions to these two "family" type institutions gave little evidence to support the familiar assumptions of deficiencies in in-

TABLE 11.6. *Security and affiliation: selected factorial analysis for early and later admissions to group care and home-reared children*

Factors	Austria: Kinderdorf				Yugoslavia: Children's Home			
	early (n=12)	later (n=54)	home (n=67)	adults (n=20)	early (n=13)	later (n=25)	home (n=72)	adults (n=53)
I$_c$. Self-Expression e.g. "Wants to be himself even though others may not like him."	2.38	2.23	2.10	2.12	1.88	2.01	1.84	1.85
II$_c$. Social Integration e.g. "Tries to work with others whenever he can." "Is cautious and carefully plans the things he does."	1.56	1.56	1.63	1.70	1.49	1.39	1.42	1.44
III$_c$. Self-Assertion e.g. "Wants to make his own decisions."	2.17	2.20	1.96	2.21	2.14	2.56	2.69	2.84
IV$_c$. Deference e.g. "Lets those smarter than he make decisions."	1.67	1.61	1.82	2.05	2.77	2.63	2.36	2.91

NOTE: The adults were asked: "Should a teenager here be just like this?" The values were: 1=strong agreement ("yes, definitely"); 2=agreement ("yes, I think so"); 3=disagreement ("no, I don't think so"); 4=strong disagreement ("no, not at all").

telligence, personality, and value development, even though the children were subject to "early and prolonged deprivation" including separation from the natural mother and many years of institutional care. While these children generally had seriously deprived backgrounds, and expressed ambivalence about "institutional living and about their present and future status, they were not markedly different in intelligence and personality variables from those who were separated from their families at a considerably more advanced age or not at all. Also, length of institutional residence (in this case, all in excess of several years) was unrelated to the present status of the child.

Supporting evidence for these conclusions is to be found in the staff evaluations of all the children in the two institutions. Asked to mark the extent to which each child came close to the wishes of the setting, the Austrian Kinderdorf staff designated 8 of the 12 early placed children as excellent achievers of whom the village is proud. One child (Johann, to be sure) was described as very distant from the expectations of the setting. The two remaining children were considered to have adequately met the expectations of the village. Of the 13 Yugoslav early admissions, 1 was described by 2 staff members as a person of whom they could be proud. The other 12 children were all average. None was classified in the category of failure.

Two Yugoslav cases provided some clinical evidence to support the aforementioned conclusions. Stephanie and Joe were not a random choice. Rather, the intent was to look at two very deprived, abandoned children. Stephanie occasionally gets mail from her father, but the contacts apparently have little substance to them. She does have warm and frequent visits with relatives.

At the time of her testing, Stephanie was slightly older than 16 years. She scored on the 24 percentile of the RPM test, about average for the institutional and home children tested in and near Belgrade. Her WISC score, standardized for Belgrade children, was 108. Stephanie's name was not on the list of outstandingly good or of problematic children.

Looking at Stephanie more carefully, the impression appears to be confirmed. Her TAT stories embody recollections of the past, pleasures of the present, and hopes for the future. The past is told in parental quarrels, child abandonment, and a search for love.

The stories are usually simple, stressing the manipulative, controlling dominance of adults (parents want the boy to become a famous violinist and force him to study; the girl wants to study but "they need help in the house and in the field" and don't let her go). They point to the crying need for love ("love between two people is the most important thing in life") and generally end on a hopeful note. Stephanie has some achievement dreams for herself. She wants to become a doctor, but quite realistically believes there is little chance of her succeeding. Friendship, mutual help, and affec-

TABLE 11.7. *Dominant value expressions of early and later admissions to group programs and of children living at home*

Sentence Completions	Austria: Kinderdorf			Yugoslavia: Children's Home		
	early n = 12	*later* n = 54	*home* n = 67	*early* n = 13	*later* n = 25	*home* n = 72
Basic morality						
One should always (have) . . .	16.7%	22.2%	13.4%	30.8%	8.0%	19.5%
A person's most important duty is . . .	16.7	16.7	25.4	23.1	24.0	26.4
One must never violate . . .	16.7	38.0	37.3	34.6	48.0	42.4
Social sensitivity						
One should always (show) . . .	16.7	5.6	14.9	15.4	4.0	7.0
A person's most important duty is . . .	33.3	40.7	37.3	23.1	4.0	9.7
One must never violate . . .	29.2	17.6	20.2	7.7	0.0	8.3
Self-control						
One should always (have) . . .	0.0	14.8	17.9	23.1	24.0	27.8
A person's most important duty is . . .	0.0	0.0	0.0	15.4	4.0	4.2
One must never (lose) . . .	12.5	8.3	12.0	11.5	24.0	14.6

tion are her concerns. She does have some close friends in the institution. Two name her as their choice for doing homework together (though four other children, perhaps more perceptive of her relatively low intelligence, reject her), three wish to share a room with her, work together, and spend leisure time with her. Among the last three is a boy, whose wishes Stephanie eagerly reciprocates. *When alone* . . . "I think about him."

All is not love and happiness in Stephanie's life. She *often has the feeling that* . . . "we are very lonely" and says that *I am often* . . . "full of sorrow," but the general impression is of a friendly, self-possessed young teenager, doing reasonable work in school, adjusting well to the institution, and reporting on her tender love for a fellow resident of the children's home. Considering the circumstances of Stephanie's early childhood and the events immediately preceding her admission to the institution, it seems that the setting has had a considerable and positive impact on her.

Joe's case is different, but it supports a cautious view that the institution has done him some good. Joe came to the institution at the age of three and a half when someone found him at the breast of his dead mother. Totally orphaned early and having no contact with relatives, Joe has lived in the institution for 13 of his 16½ years. His medical record has been normal, but he has had some problems in adjustment within the institution and in school.

At the age of 16½ Joe tested well in intelligence. With a score at the 47th percentile on the RPM, he did considerably better than most other children in the institution or the comparison group residing with their parents. His score on the WISC was 96. Staff at the institution did not find anything outstanding to report about Joe. He is neither a star nor a source of major concern.

On the TATs, Joe recapitulates his own sad beginnings: "[3BM] The boy, Rade, has neither mother nor father; his mother died and his father became a drunkard, so that he remains totally alone in the world. . . ." Other stories have a similar mood. Beginnings are bad, often even violent (people argue, son shoots father, a friend gets killed in an accident), but those who argue make up, the father forgives the son, and the mother consoles the boy whose friend had been killed. Stories end on strong, affiliative, and active notes. A strong achievement drive is particularly noticeable.

Joe wants to become an actor, has little assurance he will be one, but does think that *One must believe in* . . . "himself," that *Everyone should have* . . . "his own worth," and that *Competing with people* . . . "can be useful." He gives the impression of a somewhat sad, moody, and isolated child. He writes that he is *Often full of* . . . "sorrow," but he is not alone and knows it. He identifies one boy as his regular friend. Five children choose Joe as a roommate they want, two like to work with him, three wish to spend leisure time in his company. Only once is he rejected by anyone in all these selections. It seems that Joe is trying, and with some success, to master and implement the attitude in one of his sentences that *A person's most important duty is* . . . "to be an honorable citizen," but he still has little faith in what others will do to help him and so he believes that *When someone is troubled he should* . . . "forget about it and all that bothers him."

Joe does not, of course, present a picture of a vibrant, self-assured, creative adolescent. But for a child who was picked out of his tubercular mother's deathbed at the age of three, who has had no adult outside the institution show any interest in him, he seems to have come out remarkably well.

Lack of marked differences between the three types of children—early, later, home—may be a function of many factors. First, there is the possibility of insensitive measurement, but staff and peer judgments seem decisive. Second, the early admitted child may be less damaged than later admissions, but being harmed more than the older children by the separation, comes out about equal. Such an explanation fails to take into account the similarities between both institutional groups and the home children which may, of course, be the result of relatively normal children entering these two institutions and remaining unharmed there over a period of many years. Such a conclusion may well be supported by the findings of Pringle and Bossio (1960) whose institutional subjects were neither harmed much nor markedly helped, it seems, except through association with what they called "a firm friend outside," that is, an adult (parent or other person) with a strong interest in the child's well-being. But the intake data from the Kinderdorf and the Yugoslav children's home failed to support an assumption of normalcy at the time of entry.

A third possible explanation is made feasible by Skeels's (1966) report which showed that children can benefit from group care purely as a result of internal institutional conditions. Freud and Burlingham (1944) and Maas (1963a, 1963b) have noted the same. Life in a nursery or even absence of a parent did not appear to preclude good adjustment if the child found an adult figure with whom to form a lasting and deep relationship. This seems to be happening in the two children's institutions discussed here. The similarity between groups is particularly surprising in Yugoslavia. From all available evidence, the Yugoslav children are far more damaged at entry, and their subsequent care is not as good as that received by the Austrians. (Standard of living in general is lower in Yugoslavia.) The admissions policy of the Kinderdorf is unambiguous about excluding disturbed and otherwise difficult children. Although subject to some clinical error and to outside pressures from various authorities with children on their hands, the Kinderdorf nevertheless tends to adhere to this policy. Only three children in the sample were, like Johann, judged unfavorably at the time of admission. Although the Yugoslav institution has a similar policy, it has far less power to exclude the severely troubled. As a result, many admissions are children with very difficult past environments and, it seems, personality defects. Background materials for these children depict conditions that are in some cases unbelievably, grotesquely depriving.

Laurie and sisters: Three sisters—the mother is a prostitute. The father lives with a different woman every year and has several times been in jail. One of the girls was raped by a relative of the father. . . .

Other children have somewhat less bizarre histories, but prostitution and mental illness of related adults are common, and neglect or abuse may be reasonably assumed for all.

If these background data are accepted as evidence of serious problems in the child at the time of admission, then what has made possible the positive changes noted? There is some support for the "firm friend outside" view, but mainly it is the "friend inside" who really matters. Like Stephanie, some of the early admitted Austrians had occasional contacts with parents or relatives, and one child had a close, affectionate relationship with a parent. All others had none because their parents and relatives were dead or totally un-involved. To some extent, this is the result of agency policy, which can best be summed up by the phrase, not uncommon in the Kinderdorf, "They did enough damage already." Yugoslav early admissions show a similar pattern of relationship to outside adults. Only two children were described as having frequent, warm contacts with members of their families other than parents.

For most children, then, ties with adults must be within the institution, if they exist at all. Here the two settings diverge significantly. In the Kinder-dorf strong, affectionate ties with *Mutti* are feasible and very noticeable. Projective test responses (e.g., to TAT Card 7GF which depicts a middle-aged woman and pubescent girl) made much of the mother–child relation-ship. Ten of the 12 stories for this card were positive. Mother cares for her child, nurtures, instructs, consoles, just as a good mother should. Additional evidence of a warm, close relationship between *Mutti* and children abound-ed. In personal conversations children described *Mutti* in affectionate terms. In drawings they depicted her as a cat and themselves as kittens or other small, protected animals (Flitner, Bittner, Vollert 1965–66). Other impor-tant persons appeared to be "brothers and sisters" (a very wide age range exists in each "family"), but they were smaller lights in a child's life in this matriarchal society.

Yugoslav children face a very different adult–child situation in their insti-tution. The "families" are twice as large, somewhat less isolated physically from each other (apartment house versus cottages), and considerably less mother-oriented. The last point is of utmost significance. Ages, sex, status of the child-care people, and the ratio of adults to children all tend to preclude adherence to the familial model. The staff is younger than in the Kinder-dorf, sometimes male, usually considered or at least called "uncles" or "aunts," and much more limited in number. The Yugoslav children's responses to the same 7GF card also tended to be structured around a mother–daughter relationship, but the mother scolded, restrained, and was a picture in the memory.

Not being able to keep ties with members of their natural families, largely deprived by the institutional structure of the possibility to form close ties with a single parental figure, the Yugoslav children seem to rely on the other, often older children for their affective ties. Every "family" contains at least two or three adolescents and in some instances even young adults attending technical school or college. These become the critical "adults" in the younger children's lives. On visits to the institution, one often sees the nurturing posture of the older "brothers" and "sisters." They wash, feed, carry about the little ones, help the younger school-aged children with homework and domestic chores, and generally appear to set the tone of the place. The Yugoslav apartment lacks the security and tolerance of the mother-oriented Kinderdorf house, but still seems to create enough positive associations to promote growth. This environment and its inhabitants seem to lend further support to Skeels's (1966) findings that substantial, positive changes in early placed children are achievable not only when the environment provides for close ties with mature and stimulating adults, but also when there are others in the institution who, by virtue of their age and inclination, can be expected to fulfill some or even many parenting functions.

ADDITIONAL READING FOR PART III

Bowlby, John. *Maternal Care and Mental Health*. Geneva: World Health Organization, 1951.

Flint, Betty M. *The Child and the Institution: A Study of Deprivation and Recovery*. Toronto: University of Toronto Press, 1966.

Heinicke, Christoph M., and Westheimer, Ilse J. *Brief Separations*. London: Longmans, 1966.

Hess, Robert D., and Bear, Roberta M. *Early Education: Current Theory, Research, and Practice*. Chicago: Aldine, 1968.

Rabin, A. I. *Growing Up in the Kibbutz*. New York: Springer, 1965.

IV

Adolescents in
Group Care

12

Maturity in the High School Seminarian: An Empirical Approach

JEFFREY KEEFE

As the English public schools have shown, group care is not only a means of providing for the disadvantaged; it also can be the making of an elitist establishment intended to convey a mode of life, an ideology in conditions that exclude the distractions and infringements of the outside world. Some have argued that the very isolation needed to give the environment its effectiveness is conducive to deterioration of personal functioning. One environment subjected to such criticism is the Catholic seminary. Keefe's data, gathered in an attempt to respond to this criticism, contain little evidence to support the contention that group life is deleterious to the maturation process of the seminarians despite the generally negative outcome expectations that American society holds for settings of this type. In Chapters 13 and 15 Soviet and Israeli settings are described and positively evaluated, but these settings, unlike the seminary, had functioned in a generally accepting social environment. As extensions of collectivist societies the prophecy for them was success. Not so for the seminary. The seminary data acquire particular significance because they show the possibility of developing an atmosphere within a small societal subsegment that supports group care and shields it from the harmful consequences of pervasive negative expectations.

Theoretical Issues

Both theory and canon law strongly support the existence of the high school seminary. The Council of Trent in 1563, the Third Council of Baltimore in

Jeffrey Keefe. "Maturity in the High School Seminarian: An Empirical Approach." *The Catholic Psychological Record* 6 (1): 15–29.

1884, the latest code of canon law in 1920, and successive popes, including Paul VI in 1963, have emphasized that training for the priesthood should be carried out in specialized schools and should begin with the advent of adolescence. Certainly in the United States, the Church has translated both theory and the urgings of law into practice. The 1964 census of seminaries in the United States totaled 444, of which slightly more than 200 are high schools or include high school departments.

Despite the strong combination of theory and practice, most American clergy are opposed to, or at least have serious reservations about, the high school seminary (Fichter 1961). Long before the currents of change began to flow from Vatican II, many if not most clergy and religious could not bring themselves to enthusiastic support of the high school seminary. For a variety of reasons, pragmatic, sociological, and psychological, the rationale and execution of the high school seminary program has been questioned.

This paper presents a resumé of a Fordham University doctoral research study which sought empirical evidence bearing on a single criticism of the high school seminary—namely, the objection that the high school seminary training retards psychological maturation (Keefe 1965). The purpose of the study was to assess the relative maturity of the high school seminarian upon completion of his secondary schooling. How does he compare with his counterpart, the "ordinary" Catholic high school boy? Is the seminarian consistently more or less mature than his counterpart, or are there areas in which he is more mature, and others in which he is less so? The general hypothesis of the study was that the high school seminary product would not show poorer functioning in a majority of the several aspects of maturity investigated, and therefore should not be labeled "less mature."

There are two types of high school seminaries in the United States. In this study, the boarding school where students remain, excepting certain holidays and vacations, for the school year, is called the *minor* seminary. The day school which allows students to live at home while spending the class day at a special school for priesthood candidates is referred to as the *preparatory* seminary.

As might be expected, the minor seminary meets with heavier criticism than does the preparatory seminary, since the former involves a more restricted kind of high school environment. Therefore a minor seminary group was the pivot of the study. Three other groups were employed as well: "prep" seminarians, Catholic boys in Catholic all-male high schools, and Catholic boys in Catholic coeducational institutions. Presumably, the high school environment of these four groups can be conceived in gradient fashion, each representing a successively lesser degree of the supervision, discipline, and restricted experience which, it is claimed, adversely affect psychological maturation when brought to bear on a boy as intensively as in the seminary regimen.

Four groups of 70 boys were matched in an attempt to isolate the independent variable of high school experience. For a boy to qualify as a subject in the study he was required to be a male Catholic senior in his final semester of high school, and to have had his entire high school career in the type of school by which the group was classified. It was required that he had obtained all grammar school education in Catholic schools. By testing 449 senior boys in several institutions, data for 280 qualified subjects, 70 in each group, were obtained. In addition, group equality in intelligence and socioeconomic status was established.

The primary step of the investigation was to construct a working model of so common, yet elusive, a concept as maturity. The literature on maturity is overwhelming. Most often it resorts to illustration rather than definition. Moreover, there is a constant interchange among such terms as mental health, maturity, and normality. As one reads this literature he becomes aware of an implicit distinction between mental health and maturity. Mental health is often considered in a negative frame of reference: it is the absence of pervading anxiety and/or disabling symptoms, and provides a base line for growth in valued traits. Maturity is a positive concept. It is, as the etymology of the word suggests, an end product of development or growth in valued traits.

The valued traits which make up maturity are likewise manifold. Pius XII (1958), in writing on the minor seminary, advised that it should correspond as much as possible to a normal environment to insure development of each candidate's individuality, responsibility, initiative, and critical thinking. These characteristics would be among the hallmarks of maturity proposed by psychological theorists who commonly conceive maturity as growth in positive, productive qualities. For purposes of the present study, maturity was seen as a rubric which included core criteria proposed by leading theorists among the psychological writers.

As one reads the literature on mental health and maturity he begins to note a certain consensus in concepts despite a variety of labels. In a trim volume by Marie Jahoda (1958) the diversified approaches to full-blown mental health—i.e., maturity—have been ordered under a few general headings. The present study selected five of Jahoda's approaches to positive psychological functioning as areas of development or maturation in which to make comparisons among the four groups of boys who had varied high school experience. In brief, the research project selected certain evaluative dimensions which were considered to illustrate maturity. Note the term "selected." This study is a limited one, not only regarding the debate about the minor seminary which has ramifications in several disciplines, but limited even within the psychological area itself to *selected* aspects of maturity. It is maintained, however, that the framework provided by the five general approaches adopted from Jahoda's compendium enabled broad coverage of the multifaceted concept of maturity.

Loevinger's (1966) model of personality may add some clarity to the aim and scope of the present study. Loevinger views personality as a fourfold development: physical, intellectual, psychosexual, and ego development. Each "side" of personality is relatively independent. The present study investigated ego development, usually described in the literature in terms of self-conceptual, characterological, interpersonal, cognitive, and affective attitudes.

In the present study each general approach selected from Jahoda (1958) was reduced to a specific psychological construct. The constructs were defined in operational terms and a measure was selected to assess the relative standing of the four groups in each construct or maturity trait. Table 12.1 presents an outline of the design of the study, reference to which may add clarity to the discussion which follows here.

Factors Studied

1. EGO-IDENTITY

Jahoda reported that many authors emphasize attitudes toward oneself as a principal index of positive psychological functioning, and cited certain aspects of the self-concept recurring in the literature. One such aspect is the sense of identity. This construct exemplifying the self-attitude was adopted since ego-identity is primarily a developmental concept, and the basic concern of the investigation was possible developmental differences. Moreover, ego-identity is a self-sentiment, a cluster of related characteristics which develop sequentially, and which in Erikson's (1950, 1959) theory of ego development crystallizes during adolescence, the period of life through which the subjects of the study currently were passing.

According to Erikson, the ego (or self) develops from infancy to maturity in a manner similar to the appearance of various tissues and systems in the embryo. The developing personality meets successive crises which are common to man's life experience. The individual optimally should emerge from each crisis with an increased sense of unity. Each critical period ends with a basic attitude or value with which the individual meets future life experiences. Erikson posited eight such critical periods in life. Each critical period, successfully met, tempers the ego with a newly precipitated attitude which will provide it with more effective and wider powers of coping with life. Hopefully, when an individual reaches the threshold of adulthood, he will have developed mature ego-identity which Erikson described as "accrued confidence" and as the psychosocial equilibrium necessary to make a satisfactory adjustment as an individual in society.

Erikson postulated a criterion of positive development and one of poor development for each life crisis. For example, the first stage of life, infancy, should be marked by the development of basic trust in others, or if things go

TABLE 12.1. *Experimental Design for the investigation of comparative maturity among four experimental groups*

Maturity: the level of development of commonly proposed positive criteria of mental health.

Major Approaches to Positive Psychological Function, Classified by Jahoda (1958)	Construct	Operational Definition	Measure Employed
1. Attitudes of the individual toward self	Ego-identity	Behavioral manifestations of Erikson's positive criteria of ego-identity	Ego-Identity Scale
2. Degree of self-actualization	Positive motivation	Goal-oriented, socialized, motivating attitudes	Consistency index of TAT
3. Unification of function in personality	Integration	Correspondence of conscious and fantasy level interpersonal outlook	Variability index
4. Individual's degree of independence	Autonomy	(a) Freedom from intellectual rigidity	Intellectual Conviction Scale
		(b) Freedom from undue social pressure	Independence of Judgment Scale
5. How the individual sees the world around him	Maturity of affective response	(a) Response patterns typical of normal adults	Age Scale Perceptual Reaction Test
		(b) Lesser frequency of extreme options	Perceptual Reaction Test

awry, the developing ego would be handicapped by mistrust. Research studies have amply supported the conclusion that defective mothering between the ages of six months to two years can leave a child with a host of negative attitudes, among them mistrust (Spitz 1965). From each criterion of positive or negative development Erikson deduced attitudes which are assimilated by the ego and dynamically constitute personality. When it is predominantly positive, this dynamic integrated complexus of attitudes by which Erikson describes the ego is conceptually similar to the layman's view of a mature outlook.

Ego-identity of the four groups in the present scale was measured by Rasmussen's Ego-Identity scale (1961). This scale was chosen because it had been constructed originally to differentiate mature from immature navy recruits, who previously had been screened for psychopathology. Therefore there were similarities of sex, age, and general normality between the navy recruits and high school senior boys of the present study. Erikson had proposed that the problem of ego-identity versus ego-diffusion would be intensified during adolescence, when an individual is exposed to pressures of more than ordinary physical intimacy, energetic competition, and occupational choice. Both navy recruits and seminary groups do meet with more than ordinary pressures in these areas. Rasmussen's scale is composed of 72 items which illustrate behavioral manifestations of attitudes which, in Erikson's theory, evolve during resolution of the common life crises.

Analysis of variance, according to one criterion of classification of the Ego-Identity Scale results showed no statistically significant difference among groups in the study in overall development of this complexus of positive attitudes in self-sentiment. Actually, the results, listed in Table 12.2 were amazingly similar, with less than a single point difference separating the highest and lowest group score. The range of scores was practically identical with that obtained by Rasmussen in testing navy recruits. The cross-section of Catholic high school seniors showed comparable ego development with the slightly older navy recruits of the Rasmussen study.

2. POSITIVE MOTIVATION

Another general approach to positive psychological functioning cited by Jahoda was through such criteria as growth, development of one's potential, or as Maslow (1954) called it, self-actualization. Maslow dichotomized human motivation. He spoke of deficiency motivation, which encompasses drives toward basic physiological and psychological needs. And he spoke of self-actualizing drives which aim at development of more characteristically human potentials, the goals of which are outside of oneself, either in work or in other persons. This is reminiscent of Freud's offhand description of the mature person as one who can work and love (Shoben 1956).

Magda Arnold (1962) concluded from a wide variety of experimental samples that the common denominator for mature persons was goal-oriented rather than self-centered motivation: "We mean by maturity that the self-centered motivation of the child is gradually replaced by a more goal-oriented, socialized set of motives" (Arnold 1962, p. 185). Arnold carried out long-term empirical analyses of the Thematic Apperception Test (TAT) with many different kinds of criterion groups of successful (mature) and unsuccessful persons. From this research Arnold devised a method whereby

TABLE 12.2. *Scores of four groups of 70 Catholic high school Senior Boys on Selected Aspects of Maturity*

Variable		Minor Sem.	Prep. Sem.	Boys' School	Coed School	F
Ego identity	M	52.90	51.96	52.86	52.38	
	SD	7.97	8.09	9.81	8.20	0.14 n.s.
Positive	M	−0.09	−0.50	−0.89	−0.43	
motivation	SD	7.10	8.44	7.36	7.25	0.13 n.s.
Variability	M	54.78	56.94	60.77	55.60	
index*	SD	28.08	28.91	29.70	26.88	0.71 n.s.
Intellectual	M	−12.23	−16.33	−4.12	−6.16	
conviction*	SD	20.30	17.13	16.28	17.15	6.82†
Independence	M	9.27	10.56	9.71	9.08	
of judgment	SD	2.72	2.81	3.13	2.30	3.90†
Age scale PRT	M	23.97	25.01	30.50	25.95	
	SD	13.90	13.50	11.25	12.99	3.39†
Extreme	M	22.54	23.70	20.60	23.18	
option, PRT*	SD	9.06	9.69	8.21	9.11	1.55 n.s.

* Lower scores indicate superior functioning.
† Significant at .01 level.

a TAT story can be reduced to a motivating attitude, a principle of action held by the storyteller. It is particularly noteworthy that her empirically derived classes of attitudes have considerable conceptual similarity to the descriptive features of the self-actualizing person developed theoretically by Maslow.

For this reason Arnold's method of extracting and scoring positive motivation from the TAT was adopted as the operational approach to maturity as self-actualization. Positive motivation was considered by the investigator as the most important facet of the present study because this aspect of maturity deals with motivating attitudes rather than simply evaluative attitudes; because it was derived from a projective test, and thus less susceptible to faking; and finally, because the method has impressive research support. The process of obtaining a positive motivation score from a 10-story TAT record of each subject entailed extracting a single motivating attitude from each of 2,800 stories. A second scorer independently repeated the procedure with 250 of these stories. The reliability coefficient between scorers was .85.

Reference to Table 12.2 indicates that four groups showed no statistically significant difference in positive motivation scores. The raw mean score of each group was near zero. Since the possible range of scores was +20 to −20, the near-zero mean indicated that groups showed fairly equal degrees of positive and negative motivation. A study with male college students by Garvin (1960) also obtained a mean near the midpoint of the range. The four groups of high school senior boys showed equal development in positive motivation, that is, in mature motivating attitudes in such areas as achievement, general ethics, interpersonal relationships, and reaction to adversity. The quantitative level of attitudes which "characterize" the groups was the same. Whether the groups characteristically emphasized different areas of motivation will be subject for a future study.

3.   INTEGRATION

A third category of approaches to positive psychological functioning was described by Jahoda as unity of function among psychic processes. This unity of function has been described in various ways. Kubie (1954) offered what seems to be the simplest description of integrated functioning. Assuming that both conscious and unconscious forces enter into every action of a man, a person is considered mentally healthy or mature insofar as conscious elements dominate. When unconscious motives which are not easily accessible to consciousness dominate, the agent is inflexible and enslaved; he cannot develop mature methods of coping. The directive "Know thyself" has always been the aim and the mark of the mature man. Allport (1953) stressed that the normal individual will match the motivation appearing in projective tests with direct communication; in other words, conscious data should match preconscious and unconscious material in the integrated person.

Leary (1957) developed an operational conception and measure of integration parallel to those just cited. He chose objective and projective tests as reflecting successive levels of awareness. By transforming objective (conscious) and projective (preconscious) data to the same interpersonal variables, Leary sought to compare an individual's interpersonal perception at two levels of psychic activity. He worked out a complicated measure of interlevel discrepancy which he called the variability index—that is, the relative amount of discrepancy between conscious and preconscious outlook. General interlevel correspondence of interpersonal outlook provides an operational definition of integration, while the variability index is its operational measure.

Data for this measure of integration were obtained from the Interpersonal Check List (Leary 1957) and the TAT. The checklist provided the objective, conscious self-concept of each subject in the study. The subject's presumably preconscious self-image was obtained by tabulating the interpersonal attitudes shown by the hero of the TAT stories in terms of the same variables extracted from the adjective checklist. In simplest terms, Leary's method allows for comparison of interpersonal attitudes on two levels of psychic functioning—how closely they match—that is, how integrated they are.

The results with the integration measure revealed that the groups did not differ significantly in variability indexes. It should be noted in reading Table 12.2 that the lower the score, the greater the integration. Integration, conceptualized as correspondence of interpersonal attitudes on two levels of awareness, proved to be equally developed among the experimental groups.

4. AUTONOMY

A fourth class of the criteria of positive psychological functioning was concerned with the individual's degree of independence. The layman speaks of standing on one's own two feet; the psychologist, of autonomy.

The literature treats autonomy from two aspects. Internal autonomy is seen as freedom from rigid, rationalized conformity, a structural rather than a content feature of the mind. Dynamically, internal autonomy is flexible self-rule, a means which obviates domination either by an inflexible superego or the anarchic rule by impulse (Erikson 1959). A second aspect of autonomy discussed in the literature has an external focus: autonomy in the sense of relative freedom from undue social pressures to conform. In the light of the criticism of seminary groups, any shortcoming in autonomy might be traced either to an internal rigidity (hardly to rule by impulse!) or to excessive plasticity in respect to external forces.

To ascertain the relative degree of internal rigidity, or conversely, the degree of internal autonomy among groups, a scale devised by Rokeach and Eglash (1956), the Intellectual Conviction Scale, was employed. Rokeach's extensive research in the area of authoritarianism led him to maintain that the conformist is not betrayed by the content of his beliefs but by the manner of his believing. A conforming type of person fails to distinguish between content and source, between what is believed and the basis of belief. The conformist is the person who does not "distinguish, assess, and act independently on information received from authority" (Rokeach 1961, p. 247).

Rokeach classified adherence to conventional beliefs into rational and rationalized acceptance. The former includes open-minded adherence to authority or to inner-directed intellectual conviction. Rationalized acceptance is fear-based reliance on authority. Rokeach and Eglash (1956) devised the Intellectual Conviction Scale to discriminate rational from rationalized beliefs.

The results with this measure of internal autonomy broke the pattern of previous results which had shown no difference among groups. Both seminary groups demonstrated less willingness to subscribe to rationalizations in support of conventional beliefs than did boys from regular Catholic high schools. Table 12.2 shows that all groups obtained negative mean scores. Due to the scoring system, the more autonomous person—that is, the person who more forcefully rejects conventional beliefs which are based on rationalizations—obtains a more negative score. Therefore, all four groups leaned toward rejection of rationalized statements, and none could be labeled conformist. Each group demonstrated varying degrees of internal autonomy. But the seminary groups were much more definitive in their position. Analysis of variance showed highly significant and clear-cut group differentials. Tukey's test indicated that the two seminary groups were more internally autonomous than their counterparts from other Catholic schools. The seminary groups did not differ significantly from one another.

Assessment of external autonomy, considered as resistance to undue social pressure, was made by means of the Independence of Judgment Scale of Barron (1963). This scale was constructed of items which discriminated between groups of persons known to be independent and those who more easily yielded under social group pressure.

Results from the Independence of Judgment Scale also indicated a difference among groups. The prep seminarians had the highest group mean. Statistical analysis revealed that the prep seminary group evidenced more external autonomy than the minor seminary group and the boys group from coed institutions.

5. MATURITY OF AFFECTIVE RESPONSE

A fifth general approach to positive psychological functioning is how the individual sees the world (Jahoda 1958). Objectivity in assessing reality is axiomatic of maturity in both the professional and popular mind. But one's response to reality is not limited to cognitive assessment; it includes estimative and appetitive responses as well. The present study chose one of these sequential aspects of reality testing as an area of developmental group comparison: the evaluative, affective response which follows perception. The instrument adopted to measure the maturity of affective or emotional response was the Perceptual Reaction Test (PRT) (Berg, Hunt and Barnes 1949). Considerable research has allowed the inference that the age scale of the PRT measures maturity of affective response which is operationally conceived as correspondence to typical adult response patterns rather than patterns typical of children (Hesterly 1963).

Table 12.2 lists results from the age scale of the PRT which showed an ascending rank order of minor seminary group, prep seminary group, boys-in-coed-school group, and finally the all-boys-school group which obtained the highest—that is, the most typically adult—score. Prior expectations with this instrument were that the minor seminary group, often seen as unsophisticated and naïve by observers, would show a more overreactive and uncritical response pattern to items of the test, which pattern has been found to be more typical of children than adults. This expectation was borne out by the results; the minor seminary group, compared with the combined other three groups, scored significantly lower, that is, less adult. If seminarians as a group were compared with nonseminarians as a group, the same result held.

Therefore, on the basis of some past research, the conclusion is warranted that high school seminarians are less mature in their affective response patterns than nonseminarians.

In order to view the results from the PRT age scale in perspective it should be pointed out that seminarians did not obtain age-scale scores lower than expected for their age from standardization norms; what made the difference was that the all-boys-school group scored considerably above norms for their age. The age-scale was standardized on samples of adults from a different section of the country than subjects of the present study. The development of adult norms from persons more comparable to the subjects of the present study would allow for more definite statements in this area of affective maturity.

Other studies have provided a somewhat different approach to maturity assessment with PRT test data. Studies have shown that, when a rating scale is employed, predominant choice of extreme ratings is characteristic of maladjusted adults, and of both normal and maladjusted children (Zax, Gardiner, and Lowy, 1964). The choice of extreme ratings seems to be a reflection of the immature, childish tendency to assess the world in terms of polarized extremes, to see things as black or white. On this rationale, the incidence of extreme-option choice in ratings designs of the PRT was used as an index of a subject's tendency to oversimplify, to affectively overreact. The group means listed in Table 12.2 showed no significant difference among groups in their penchant for extreme affective reactions.

The Intercorrelation Matrix of Basic Measures

In a multivariable study, the opportunity is present to learn more about the instruments as well as about the subjects of the study. To achieve the former end an intercorrelation matrix of all the variables and subscales was calculated. [Table 3, showing intercorrelations, and the explanatory text are omitted in the interest of brevity. The author's conclusions about the data in this table follow (M.W.).]

The matrix of Table 3 showed that significant covariation among the measures was relatively infrequent, low, and in some cases, negative. Approximately 40 percent of possible intercorrelations of basic measures proved significant, though most of these were meager in size. The small correlations may be evidence that maturity, like intelligence, is multidimensional, and that various aspects of maturity, like intelligence, develop without commensurate progress in all of its manifestations.

Summary

The present investigation was undertaken to test empirically the frequent criticism that high school seminaries retard psychological maturation. The experimenter adopted the position that maturity was a general rubric illustrated by many valued traits. Relative maturity was conceived as comparative development in positive attributes which had been proposed by leading theorists as criteria of sound ego functioning. Four equated groups of high school senior boys, representing minor or boarding seminaries, preparatory or day seminaries, Catholic boys' schools, and Catholic coed schools, were tested in five dimensions of maturation.

The principal hypothesis of the study stated that high school seminarians would not show generally poorer performance in the aspects of maturity under consideration. The results sustained this hypothesis. All four experimetal groups showed an equal level of development in constructs of ego-identity, positive motivation, and integration. Both groups of seminarians registered superiority in one autonomy measure, internal intellectual conviction, while in a second autonomy measure which reflected resistance to undue social pressure, the prep seminary group evidenced a significantly higher score than two of the other groups. Conversely, seminarians scored lower than nonseminarians on a scale considered to tap maturity of affective response, although with a second current approach to data from the instrument employed, the groups did not show differential levels. Conclusions about maturity of affective response must remain guarded.

Correlational data established that one instrument, the Independence of Judgment Scale, could not be retained as a linear measure of mature autonomy. Reconsideration of the variability index, the measure of integration, led to the conclusion that it is more accurately a neutral measure of mental health, and insufficient by itself to meet the present study's definition of maturity as positive functioning in a valued attribute. However, even with these reservations, results for the four groups revealed more similarity than differences in maturity. Differences did appear, but when greater development for one group was indicated by one measure, the general picture was balanced by a lesser development indicated by another measure. Thus the general conclusion was that no single experimental group was outdistanced by any other(s) in progress toward psychological maturity. It would seem that debates on the advisability of the high school seminary should be shifted to grounds other than psychological maturity as measured in this study.

13

Reaction to Social Pressure from Adults Versus Peers among Soviet Day School and Boarding School Pupils in the Perspective of an American Sample

URIE BRONFENBRENNER

One of the main dangers of institutional care lies in the peer group. Ever-present, it envelops the inmate and carries him to doom or glory. Since most group environments have been for the undesirable, the individual usually is pressed to move in the direction of behaviors that the larger society depreciates or even resents. Polsky (1967) found this to be so in Cottage Six; others have made similar observations before and since his excellent study. The group is omnipresent, hence omnipotent. Its power is so great that adult leaders are unable to act as a balance, so that they, too, actually become co-opted and not only accede to but often participate in the behavior that society has charged them to reduce or eliminate. The fact has led to its assumption.

Some settings, however, do not begin with the assumption that adolescent

Urie Bronfenbrenner. "Reaction to Social Pressure from Adults Versus Peers among Soviet Day School and Boarding School Pupils in the Perspective of an American Sample." *Journal of Personality and Social Psychology* 15 (3): 179–89. Copyright 1971, American Psychological Association. Reproduced by permission.

This article was first presented at the Symposium on Social Factors in Childhood and Adolescence at the XIXth International Congress of Psychology, London, England, July 28 to August 2, 1969. The research was supported by a grant from the National Science Foundation. The experiments reported in this paper were carried out with the cooperation of Soviet colleagues while the author was an exchange scientist at the Institute of Psychology in Moscow.

peer societies will evolve conduct unacceptable to adults nor that pressure of age-mates will confirm the young person in his misbehavior. Clearly the kibbutz youth group is predicated on the opposite premise—namely, that peers will clarify and cajole, push and reward in order to move a member toward adult values. In this effort they seem to succeed (see Chapter 15), but more than that, if unconstrained in their youthful exuberance and ideological purity they may well push and succeed to excess. In his studies of adolescents Bronfenbrenner also finds a lack of divergence between the culturally approved values and those that Soviet school children accept. In boarding schools where peer pressure is bound to be intense conformity to societal values is even greater than among children who live at home, whose environment contains a diversity of socializing agents.

Background of the Problem

In a previous experiment (Bronfenbrenner 1967a), the author reported systematic differences in the degree and stability of orientation toward peers versus adults among Soviet and American school children. Specifically, in comparison with their Russian age-mates, American 12-year-olds indicated substantially greater willingness to engage in adult-disapproved behavior. In addition, the effect of the peer group (one's friends in school) was quite different in the two societies. When told that their classmates would know of their actions, American school children were even more willing to engage in misconduct. Soviet youngsters showed just the opposite tendency. Knowing that their peers would learn of their actions increased the level of socially approved responses.

In discussing the results, the author pointed out that the two samples being compared differed not only in cultural background (Soviet versus American) but also in the type of school attended, all of the Russian children being enrolled in boarding schools. This fact, it was noted, probably enhanced the observed cultural contrast, since one of the stated purposes of Soviet educators in introducing *internats* or boarding schools into the regular educational system was to make possible more effective character education. "It is therefore possible that pupils in the internats are more strongly identified with adult values than those attending ordinary day schools [Bronfenbrenner 1967a, p. 205]." Fortunately, there was a way to clarify the issue by replicating the experiment in Soviet schools of the conventional type where pupils live at home, and in the original study, the author indicated that such an investigation was already being carried out.

Theoretical Orientation

The present work reports the results of the promised replication. The research is of interest from two points of view. First, it does clarify the extent to which the findings for the Soviet sample in the earlier experiment are attributable to Russian children in general versus boarding school pupils in particular. But in addition, and perhaps more significantly, the results shed light on an important theoretical (and increasingly practical) issue in studies of socialization; namely, the impact of group upbringing when the influence of the family is minimized. During the school year, pupils in Soviet boarding schools see their parents only about once every two weeks. Thus the school, or more specifically, the children's collective, plays the primary role in the process of socialization.[1]

With respect to this issue, in the course of previous research (Bronfenbrenner 1961, 1962, 1967a, 1969; Devereux, Bronfenbrenner, and Suci 1962) a general hypothesis was formulated that could be tested by the experimental comparison of day school and boarding school pupils. The hypothesis focuses on the differential impact of upbringing by one versus two or more primary socializing agents on the child's capacity to resist social pressure. Specifically, it was proposed that a child is more likely to be able to resist social pressure if, in the course of growing up, he has been exposed to more than one major socializing agent. The assumption is that exposure to divergent influences in the course of growing up makes it easier for the child to resist pressure to conform. Thus, a child who has been brought up by a single socializing agent (e.g., one parent instead of two) is not only likely to become more dependent but also more anxious at the prospect of differing from his sole source of emotional support. In contrast, a child raised by more than one upbringer is apt to learn that you "can't please everybody" and that deviation does not jeopardize one's major source of security. As a result, the child reared by multiple agents may not subscribe as fervently to his upbringers' values but is more likely to remain true to his own views, whatever they may be, when these are subjected to pressure for change.

The contrast between Soviet boarding and day schools provides an opportunity to examine the impact of what might be called *pluralistic* versus *monistic* socialization at yet another level. Pupils in Soviet boarding schools are subject to a highly homogeneous pattern of socialization with minimum exposure to extraneous influences. To begin with, the influence of the family is reduced. Not only are visits with parents restricted to once or twice a month, but in addition, admissions policies give priority to families in the following categories: *(a)* one parent is missing (through death or divorce), *(b)* the parents' job requires extended periods away from home (e.g., work as truck driver, soldier, geologist, airline stewardess, etc.), *(c)* the two parents work on different shifts. In other words, these are families in which, even when the child is at home, opportunities for parent–child contact are limited. Moreover, such families also receive priority in entering their children in nurseries and kindergartens, so that a higher proportion of boarding school children will also have attended boarding or day nurseries and preschools, some from as early as eight months of age. When the children enter boarding school (almost always in the first grade), they are assigned a teacher and an upbringer who continue with the same group year after year.

Such continuity in staff and group membership takes on added significance in view of the explicit responsibility borne by both of these parties in the Soviet system of childrearing. The principles and procedures of upbringing to be employed in all Soviet schools are outlined in detail in official manuals prepared for the different age levels. As a result, there is far greater similarity from one classroom to another in the way that children are treated in Soviet schools than in American schools, where such matters as standards of conduct, training in character development, social organization of the classroom, etc., are largely left up to the individual teacher, who may not choose to do very much about them.

In Russian schools, such matters become the major concern not only of the staff but also of the children's collective, which in the Soviet educational system functions as the agent of adult society in maintaining standards of conduct and dispensing rewards and punishments. The latter typically take the form of group sanctions expressed through public criticism and ultimately the threat of excommunication. In the boarding school, the role of the collective is deliberately emphasized. In addition, the influence of this group extends beyond the classroom into all aspects of the child's life. Whatever he does—be it academic, recreational, or social—he does not as an individual but as a member of his collective, which corresponds in membership to his school class. Thus for boarding school pupils, the classroom collective— which in turn is an integral part of the *druzhina,* or collective of the entire school—becomes a pervasive, enduring, and primary source of the child's security and satisfaction.

Although children enrolled in day schools are in a similar situation for much of the day, once they are dismissed in the middle of the afternoon they fall under the influence of two other major settings. The first of these is of course the family; the second is the *dvor* or courtyard, a place where the informal peer group holds sway. Moreover, a lower proportion of these children will have attended boarding or day nurseries before entering school, or have parents who are often away from home. In short, in comparison with boarding school children, Russian pupils in day schools experience, both in past and present, substantially greater diversity in types of socializing agent. Thus the contrast between the two types of institution provides an opportunity to test out the theoretical orientation, which gives rise to two specific hypotheses.

Hypothesis I. Children being raised primarily in a single socialization setting (the boarding school) subscribe to culturally approved values to a greater extent than those exposed extensively to a greater variety of socializing agents (day school pupils).

Hypothesis II. Children being raised primarily in a single socialization setting (the boarding school) are more likely to conform to changing social pressures in their immediate environment than those exposed extensively to a greater variety of socializing agents (day school pupils).

A third hypothesis deals with the relation of the Soviet findings to analogous data previously obtained from an American sample (Bronfenbrenner 1967a).

Hypothesis III. Intracultural differences (Soviet boarding versus day school) are smaller than intercultural differences (Soviet versus American); specifically, Soviet school children, whether from boarding schools or day schools, differ from their American age-mates in the two respects previously reported: *(a)* Russian children show less willingness than American children to engage in antisocial behavior; *(b)* when told that their misconduct will become known to their classmates, Russian and American children react in opposite ways, the former being less ready to engage in misconduct, the latter more willing to do so.

Method

The primary experiments reported here were carried out in 12 5th-grade classes equally distributed among 3 boarding schools *(N = 188)* and 3 day schools *(N = 165)* in Moscow. With the aid of Soviet colleagues, the boarding and day schools were selected so as to be comparable in educational and economic background of the children's parents, the majority of whom had completed secondary school and were employed in service occupations or skilled trades. The control was accomplished by picking schools serving the same or adjacent neighborhoods known to house families of a generally similar socioeconomic level. Unfortunately, it did not prove possible to check on the degree of comparability by securing systematic data on parental education, income, or occupation. Nor could information be obtained on other relevant background factors such as family structure, parental treatment, or previous educational history of the child.

The experimental procedure was identical to that employed in the earlier research and consisted of the following elements.[2] Children were asked to respond to a series of conflict situations under three different conditions: *(a)* a *base* or *neutral* condition, in which they were told that no one would see their responses except the investigators conducting the research; *(b)* an *adult* condition in which they were informed that the responses of everyone in the class would be posted on a chart and shown to parents at a special meeting scheduled for the following week; and *(c)* a *peer* condition, in which the children were notified that the chart would be prepared and shown a week later to the class itself. The conflict situations consisted of 30 hypothetical dilemmas such as the following.

The Lost Test

You and your friends accidentally find a sheet of paper which the teacher must have lost. On this sheet are the questions and answers for a quiz that you are going to have tomorrow. Some of the kids suggest that you not say anything to the teacher about it, so that all of you can get better marks. What would you really do? Suppose your friends decide to go ahead. Would you go along with them or refuse?

REFUSE TO GO ALONG WITH MY FRIENDS

absolutely certain	fairly certain	I guess so

GO ALONG WITH MY FRIENDS

I guess so	fairly certain	absolutely certain

Other items dealt with such situations as going to a movie recommended by friends but disapproved by parents, neglecting homework to join friends, standing guard while friends put a rubber snake in the teacher's desk, leaving a sick friend to go to a movie with the gang, joining friends in pilfering fruit from an orchard with a "no trespassing" sign, wearing styles approved by peers but not by parents, running away after breaking a window accidentally while playing ball, etc.

The items had been developed through a series of interviews and pretests in which parents, teachers, and schoolchildren had been asked to indicate the kinds of behaviors about which adults and children disagreed. Two criteria were employed in selecting from a large number used in the pilot studies the 30 dilemmas employed in the experiment proper. The terms chosen were those which *(a)* in pretest experimental runs had showed the greatest shift between *adult* and *peer* condition; *(b)* in a factor analysis had highest loadings on a general factor of adult-approved versus -disapproved behavior and lowest loadings on factors specific to a particular type of situation.

With the cooperation of Soviet colleagues, a Russian-language version of 30 items was prepared, with minor variations to adapt to the Soviet cultural context. Each response was scored on a scale from -2.5 to $+2.5$, a negative value being assigned to the behavior urged by age-mates. To control for a positional response set, scale direction was reversed in half of the items. The situations were divided into three alternate forms of 10 items each, with a different form being used for each experimental condition. Thus under any one condition a child could obtain a score ranging from -25 to $+25$ with 0 representing equal division between behavior urged by peers and adults. Split-half reliabilities for the 10-item forms (based on American samples only) ranged from .75 to .86 under different experimental conditions; the reliability of the total score (i.e., sum across all three conditions) was .94. All reliability coefficients are corrected for length of test by the Spearman-Brown formula.

The basic research design involved a double Latin square with experimental treatments constituting the three rows, classrooms appearing in the columns, and forms distributed randomly, with the restriction that each form appear only once in each column and twice in each row. This basic pattern was repeated twice in each sample, once for boys and once for girls, for a total of four sets of double Latin squares (3 Conditions × 6 Classrooms in 4 Sex × School-Type combinations). In order to equate for varying numbers of boys and girls in each classroom, the individual cell entries used for the primary analysis of variance were the mean scores obtained by all boys or girls in a given classroom under a particular experimental condition. In this model, classrooms and forms were treated as random variables, and type of school (boarding versus day), experimental treatment, and sex of child, as fixed effects. It is, of course, the latter three which constitute the primary focus of interest in the experiment.

For interpreting the results, the reader must bear in mind that a high mean score signifies going along with adult-oriented alternatives; and a low score with adult-disapproved actions being urged by the peers described in the item itself. This does not mean, however, that the behavior in question is necessarily approved or disapproved by the particular adults or peers who supposedly get to see the child's responses under the experimental conditions. Indeed, it is the purpose of the experimental procedure to reveal to what extent and *in which direction* adults and peers do in fact influence the child's responses in a given situation.

Results

Mean values obtained by boys and girls in each type of school under the three experimental conditions are shown in Table 13.1. Tests of significance, together with relevant means and differences, appear in Table 13.2. Several findings emerge from this analysis.

First, the reliable difference in total score favoring boarding school pupils (Table 13.2, line 1, column 4) indicates that across all three experimental conditions, this group was more committed to adult-approved standards of behavior than pupils enrolled in day schools.

Second, the reliable sex difference in total score (Table 13.2, line 2, column 3) reveals that girls gave more adult-oriented responses than boys. Although this difference was higher for the boarding school than for the day school sample, the interaction effect (Table 13.2, line 2, column 4) was not significant.

Third, the absence of any significant differences in line 3 of Table 13.2

TABLE 13.1.   *Mean scores obtained by Soviet boarding and day school pupils under three experimental conditions*

Ss	Experimental Conditions			
	base	adult	peer	average across conditions
Boys				
Boarding	12.54	14.21	13.18	13.31
Day	11.25	12.08	11.38	11.57
Difference	1.29	2.13	1.80	1.74
Girls				
Boarding	15.11	17.02	16.90	16.34
Day	12.36	12.89	13.26	12.84
Difference	2.75	4.13	3.64	3.50
Both sexes				
Boarding	13.82	15.62	15.04	14.83
Day	11.81	12.49	12.32	12.20
Difference	2.01	3.13	2.72	2.63

NOTE: A high score indicates an adult-oriented response.

shows that there was no reliable tendency for Soviet children to respond differently under pressure from peers versus adults.

Lastly, the presence of a reliable difference in line 4 of Table 13.2 demonstrates that Soviet children did respond to the experimental manipulation. The difference in question measures the shift in response between base condition and the two social pressure conditions taken together. The significant positive value in column 3 thus indicates that across both school settings, Soviet children became less willing to engage in antisocial behavior when told that their actions would be known to others, including both peers and adults.

Discussion

What are the implications of these results for the three major hypotheses of the study?

HYPOTHESIS I

To begin with, the higher total score achieved by boarding school children supports the first general hypothesis; namely, children raised primarily in a single socialization setting (i.e., a boarding school) did subscribe to adult-approved values to a greater extent than those exposed to multiple settings (day school pupils). An additional line of evidence bears directly on the same hypothesis. It is reasonable to suppose that greater conformity to

TABLE 13.2. *Means and differences in total score and in experimental effects by type of school and sex*

Scores	Boarding School	Day School	Average across Both Settings	Difference by Type of School (Boarding-Day)
Total (across 3 experimental conditions)				
Both sexes (girls + boys)*	14.83	12.20	13.51	2.63§
Sex difference (girls — boys)	3.03§	1.27	2.15§	1.76
Shift (girls + boys)†				
Adult-peer	.58	.17	.38	.41
Experimental-base‡	1.51§	.59	1.05§	.92

* A high score indicates an adult-oriented response.

† None of the experimental effects showed a significant interaction by sex.

‡ Difference between the mean of adult and peer conditions combined and the mean for the base condition.

§ $p < .05$.

adult-approved standards of behavior would be reflected not only in a higher mean score but also in reduced individual differences about that mean. In other words, the hypothesis predicts an inverse relationship between mean and variance with the boarding school pupils showing a smaller spread than the day school children. In view of the large sex difference in total score observed in both samples, with girls being appreciably more adult-oriented than boys, the variances have been calculated separately for each sex. The results, shown in Table 13.3, document the predicted inverse relationship between mean and variance not only for the two school settings, but for the two sexes as well. In both types of schools, girls showed greater convergence about the mean than boys. This fact, taken together with their higher level of response (Table 13.2, line 2), adds further weight to the conclusion of the author's earlier study that it is Soviet girls in particular who conform to culturally approved standards of behavior.[3] Finally, for both sexes, individual differences were smaller in boarding schools than day schools (significantly so for girls). Thus there is further corroboration for Hypothesis I and its prediction of greater conformity to adult-approved norms among Soviet boarding school children.

HYPOTHESIS II

The research data yield several independent lines of evidence bearing directly on the hypothesis of greater susceptibility to social influence on the part of boarding school children. First, the fact that such children showed greater

TABLE 13.3.   *Variances in total score for boys and girls in boarding and day schools*

Schools		Boys	Girls	F Ratio Boys/Girls
Day schools		201.55	125.96	1.60*
Boarding schools		179.19	53.63	3.34†
F ratio	Day schools	1.12	2.35†	
	Boarding schools			

*p < .05.
† p < .01.

conformity to cultural norms is of course consistent with the notion of a higher level of susceptibility in general, and to this extent the confirmation of Hypothesis I also constitutes necessary but not sufficient support for Hypothesis II. For further evidence on this general proposition, we turn again to the data of Table 13.2. In line with the prediction of greater responsiveness among boarding school pupils to changing social pressures in the *immediate* environment, this group should show larger shifts in response to the experimental conditions than the day school children did. Although the trends in the data are all in the expected direction, none is reliable. Thus the shift scores in Table 13.2 (lines 3 and 4) are both higher for boarding school than for day school pupils. In the case of the shift from the base condition to the two experimental conditions (line 4), the difference was significant for boarding school pupils and not for day school children, but the interaction (column 4, line 4) was not reliable. Similarly, the total variation in response to social pressure, measured by the mean square for conditions, was more than six times as great for the boarding school sample (40.13) as for day schools (6.04), but the *F* ratio falls short of significance.

But experimentally induced social pressures were not the only ones conceivably operative in the present research situation. In addition, both boarding school and day school pupils were exposed to another potential source of variation in school atmosphere deriving from naturally occurring rather than deliberately manipulated variables. Each sample, it will be remembered, consisted of six separate classrooms possibly characterized by somewhat different group climates and social norms. If the general hypothesis is correct, then boarding school pupils should be more susceptible to this source of variation than children enrolled in regular schools. Such susceptibility would be reflected in significant differences among classroom means, and indeed there were such reliable differences among the six boarding school classes *(p > .05)*, but not among the six classes in day schools.[4]

We can now carry this logic one step farther and ask under which experimental condition the classroom variation among boarding school children should reach its maximal level? In other words, was there a significant inter-action effect? Specifically, if we are correct that children raised in a single socialization setting are especially vulnerable to the social climate of the moment, then the introduction of experimentally induced social pressures should have the effect of superseding and weakening whatever social influences may have been operating prior to that time. In other words, in the boarding school sample, differences in classroom atmosphere should be maximal under the base condition and much attenuated under the peer and especially the adult condition, since it is here that pressure on all children to conform to general cultural norms should be at its peak, and the influence of diverse classroom climates least salient. In terms of experimental design, we are positing a particular significant Condition × Classroom interaction for boarding schools, and none for day schools. Again the prediction is borne out by the analysis. The relevant interaction mean square is significant ($p \leqq .01$) only for the boarding school sample and the relative magnitudes of variance estimates for classroom means under each of the three conditions correspond to our expectations. The highest and only signficant value occurred under the base condition ($\sigma^2 = 8.68$), the next largest occurred under pressure from peers ($\sigma^2 = 2.07$), and the smallest under pressure from adults ($\sigma^2 = .35$).

Taken as a whole, the evidence cited above supports the prediction that boarding school pupils would be more susceptible to social influence than children attending day schools. This conclusion, in turn, is consistent with the general hypothesis that children brought up primarily in a single socialization setting are more likely to conform to the social pressures in their immediate environment.

HYPOTHESIS III

Finally, we return to the unresolved question posed by the earlier research: To what extent are the cross-cultural differences reported in the previous study specific to Soviet boarding school pupils as distinguished from Russian children attending conventional schools? The answer to this question is almost self-evident from Table 13.4, which presents scores for all three samples of 12-year-olds: American children attending public grade schools, Soviet boarding school pupils and Russian day school children. The cross-cultural differences (and corresponding significance levels) between the American and the two Soviet groups are documented in Table 13.5. In addition, for purposes of comparison, we repeat in column 5 the intracultural differences between boarding schools and day schools originally cited in Table 13.2. The pooling of the two Russian samples was indicated by the absence of any significant differences except in total score (as already shown in Table 13.2); in addition, the error terms showed no heterogeneity in variance.

The most striking fact which emerges from these tables is the wide gap in

TABLE 13.4. *Means and shift scores obtained by children from Soviet boarding schools, Soviet day schools, and American public schools*

Item	Setting		
	Soviet boarding	*Soviet day*	*U. S. public*
Across experimental conditions*			
Girls	16.34	12.84	3.52
Boys	13.31	11.57	.92
Both sexes	14.83	12.20	2.22
Sex difference (girls—boys)	3.03	1.27	2.60
Within experimental conditions (both sexes)*			
Base	13.82	11.81	2.43
Adult	15.62	12.49	2.96
Peer	15.04	12.32	1.27
Shift scores (both sexes)†			
Adult–peer	.58	.17	1.69
Experimental–base	1.51	.59	−.31

* A high score indicates an adult-oriented response.

† These data are not given separately for boys and girls, since none of the experimental conditions showed a significant interaction by sex.

total score between the Soviet and American samples. Russian children, whether in boarding schools or day schools, are substantially less ready to engage in antisocial behavior when tempted by peers than their American age-mates. In both societies, girls gave more socially approved responses than boys, but there was no significant interaction effect of Sex × Culture, which indicates that the sex difference was no larger in one country than the other. As stated in the earlier report (Bronfenbrenner 1967a), "It is noteworthy that despite the differing conceptions of the role of women in the two societies, females in the Soviet Union as in the United States lay greater claim to virtuous behavior, at least up to the age of twelve [p. 203]."

A second salient feature of the data gives further support to the third hypothesis: the differences between the American and combined Soviet samples are larger and more reliable than those between the two Soviet samples. In short, intercultural differences exceed intracultural differences. Indeed, as is especially evident in Table 13.4, the contrasting character of the American data highlights the similarity in the pattern of results for the two Soviet samples. The differences between them are entirely in degree, and not in direction. The boarding school children exhibited the same responses as the day school children, but in more extreme form. Specifically, they show a higher mean in total score, their shift scores are consistently in the same direction but always larger, and—as noted previously—classroom effects and sex differences in variance are more pronounced. In a word, the boarding school data constitute a magnified version of the day school results. This fact is not without significance for Soviet society. At least so far as the variables measured in the present experiment are concerned, the expectations of Russian educators are fulfilled: in the Soviet boarding school, the effects of collective upbringing are "writ large."

In contrast, American children showed a different pattern of response. Not only were they far less ready to subscribe to adult-approved standards (Table 13.5, line 1), but they reacted otherwise to the experimental conditions (Table 13.4, lines 5–9, Table 13.5, line 4). Although both Russian and American youngsters obtained highest scores under pressure from adults, they responded differently to the peer condition. When told that classmates would see their answers, American pupils indicated greater readiness to engage in socially disapproved behavior, whereas Soviet children increased their commitment to adult standards. In short, in the Soviet Union, as contrasted with the United States, the influence of peers operated in the same direction as that of adults.

What should be the impact of experimentally induced social pressure on classroom differences in American schools? Since pressure from peers does not invoke adult values in the American setting, it should not have the same dampening effect on classroom variation which we observed in Soviet boarding schools. On the contrary, awareness that one's responses will be-

TABLE 13.5. Mean differences between American and Soviet children

Scores	Combined Soviet Sample	American Sample	Average across Both Cultures (Soviet + American)	Soviet Minus American	Boarding School Minus Day School
Total (across 3 experimental conditions)					
Both sexes*	11.51	2.22	—	9.29 ‖	2.63§
Sex difference (girls — boys)	2.15	2.60	4.75 ‖	−.45	1.76
Shift scores†					
Adult–peer	.38	1.69	2.07§	−1.31	.41
Experimental–base‡	1.05	−.31	.42	1.68§	.92

* A high score indicates an adult-oriented response.
† None of the experimental effects showed a significant interaction by sex.
‡ Difference between the mean of adult and peer conditions combined and the mean for the base condition.
§ $p < .05$ (one-tailed test).
‖ $p < .01$ (one-tailed test).

come known to classmates should increase conformity to the norms of the particular group, with the result that among American children, classroom differences should be even greater under the peer condition than under the base condition. In statistical terms, we are once again predicting a significant interaction of Classroom × Condition but differing in pattern from that observed in the Soviet boarding school sample.

The actual data are nicely in accord with expectations. The Class × Condition interaction is again highly significant $(p \leq .01)$, but as shown in Table 13.6, classroom variation in the American sample, in contrast to Soviet boarding schools, was even greater under the peer condition than under base condition. As in the boarding schools, classroom differences were almost completely suppressed under the adult condition. Clearly in both societies the influence of parents can counteract pressure to conform to peer-group norms, at least up to the age of 12.

In the perspective of the Soviet material, one other aspect of the American data takes on special significance. In all probability, the average Westerner would expect Russian children to be more conforming than American youngsters. How does this stereotype stand up to the research findings? Do Russian children conform more? The answer must be another question: Conform to what? It is certainly true that Soviet youngsters show greater acceptance of adult-approved standards of behavior. But if conformity means susceptibility to social pressure, the American children in the present sample were as ready to yield as their Soviet age-mates. Although American and Russian children reacted differently to the experimental conditions, the absolute amount of shift measured by the mean square for conditions was only a little smaller in the American group $(MS = 35.78)$ than that observed in Soviet boarding schools $(MS = 40.13)$ and considerably greater than that obtained in Soviet day schools $(MS = 6.04)$. As is clearly apparent from Table 13.6, a similar picture emerges when one turns from experimentally induced social pressures to those that occur spontaneously in children's groups. The tendency to be influenced by the climate of a particular classroom was at least as strong in the present sample in the American public

TABLE 13.6.   *Variation among classroom means under three experimental conditions*

Experimental Condition	Estimated Classroom Variances	
	American public schools	*Soviet boarding schools*
Base	6.26*	8.68*
Adult	.56	.35
Peer	11.52*	2.07

* Classroom differences significant at the .01 level.

schools as in the Soviet boarding schools, and considerably stronger than in Soviet day schools. In short, like the Russian boarding school pupils, American youngsters show a high degree of conformity to the social pressures operating in their immediate environment. The only difference is in the nature of the pressure. In the Soviet Union it is deliberately directed to increase the child's adherence to norms established by the larger society; in the United States, it reflects the spontaneous interests and impulses of an age-graded peer group.

But if American children do show a high degree of susceptibility to social pressure, how does this square with the thesis that such heightened susceptibility tends to develop when children are brought up in a single socialization context rather than jointly in the family and children's group. Most of us think of the United States as a society strongly committed to the family as the primary agent of child rearing. Yet our research results document the potency of peer-group pressures in influencing the responses of American children.

The resolution of the paradox is to be found in a mistaken stereotype. As documented elsewhere (Bronfenbrenner 1970), there is evidence to indicate that over recent decades the American family, primarily as a result of urbanization and technological changes in the larger society, has been losing power as a major socializing agent in the lives of children, and the resulting vacuum has been filled by the age-segregated peer group. As for the Soviet Union, contrary to popular impression the Soviet family has not "withered away." To quote from the comparative study of childrearing in the two countries (Bronfenbrenner 1970):

> Given the prevalence of institutional upbringing in the U.S.S.R., one might conclude that American parents are closer to their children than their Russian counterparts. Paradoxically, our observations fail to support such a conclusion. Collective upbringing notwithstanding, emotional ties between Russian parents and children are exceptionally strong. Maternal over-protection, overt display of physical affection, and simple companionship between parents and children appear more pronounced in Soviet society than in our own. Although, because of longer working hours and time lost in shopping and commuting, Soviet parents may spend less time at home, more of that time appears to be spent in conversation, play, and companionship with children than in American families [p. 99].

Viewed in this perspective, the American subjects in the present experiment responded in a fashion quite consistent with theoretical expectations. Like Soviet boarding school pupils, they showed the effect of being brought up under strong peer group influence and weakened parental power: they were highly susceptible to social pressure. In contrast, Russian day school pupils, whose parents continue to be highly involved in the lives of their children, exhibit a greater degree of stability in the face of divergent social influence.

Precisely because these results are in accord with the hypotheses, it is important to stress the limitations of the study. First, although the size of the sample from Soviet society now has been doubled, the fact remains that the conclusions are based on but a few classes and fewer schools in each culture. Second, both samples were essentially accidental, the Russian classrooms coming from three boarding schools and three days schools in Moscow, and the American from two public schools, in middle class neighborhoods of a small city in upstate New York. Since these data were gathered, the same experiment has been replicated, in slightly modified form, in 39 classrooms spread over 18 different schools in another city in the same region with a population of over a half-million, and preliminary analyses indicate close comparability with the findings for the smaller American sample reported here. Unfortunately, an effort to repeat the experiment in another Russian city (Kiev) has not yet proved successful.

Relevant indirect evidence, however, comes from the author's work in other countries. Through the collaboration of research colleagues, this same experiment has now also been carried out in half a dozen more nations in East and West, including Great Britain (Halla Beloff and Xenia Paton), Holland (Herman Hutte), Hungary (Sandor Komlosi), Poland (Edda Flesznerowa), Switzerland (Kurt Luscher), and West Germany (Franz Banhegyi). Preliminary analyses reveal a consistent cross-cultural pattern. For example, mean scores from all three East European countries were substantially higher (range: 6.14 to 14.83) than those from the West (range: −2.09 to 2.83). In other words, children from Eastern Europe gave many more adult-oriented responses. In terms of reaction to experimental manipulation, the Soviet youngsters stood out from all the rest. Only the Hungarians resembled them in scoring reliably lower under the base condition than under pressure from peers and adults, and the Russian sample was the only one out of eight countries that failed to show a significant difference under pressure from peers versus adults.

The fact that the Soviet-American results fall meaningfully within a larger cross-cultural pattern lends credence to their validity. But even if the facts are right, the interpretation given them may still be wrong. It has been argued, in effect, that different patterns of socialization, both within and between cultures, produce different types of character structure over time. Specifically, the obtained results have been interpreted as implying that children raised primarily in a single socialization setting, as compared with those exposed to diversity in agents and contexts of upbringing, are more likely to develop conformist personalities, and, like chameleons, adopt the coloration of their immediate environment. The present results are indeed consistent with that interpretation. But, as indicated, for that very reason, the author is obliged to seek alternative explanations.

One possibility that challenges the basic assumption at its very core derives from Lewin's field-theoretical orientation and its injunction to seek causal forces in the immediate situation rather than in some historical process (Lewin 1936). Proceeding from this perspective, one might argue as follows. The obtained results do not necessarily imply any differences in personality between Soviet and American children. Children in every culture are basically the same. They all adapt to the situations in which they find themselves. When in a given society a child is confronted with different socializing agents with different expectations, he reacts accordingly. Thus, in the United States, where the peer group is relatively autonomous and stresses different values and behaviors from those expected by parents and other representatives of the adult society, children give different responses when exposed to the one and to the other. In contrast, in the Soviet Union, where standards of conduct are more homogeneous, and the children's collective is deliberately used as an agent for teaching and enforcing cultural norms, the child reacts in the same way toward his collective as toward his parents; only when no one will know of his actions (except those he might privately choose to tell) is the child willing to indicate some slight readiness to act against adult-approved standards.

What conclusions do we reach if we now try to apply the same logic to explain the greater variation observed under different social conditions within the Soviet boarding schools versus day schools? Again, the argument would run that the children in the two settings did not differ in susceptibility to social influence, but that the objective pressures to conformity were greater both within boarding schools in general and in a given classroom collective.

Although the theorizing which led to the present experiment assumed a socialization process over time, the available evidence does not rule out a purely situational explanation. A real test between a developmental versus field-theoretical hypothesis would require transferring children from one setting to another and observing whether they changed their pattern of response accordingly. If each group soon began to exhibit the previous reaction of the other, the situational hypothesis would be vindicated. In contrast, persistence of the prior pattern would constitute evidence for the development of a stable personality trait.

Finally, there remains the possibility that neither of the foregoing theoretical explanations accounts for the observed results, that the obtained differences are attributable primarily to some as yet unidentified and uncontrolled factors which were unevenly distributed across the two cultures and school settings. The backgrounds of Soviet boarding school versus day school pupils—not to mention Russian versus American children—surely differ in many respects besides those considered in the present research, and some of these may have in fact produced, or at least influenced, the significant effects found in this study. Indeed, such a likelihood is enhanced by the small size and "accidental" character of the samples used. At the moment, all one can do is alert the reader to this possibility.

But whatever is the true explanation of our findings, this much is clear: Soviet children show considerably greater conformity to adult-approved social norms than their American age-mates, with the difference being maximized in the case of Russian boarding school pupils. Moreover, the results from both cultures underscore the importance of the children's group as a force shaping behavior and development. Specifically, where the peer group is to a large extent autonomous—as it often is in the United States—it can exert influence in opposition to values held by the adult society. In other types of social systems, such as the Soviet Union, the peer group—and its power to affect the attitudes and actions of its members—can be harnessed by the adult society for the furtherance of its own values and objectives. This fact carries with it significant educational and social implications. Thus it is clear that in the Soviet Union the role of the peer group is in large part the result of explicit policy and practice. This is hardly the case in the United States. In the light of increasing evidence for the influence of the peer group on the behavior and psychological development of children and adolescents, it is questionable whether any society, whatever its social system, can afford to leave largely to chance the direction of this influence—and realization of its high potential for fostering constructive achievement both for the child and his society.

NOTES

1. For a description of Soviet techniques of collective upbringing see Bronfenbrenner (1970).
2. This procedure was developed by the author in collaboration with E. C. Devereux, Jr., G. J. Suci, and R. R. Rodgers.
3. The sex differences in socialization practices which contribute to this phenomenon are discussed in Bronfenbrenner (1970).
4. In neither sample were there any significant differences by school.

14

Group Care: Friend or Foe?

MARTIN WOLINS

In the early 1960s two eminent psychoanalysts mounted literary platforms to set down their opposite views on nonfamilial childrearing. One (Kardiner 1961. Also Chap. 5) noted the dangers to personality involved in such an experience and described a conversation with a kibbutz adult who seemed thoroughly devoid of any capacity for human relationship. The other (Bettelheim 1962), although he had not yet visited any kibbutz, nevertheless was of the opinion that group care in such a setting could and should be conducive to healthy human development. Strangely, argument about group care often has had this kind of surrealistic feel about it, even though group care for better or for worse certainly existed, and some evaluation based on evidence could be made; Trotzkey (Chap. 2) showed the way long ago.

Chapter 14 is an attempt at such evaluation of group care programs whose sponsors in Austria, Poland, Yugoslavia, and Israel claimed to be successful. Though the programs themselves, the attributes of children involved, and the nature of the surrounding milieu varied markedly from one country to another, one factor was common to them. All the programs were based on the premise that culturally normative expectations will yield socially desired behavior and its psychological underpinnings. While this goal was not always obtained, and the probability of very positive results in group care may be lower than its advocates are willing to admit, some settings are obviously successful. Group care as assessed in this paper tends to justify some of Kardiner's and some of Bettelheim's positions; yet in the hand of devoted staff it seems to be more a friend than a foe of the growing child.

Martin Wolins, "Group Care: Friend or Foe?" *Social Work* 14 (1): 37–53. Reprinted with permission of the National Association of Social Workers.

Introduction

Group Care is plainly many different things. It is the preschooler in a day care center, the adolescent in a juvenile hall, the scholar in a boarding school, the disturbed in a mental institution. For us in this project, group care is the preadolescent and adolescent from a disrupted familial or deviant cultural background in a setting with rather standard, though often quite severe expectations. In regard to physical growth, cognitive development, psychosocial adjustment, and acquisition of values, the young people described here are considered eventually capable of normal functioning, if the group setting does its job.

The question before the research described here was whether evidence supports this assumption. Excluding the matter of physical health, which was not in dispute, we assembled data on group care and comparison children in Austria, Yugoslavia, Poland, and Israel.

Study Settings

The study settings were for predominantly normal children from toddler to adolescent and can be arranged rather well on a dimension of critical importance in child care—namely, their proximity to a familial model. Most familial are the Austrian *Kinderdorf* villages. These are rather large institutions divided into family unit cottages, each consisting of nine children of both sexes and varying ages and a *Mutti*. Children enter this program mainly because of familial incapacity and are expected to remain to maturity. The study sample is from one such *Kinderdorf* located near Vienna.

Sample 1: Austria—SOS Kinderdorf. This sample consisted of 65 children, mostly dependent, neglected, or abandoned wards of the welfare department who were sent to the Kinderdorf for care. Few maintained substantial ties with their natural family, and many had been born out of wedlock. Physically handicapped and seriously disturbed children are not admitted. Maximum entrance age is about 12 years, but the Kinderdorf's emphasis is on early admissions and most are admitted much earlier, even in infancy. The ages of children in this sample ranged from 12 to 18 years.

Sample 2: Austria—children living at home. This sample consisted of 67 children from families living in the same small suburban middle class community where the Kinderdorf studied is located. These children and the younger children in the Kinderdorf attend the same school (and church). Because older Kinderdorf children attend numerous schools, matching them with classmates was beyond the project's capability. The home children had the advantages of family stability—at least they had lived with their parents from birth—and a higher socioeconomic background, which should be expected to affect test results. These children represent the type of population to which the Kinderdorf child would most likely wish to belong on growing up. Ages of the sample ranged from 12 to 15.

Somewhat different in structure is the Yugoslav *Djete Dom* (children's home), which is typically a large apartment house divided into family residences, each containing about 16 to 18 children of both sexes and various ages and an adult "aunt" or "uncle."

Sample 3: Yugoslavia—children's institution. Somewhat over 100 children living in four institutions in or near Belgrade comprised this sample. The majority came from broken and disrupted lower or lower middle class homes and were sent to the institution by local centers for social work. Children attend local schools in the neighborhood up to the age of 14, at which time they must choose a high school or trade school that may be outside of the neighborhood. To the limited extent that parental contact is possible, children are encouraged to maintain family ties. Children are placed in the institution from infancy on into adolescence, but the age range of the sample is restricted to 11 to 19 years.

Sample 4: Yugoslavia—children living at home. This comparison sample consisted of 76 children living with their parents in the same area as the Belgrade institutions. Families of these children were predominantly of the lower or lower middle class. Ages of the sample ranged from 12 to 19 years.

Further from the familial model is the Polish *Dom Dziecka* (children's home), which makes no attempt to structure a relatively small number of children around an adult but does have a considerable age range (although sex separation) in the various units of the institution. Like the *Kinderdorf* and *Djete Dom,* the *Dom Dziecka* consists mainly of children whose families have disintegrated. Although not expected to stay to maturity, many a child remains in the institution for 10 or more years.

Sample 5: Poland—children's institution. This sample consisted of 34 abandoned and/or neglected children from the city of Warsaw who were sent to the institution by the local educational and judicial authorities. Most came from inadequate or disrupted families of low socioeconomic status. Entrance into the Polish program is possible from the age of about five years and on into the teens, but most children are admitted during the first few years of grade school. Ages in the sample ranged from 11 to 19 years.

Sample 6: Poland—children living at home. The Polish comparison group contained 49 children who lived in the neighborhood of the institution and attended the same schools as the institution children. They were mostly of low socioeconomic status and reasonably equivalent in background to the institution children. Ages ranged from 10 to 14 years. It was not possible to test a comparison group of exactly the same age as the older institution children.

The Israeli youth village is still further from a familial structure. Composed predominantly of new immigrants in their teens whose families were usually intact, such a group aims at rapid socialization. Most children stay only two to four years, learn the new language, progress in academic work, and move on. The resident group is quite large, somewhat varied in age, and in the charge of an adult with "big brother" status.

Sample 7: Israel—youth village children. This sample included 79 children ages 13 to 17 from various social strata though predominantly in the lower socioeconomic groups. Many were children of new immigrants. Length of residence in the village was two to four years.

Least like a family is the kibbutz youth group. This is an unfamiliar entity and must not be confused with the kibbutz-born children described by Spiro, Rabin, and others. For the groups in this study the kibbutz is a "foster mother." The groups consist of up to 40 young people of both sexes who enter in early adolescence and remain together for 3 to 5 years. They come mainly from deprived Israeli families; in most cases both parents are living and maintain ties with the children. All of the young people and several adults (Madrichim, teachers) are expected to form a chevra (group, society), initially of near-equals and eventually of equals. It is hoped that the young people will remain and join the kibbutz as members.

Sample 8: Israel—kibbutz youth group. The Israel kibbutz youth sample was comprised of 155 children mainly of low socioeconomic status from major Israeli cities and development towns who entered group care in the kibbutz at approximately 13 years of age and remained there 3 to 5 years.

Sample 9: Israel—kibbutz-born children. This sample included 33 children born and reared in several adjacent kibbutzim and attending a regional kibbutz school at the time of testing. The children ranged in age from 15 to 17 years and were used as a comparison group for the group care children.

Sample 10: Israel—children living at home. Approximately 112 children of recent immigrants settled in development towns constituted this sample. They were attending a day care vocational program operated by the same organization (Youth Aliyah) as the two group care programs mentioned above. Because of language inadequacies and other reasons, these children—much like those from the kibbutz youth group and the youth village—did not fit into the regular public school program, even though they were of school age. In some instances, these children living at home and attending the day center had actually been rejected for admission to a Youth Aliyah residential program because space was scarce and family competence was judged high enough to offer needed care. In terms of background and socioeconomic status, these children constituted a reasonable comparison for the two group care samples. The sample ranged in age from 14 to 18 years.

Aside from the family–egalitarian group dimension, these programs differ from one another in many additional ways. They attempt to transmit different ideologies. They place unequal emphasis on academic as contrasted with socially integrative achievement. Their attitudes toward work, ties to the outside community, and relations between the sexes and between man and authority are extremely disparate. Yet they all claim to be successful. Are they?

Methodological Questions

Riecken (1952) once defined evaluation as "the measurement of desirable and undesirable consequences of an action that has been taken in order to forward some goal that we value." The definition highlights some formidable methodological problems pertaining to comparison groups, age-related variables, cultural differences, and variability of expectations that cannot be discussed adequately in the present paper. In general, an attempt was made to compare group-reared children with age-mates reared at home. Age was held constant whenever possible, and cultural and value differences were dealt with when essential.

A major question in such a study pertains to attributes that are to be compared. Prior studies of children in group care have usually been focused on one or more of three constellations of characteristics roughly designated as functioning intelligence, personality maturity, and social integration.[1] That pattern was followed in this study, since it allows comparisons with earlier work and also appears to address reasonable practice concerns about the negative effects of group care in all three areas.

Several studies exist that seem to support the view that group care may retard intellectual growth.[2] There also appears to be some basis in prior research for the position that institutional residence may cause personally maladjustments (Edmiston and Baird 1949, pp. 482–88; Pringle and Bossio, in Pringle 1965). As to social integration and social competence, in general the evidence seems more favorable. Institution-reared children are found to be more socially competent when compared with ordinary children, although the data are not uniformly one-sided (Edmiston and Baird 1949; Bodman et al. 1950, pp. 173–76).

Intellectual Development

Gross data from the five study settings fail to support the hypothesis that group care children are less able to deal with the intellectual requirements of the Raven Progressive Matrices Test (RPM, Raven 1960) than are the family-reared controls. The group care subjects in Poland and Israel have scores at least equal to and in some instances markedly exceeding those of children living at home. Austrian and Yugoslav institutional children have scores that are slightly lower than their controls. But the findings leave several unanswered questions: Are the differences between group care and home children the result of initial capability or of impairment or gain attributable to the group setting? Is there a possibility of selective removal from care that acts to raise or lower institutional mean scores? Is length of stay in the group program associated with depressed intellectual capability?

Unfortunately, the study samples do not permit an analysis of these three issues in every setting, but there is considerable evidence to offer a fairly defensible position on each question. In Yugoslavia and Israel data were obtained on intake groups consisting of children whose stay in the respective programs has been relatively brief (one to three months in Israel and up to six months in Yugoslavia). When compared with the long-stay children's scores, no drop is shown following a stay in each setting; in one instance a considerably higher score is seen. Mean RPM percentile scores for new entrants are as follows: Israeli kibbutz youth group, 31.92; youth village, 57.58; Yugoslav institutions, 31.09. Comparing these scores with those of long-term residents in the three settings, the Yugoslav scores were found to be the same (remember, these are *not* the same children), the youth village showed a positive difference of some 8 percentage points, and the kibbutz youth group an amazing positive difference of 21.5 points. The outlook for group care children seemed good, but the comparison may be improper, matching low intelligence intake of 1964 (when the testing was done) with much brighter children admitted in earlier years. Israeli and Yugoslav staff state that such is not the case, and some data exist to support their contention, at least with regard to the kibbutz youth group. The data also speak to the question of selective withdrawal from the program.

During 1964–65 the researchers tested 137 newly admitted children who had joined 4 kibbutz youth groups. At that time their mean RPM percentile-score was 31.92. Two years later, 58 of these children were available for retesting (most of the others had withdrawn from the program). Two things were discovered: (1) Their original scores were lower than the mean for the total group (1964 RPM percentile mean for those later retested was 29.12). (2) Their new scores were significantly higher (RPM percentile mean, 37.19). The latter is still a long way from the 53.32 observed in the kibbutz youth group longer-stay children, but it certainly points in that direction. As may be anticipated, this encouraging mean hides marked advances, some standstills, and even regression for some of the children, but the general trend is positive. (See Table 14.1.)

The third and last question is about the relationship between intellectual capability and length of group residence. Pringle and Bossio suggest, contrary to earlier assumptions, that "if institutionalization takes place after the age of five years, the longer it lasts the higher a child's tested intelligence (in

TABLE 14.1. *Mean Raven percentile positions of children in long-term group care (two or more years) compared with children living at home**

Sample	Number	Mean Age (Years)	RPM Percentile†	
			Mean	Standard deviation
Austria				
Kinderdorf	65	15.8	45.71	26.3
Home	67	13.9	54.12	23.7
Yugoslavia‡				
Institution	119	14.8	28.85	24.4
Home	76	15.3	37.30	19.5
Poland				
Institution	34	14.4	53.03	29.0
Home	49	12.5	50.96	30.2
Israel				
Youth village	79	16.2	65.37	19.6
Kibbutz youth				
group	155	17.3	53.32	25.2
Kibbutz-born	33	16.5	71.73	18.7
Home	112	15.7	29.24	22.7

* The Yugoslav institution includes 49 children with a stay of less than 2 years, but their RPM's are not different from the others.

† This is an age-adjusted value. Correlation of age and percentile on RPM is quite low (e.g., $r = 0.05$ for the Austrian children).

‡ Because there was some question about the Yugoslav children's performance on the RPM, as many as possible were retested on a locally standardized version of the Wechsler-Belleview. The following are the results of the retest.

Sample	N	Mean Age	RPM Percentile Mean	IQ Mean
Institution	73	14.6	27.6	96.1
Home	26	14.8	30.2	105.3

Pringle 1965, p. 26). The data are ambiguous on this issue, although generally in line with the above conclusion (at least for the older child) rather than with the assumption of regressive consequences earlier attributed to extended group care. The kibbutz youth group sample provides the strongest positive evidence. Assuming comparability of the cross-sectional groups, which there is no reason to doubt, these young people seem to advance from an entering position near the 30th percentile to the 37th percentile 2 years later and to the 53rd percentile 4 to 5 years later. However, these data are possibly suspect on methodological grounds, especially because of the researchers' inability to control for age (except, of course, by percentile conversion) while varying length of stay. On the other hand, there is some evidence of an upward drift in RPM scores associated with age, which holds only for the kibbutz youth group long-term residents and not for new entrants or for youths living at home. Age alone, then, does not account for the gains noted in the kibbutz youth group. (See Table 14.2.)

TABLE 14.2.   *Mean Raven percentile position at seven age levels for Israel home children, new entrants, and long-stay members of kibbutz youth groups*

Sample	Age (in Years)						
	12	13	14	15	16	17	18
Kibbutz entrants	33.91	31.38	22.77				
	(N=43)	(N=79)	(N=13)				
Home children			25.63	33.53	27.13	25.29	
			(N=16)	(N=40)	(N=39)	(N=17)	
Kibbutz residents (two or more years)					50.75	51.76	57.68
					(N=44)	(N=83)	(N=25)

Whatever may be concluded from the kibbutz data, one thing is certain —protracted stay *does not reduce* RPM scores. (Incidentally, delay in entering may have such an effect.) Evidence from the Yugoslav institution supports such a conclusion. The mean RPM percentiles for 5 groups of children, arranged by length of stay and each with an average age of 14 to 16 years, shows no significant relationship between these two variables. (See Table 14.3.)

Measured by the RPM, intelligence of children living in a variety of group programs and over relatively long periods of time is generally equivalent to that of normal children residing with their parents. Two instances of

TABLE 14.3.   *Mean Raven percentile position of Yugoslav children related to length of residence in group care*

Length of Residence (Months)	Age at Entry (Years)	Present Mean Age	RPM Percentile	
			mean	standard deviation
0–11 (N=22)*	13.6	13.7	31.09	22.1
12–23 (N=28)	13.4	14.4	25.52	22.2
24–47 (N=28)	11.9	14.6	27.46	25.3
48–119(N=23)	9.1	15.7	31.74	25.5
120–179(N=19)	4.4	15.8	24.26	23.5

* All children were in residence for less than six months.

$F = .42$, not significant.

somewhat disadvantageous results (Yugoslavia and Austria) are offset by some remarkable gains that seem to be made in the kibbutz youth group. These findings conform with those of Keefe (see Chap. 12), Rabin (1965), Smilansky et al. (1966), Skeels (see Chap. 10), and others who contend that a stimulating group environment can not only prevent intellectual regression but may lead to substantial achievement.

Psychosocial Maturity

Earlier it had been noted that some available evidence and the bulk of clinical opinion support the position that marked psychosocial handicaps arise from group care experience. In practice, Bowlby's original formulation is still substantially adhered to. It should be underscored that Bowlby (1950, 1952 ed.), even in the original WHO report, clearly distinguished between the impact of separation and group care on the very young and the older child, but even in the older he expected "unhappiness and very unfavorable social attitudes [p. 57]." Earlier, Edmiston and Baird and later Pringle and Bossio arrived at a similar position, which they supported with projective tests and clinical observations. The present author's data, limited here to the Austrian, Israeli, and Polish subjects, fail to uphold this negative view. Reliance is mainly on two analyses of projective test materials. In the first, Thematic Apperception Test protocols are classified using Erikson's (1950, 1963) stages of human development, and the group data are subjected to statistical comparison. In the second analysis, pairs of children from group care and own homes are matched, and all available information is used to arrive at a clinical decision about each member of the pair.[3]

Stages of Development

Returning now to the first approach, it was found that a classificatory scheme for assigning children's protocols to the several stages and to positive or negative tone could be implemented. Two independent coders, one a clinical psychologist, the other an education student, were able to assign the children's stories to themes of basic trust versus mistrust (Stage I), autonomy versus shame (Stage II), and so forth, with an intercoder reliability (perfect agreement) of 69 percent. Agreement was 93 percent when judging whether the protocol tone was positive or negative.[4]

Comparisons of all group care children with their home controls in the three countries leads to quite encouraging conclusions. In most instances the mean stage of responses for each of the eight cards presented is not significantly different for the subjects and their roughly age-quivalent controls. When statistically significant differences do occur they invariably favor the group care children. Specifically, on four TAT cards the kibbutz youth group scored higher than controls, twice the Israeli youth village did, and once the *Kinderdorf*. Similarly, the percentages of positive tone favor the children in group care whenever a distinction does exist.

From a first-hand familiarity with these group care programs and with the parental homes of the controls, the author would conclude that in every instance the staff has accomplished its objective of emulating the parental home or, if that is its choice, drawing a model quite different from it. The *Kinderdorf* wants to duplicate the atmosphere and values of suburban Austrian middle class home life. It accomplishes that with considerable success. Israeli and Polish settings attempt to inject the programs with satisfactions and tensions that are usually foreign to the families from which their wards are drawn. They emphasize ideology, stress educational achievement and group membership, and, while concerned with rudimentary physical safety and good health, do not shun heavy work. On the contrary, their slogan could well be "Labor, education, group membership, and ideological commitment."

Perhaps as a result of these challenges, which are, after all, usually tempered by a sympathetic staff who work and live with the children, both the kibbutz and institution residents in Israel are responding with some higher stage stories than their controls. This higher stage does not seem to be a function of intellectual difference or age, although it was not possible to control the age factor fully.

Some examples from the Kibbutz and institution illustrate the mature way in which the situations in two of the four discriminating cards are projected. Card 4, showing a young couple, yields many heterosexual affiliative themes; 13B, depicting a young boy in a doorway, evokes statements of independence, autonomy, aspiration, and recognition. While similar stories may also be found in the home group, they are rarer, usually less mature and less sophisticated.

A 17-year-old girl who had been in a socialist kibbutz for nearly 4 years wrote the following about Card 4.

> Family problems. A young couple is married. The husband was sent away from his work and demoted because he used to be late. He expresses this to his wife. She tries to make him feel better. She tells him that he should look for another job, that it is not all lost yet, that there is still hope. The husband is still angry and cannot even listen to her. He is very mad, angry at her without knowing why, simply because he is angry and sorry. He leaves his house and goes outside to calm down. His wife understands him completely and is waiting for his return. *Score: Stage III, positive*

A 17-year-old boy, with 4 years in an Israeli youth village, described Card 13B in this way.

> Outside it is warm. The sky is blue. All the children are playing social games, all the boys and girls except Dani. Dani doesn't have any interest in these games. He thinks about more important things, so in order not to be disturbed

he goes to a storeroom in a backyard, sits in front of it and concentrates on his thoughts. He wants to be an important man just like his father. He almost wants to fly in the sky above everybody and look down with happiness. He wants to be like his father, good and a friend to everybody. When will all these thoughts come true? That is what he is sitting and thinking now. *Score: Stage V, positive*

With an objective quite different from the Israeli programs, the Austrian *Kinderdorf* appears to have succeeded to a considerable extent in recreating the hearth and mother. These comforts are associated with the highest proportion of positively toned stories of any group in the project.

Considering only that all of the children in the *Kinderdorf* come from shattered familial situations, their consistently high positive tone, often exceeding that of the comfortable Viennese suburbanites with whom they are compared, is surprising. But this is not the case on further reflection. The setting in which these children are reared—the lovely cottages, the constantly present mothers, the smell of good food in preparation, and the *Grüss Gott* ("God be with you") in the air—seems to have had its effect. Understandably, these children respond quite often with stories expressing simple trust on the most basic developmental level. For example, in response to Card 14 (a figure silhouetted against a window or door) the story of a 14-year-old boy in the program for 5 years is quite typical.

A boy returns from school and has no assignments. He seats himself comfortably at the window, resting one of his hands on the wall. He looks out at the garden until it gets dark. *Score: Stage I, positive*

A story of this kind could just as well have come from a child living with his parents. There is little difference in stage between the *Kinderdorf* and the home children. The author's conclusion is that, as concerns TAT performance, parity exists between the *Kinderdorf* children and those from suburban middle class families.

In one respect the *Kinderdorf* children appear to show more maturity than their controls. Card 4 yields 18 percent Stage V or VI responses in the home group and 30 percent among the *Kinderdorf* children. The numbers are quite small and the difference is not statistically significant, but the occurrence deserves note by virtue of themes involved—affiliation, intimacy, devotion, and fidelity—and an overwhelming 65 percent of these expressed in positive tone. Since one of the main concerns of *Kinderdorf* critics is with the suitability of this setting for the development of heterosexual expectations and sex role clarity (remember, there are no "fathers" in these households), this finding may be significant. The boys and girls of the *Kinderdorf* can and do respond with heterosexual themes.

All of the Polish children in the sample wrote TAT stories of a low developmental stage, lower than either the Austrians or Israelis of similar age. For example, a boy living at home described Card 3BM as follows.

> A boy sits on the ground and cries. He leans against the sofa. Probably something bad happened to him. *Score: Stage I, negative*

A young boy in the institution described it thus.

> The boy in the picture is crying. He is leaning on the couch and sitting on the floor. *Score: Stage I, negative*

The positive story on the same level is equally basic and simple. The following is told by a young girl in the institution.

> In this picture I see a boy in a beret and a coat. He is eating outdoors next to a bench. Next to the bench lies something that must have fallen from his pocket. *Score: Stage I, positive*

Coming from low socioeconomic strata and living in a newly forming socialist state built on the physical and moral rubble of World War II, these children have suffered considerable privation. In addition, those in the institution have been abandoned, abused, and neglected by their parents. The institutional children with this double handicap appear to equal their home age-mates in development. The major difference between them—favoring the group in care—is in tone. Within the institutional program, when the child begins to feel secure he appears to shift from basic physical or psychological mistrust to security and trust, but maturity comes more slowly—if, indeed, at all.

Global Clinical Judgments

Statistical analysis of the children's TAT performances left unresolved issues pertaining to representativeness of the content, reliability of the classification, and comparability of subject and control groups. Another approach seemed indicated: one that subjected to judgment all available data about the child, used a different classificatory scheme, and compared matched individuals.

A clinical psychologist, temporarily on the project staff and unacquainted with the materials and distinguishing characteristics of home and group care children, was given pairs of cases matched for sex, age, intelligence, and (in Israel, where this factor is important) prior nationality. Each case record included all material available on a child except clues to his location. Specifically, the psychologist reviewed in the order named the responses to the Raven Progressive Matrices Test, a 60-item Value Inventory, a 41-item Sentence Completion Test, and protocols to 8 TAT cards. Each subject was then described in terms of five dimensions:

1. The level and type of cognition with emphasis on questions of flexibility and complexity of function.

2. The degree of egocentrism with specific consideration of self-absorption, energy, and optimism.
3. Extent of manifest conflict, noted in terms of the subject's defensive structure, his rigidity or constriction.
4. Social conformity as evidenced in commitment, purpose, identity, and goal directedness.
5. Relationships with same and opposite sex peers and in particular ability to tolerate intimacy and be cooperative, trusting, and empathic.

Subsequently, the other member of the pair was similarly described and a decision was made on which of the two was more mature.

Reliability and validity of these decisions were checked in several ways. First, the material was reexamined after a lapse of some time and independently rated again. Original and subsequent impressions were then brought into agreement. Second, another psychologist was given a random sample of 25 pairs of records and asked to rank members of each pair for relative maturity. (Interrater agreement was 79 percent.) Finally, the psychologist's global descriptions of children in group care were compared whenever feasible with staff judgments given in the field to the investigator. The correspondence is highly revealing and encouraging. For example, comments of a *Madrich* and the psychologist about a 16-year-old Israeli girl with an RPM score at the 60th percentile run as follows.

> MADRICH (based on observation). She did not achieve her full potential. This is a girl with considerable ability. She is subject to a serious conflict in values between those espoused in her home and in the kibbutz, and she feels this very deeply.
>
> PSYCHOLOGIST (based on tests). A confused adolescent struggling to obtain an independent identity. She is divided between the various roles she thinks are expected of her by both her peer group and her parents. She fears that a role which would differentiate her sufficiently from her peers would also isolate her. She is, however, concerned with her future as a professional and is committed to a specific goal. Despite her different environmental pulls, she is a highly conscientious and determined adolescent.

A total of 50 pairs of children from Austria, Poland, and Israel were compared. Austrian children tested at the *Kinderdorf* and their classmates living at home seem about equally mature, as do the home and youth village children in Israel. However, such is not the case regarding members of the Polish children's home or the Israeli kibbutz youth group. Kibbutz youth group children are judged as significantly more mature than those living at home. In Poland the converse is true—the home children appear to be significantly more mature than residents of the institution. (See Table 14.4.)

Comparing the two sets of data on psychosocial development, general agreement and one possible discrepancy are noted. Both the statistical (Erik-

TABLE 14.4.   *Judgments of maturity by setting within country*

	Total Pairs	Setting		Level of Significance*
		home more mature	group more mature	
Austria	16	9	7	n.s.†
Poland	8	7	1	.070
Israel				
Kibbutz	13	2	11	.022
Village	13	7	6	n.s.

* These probabilities were calculated using a two-tailed binomial test.
† Not significant.

son stages) and clinical (matched pair) procedures led to the conclusion that the Austrian *Kinderdorf* children are as mature as their peers in the same neighborhood. They are, in fact, about what the leadership of this organization wishes—indistinguishable from the normal child reared at home. Polish children in the institution are now assessed less favorably than they were when statistical comparisons of stages on the TAT alone were used, although they did not appear mature on the previous test either. Israeli youth village adolescents are little different from their controls—a slight reduction from the earlier (stages of development) assessment in which some difference was noted in their favor. Finally, global clinical evaluations of the kibbutz youth group children fully conform with the earlier statistical evaluation. However, the clinical judgment data go beyond the earlier optimism shown about the development of these young people, who seem to possess many of the qualities their setting—the kibbutz—aims to achieve.

In sum, group care need not necessarily result in marked psychosocial handicaps. Two of the four settings reviewed, namely, the *Kinderdorf* and the kibbutz youth group, yield especially encouraging results. The former, primarily focused on the developmental needs of the latency-age child, appears to overcome initial deprivation and the assumed handicaps of a contrived, fatherless family. Although it is not as stimulating as the kibbutz youth group, it does, nevertheless, seem to achieve its aims, even with children of a more difficult age. As to the kibbutz, it appears to suit the adolescent years better than any of the settings studied and possibly better than any child care setting in existence.

Both settings are examples of the effectiveness of constant and clearly formulated social relationships and ideology. In the *Kinderdorf,* mother, family, and Catholic values are all firm foundations on which a child's security can be made to rest. Within the kibbutz, adults, peers, and socialist values have similar permanence and visibility. Although the former is more an adult-oriented and the latter more a peer-oriented society, both accept the person for what he is and provide numerous affiliative possibilities and unambiguous conceptions of desirable behavior. Emotional maturity appears to be their reward. Although it may be, as Hilgard et al. (1960) have noted, that traumatic childhood experiences, the one constant for all the group care children, will leave "scars that can be opened up at a later time," present adjustment shows little evidence of it. Along with Skeels, it was found that marked early deprivation can be overcome and long-term mental health should reasonably be anticipated following *good* group care (see Chap. 10).

Development of Values

As an agent of its society, every child placement service is centrally and unavoidably involved with the development of values. Children's institutions are either "people-making" or "people-changing" social systems, and as such they have a primary responsibility for rearing children who have culture-appropriate values and sound moral character (see Wheeler 1966; and Street, Vinter, and Perrow 1966). It has not been fashionable to deal with such issues in recent years because morality and—to a large extent—values were seen as the province of familial and church activity and to be carefully avoided by any public socializing institutions (Kohlberg 1966). While such a stricture could not very well apply to childrearing institutions functioning in lieu of the natural family and often as an arm of a religious establishment, the general orientation toward issues of this kind has had its effect. Little is known about the capacity of the group care setting to imbue its charges with proper values and sound character.

Early theoreticians, writing before the issue fell into obscurity, generally believed that the isolation of such settings, the scarcity of adult models, and the lack of progressively increasing social responsibility caused the institution-reared child to emerge seriously deficient. Folks (1896), writing mainly at the turn of the century, well represented this view of "the inherent tendency of the system" of institutional care to fail in developing proper values and good character. His preoccupation with the issue was timely, but somehow little attention was paid to values and their development in group settings for the next 50 years. The issue surfaced again in the 1950s and 1960s in a series of publications on the immoral behavior of American prisoners of war in Korea (Kinkead 1957, 1959; Segal 1957) and in new theoretical and empirical work in developmental psychology.[5]

But new thinking catches up slowly with children in care. The literature on what happens to their values and how moral they become is remarkably sparse. Small exceptions to this general lack of data are some British studies of social development, which generally deal with attitudes, values, and morality but are more focused on interpersonal relationships descriptively labeled by the authors as "social adjustment" or "social maturity" (Dunsdon 1947; Pringle 1951). Finding somewhat greater social competence in group care subjects than was generally anticipated, the researchers handle the data with some distrust, cautioning, as Pringle and Bossio have done, that "this is often achieved at some cost, indicated by emotional disturbance, including delinquent manifestations [in Pringle 1965, p. 22]." What emerges from this writing is a distinction between social competence—that is, ability to get along in a group—and values or morality acceptable to the larger society.

The emphasis in the present study is on the values expected of the children.[6] It was assumed that children who live in group care programs are responsive to the demands of their setting and that this means, in turn, an awareness of values that may appropriately be held and a desire to act in accordance with them.

While numerous values appeared to permeate the atmospheres of the group care programs, major concern was usually expressed around two issues: inequality versus egalitarianism and inner versus outer orientation. With numerous correlated values, these concerns formed the main core of emphasis in the socialist kibbutz and youth village, the Catholic *Kinderdorf,* and the Communist children's homes of Yugoslavia and Poland. In discussions and the literature there is repeated mention of the importance of balancing the inner needs of the child (and the possibility of self-expression and even withdrawal) against the desirability of active participation, involvement, and sensitivity to others. On the other major dimension there is also concern for balancing individual difference and competitive and acquisitive drives with a commitment to cooperation, sharing, and equality. But the desired weights for these various positions are markedly different in the several group care settings.

The researchers' efforts to develop some discriminating measures in these areas have proved fairly rewarding. A value inventory listing a series of attributes (e.g., "A enjoys competing with others to find out who is best," "N always puts the wishes of others ahead of his own") and following it with the question, "Should a teen-ager here be just like this?" yielded several factors that clearly differentiated the expectations of staff. Composed of five to eight items each, these relatively uncorrelated factors designate expressed value preferences of the adults most immediately involved with the children and youths in group care. Since the questions were followed by a four-point scale of agreement (from "Yes, definitely" to "No, not at all") it is possible to represent the adult expectations on a strong agreement–strong disagreement continuum on each factor. Further, the adult position may then be matched with the one taken by institutional and home children in response to the identical items but followed by the question, "Should I be just like him?"[7]

At this point a brief digression is needed into the matter of criteria. While in regard to intellectual development and psychosocial maturity it may generally be assumed that the desirable is unidirectional—the more intelligent and the more mature the child becomes, the better—no such assumption makes sense regarding values. What then? It does make sense to ask about the position of some criterion groups and to compare the children's responses with them. But this does not always resolve the matter. When the Austrian *Kinderdorf* clearly specifies that identity with children living at home is the perfect outcome, that should clearly be the criterion and the group care children's responses should be expected to lie between those of the *Mütter* and the home children and, ideally, close to the latter. The matter is indeed quite simple there. It is not in the other settings. Yugoslav and Polish institutions and the Israeli kibbutz and youth village do not accept the home children as a sufficient model. Ideally they wish to bring their charges closer to the expressed images of the kibbutz adults than to those of children in the surrounding community. In some respect they function not only as socializing agents for the existing norms, but as proponents of new norms. While they may want to retain some values held by children living with natural parents, these settings may also have their own value axes to grind.[8]

A case in point are the youth group children in the kibbutz. Since a major objective for the founding and maintenance of this program is to yield new membership for the kibbutz, the value expectations are obvious—conformity with the values of the kibbutz even when this means divergence from the values held by young people in the communities of origin.

Findings on Values

It is expected that the values desired are reasonably well known to the children in these settings. Using the four-point scale on five factors the study findings are as follows.

1. The several factors yield substantial differentiation cross-nationally. This is important if one is going to assume that differences in emphasis among the various settings actually do exist, and they do. Adults give the clearest indication of these differences. The Yugoslavs, for example, are more in favor of other-orientation (Factor IA), controlled achievement (Factor IIA), and competitive achievement (Factor IIIA), but they are more against individualism (Factor IVA) than adults in any of the Israeli settings. The children also show variability that generally follows the adult alignment in emphasis. (See Table 14.5.)

2. When adult expectations differ from those of the children living at home, the group care children are like the home children in Austria and Yugoslavia, but *not* in Israel. In Israel children tend to conform more to

TABLE 14.5. *Mean position of adults and children on 5 adult factor scales derived from the 60-item value inventory**

Sample	Number	Factor IA[†] Other-Orientation	Factor IIA Controlled Achievement	Factor IIIA Competitive Achievement	Factor IVA Individualism	Factor VA Detachment
Israel						
Home	72	2.05	2.02	2.48	2.55	2.32
Kibbutz						
Entering	137	1.83	2.06	2.59	2.80	2.32
Retest group	57	1.99	2.23	2.63	2.90	2.55
Long stay	155	2.01	2.05	2.67	2.67	2.57
Kibbutz-born	33	2.06	2.17	2.65	2.82	2.85
Adults	42	2.22	1.92	2.73	2.42	2.97
Youth village						
Long stay	77	1.92	1.92	2.50	2.84	2.53
Adults	18	2.37	1.68	2.32	2.24	2.90
Austria						
Home	67	1.68	2.02	2.18	2.37	1.99
Kinderdorf	66	1.63	2.00	2.17	2.36	2.09
Adults	20	1.89	2.06	1.74	1.99	2.68
Yugoslavia						
Home	72	1.71	1.79	1.95	2.85	2.13
Institutions	93	1.76	1.78	1.94	2.77	2.00
Adults	51	1.94	1.43	1.77	3.09	2.61
Poland						
Home	(No test data available.)					
Institution	34	1.60	1.76	2.19	2.52	2.27

* 1 = strong acceptance; 4 = strong rejection.

† See footnote 7 for a listing of the five factors with their defining items from the value inventory. (Factor numbers are listed there without the A, which designates them as adult factors; i.e. based on adult's responses.)

adult expectations than to models of children living at home on the factors of controlled achievement, competitive achievement, and detachment. The tendency to accept the first, mildly reject the second, and reject the third is especially noticeable among the kibbutz youth group children. The last is especially important. Young people in any group care program inevitably seek some detachment—they want to be left alone, not to bother with others' opinions, work for their own welfare, and so on. No group care program can tolerate such a position for long. All adults, regardless of setting or country, are more or less opposed to it. However, the group care children in Austria and Yugoslavia do not respond. At the end of many years in care they still resemble children living at home. The Israeli programs do get some response away from the home children and toward the adult expectations. To be sure, the children are nowhere near rejecting detachment as much as do the kibbutz-born children (see Table 14.5), but they move in the desired direction.

3. As with intelligence and psychosocial maturity, again the *Kinderdorf* and kibbutz children move toward the expectations of their respective settings or actually meet these expectations. Austrian home and *Kinderdorf* children are almost indistinguishable on any of the five factors. Although the staff would like them to be more competitive and more individualistic than they are and considerably less detached, the fact is that they resemble other children who live under conditions and with expectations the *Kinderdorf* tried to emulate. *Mutti* has achieved her objective, but she does not seem to realize it. Even her failure to break down some of the detachment is a good omen, since the children will soon be leaving the institutional nest.

Kibbutz youth groups show a similar capacity to convey to the child whether he "should be just like him." It is instructive to look at the relative positions on each factor of the home children, those just entering the setting, some of those retested about two years later, similar teen-agers tested some three to five years following admission, and kibbutz-born adolescents (Table 14.5). On Factors III and V—competitive achievement and detachment— when home and kibbutz values are divergent, a progression toward the kibbutz values is noted that seems to begin with entry and to continue over the next two test periods. While on the matter of detachment progression is slow and obviously inadequate from the kibbutz point of view, it is nevertheless there and in an area that is highly difficult for the children.

In the other two settings home values generally prevail.[9] Despite staff attempts to achieve some differences, as indicated by their positions on all five factors, the group care children show no movement in the direction of staff expectations, except that the youth village residents seem to move somewhat on the detachment dimension.

Values of children in group care do seem, then, to move into some conformity with expectations. In general they have substantial knowledge of the behavior expected and a positive stance toward such expectations. Kibbutz youth group children tend to draw nearer (at least in their pencil-and-paper answers) to kibbutz-born children and to adult expectations. Austrian *Kinderdorf* residents appear much like children living at home. The other settings also show that they have made some, although apparently less, impact on the values of children in their care. We should not be surprised. These are, after all, what Bloom (1964) has called "powerful environments."

Although numerous earlier studies seem to show basic stability of value development, the settings studied may not meet the conditions of a powerful environment pushing toward change.[10] Usually the child observed lives in the family and whatever influences are aimed at him are diffuse and often mutually neutralizing. Even when a clinical effort is made, it juxtaposes adult healer versus adolescent patient—a condition not known for its effectiveness. By contrast, value changes do occur as a result of social participation with persons of like position who hold the values to be acquired (Newcomb 1943; Wilson 1959; Coleman 1961; Coleman et al. 1966). From his own research Kohlberg (1966) has concluded, after experimenting with groups equated for social class and intelligence,

> that children with extensive peer-group participation advance considerably more quickly through the Kohlberg stages of moral judgment than children who are isolated from such participation [p. 17].

This leads to a possible explanation of the present findings.

Bloom (1964) notes three critical components of change. One is alluded to by Kohlberg's findings pertaining to the social environment surrounding the child.

> The major point to be made about such environments is their pervasiveness, that is, the individual is completely engulfed in a situation which presses him from every angle toward a particular type of development or outcome [Bloom, p. 212].

The other components are age and novelty of impact: "There appear to be marked changes in some characteristics at the adolescent stage or in the early stages of encounter with a markedly different environment [Bloom, p. 193]."

This combination of forces is most evident in the kibbutz youth group and least evident in the Yugoslav institutions. In the kibbutz youth group, age of entry, drastic difference of the new setting from the old, continuous and intense interpersonal engagement, and isolation from outside influences all serve to produce change. In the Yugoslav institution, age of entry is highly varied, education is in the community, and certain hierarchical and even political considerations did not (they may now) allow an open review of various value positions. In brief, the institution's powers to push for change are substantially impaired. The present data appear to support the position taken by Bloom that value changes will occur when the program contains the appropriate ingredients of child and environment.

Summary and Discussion

Children reared in five different types of group care programs appear to show little or no intellectual or psychosocial deficiencies when compared with controls from home environments. Although Yugoslav and Austrian group care children do seem somewhat lower in intelligence and Polish institution children appear psychosocially less mature, the general conclusion appears justified. Further, the group care setting seems to have the potential to change values. Examining these conclusions in the light of previous research, considerable support is found for the decision about intellectual development and less about the absence of marked negative psychosocial conditions and the acquisition of values attributable to group care. Perhaps the discrepancies that exist are the result of several still uncontrolled variables.

1. Certainly there are marked differences in settings and thus in the characteristics they promote or suppress. The *Kinderdorf,* for example, is little concerned with intellectual achievement but highly emphatic about warmth, security, and comfort for its children. In the Warsaw children's home, the emphasis is almost reversed. Ratios of adults to children are far smaller. Staff changes often. Building and grounds are shabby, and ideology is not especially clear. Academic achievement and the whole academic experience serve as basic organizing principles in the institution. The RPM and TAT results seem to reflect these institutional atmospheres.

2. Also to be noted are the different initial populations the settings attract or are compelled to serve. The Yugoslav, Polish, and Austrian institutions generally admit much younger and more seriously hurt children than is the case for the two Israeli programs; while some of the Israelis may be quite dull or emotionally disturbed or socially incapable at the time of admission, their proportions are not as high, and their impairment generally is less severe. Good outcomes are therefore more to be anticipated in the latter settings.

3. Of critical theoretical and practice consequence is the fate of the younger children entering the several programs. Thus far the data and discussion have treated them as part of the total sample in each setting. There exists, however, a separate analysis of Yugoslavs and Austrians who entered the group programs by the age of five years. Space limitations do not permit any detailed reporting here, but contrary to usual expectations, the evidence generally points to little or no difference between early and later admissions. (See Chap. 11.)

Finally, a question uppermost in the mind of any practitioner concerned with the placement of children must be this: If some or all of these settings are conducive to good results, what are the ingredients of success? There is not space here for an extensive and elaborate analysis, but several previously noted observations may be restated.

First, and perhaps most ironically obvious, is the nature of expectations. The more successful of the settings do not even concede the idea of failure for the enterprise, although they will, of course, grant the possibility of individual failures. Rejecting the pessimism of Freudian theory based on the assumption of early, massive, and nearly irreparable damage to a child subject to maternal deprivation, these settings believe optimistically in modifiability.

Second, some of these programs, and in particular the *Kinderdorf*, assume that separation, permanent and unequivocal, with a simultaneous commitment to rear each new child to maturity, is more constructive than an unpredictable alternative. Having begun with an evaluation of parental deficiency in each case, they make no claim about modifying it or even living with it. Then, free of the encumbrance, they plan a long-range program for the child in their setting. A kibbutz youth group, although far less separatist, nevertheless has a similar long-term impact in both its means and goals. The former are reflected in a social pattern and value system markedly different from the child's family, and the latter is seen in the focus on the child's future membership in the kibbutz, which clearly aims toward ultimate separation from his family.

Third, social integration within the large milieu appears to mark the successful program. *Kinderdorf* children are not only members of their own family and their children's village but also of the town where they live, the local church in which they worship, and the neighborhood school they attend. Similarly, the kibbutz youth group members become over time not only members of their own peer society but also of work units, the total kibbutz *chevra*, and even of family units within it.

Fourth, peer impact is an important factor. Since the children's society is generally viewed as healthy and accordingly endowed with rights and responsibilities, pressures are exerted by peers in the direction of adult expectations. This influence is especially important in the kibbutz where much evidence exists of peer group power.

Fifth, socially constructive work is of major importance in giving the children both the sense of competence they so badly lack initially and the feeling of ownership. "We built this garden, or classroom, or barn" is not uncommonly heard in a kibbutz youth group. Even more prevalent, in fact universal, is the assumption of various work responsibilities in the adult society. Some youth group members become so proficient at their tasks that their prospective departure is treated with considerable gravity and serious recruitment efforts are made.

Finally, there is ideology. An ideologically confused setting ill-serves the emotionally and socially uprooted child. It offers him no moral anchorage and little hope of finding a firm idea to which he can hold. Kibbutz and *Kinderdorf* children are most privileged also in this respect. Whether it is the socialism of the kibbutz or the Roman Catholicism of the *Kinderdorf* may not be crucially important to healthy psychosocial development. Its pervasiveness, benign interpretation of human behavior, and the abundance and consistency of adult models seem to be.

If these are the requirements of a powerful environment conducive to change, where does the American child-care practitioner stand on them? It seems that for reasons of faith, history, and political propriety he may have difficulty with every one of the six conditions that seem to lead to the results seen in the most successful group care settings. Adherence to traditional interpretations of Freudian theory predisposes him toward familial rather than group substitutes. This also precludes clear separation and social integration of institutional children. He is cautious about peer influences, believing that in adolescence they are directed away from or against adult values. Historically he has had an abhorrence of child labor, since it evokes in him images of English spinning mills and American sweatshops. He fears strong ideology because in a pluralistic environment it leads to disagreement, which our society, operating under the "unity-in-diversity" motto, has yet to harness successfully to productive purposes. Yet these seem to be the ingredients of good group care for some children.

NOTES

1. See, for example, the studies Pringle (1965) mentions or describes.

2. See, for example, Crissey (1937); Dennis and Najarian (1957); Kirk (1958); and Pringle (1965).

3. Because the validity of such analyses is always open to question, the researchers are now embarked on yet a third and rather different assessment of these materials.

4. Details on the classification, scoring, and evidence of probable validity will be supplied on request.

5. See, for example, Bronfenbrenner (1968, 1967a, 1963); Kohlberg (1958); and Peck, Havighurst et al. (1960).

6. Unfortunately, Kohlberg's imaginative work on stages of moral character development and the seemingly universal applicability of a certain hierarchy of morality did not come to the author's attention in time to be incorporated into the present research, although it might well have been of considerable importance (see Kohlberg 1963).

7. The following are the five adult factors and the items of the value inventory that define them.

Factor I, *Other-Orientation*. Wants to devote his life to helping other people. Has strong ideas about how people should live. Is always willing to help anyone no matter how great the price. Is someone everyone comes to for advice and help. Is always ready to share what he has with others. Has a definite set of rules of how to act. Works for the good of others and not himself.

Factor II, *Achievement (Controlled)*. Is always the last one to ask for help; he likes to do things for himself. Tries to be the best in whatever he does. Tries to work with other people whenever he can. Is never emotional about things and always stops to think things through. Is not ambitious and does not care what he does when he gets older (negatively associated with the other items of Factor II). Always looks for new ways to do something.

Factor III, *Competitive Achievement*. Treats everyone he meets as an equal, no matter who they are (negatively associated). Enjoys competing with others to find out who is best. Wants to be someone who is looked to for leadership. Is cautious and carefully plans the things he does. Always decides for himself what is right and what is wrong (negatively associated).

Factor IV, *Individualism*. Tries to follow the sure and proved way of doing things (negatively associated). Would rather be different from others than just like them. Likes to have a place where he can go and be by himself. Is a religious person. Is someone who likes to be alone with his thoughts. Does not like to do things that others might think unusual or strange (negatively associated).

Factor V, *Detachment*. Obeys right away and never argues with adults. Likes to be left alone to do just what he wants to do. Would rather work by himself and does not care too much about working with others. Spends a lot of his time by himself reading and thinking about things. Lets those smarter than he make the decisions. Always avoids telling other people what they should do. Is never bothered by what others think of him. Works for his own welfare and encourages others to work for themselves.

8. An extreme but most illustrative example of such use of group care may be seen in the Soviet boarding schools. Established under Khrushchev, they were intended to produce the "New Soviet Man." See Chapter 4 and Ambler (1961) for a description of this program.

9. Poland is omitted because the samples of children are small and no data on adults' expectations exist.

10. Peck, Havighurst et al. (1960) have found that "the child of each character type starts very early to develop along that type of path, and that growth simply makes him more and more that kind of person [p. 157]." Kagan and Moss (1962) arrive at essentially the same conclusions. Meyer, Borgatta, and Jones (1965) go even further and show the lack of impact made by a substantial program of clinical intervention on delinquency-prone adolescents.

15

One Kibbutz as Foster Mother: Maimonides Applied

MARTIN WOLINS

Extreme cases probably mean little operationally, but for theoretical purposes they are the classic situations that clarify reality, shedding light on the feasible—the potential of the human spirit to melt the iceberg of social indifference and neglect. Chapter 15 is a description of an outstanding group care success in a sensitive and intensely invested environment.

Unlike most group programs that admit, try to modify, and send back into "the real world" those designated to their care, the kibbutz aims to retain. The epitome of success is therefore the acculturation of an adolescent to the norms of the setting not only for the period of treatment but also for life. Members of the Cactus youth group described here were mostly former slum dwellers designated for the scrap heaps of humanity in the manner of urban young people like them throughout the world. They came to Ramat Yedidim with few illusions, and few were harbored about them. The first contacts were wary and painful; yet, as this book is being prepared for press —12 years after the arrival of Cactus—its former members comprise a significant and productive part of the kibbutz. How did it happen?

> The function of socialization is to transform the human raw material of society into good working members; the content can be considered and analytically to include an understanding of the society's status structure and of the role prescriptions and behavior associated.
>
> (BRIM 1966)

Martin Wolins. "The Kibbutz as Foster Mother: Maimonides Applied." In *Group Care: An Israeli Approach,* eds. Martin Wolins and Meir Gottesmann, New York: Gordon and Breach, 1971. Reproduced by permission.

There are eight levels of zeddakah. The highest virtue is to take the hand of an Israelite who has fallen, give him a gift or loan or enter into a partnership with him, or find him work.

(MAIMONIDES, 12th century)

Socialization and resocialization are unavoidable in any community that seeks to survive. When, as in Israel, the community is bent on "ingathering of exiles," the task acquires urgency and great national significance. New members coming from highly disparate environments must be admitted, transformed, and allowed to enter the national partnership. Every new nation built on immigrants must confront this task so familiar to generations of new Americans tossed more or less gently into the proverbial melting pot. The experience also is common for many Israelis, but they, in the words attributed to former Prime Minister Ben Gurion, were put into a "pressure cooker"—a more intense socializing experience. One of the high-pressure instrumentalities has been the kibbutz.

This form of collective settlement, whose development since the early part of the century is almost synonymous with the rise of Israel, has served many functions. As an agricultural entity it has nourished the body and spirit, converting progeny of untold generations of small shopkeepers into tillers and lovers of the soil. As a community of the young it formed the backbone of a defense establishment. As aggregates of self-selected ideologists, the kibbutzim have been the mainstay of several political parties. It was only natural, then, that the demands of immigrant acculturation should find a response in the kibbutz, which has shown a particular receptivity to young people. So it was that the early victims of Nazi policies in the 1930s—children whose parents sent them out of Germany—found their way into kibbutzim. What they started ultimately became a major program as thousands of children in hundreds of youth groups entered kibbutz settings. There they studied and worked, and ultimately many became members.

More recently, though, the pattern has changed. Immigration slowed down. Children arrived with their parents. If disadvantaged culturally or economically, they filled the poor quarters of cities and the sluggish streets of development towns. They began to drop out of the mainstream of Israeli life, despite the efforts of a concerned government. The old parental values and behavior did not fit, and the new were either unknown or beyond capability, leaving few open alternatives that were both socially acceptable and personally feasible. One of these has been the kibbutz, its objective—socialization into membership.

Like any goal in societal intervention, membership is but a clear-cut, measurable end product with many bench marks along the route. In order to become a member the young adolescent going into a kibbutz must change substantially. Although the kibbutz is willing to take his hand and lead toward partnership, it watches critically for indications of growth in intellectual capability, psychosocial maturity, and the acquisition of values consonant with kibbutz life. And in the most capable settings these do take place. Young people who move from parental homes in development towns and urban slums and remain in kibbutz youth groups for periods of two to five years change in the direction of kibbutz-born children. Their intellectual capability shows a marked increase; they gain substantially in maturity; and when confronted with open-ended questions that allow for various value expressions, they answer on several important dimensions neither like their former nor yet like their current role models but predictably in between. Nor is this the only evidence of such change. Amir (1967), reviewing the adjustment of soldiers in the Israeli armed forces (and using apparently sizable samples), comes up with a similar in-between position for the youth group members. On dimensions of competence, rates of volunteering, and adjustment to the service they score better than the general (not just low socioeconomic) Israeli population. "The evidence," the author concludes, "shows the impact of kibbutz life upon youth placed after the age of ten years [p. 258]."

Reasonable yet somewhat inconsistent with other evidence and developmental theory, these data require attention. By and large, we have come to expect perseveration. Rightly so. Bloom (1964) has found it to exist along several dimensions, which are characterized by a "period of most rapid growth . . . likely to be in the early years and . . . followed by periods of less and less rapid growth [p. 204]." Since rate of growth and environmental impact are closely interrelated, little change should be expected once the trajectory of a growth curve flattens out. This, indeed, is what we are told by some researchers. For example, Peck, Havighurst et al. (1960) write that "the child of each character type starts very early to develop along that type path, and . . . growth simply makes him more and more that type of person [p. 157]." Although the authors explain this phenomenon by adding that "the family influence is usually continuously the same . . .," there is evidence of perseverance even when environment is changed. Another study shows that when delinquents move from the city to a corrective treatment institution, they seem to maintain (and even accelerate and impose) their behavior despite a change in environment and in the face of usually contrary staff values (Polsky 1962).

Persistence of such childhood patterns is reasonably attributed to frequency of learning situations, primacy in the life of the child, the powerful nature of rewards, and the probability that much of the personality becomes relatively inaccessible as unconscious material (Brim 1966, p. 21). However, this is only part of the story. While evidence for continuity exists, "the larger proportion of the variance in personality at later times remains unaccounted for [p. 23]." In brief, there is room to maneuver. And the question seems to revolve not so much around the likelihood that an adolescent can change but rather around the conditions under which he is apt to change in the direction desired. Having seen this happening to foster children in the kibbutz, we may well ask: How is it that the earlier traits did not persevere? What has made the kibbutz as a foster mother different from Polsky's Hollymeade and the youth group unlike the members of *Cottage Six?* (Polsky 1962).

Ramat Yedidim may help us describe the phenomenon more precisely and perhaps explain it. As its half-plagiarized name is intended to imply *Ramat Yedidim* is a close relative of Spiro's (1956) *Kiryat Yedidim.* Both are members of the same political movement and belong to the same kibbutz federation. Kibbutz members *(chaverim)* are still relatively young at *Rama,* just as they were at *Kiryat Yedidim* in the early 1950s. There are quite a few young children, almost no adolescents yet, and nearly all adult members are married. The social and political ideology Spiro described in his Yedidim is still relevant to *Rama,* where in spite of considerable attenuation and great disappointment with the "mess the Russians have made of Marx," it powerfully affects the kibbutz. *Rama's* slogans are equality, humanity, productivity and, in the face of the current politico-military situation, nationalism. This ideology it would rather not espouse, and the children in class are still taught to love all mankind.[1] Ideological enemies are also quite well defined: authoritarianism, privilege, parasitism, indolence. Increasing affluence, a general acceptance of the values, and a pruning away of some irrelevant, largely ceremonial aspects have muted the proclamations and possibly reduced some of the ardor; but the core holds fast at *Rama,* though possibly not in the kibbutz movement generally (Rettig 1966). Although, as Karl Mannheim (1936) so insightfully observed, the "utopia" of the fathers is becoming the "ideology" of their children, the ideology is strong and an essential part of the setting into which the youth group enters.

Rama's physical environment is also common to kibbutzim, although perhaps more attractive. Arranged in several nearly complete concentric circles somewhat displaced by a rather rugged topography, the kibbutz is physically as well as socially centered around the dining/assembly hall. In the first circle are the young children's houses, followed somewhat further away by family rooms, the youth corner, and all surrounded by implement buildings, storehouses, barns, and then fields, orchards, and pastures. It is an attractive place. Trees planted in the forties have grown large. Annual and perennial flowers abound. The view of the surrounding hills and valleys is grand, often in the late afternoon sunsets even breathtaking.

Although life is hard, and this is obvious from even cursory observation of *chaverim* at work, it is also secure. Confident capability seems to match existing problems. While "utopia" is off the masthead, the good life can be had if members can be attracted to expand the social circle of *chaverim.*

Here is where the youth group fits the designs of the kibbutz. A precedent has existed from the very beginning when young people entering as foster children turned into members and at times even founders of new kibbutzim. But then the arrivals were different. Europeans, often members of political youth movements, mostly middle class in origin, generally articulate and even highly literate—those young people fitted well with the existing membership. Now the available population has changed. Representing more recent waves of *aliyah* (immigration), children are mainly African-Asian in origin, lower class in status, politically uninvolved, academically backward, and ideologically somewhat adverse to kibbutz life. Probability of success is unknown, but the membership problem is severe. In the 10th year of its existence, *Rama* was prepared to try.

The first group was far from an unqualified success. It was small, predominantly male, and quite advanced in age. Accepted with some reluctance by the kibbutz and assigned a peripheral member as their *madrich,* these young people stayed for only a year before joining the armed forces as a military-agricultural unit. Surprisingly, more than half of the young people kept their ties with *Rama* and returned as members following military service.

The second attempt—the Cactus group—involved more children, a much larger kibbutz investment, and a greater risk, which seems to have paid off (see Table 15.1). What were the ingredients of this success? They seem to lie largely, if not exclusively, in the structural-functional components of the youth group and its relation to the encompassing kibbutz. An exploration of the context in which the youth group functioned will comprise the remainder of this paper. First, briefly, a look at the validity of the success assumption.

During a two-year period (mid-1960 to mid-1962), "Cactus" (the self-designation of our youth group) admitted 69 members. Although born in 18 countries ranging geographically over Western Asia, North Africa, and all of Europe, the entrants were not newcomers to Israel. Most had been in the country several years, spoke Hebrew more or less well, and had attended schools in various cities and towns before joining "Cactus." Their school reports made rather dismal reading. Although theoretically sixth and seventh graders, in actuality many were considered failures, and scholastic inadequacy was given as a major reason for joining the group in more than half of the cases. (Estimated intelligence test performance based on scores of similar groups is at about the first quartile.) Other children came to Cactus because their families were unable to keep them, their physical environment was dangerous or harmful, and a few—very few—because their parents wanted them to grow up in a kibbutz.

First- and second-year withdrawals and admissions[2] led to considerable changes in Cactus membership, but slowly a hard core evolved. In the fifth year, when the young people were preparing to complete their *hakshara* ("making fit"—socialization process) and enter the army, everyone considered the group a success. The long-stay members who remained were bright (mean Raven Progressive Matrices percentile 55.4), their expressed values came close to the kibbutz ideal, they were heavily involved in various activities of *Rama,* and they were expected to become members.

TABLE 15.1. *Comparison of development town, kibbutz youth group, Cactus, and kibbutz-born young people on selected variables**

	Devel. Town Youth	Kibbutz Youth Groups	Cactus† Members	Kibbutz-Born
Number of subjects	112	155	28‡	33
Mean age when tested (years)	15.7	17.3	17.2	16.5
Raven Progressive Matrices mean percentile	29.2	53.3	55.4	71.7
Percent judged more mature (13 matched pairs)	16.0	84.0	—	—
Factor scores:				
Other-orientation	2.05§	2.01	1.81	2.06
Controlled achievement	2.02	2.05	2.14	2.17
Competitive achievement	2.48	2.67	2.73	2.65
Individualism	2.55	2.67	3.02	2.82
Detachment	2.32	2.57	2.84	2.85
Sentence completion (in percent of endings):				
Self-control	16.4	22.3	17.9	30.3
Occupational achievement	56.4	40.8	32.1	21.2
Belief in abstractions	9.1	19.1	32.1	39.4
Social affiliation	16.4	22.9	25.0	27.3
Satisfaction in group activity	9.1	27.4	17.9	42.4
Optimism	9.1	26.1	35.7	48.5
Morality of sharing	14.5	26.8	21.4	30.3
Control of one's wishes	29.1	45.9	39.3	51.5

* More details on the groups and the variables are given in Chapter 14.

† Cactus is the name of a youth group placed in Kibbutz *Ramat Yedidim.*

‡ Only long-stay members (mean stay 3.8 years) are included in this tabulation.

§ 1=maximal acceptance; 4=maximal rejection.

To be sure, some problems existed. They overemphasized some kibbutz doctrine (e.g., other orientation) or too strongly opposed traditional kibbutz enemies (individualism, competitive achievement). This typical enthusiasm of the convert did not spread throughout, however. Self-control and control of one's wishes still remained low, and satisfaction in group activity, a major theme of *Rama* life, was probably less than the *madrichim* would have wanted. But the drive for occupational achievement—a prime reason for leaving the kibbutz—had been reduced; belief in abstractions—equality, humanism, etc.—had risen markedly; and expressions of social affiliation were high. Considerable optimism was expressed by Cactus members and by *Rama chaverim*.

On the whole, test results justified the prediction of ultimate success—that is, kibbutz membership. In 1965, shortly after the tests were administered, nearly all members of Cactus entered the Israeli army as a *nahal* unit. Three years later, three-quarters joined *Rama* as *chaverim,* bringing with them several wives and husbands and one or two friends—a very measurable yield of 39 percent of the total number of children and young people whose names had ever graced the Cactus roster. And they now have good status in the kibbutz. Where *chaverim* are regularly and often even openly evaluated by the community, the former members of Cactus are no exception. Asked to rate the returnees on the attributes of intellectual capacity, emotional adjustment, acceptance of *Rama* values, quality of group membership, and attitude toward work (see Table 15.2), several old *chaverim* rated them high.[3] None of the Cactus group scored low in all categories; 1 member received a perfect 15, meaning high in all 5 areas; and 3 others scored nearly perfect 14s. Further, there was no difference in standing associated with continent of birth—a matter of considerable pride now, as it once had been a source of real concern.

TABLE 15.2. *Cactus performance as kibbutz members by continent of birth**

	Africa/Asia	Europe	
Above median	7	6	13
Below median	8	6	14
	15	12	
Possible range:		5-15	
Actual range:		7-15	
Mean score:		10.8	

* Scores consist of the sum of evaluations (high=3; average=2; low=1) in each of the following categories: intellectual capacity, emotional adjustment, acceptance of kibbutz values, quality of group membership, and attitude toward work.

So much for achievement. Maimonides' prescription for the highest form of *zeddakah* has carried the day in the midst of Marxist slogans, but why did it work? The answer seems to lie in large measure in the teleological implications of the goal—membership—and the ideological context of its pursuit. Having established an anticipated status for children who joined the Cactus group, the kibbutz then allowed it to dictate means, thus effectively producing a "self-fulfilling prophecy" (Merton 1957) atmosphere.

Most powerful in its implications was the definition of the program. Having received a busload of disheveled, unruly, often neglected, and occasionally disturbed kids, *Rama* could have defined them in the manner of many U.S. welfare settings as abandoned, delinquent, or sick. The definition would then imply an appropriate environment emphasizing, respectively, custody, resocialization, or treatment (Street et al. 1966; Wheeler 1966). In fact, *Rama* chose a different route and defined the situation as normal children in need of socialization.[4]

At this point the old, nearly trite Marxian slogan came to be important. In the early days of the group, kibbutz input clearly exceeded return—a matter of immense consequence in a very rational, cost–benefit economy. Eventual benefit had to be implied, or the effort would collapse. When the situation was defined as "from each according to his ability, to each according to his need" and a long-range view was taken, then the children could be seen as having rights from the outset and obligations for productivity deferred. Kibbutz contributions to the group could then be entered as a kind of long-term social welfare investment not very different from childrearing in a natural family. If the best meeting of needs leads to subsequent optimal ability, then justification exists not for just minimal but for high investment. Cactus thus got nice buildings, good classrooms, a laboratory, musical instruments and, most important, some of the best and most influential *chaverim* as *madrichim,* teachers, and other adults directly responsible for the group.[5]

Although the initial definition labeled all entering children as normal—capable of functioning in a socialization medium—in reality it was not so. Within a short period of the group's entry some children were clearly designated as unfit. Usually such status was earned by those who violated cardinal rules of kibbutz life. Physical and verbal aggression, theft, and withdrawal usually led to adult and subsequently peer pressures. While the choice before the deviant to stop or leave was always modified by a concern for his personal circumstances and the alternatives open to him, the closed character of the group and the ever more intense patterns of interrelationships made it difficult to deviate and remain. Failures tended to leave.

Considerable effort also was made to keep successes who inclined toward returning home because of personal objectives or family obligations. Although *Rama* usually had not been able to retain young people who, having gained maturity and competence, opted for occupations not open in the kibbutz or chose to return home to meet filial responsibilities, strong efforts were made, including commitments for further, nonkibbutz occupational training and financial as well as other help to Cactus members' parents when the need was very great and endangered a child's continued stay at *Rama.*[6]

Community status of the group is obviously affected by the membership goal and the normalcy implications. To be sure, the young people never feel equal in competence and status to the young elite whom their kibbutz-born peers represent in Israel, and their self-image is probably justified (Amir 1967; Wolins 1969). Some members of Cactus, even after becoming *chaverim,* still refer to their youth group days as second-class citizenship. It comes down to simple things: "The girls say that everyone in *Rama* has high fur boots for the winter except us. Everyone has a flannel shirt except our members."[7] But the bulk of this problem lies mainly in the youth movement of the kibbutz federation where youth group and kibbutz-born teenagers participate together.

At *Rama,* as in any other setting, adults who work with deprived children can conceptualize their task as mainly a skilled job or an act of dedication. The probability of defining the situation as expert function or noble cause varies with the type of subjects, objectives, attributes of the staff, and ideological state of the setting. A hospital for mentally ill patients, which provides largely custodial care with some professional intervention and is accustomed to a generally poor prognosis, will predispose staff to dissociate from the setting and the patients and to define their role functionally. At best, emphasis will be given to skill, licensed competence, and the proper performance of duties. At worst, staff will try only to survive (Goffman 1961). American settings for deprived children, while not extreme examples of such functional role definition, are strongly influenced in that direction.[8]

Chaverim of *Rama* who took charge of Cactus saw their role quite differently. First, they were not really professionals in the usual sense: while some had broad academic training, it lacked specific emphasis and technical skill. Second, the subjects having been perceived as normal and the goal as membership, the usual childrearing role definitions applied: devotion, affect, and understanding were seen as far more important than technique. Finally, the attempt to bring the children into a faithfully held doctrine gave the task a sense of evangelical ministry. The total effect was a strong cause orientation, which generally aided though on occasion also overwhelmed the children by its intensity.

The cause orientation of staff could be used most effectively in the isolation imposed on Cactus by temporal, geographic, and ideological factors. Entry into Cactus had the total immersion qualities so well described by Goffman (1961), but the conditions surrounding Cactus were, it seems, the more powerful. As noted, one factor in the group's total immersion is temporal. Half of Cactus members tested in the fifth year were there from the first month. The emphasis was always, as one supervisor wrote in the record, "to complete the group as soon as possible." Once the child was moved to the kibbutz, his preexisting social supports were undercut. He had to search for new ones, and the ongoing group provided the ties and claimed his allegiance. A serial pattern (Wheeler 1966, pp. 60–64) of admissions would have allowed greatest peer influence. A disjunctive one (as initially in Cactus) gave more power to the staff. The children coming to *Rama* in the fall of 1960 had to find their own way. Faced with obviously improper old direction signs (leading toward private property, occupational or competitive striving, or even religious thought and observance), they had to look for new signs. These, however, were not in an existing peer group, which had learned to attenuate *Rama's* expectations, but in the *chaverim* themselves.

The dependence on *chaverim* for clues to proper behavior was further intensified by the geographic isolation of the kibbutz. Its scenic grandeur derives from a hilltop setting, to be sure, but no less from the sparse habitation all around. And this had social significance. Parents were hours away by bus and so were the soon-to-be-forgotten former friends who were seen only during the four regularly scheduled brief vacation periods a year or during special occasions arranged at the kibbutz. While the attitude toward parents was friendly[9] and careful attempts were made to keep them informed, their influence was not great except when the children went home. Reduction of outside cues increased the salience of those that remained. In this context the effect was further amplified by the minimal pull on the youth to resolve "the dilemmas of adolescence" in the family as well as with the peer group (Sherif and Sherif 1965, p. 282).

Finally, the powerful ideology of *Rama* contributed to the isolation and immersion of the Cactus young people. As Eisenberg and Neubauer (1965) have pointed out:

> . . . kibbutz society makes its expectations for its youth explicit. Its pioneers made a conscious, ideologically motivated choice of a way of life, in heroic disregard of hardships that would have deterred the fainthearted. Having brought its ideals of social justice to a remarkable, if necessarily incomplete fruition, it is not prepared to consider abandoning them. In consequence it heralds its goals for its youth in unmistakable fashion [p. 430].[10]

This call crosses the boundary between the kibbutz-born children and foster children, and powerful ideological demands that were often quite divergent from those of their earlier youth immediately surrounded the incoming Cactus members, thus intensifying the sense of isolation from the past and immersion in the kibbutz. As one of the most successful members of Cactus put it quite literally: "When I first came here I felt as if I was drowning. Man breathes air, I thought, and my air was in the city. But Cactus soon found the oxygen in this atmosphere. If it had not been for my friends and Moshe [the *mandrich*] I would never have made it."[11]

Ideological demands made on children who enter the kibbutz youth group are expressed in terms of expectations that can apply only to healthy, mature persons. Three such expectations are embodied in common phrases flown on the masthead of every group: *Chevra, Avoda, Limudim*—society, work, studies. A fourth, the family, while more covert, nevertheless permeates kibbutz functioning. These four pillars of the kibbutz also serve as the base on which the youth group functions. Work and family bring the young people—children, really, at the time of entry—into the mainstream of kibbutz life. Society, used here in the sense of group interaction, and study remain for the duration largely within the youth group.

Within these two social circles the Cactus members learned the prerogatives and obligations of a *chaver* in *Rama*. Several conditions this arrangement dictated clearly distinguished them from the kept status that normally and properly characterizes a child fostered by adults related or unrelated to each other. Since acting out membership in the larger society (i.e., *Rama*) started from the very beginning, taking the form of work, social participation, and self-improvement, each of the child's activity could be seen as a contribution to *Rama*. The considerable significance that the work of Cactus members eventually acquired in the total life of the kibbutz is difficult to overestimate.[12] Visible to *chaverim* and children alike, it served continually as a status symbol denoting mature responsibility as contrasted with tolerated dependency in the usual foster care setting.

In a similar manner, the "attachment" of Cactus children to kibbutz families served to enhance status. A child coming into the youth group was introduced to a family whose rooms he could visit. This relationship conferred on many the status of oldest sibling and often elicited appropriate role behavior. It was not unusual to see Cactus youth visiting their young "brothers" and "sisters" in the children's house, playing with them after work, or, consistent with their oldest child role, being aided, counseled, or rebuked by the "parents."

By tying family and work situations into the life of the Cactus child, *Rama* was providing him not only with symbols of status and avenues of ego satisfaction but also with very proximate models of adults doing the expected as a matter of course. However, the self-evident to *chaverim* was by no means so to the newly entering child. He needed the society of peers in which to hammer out the issues and gain some competencies. This, of course, was the major function of the Cactus social organization—the inner circle that surrounded each child from the outset and with ever-increasing power carried him toward the objectives of the kibbutz. Since Cactus was a collective within the collective of *Rama*, it served not only as a means of social control and a base from which to venture with increasing frequency and consequence into the outer circle of *Rama* but also as a miniature society similar to *Rama*. It was in this manner an excellent training environment for adult roles in an egalitarian society. To be effective, Cactus had to exert considerable peer power, act largely in lieu of adults, though with their benevolent and helpful guidance, and direct group goals toward convergence with those of *Rama*.

In performing these functions, the Cactus youth group took on most, though not all, of the characteristics Bronfenbrenner (1962) described as operating in the Soviet classroom.

1. The collective—*chevra*—with adult leadership became the primary vehicle of socialization.

2. Behavior of Cactus members was evaluated in terms of appropriateness to the goals of the group and—somewhat more remote but never disregarded—the purposes of *Rama*.

3. Reward and punishment were group directed; that is, everyone benefited or suffered from the behavior of individuals.

4. Evaluation of members moved quickly from *madrichim* to peers within the collective.

5. Principal sanctions were expressed in the form of group recognition or disapproval; the ultimate was the award of a leadership role or a vote for expulsion.

6. Open group criticism was the beginning of internalization and ultimate honest self-criticism along the criteria established by the collectivity.

Another attribute, intergroup competition, usually employed in the Soviet collectives as a means for stimulating socialization of all members, was of minor importance in Cactus partly because of isolation and in large measure by virtue of the negative value attached to competitive behavior in kibbutzim. However, in a limited sense even that was present. Strong group identity eventually required some determination of relative status, and Cactus members were fond of comparing their group achievements (in encampments, for example) with those of other youth groups.

As *Rama's* norms permeated the behavior and, by implication, the personality structure of Cactus members, the motive force moved from compliance to identification to internalization, as Kelman (1961) had described it for other settings of social influence. Initially, a child did what was expected because someone, usually a *madrich,* told him to. Rather quickly the focus moved from request to example and the models from solely adult leaders to *chaverim* as well as the more lauded members of Cactus itself. It was somewhere in this phase that the convergence of *Rama* and Cactus goals became clear[13] and the boundaries between foster child and member status became increasingly indistinct. To be sure, formal entry into *Rama* membership could not yet take place, but ever-increasing opportunity for as-if behavior existed, which culminated in a kind of initiation rite[14] that had the earmarks of a *rite de passage,* to be sure, not from Cactus youth to *Rama chaver* but more from identification with to internalization of the ideological essence of kibbutz life. Following is the initiation of Ehud. He was 17½ years old then, had been in Cactus about 4 years, and was of low average intelligence.

CACTUS 1: Ehud's position in the group is that he is easily influenced and does everything he is told.

MADRICH 1: There are many who have much capacity, others who have limited capacity but contribute what they can. Ehud gives all he can. His work is very good. He wants to learn.

CACTUS 2: Ehud has a serious problem at home, great pressure to come back. And the question is how long and in what way he will be able to withstand it.

[Ehud comes in.]

CACTUS 1: We are trying to summarize the period you have spent with us. How do you see your future in the group?

EHUD: As I see it, it's okay. No one bothers me. I'm fine in committees.

CACTUS 1: You show no initiative in the group. You are under pressure from home.

EHUD: I want to remain and I will struggle with my parents.

Madrich 1: This is the group in which you grew up, and you are now at the conclusion of your adolescence. You stand at the crossroads. Which way do you want to go? Is this a group where you feel comfortable? Do you want to remain in the kibbutz? Ask yourself.

CACTUS 2: Do you feel any indication that your parents will win out or you? When the chips are down, will you break or overcome?

Madrich 2: The test is to be in *Rama* and yet not cut ties with parents.

Madrich 1: Ehud, why do your parents want to take you out?

EHUD: They want to prepare me for a trade.

CACTUS 2: You must explain to your parents your way of life.

Madrich 1: When we get the "Symbol of Maturity" and become graduates, what is our connection with *Rama* or some other group?

EHUD: I'd like to be attached here.

CACTUS 1: What is your attitude to Nahal?

EHUD: I want to join.

CACTUS 2: There is a condition of surrender and a condition of "I want and will make an effort."

EHUD: I've chosen the second.

CACTUS 1: Do you have some kind of a problem? Some kind of a question?

EHUD: To continue work in the dairy barn.

Madrich 1: Ehud has adopted the values of our movement and the question is whether there are doubts or not.

Conclusion

There are no doubts so far as the Cactus group is concerned. There is nothing negative about Ehud except for the difficulty at home.

They made no error. Ehud went off to *Nahal*, returned to the kibbutz, and now in his early twenties is rated as a good young member. His work and group membership are outstanding; and although he is not quite so imaginative or intellectually tough as others from Cactus, he is considered to be well adjusted and well accepted in *Rama*.

Ehud's vacillation, other members' acting out, the general lack of intellectual capacity, and the absence of appropriate values have not prevented Cactus from remaining at *Rama* and moving gradually from foster child to *chaver* status. In the face of foster care failures elsewhere (Eisenberg 1962; Jeter 1963; Maas and Engler 1959), the success of Cactus seems due to the play of a powerful combination of forces, including a sensitive age, a strong setting, and a goal that goes beyond the limits of the custody–treatment continuum (Polsky and Claster 1968; Street *et al.* 1966) and is anchored instead in membership. This goal softens the great pressures of the environment and, given a group context, makes them endurable. The power of this environment results from several factors easily discernible in Cactus: adolescent age, a markedly different setting, and a pervasive environment that totally envelops the member. As Bloom (1964) has pointed out, "in such powerful environments only relatively few individuals are able to resist the effects of environmental pressure [p. 212]."[15]

Consistent with such power is considerable self-assurance, an attitude well reflected in the invitation Cactus extended to visitors who came to call on World Child's Day a few years ago.

Peace be with you and welcome to our house—your house.

This corner shows the undeniable contributions of the kibbutz and Youth Aliyah, but its major component is the young men and women who built it, have been and will be built within it. We believe in the powerful spirit of man. We believe in his ability to do good for himself and others and that this, our way, will bring us to our goal.

Come, let us be *chaverim* in the struggle and . . . the hope [*Rama,* Cactus group, 1965].

NOTES

1. Given present conditions, this leads to serious intrapersonal conflict when the young people are confronted with wartime choices of killing or dying. See *Talks with Warriors* (1967), a collection (in Hebrew) of vivid interviews with kibbutz participants in the 1967 Six-Day War.

2. The reductions in youth group membership do not seem to correlate with intellectual or psychosocial competence. While some members of youth groups leave because of group pressures, most withdrawals are caused by outside, usually familial factors.

3. It is helpful to recall in this connection Brim's (1966) three prerequisites of satisfactory role performance: knowledge, ability, and motivation.

4. This, by the way, is not true in all kibbutzim. In the older, more established ones another of the definitions may be applied, usually leading to failure.

5. At one point a Youth Aliyah supervisor, taken aback by the staff *Rama* proposed for Cactus, called it "an embarrassment of riches."

6. Desired and undesired departures from the youth group appear to balance out, so that at least some intake attributes of those who remain and those who leave during the first two years seem to be identical (Wolins 1969).

7. "Cactus" newsletter, January 1964.

8. This tendency was particularly encouraged in social work by the gleeful elevation of functional competence over commitment to causes that took place in the 1930s through 1950s. Porter Lee's (1937) article on social work as cause or function is a prime example.

9. "The spring has come, winter's gone, and we invite you to our home." So goes a brief poem in a newsletter to the parents, which tells them also about the group's activities, need to renew certain documents, and forthcoming events in Cactus.

10. The search for fidelity in these circumstances should certainly be less burdensome than that described by Erikson (1962) for other youth of the same age.

11. See Schachter (1959) for evidence and discussion of a similar phenomenon. The sense of joint immersion serves to heighten the intensity of relationships leading to even more powerful peer influence than would ordinarily exist here.

12. Toward the end of its five-year existence, the members of Cactus were contributing some 20 percent of *Rama's* man-hours of work in the collective's production and service branches.

13. Goal convergence and increasing participation in goal setting by Cactus members had an additional positive effect on the socialization process. See Wheeler (1966), pp. 69–72, for relevant discussion.

14. Eisenberg and Neubauer (1965, p. 438) have pointed to its practice among kibbutz-born children and expressed their trepidation by calling it a "purification ritual." The event referred to here is neither so dramatic nor likely to be so traumatic as they indicate.

15. Bloom further writes that "there do appear to be marked changes in some characteristics at the adolescent stage or in early stages of encounter with a markedly different environment (. . . placement in a foster home . . .) [p. 193]."

ADDITIONAL READING FOR PART IV

Bloom, Benjamin S. *Stability and Change in Human Characteristics*. New York: John Wiley & Sons, 1964.

Kohlberg, Lawrence. "Stage and sequence: The cognitive-developmental approach to socialization," in *Handbook of Socialization Theory and Research*, edited by David Goslin. Chicago: Rand McNally, 1969.

Makarenko, Anton S. *The Collective Family: A Handbook for Parents*. Garden City, N.Y.: Doubleday-Anchor Books, 1967.

Polsky, Howard W. *Cottage Six: The Social System of Delinquent Boys in Residential Treatment*. New York: John Wiley & Sons, 1967.

V

Meliorative Environments

16

Evaluation of the Educational Process in *Mechinot* (Preparatory Classes of Disadvantaged Children)

CHANAN RAPAPORT AND
RIVKA ARAD

Mechinot (singular: Mechina) means in the present context preparatory environments of the kind Feuerstein (1971) conceptualized. The task is cognitive and academic upgrading of adolescents so that they may return to the usual schools and continue normal progress. Although the gains in the Mechinot often have been dramatic—on the order of three–four years of academic achievement in a single school year—Israeli specialists have contemplated with some trepidation the prospect of "graduates" immediate return to the previous environment. As an alternative they placed the "graduates" of Mechinot in kibbutz youth groups (See Wolins, Chap. 15) for several years, thus maintaining them in a group environment for up to five years. Rapaport and Arad evaluate the impact of this tandem group care arrangement in which academically oriented youth village life is followed by a more socially demanding period in a kibbutz.

Introduction

The Israeli educational system is typified by a strong faith in man, in the educational process, and in a relentless, untiring push with total commitment to raise all strata of society to levels that will enable them to participate ac-

This paper is an abridged form of Research Report No. 136, published by the Henrietta Szold Institute, Jerusalem, April, 1969. Chanan Rapaport and Rivka Arad. "Evaluation of the Educational Process in *Mechinot*." In *Group Care: An Israeli Approach,* eds. Martin Wolins and Meir Gottesmann. New York: Gordon and Breach, 1971. Reproduced by permission.

cording to their potential in the creation of a nation and a state in this underdeveloped part of the world. The great faith in the educational process is reflected in the lion's share of national attention and economic and financial effort invested by this society in the educational sphere. The total commitment is carried out across the entire educational age span. When we observe the Israeli educational system we find many programs, some institutionalized and others experimental, from near birth, in the nursery and kindergarten, in the various stages of elementary school, in high school, army service, and finally postarmy preparatory courses leading to higher education.

The Szold Institute has carried out and is carrying out experimental research projects on many of the currently established programs, plus others still being tested. None of the above programs, however, was so bold yet carried so little founded hope as the Mechinot experiment of Youth Aliyah. Here children were gathered from all over the country—children who had failed time and again in different educational settings and who even in early adolescence (13–14 years) displayed an educational achievement level at only the first to third grades. Continual experience of failure at the elementary school age unfortunately discourages educators from additional efforts and in practice determines the futures of such children. This was not the reaction of Youth Aliyah, who believed in the educational force of the powerful environment in a youth village[1] and kibbutzim. The "educational rehabilitation" of such a population presented a real challenge. We studied this attempt at rehabilitation.

Our initial assignment was to study "the reasons for the high rate of dropping out from kibbutz youth groups and the situation of the dropouts from an educational, economic and social point of view." In order to compare our findings with another analogous study[2] we looked at intelligence levels, attitude and values, and personality traits of the wards at the preparatory classes. For the above attributes the same instruments were used in both studies. We, for our part, added tests in the spheres of work, education, and social life.[3] Material was then evaluated for the dropouts from the preparatory classes and those who remained to the end of the program.

Generally speaking, we assumed that the population of the preparatory classes was marked by a number of features that singled it out from the other population of Youth Aliyah. We accepted these background variables as the independent variables in this research. What happened to the wards in Youth Aliyah was considered as independent and intervening variables. The reason for this was our recognition of the fact that with regard to part of these variables Youth Aliyah had no alternative other than to accept them as given. Regarding others, changes could have been made. It is obvious, for instance, that the size of classes or the teaching of a certain subject in a kibbutz could differ in accordance with the educational approach. Finally, the dependent variables were the more or less explicit goals of Youth Aliyah (see Table 16.1).

TABLE 16.1. *Independent, intervening and dependent variables of the study*

Independent Variables	Independent and Intervening Variables	Dependent Variables	
Ethnic origin Sex	Teaching of a subject in the kibbutz	Attitude toward work	Attitude toward the kibbutz as a way of life
Year of immigration to Israel	Stability in work in the kibbutz	Ward's estimation of his achievements at work	Nature of *madrich*–ward relationship
Economic situation of the family	Size of class in the village and the kibbutz	Changes in level of intelligence	Self-image Expression in values
Health situation of the family	Class homogeneity at the village and the kibbutz	Changes in educational achievement	Attitude of the family toward the kibbutz and Youth Aliyah
Mental condition of the wards	Personality of *madrich* teacher	Self-image of the ward as a pupil	
Intelligence		Ward's estimation of his educational achievement	Dropping out—remaining
Level of studies	Contacts with members of the kibbutz		Professional work in town
Reasons for joining Youth Aliyah	Value system of the kibbutz society	Social activity	Stability of work in town
Ward's Personality	Attitude of the family toward the kibbutz and Youth Aliyah	Attitude of society toward the ward	Scope and intensity of social contacts in town
			Study in town
			Plans and activity in the army

The Research Population and the Educational Framework

THE POPULATION

The subjects for this evaluative study were 91 wards who participated in the first 2 years of the *Mechinot* and transferred to youth groups in kibbutzim during 1960–62. At the time of the research, 26 wards (28.6 percent) were still at the kibbutz, 65 wards (71.4 percent) had dropped out. A dropout was defined as a ward transferred from the *Mechinot* to a kibbutz who subsequently dropped out during his stay at the kibbutz. The average period spent by the dropouts in the kibbutz was 18 months. Approximately 18 percent of the wards were asked to leave the youth groups against their will.

Most wards came from Oriental immigrant families (84 percent) and from poor economic environments. Approximately two-thirds of the population came from homes where economic conditions are most critical. One-fourth came from conditions approaching the comfortable, and only about one-tenth from homes where conditions were fairly good. In a number of cases one of the parents was mentally ill and hospitalized for some time; in other cases the parents were separated. A majority of the families were very large (see Solberg 1961).

The *Mechinot* were intended from the outset for wards who suffered from backwardness in their studies. One of the guidelines in the classification of this group was "to avoid absorbing youths suffering from mental problems whose origin did not lie in backwardness in study [Solberg 1961]." Wards suffering from mental disturbances are generally directed by Youth Aliyah to special treatment centers. A study of the personal files revealed that in spite of this directive a number of wards whose mental problems could have been expected to be more complicated than those of the group in general had been accepted into the group. Approximately 25 percent of all the wards suffered from serious mental problems, 40 percent suffered from mental problems of a moderate nature and some 35 percent showed no mental problems. The files also revealed that some wards had been caught in acts of delinquency prior to their acceptance by Youth Aliyah. Others had not actually been caught in criminal acts but, according to the evidence of their families, had associated with juvenile delinquents.

The *Mechinot* group was characterized mainly by serious backwardness in education. Despite their backwardness in studies, these pupils were subjected to the educational policy existing in schools of limiting the repetition of grades. As a result, the wards advanced from one grade to the next in spite of the fact that they did not manage to keep up with the level of work. Moreover, the more a pupil rose in grade, the wider became the gap between the level of the grade and his own performance. Approximately 43 percent of the wards performed on the first and second grade level when accepted at Ramat Hadassah. Twenty-eight percent had reached third grade and the remaining 30 percent had reached fourth grade level. At the time of admission, the wards were on the average of 13 years old, an age which is generally represented in eighth grade. In fact, three-fourths of them had attended sixth, seventh and eighth grade.

Psychologists at Youth Aliyah are aware that numerous diagnostic instruments are not suitable for estimating the educational level of children who belong to backward cultural and social groups. They are familiar with many children who, as a result of unsuitable psychometric tests, had been directed to educational institutions for the retarded, in spite of their normal intellectual potential.[4] They therefore employed a special method for testing deprived children. By means of this method they identified a normal educational capability among many children who had been defined as backward by the accepted diagnostic procedures (Feuerstein and Shalom 1967).

As a result of the foregoing, we are confronted with a rather gloomy picture of the nature of the wards at the *Mechinot*. Two main groups of variables may be discerned. The first group includes the environmental variables: the great majority of the wards came from immigrant families whose economic condition was extremely poor. When in Israel, most of the fathers were employed in unskilled, seasonal, public work projects or were unemployed. In some cases the family was broken because of the death or mental illness of one of the parents or due to separation. The families also had many children. Most of the wards came from Asian-African countries.

The second group of variables consisted mainly of personal ones: the wards suffered from the most serious backwardness in education which was evident particularly in the spheres of language (reading and writing) and arithmetic; they were older than their classmates; their intelligence (IQ) was very much below average; some of them even showed signs of mental disturbance; their behavior was at times asocial; they associated with negative elements and some of them were even caught in delinquent activities; they were on the threshold of adolescence. All of the above attributes are good predictors of juvenile delinquency and deviance in general. It would appear that such a future would have been in store for a large proportion of our wards as well.

THE EDUCATIONAL FRAMEWORK

The treatment of the *Mechinot* group took place in two stages: Stage A—the village; Stage B—the kibbutz.

The transfer of the ward from his former environment which had caused him great frustration to a completely new one which held out many promises is the beginning of social rehabilitation. The problem of frustration in class due to backwardness in studies is solved by the creation of relatively small classes whose learning standards are suited to the pupil's level, and which were as homogeneous as possible. The pupil's sense of backwardness in study disappears almost entirely within the framework of such a class. He is now in a class of peers whose age is equal to his own and whose knowledge is parallel with his. He may once again devote his energy to studies in the knowledge that he is now in a position of fair competition with others of equal ability. The pupil is indeed aware that he is a member of a group which is objectively backward relative to a normal class. However, the feeling that he constitutes a part of a group which, despite its backwardness, is benefiting from a positive approach and assistance from its teachers encourages him.

In the wake of restoration of confidence to the ward in his capacity as a pupil, a feeling of social confidence is also achieved indirectly in the class. In the village the ward who was rejected socially by his former classmates becomes a desired friend of his new ones. Naturally, intentional activities aimed at insuring the social confidence of the ward are also undertaken. Unlike in town, the ward is in an intensive social framework for the entire duration of his stay. Life is, in fact, organized socially. The ward is together with his mates in class, at work and during social activities.

This arrangement gives great importance to the age group as an educational instrument. By means of his age group the ward acquires self-confidence, is more successfully aware of his self-identification, integrates the group values and judges society in general and his own society in particular in the light of the criteria he has acquired in his age group and under the guidance of older *madrichim.*

At the end of one school year the wards in the present study were transferred to kibbutzim. The year in the village could thus be seen as an intermediate stage between home and kibbutz. This intermediate stage enables the wards to crystallize socially as an age group. Their new society is the warm home and shelter when they find themselves in the midst of the life of the kibbutz. Here they no longer constitute the focal point but one of several frameworks organized within it for a special purpose. It has been noted that

> The kibbutz society has a modern and industrialized character and the relationships between its members are based on a mixture of a practical-purposive relationship and personal-emotional attitudes of one member to another. The society of the kibbutz overcomes this conflict by means of a mechanism of localization and diagnosis. In other words, it confines the objective-authoritative relationships within one sphere—that of work and public activity—whereas the personal-emotional relationships are isolated in a second sphere—that of the family and friendship [Bar-Yosef 1960, p. 23].

The nature of the relationships between the youth group wards and the adult society in the kibbutz can be roughly divided into the same two spheres. On the one hand, the ward, through his identity as a member of the youth group, enjoys particular, purposeful contacts in the form of work and satisfaction of his remaining needs by the adult world. On the other hand, three channels have been provided for purposes of personal, emotional relationships: the foster family, the *madrich,* and the peer group.[5]

Work and Study

The daily timetable of the wards in the kibbutzim is similar to that in the Village but different in proportions and emphasis. The wards devote part of their day to study, part to work, and the remainder to social activity. Study is indeed regarded as important, but less important than work. While study is the main activity in the village, its importance declines in the kibbutz due to the stress put on work. The social acceptance of a ward is determined by his approach to work.

According to the interviewers' reports, it is clear that in a considerable portion of the households from which the wards came there existed unemployment of the father and other members of the family. This unemployment had not always been forced upon them but was sometimes the result of free choice arising out of a negative attitude toward work. Yet, after a stay in the kibbutz, half of the wards had a neutral attitude toward work and over a third had a very positive one, while only a sixth of the population had a negative attitude. That such a small proportion—some 16 percent—of the wards expressed a negative attitude toward work in the kibbutz is a most encouraging finding and points to the educational success of the kibbutz framework in general and of the youth group in particular.

It may be assumed that the central place of work in the kibbutz adult society, and the atmosphere resulting from it, together with the more direct educational influences are the factors which led to the attitudes described above. On the other hand, the fact remains that almost half of the wards regarded work neither positively nor negatively. In contrast to the achievement previously mentioned, this phenomenon raises the question of its origin. It is possible that we may understand it on the basis of findings in connection with the study of a vocation in the kibbutz and permanency at work. We found that only a third had learned a vocation and only half of the wards worked steadily in one branch. These facts may have had their influence on the ward's attitude toward work.

We assumed a connection between a positive attitude toward work in the kibbutz and remaining within its framework. Since work is one of the supreme values of the kibbutz, full identification with such a central value would facilitate identification with the community as well.

TABLE 16.2. *Stayers-leavers and attitudes toward work. Information from the wards (percent distribution)*

Category of Youth	Negative	Neutral	Positive	Total Percent	N
Stayers	0	46.1	53.8	99.9	26
Leavers	26.3	50	23.7	100	65

Significance $P < 0.1$ $x^2 = 10.98$
$df2$

Not one of the wards who remained in the youth group expressed a negative attitude toward work, whereas a quarter of the dropouts revealed such an attitude. Three-quarters of the dropouts fall into the "neutral" and "negative" categories. (We also know that 75.6 percent of the dropouts declared that they had not learned a vocation.) Only 46.1 percent of those who remained fall into the neutral category (the same number of those remaining who claimed that they had not learned a vocation). There appears to be a close correlation between learning a vocation and attitude toward work. To create a positive attitude toward work in a ward the kibbutz must grant him the possibility of learning a vocation. Wards who feel that they have learned a vocation in the kibbutz have a sense of creativity, of belonging to the kibbutz framework, and of responsibility toward it. Due to the centrality of work in the kibbutz, these wards feel accepted by their society, a fact that encourages them to remain in the kibbutz. The absence of vocational study leads to a feeling that time is being wasted, a negative attitude toward work, and numerous other frustrations, all leading to leaving.

TABLE 16.3.   *Mean RPM percentiles at placement and retest*

Group	at time of placement 13–14 years old	Test Period leavers— average stay in kibbutz 1–½ years	2 years	stayers— average stay in kibbutz 3 years
Mechinot wards	6*	27.5		35.2
Usual youth group in kibbutz†	29.12		37.19	
Usual youth group in kibbutz‡	31.93			53.32

 * Results received from extrapolation of the Raven Progressive Matrices (RPM) tests in examinations carried out on entry to the village.

 † In this measurement one group is compared in two periods: the first on its entry, the second after two years in the kibbutz (from Wolins 1969).

 ‡ In this measurement two different groups of Youth Aliyah are compared in their average achievements at different ages. The underlying assumption of this comparison is that of equal populations: in other words, that the two groups come from the same population pool and possess the same identifying marks which set them apart from other types of population (from Wolins 1969).

As in attitude toward work, there were also changes in cognitive capability. The group which at first was at a stage of deep backwardness had moved into the range of normal to average. Furthermore, the stayers were considerably above the leavers (mean RPM age-adjusted percentile of 35.2 as contrasted with 27.5).

The fact that all groups advanced intellectually over and above what was expected and accepted during adolescence reinforces the view of possible reversibility even after a long period of deprivation (see Bloom 1964; Hunt 1961; Smilansky et al. 1966). The progress of the *Mechina* wards who in any other framework would have been treated as retarded was particularly encouraging. Their advancement calls for a review of examination procedures the results of which decide whether a child is sent to school for retarded children.

The *Mechina* framework and the special youth groups which followed were created with the purpose of responding to the particular needs of youths who had not been absorbed by the general system of education or had even been rejected by it. These youths, two-thirds of whom at the ages of 13–14 years had revealed a level of achievement equal to that of the first–third grades, constituted a most serious pool for the supply of candidates for street gangs and juvenile delinquency. But in the village achievement rose substantially. In effect the youths were being recycled into positive channels.

TABLE 16.4.   *Grade levels on entering and leaving the village*

Time Period	1st–2nd Grade	3rd Grade	4th Grade	5th Grade	Total Percent	N
On entry	42.6	27.0	29.5	—	100	91
On leaving (A year later)	—	7.4	39.7	52.9	100	91

The findings demonstrate that the year's study was most fruitful. First, the pupils whose level on entry was that of the first and second grades advanced. Second, whereas only 7 percent remained at the third grade level, the low level pupils achieved far more than one year's growth. Third, and most important, over half of the pupils reached fifth grade level even though less than one-third were previously at the fourth grade level. Here, too, it is clear that this year contributed more than a normal year's progress.

Following the village experience the youth continued their academic program. However, we can examine only the achievements of those remaining in the kibbutz since the dropouts left at different periods and their progress was not uniform. The achievements were determined on the basis of the teacher's evaluation. The latter were based on examinations in the course of the final school year.

On entering the kibbutz, approximately two-thirds of the pupils were at fifth grade level. Three years later 78 percent had reached eighth and ninth grade level. Here, too, the advancement is more rapid than in normal school years. Nevertheless, there is a group—albeit small—which reached the fifth grade level only at the conclusion of the same period. As regards the drop-

TABLE 16.5. *Stayers' grade levels on leaving village and in the kibbutz*

Time Period	3rd–4th Grade	5th Grade	6th Grade	7th Grade	8th Grade	9th Grade	Total Percent	N
On leaving village	34.6	65.3	—	—	—	—	99.9	26
When examined in kibbutz	—	13	—	8.7	47.8	30.4	99.9	26

outs, it was the opinion of teachers and *madrichim* that over 60 percent had reached sixth–seventh–eighth grade levels. Even if these estimates are treated with caution, they still indicate progress. Given the reduced emphasis on study as compared with the normal school or the village, this progress in the kibbutz youth group is even more outstanding.

The Person, Group and Society

In the modern, western, industrial society the values underlying social association are not as clear as those of work and study. Furthermore, when such a demand is presented, the youth is not sufficiently aware of the criteria of success. This group of variables appears to stretch on a continuum, however, according to the degree of intensity of the demands of social association and affiliation. The large city, whose social demands of the individual are minimal, is at one end, and the development town, the *Moshav* (smallholders' settlement), the kibbutz, and finally the youth group within the kibbutz are at the other.

If the assumption that one of the features distinguishing the group of "society variables" from the others is the lack of sufficient clarity regarding ends, means, and criteria of success is correct, then the *Mechinot* wards should be greatly perplexed as to the way to behave. These youths come from broken families and being new immigrants confront a society with a value system different from the one their parents knew. Hence, social workers, psychologists, and various officials strongly request the placement of these youths in that framework which is so clearly distinguished by the stability of its value system, levels of demands and way of life from the unstable society from which these youths came. They urge kibbutz placement.

We have so far dealt with a number of social aspects typical of the group of wards in the *Mechina* as a whole. We shall now see how these variables are expressed when we distinguish between those who remained and those who dropped out.

Following placement in the kibbutz about half of the wards became markedly active in group life. Furthermore, there is a difference between those who remained and those who left. It was assumed that wards who are socially accepted, active, and popular will presumably be those who remain, whereas the wards who are neither accepted nor active will be rejected by the tone-setters in the society and tend to drop out (Kaneti-Baruch 1960; Stock and Theler 1958; Jennings 1950).

TABLE 16.6.   *Stayers-leavers and their place in society as judged by the* madrichim *in the village and kibbutz*

Category of Youth	Unpopular	Tolerated	Popular	Total Percent	N
Stayers	11.4	19.2	69.1	99.7	26
Leavers	30.9	33.3	35.6	99.8	65

Significance $P < .05$ $x^2 = 7.47$
$df2$

As Table 16.6 shows, three times as many leavers as stayers were unpopular in their groups—a factor which may have contributed to their leaving. However, a significant number of popular youth also failed to stay.

Despite (or possibly because of) the great difference between the forms of social organization in the town and the kibbutz, Youth Aliyah succeeded in attaining a considerable portion of its objectives. The totality of the educational system in the kibbutz as expressed by education through life and in the midst of life itself, employing every possible channel for passing on values, led the wards to identification with and introjection of the values confronting them. They developed a positive attitude toward their society, and many became active within the youth group.

The Madrich *and the Ward*

The *madrich* (group leader) has great significance to young people in the village and kibbutz, and a good relationship with him is associated with staying in the group. Table 16.7 describes the association between staying-leaving and the *madrich*–ward relationship as seen by the youth.

Half of the dropouts regarded their relationship with the *madrichim* as negative. Here it should be noted that a considerable portion of the dropouts did not leave of their own free will but were expelled by the *madrichim* for reasons of unsuitability. It is not surprising that a ward who is taken out of the group by the *madrich* will define his relationship with the latter as unsatisfactory. As compared with half of the dropouts, only one-tenth of those who remained defined their relationships with the *madrichim* as "not good." A major difference is to be found in the category which defines the relationship with the *madrich* as "very good." Approximately 58 percent of those

TABLE 16.7. *Stayers-leavers and the relationship between wards and madrichim. Information from the ward*

| Category of Youth | Quality of Relationship | | | | |
	Not Good	Good	Very Good	Total Percent	N
Stayers	11.5	30.7	57.6	99.8	26
Leavers	50	31.6	18.4	100	65

Significance $P < .01$ $x^2 = 13.6$.
$df2$

who remained defined their relationship with the *madrichim* as "very good," as compared with only 18 percent of the dropouts.

Values and Aspirations

Every environment attempts to instill its values in the children it rears. Regarding our wards we assumed there existed value positions to which young people would be expected to adhere. Some of these were discussed earlier in the sections on work, study, and peer associations. Others less palpable were probed by means of a value inventory developed and factor analyzed by Wolins (1969).

In three of the five factors (I, II, IV) there is almost complete identity between the *Mechina* wards and the youths born and reared in the kibbutz. The average is nearer to the answers of the kibbutz youths than those of the regular youth group of Youth Aliyah. The two remaining factors (III, V), which represent competitive achievement and detachment, were not rejected by the *mechina* wards in the same degree as by other groups. It may be as-

TABLE 16.8. *Mean factor scores for youth and adults in Mechinot and kibbutzim*

No. of Factor	Name of Factor*	Mechinot	Kibbutz Youth Groups	Kibbutz Born and Reared	Adults (mainly madrichim)
I	Other orientation	2.05	2.00	2.07	2.19
II	Controlled achievement	2.13	2.05	2.17	1.92
III	Competitive achievement	2.52	2.68	2.67	2.64
IV	Individualism	2.74	2.68	2.82	2.44
V	Detachment	2.40	2.57	2.84	2.93

* For content of each factor, see Wolins (1969 or Chap. 14).

sumed that the background, from which these wards came, still had some influence on a certain acceptance of competitive and individualistic values. In general, however, the kibbutz and its *madrichim* seem to have succeeded in attaining the value goals which they had set for themselves.

Values changed in yet another way. In general, cultural deprivation and retardation are known to lead to negative reactions. One of these is the retreat of the youth into himself as a result of a lack of faith in his future which is at times accompanied by syndromes of apathy and depression. The other is asocial behavior in the framework of delinquent groups or as isolated activity. The findings on *Mechina* wards point in a more positive direction.

First, there is a rise in aspiration levels compared with parental economic status. Eighty-two percent of the wards aspired and hoped that their economic situation would be "better" or "much better" than that of their parents. The wards do not accept their families' economic position as an unchangeable fact as do the young people in Adler's (1965) study of a slum. They are not in a state of apathy concerning the possibilities open to them. Life in the kibbutz which represents a higher standard of living than that of the parents, the education in the kibbutz, work and social activity all succeeded in bringing about a change in aspirations.

Second, the kibbutz as a mode of life appealed to a considerable proportion of the wards. Even though it was not one of the declared goals, the kibbutz, as a life complex and totality, succeeded in influencing more than one-fifth of the wards to regard it and want it as a home and a permanent way of life. Compared with the percentage of those attracted to the style of life in the kibbutz among the population of youth movements which educate toward it the percentages revealed in the research population is quite high. It would be worthwhile to reexamine this point a number of years later when the wards have the possibility of putting their aspirations into practice.

TABLE 16.9. *Wards' attitude to life in the kibbutz. Information from the wards*

Do not Like the Kibbutz	Like the Kibbutz but Want to Live in Town	Want to Remain in the Kibbutz until Conscription	Want to Live in Kibbutz after the Army	Total Percent	N
33.3	21.2	24.2	21.2	99.9	68

Attitude of the Family toward the Kibbutz

It should be noted that the parents also came to appreciate the kibbutz. Only 6 percent of the parents regarded the fact that their children were in a kibbutz in a negative light. The reasons were mainly of a religious nature (nonkosher food) or connected with families who insisted that their children assist them financially. On the other hand, some 85 percent revealed a positive attitude to the period spent in the kibbutz. The reason for such an evaluation by these parents was not only the fact that this period had lightened their economic burden but also because they believed, almost blindly, in the capacity of the kibbutz to educate their children and turn them into "human beings." Many of these families could indeed have benefited from the financial assistance of their children had they left the kibbutz. The period in the kibbutz thus constituted a painful concession on their part for the sake of their children and the educational framework. The understanding behavior of parents should be attributed, in good measure, to Youth Aliyah's *madrichim* who saw to it that contact was maintained with the families.

And the Dropouts?

Generally speaking, the phenomenon of dropping out is regarded as a negative one. Dropping out from one's framework is taken to indicate a lack of capacity to continue coping with its demands. In this context, there was not always justification for such a view. The impact of the *Mechina* and kibbutz on dropouts will be assessed in relation to work and social position. In general, even their situation is quite positive. Approximately 86 percent of the boys worked in various skilled occupations and 85 percent of the girls were employed in occupations which required some professional knowledge in a defined field. This is in marked contrast to Adler's (1965) findings for slum youth who, after dropping out of school, find employment in marginal occupations. Furthermore, four-fifths of the dropouts worked permanently at their place of employment or had changed it to a small extent only.

Placement in the village and kibbutz though interrupted before completion of the term also had a positive effect on the social orientation of the wards. Many stressed that on their return home they made efforts to contact a more positive peer group than the one they were connected with socially prior to their joining Youth Aliyah. The wards repeatedly asserted: "I looked for good friends," "I did not want to return to my old criminal friends," and the like. This aspiration to associate with socially oriented peers compelled the wards at times to ignore their immediate environment and look for friends at work or from more outlying districts. At the same time, only a very small portion of the dropouts tried to form a more permanently consolidated social framework such as a youth movement or a social club.

More than one-third of the dropout wards managed to break through the narrow circle of the family and neighborhood and become friendly with a wider circle: workmates, friends from other districts, etc. Nearly half of them spent their time within the neighborhood with old or new friends. However, about one-fifth of the wards suffered from serious social isolation. It may be assumed that this group also contained those wards who decided to forego their old friendships but have not yet succeeded in forging new ones.

Conclusions

This research provides yet another confirmation of the necessity for clarity in the demands presented to the child and adult and for establishing clear criteria to test their achievement. In each and every phase of man's life, but particularly in the course of his growth and development into a member of adult society, a clear presentation of what is "desirable" and "not desirable" and of what is "correct" and "incorrect" is required. This clear presentation enables (does not necessitate) a clear decision on the part of the youth. Following the provision of criteria for coping with these requirements, the child and the youth are able to judge themselves with regard to their achievement, their success in coping with society's demands. Every presentation of demands that is unclear, vague or highly transitory and unstable does not allow clear judgment.

In the absence of criteria for success, both judgment and decision are difficult. Such a situation compels the child or the youth to try and create for himself inner anchorages of norms of conduct and thinking. If there is a strong ego or if norms of behavior and thinking have already been introjected, the youth will discover a possibility of navigating his ship in the sea of capricious and vague demands. If, on the other hand, the child is very young and has not yet managed to stabilize and introject a clear system of judgment and decision, then the different and varying demands will lead, in extreme cases, to schizophrenia.

Clarity and consistency are of particular import in special cases such as the transfer from one country to another, from one cultural sphere to another or from a social framework in which one system of norms prevails to another framework with an entirely different system of norms. Clarification is most important in order to enable judgment and decision and prevent disorientation, despair, withdrawal, seclusion or "emigration."[6] In the *Mechinot* Youth Aliyah has succeeded in presenting its wards with clear demands and criteria for testing their achievements. In this lies some explanation of their positive results. The *Mechina* has proven itself to be an educational project which led to most important achievements in several dimensions. Incoming wards were on such a low intelligence level at the time of admission that they fell below the line of the normal average. By the time of the retest, the wards had advanced to the normal average range, although they were still below the median as a group.

Progress was particularly outstanding in study. At the time of their acceptance most of the wards revealed syndromes of serious backwardness in study manifested by great difficulties in reading, writing, and arithmetic; their grade level was equal to first to third grades. According to the reports of teachers and *madrichim,* most of the wards reached the level of the eighth grade and even a little higher. The study achievements were more marked among the wards who remained than among those who dropped out. (The dropouts reached the level of the sixth to eighth grades.)

The advance in the level of intelligence, together with the considerable advance in study achievements prove that Youth Aliyah was justified in selecting a special framework for these youths who revealed considerable study and intelligence potential. It has once again been proven that reversibility is possible and that youths who are backward and failures due to environmental causes can be advanced and promoted by environmental rearrangement.

In the sphere of work Youth Aliyah scored another success. Two-thirds of the wards revealed a positive attitude toward work in the kibbutz. This was even reflected in the employment picture of the dropouts where the influence of the previous education was marked. Most of the boys and girls worked in productive-vocational employment. A good part of them was even employed in stable and permanent work.

In the social sphere some gains were also made. The educational framework succeeded in crystallizing a youth group from various, single individuals. Moreover, the social education prevented the kind of decline which is possible among slum youths. The majority of the wards revealed a positive attitude to society, and half of them were even active in its framework. The majority claimed that it would have attained less had it not gone to Youth Aliyah. These young people in contrast to the expectations for them revealed faith in the future and a higher level of aspirations than that of their parents in both the economic and social spheres. They also showed considerable introjection of the system of values which is represented by the kibbutz.

In the main, the youths oriented themselves toward achievement and not to the former ascription; to more productive vocations rather than service occupations; and to the national-collectivist approach as opposed to the former individualistic approach. Even though all the channels of communication at the disposal of kibbutz society contributed their share to the acceptance of these values, it appears that the major contribution is the *madrich's*

The *Mechina* is an exemplary model of an educational project relying on great faith in education. We propose its continuation, and expansion.

NOTES

1. Reference throughout is to a single village—Ramat Hadassah—the village.

2. See M. Wolins (Chap. 14.)

3. Instrumentation consisted in part of that Wolins used, and in part of our own tools. These were: (1) the Raven Progressive Matrices Test (without time limit); (2) a sentence completion test; (3) an attitude and value questionnaire; (4) a self-image test; (5) part of the Thematic Apperception Test. Other materials included a comprehensive structured interview with the wards, an evaluation questionnaire on the ward answered by the *madrich* at the village, an evaluation questionnaire on the ward answered by the *madrich* at the kibbutz, an interview with the *madrich* on each ward, and information taken from the wards' personal files.

4. The wards of the *Mechinot* under discussion passed through a filtration process such as the one described by Feuerstein and Shalom (1967) and proved themselves to be possessors of a better intellectual potential than that expressed in their educational achievements. By contrast, their scores on the Raven Progressive Matrices (RPM) test (Form A ab B) were expectedly low.

5. For more details about youth groups in the kibbutz, see Chapters 14 and 15.

6. Emigration is mentioned here because, in our opinion, in the case of immigration to Israel, or, for the sake of this general discussion, any voluntary immigration, the adult, too, faces a reeducational process. If the absorbing society succeeds, through all its channels of communication, to present itself clearly and offer the immigrant appropriate opportunities of testing to what extent he has settled down in it, there are chances of preventing despair, seclusion, withdrawal, and emigration.

17

Helping Disturbed Children: Psychological and Ecological Strategies

NICHOLAS HOBBS

Hobbs' model for the care of emotionally disturbed children is both similar to and different from Feuerstein's (1971) on which the Mechina of Chap. 16 is based. Their similarity is in the optimism that distinguishes both models from traditional group care approaches. Both begin with the assumption that life is to be lived and that the mere designation of disability does not necessitate a moratorium on responsibility. They stress the importance of the group, the therapeutic implications of increasing competence in academic and work pursuits, and the meaning of trust to the vulnerable child.

The divergence of the two models is also significant. Unlike the Israeli programs described in Chapters 14, 15, and 16, Project Re-Ed leads to a rapid return home. Such is neither the aim nor the outcome in the Israeli settings, where familial and environmental incapacity are assumed to be long-term—perhaps permanent. Thus while most Israeli group programs (as well as Soviet boarding school and SOS Kinderdörfer) are predicated on a near-substitution of the child's ecosystem, Project Re-Ed is based on a modification—an expansion—of the environment. Greater capability in the child, his family, or other parts of the milieu are then expected, and Re-Ed withdraws from the scene.

Nicholas Hobbs. "Helping Disturbed Children: Psychological and Ecological Strategies." *American Psychologist* 21 (12): 1105–15. Copyright 1966, American Psychological Association. Reproduced by permission. This was an address of the President to the Seventy-Fourth Annual Convention of the American Psychological Association, New York, September 3, 1966.

The Problem[1]

"Project Re-ED" stands for "a project for the reeducation of emotionally disturbed children." Re-ED was developed explicitly as a new way to meet a social need for which current institutional arrangements are conspicuously inadequate. It is estimated that there are some 1.5 million emotionally disturbed children in the United States today, children of average or superior intelligence whose behavior is such that they cannot be sustained with normal family, school, and community arrangements. There is one generally endorsed institutional plan for the care of such children: the psychiatric treatment unit of a hospital. But this is not a feasible solution to the problem; the costs are too great, averaging $60 a day, and there are not enough psychiatrists, psychologists, social workers, and psychiatric nurses to staff needed facilities, even if the solution were a good one, an assumption open to question. There is a real possibility that hospitals make children sick. The antiseptic atmosphere, the crepe sole and white coat, the tension, the expectancy of illness may confirm a child's worst fears about himself, firmly setting his aberrant behavior.

But worse things can happen to children, and do. They may be sent to a state hospital to be confined in wards with psychotic adults. They may be put in a jail, euphemistically called a detention home, or committed to an institution for delinquents or for the mentally retarded; or they may be kept at home, hidden away, receiving no help at all, aggravating and being aggravated by what can become an impossible situation.

The problem is further complicated by the professional advocacy of psychotherapy as the only means of effecting changes in behavior and by the pervasive and seldom questioned assumption that it takes at least two years to give any substantial help to a disturbed child. Finally, the availability of locks and drugs makes children containable, and the lack of evaluative research effectively denies feedback on the adequacy of approved methods. We became convinced eight years ago that the problem of the emotionally disturbed child cannot be solved by existing institutional arrangements. The Re-ED program was developed as one alternative, surely not the only one or even the most satisfactory one, but as a feasible alternative that deserved a test.

The Re-ED Schools

The National Institute of Mental Health made a test possible by a demonstration grant in 1961 to Peabody College to develop residential schools for disturbed children in which concepts of reeducation could be formulated and tried out, and to provide for a training program to prepare a new kind of mental health worker, called a teacher-counselor, and for a research program to evaluate the effectiveness of the schools to be established.

Cumberland House Elementary School in Nashville received its first students in November of 1962, and Wright School of Durham in January of 1963. The schools are located in residential areas not far from the universities (Vanderbilt and Peabody, Duke and North Carolina) that provide personnel and consultation. They are pleasant places, open, friendly, homelike, where children can climb trees and play dodge ball, go to school, and, at night, have a good meal, and a relaxed, amiable evening.

Both schools have nearby camps that are used in the summer and on occasion throughout the year. The camps are simple, even primitive, with children erecting their own shelters, preparing their own meals, making their own schedules. For staff and children alike there is a contagious serenity about the experience. Cooking is a marvelously instructive enterprise; motivation is high, cooperation is necessary, and rewards are immediate. Children for whom failure has become an established expectation, at school and at home, can learn to do things successfully. In this simpler setting, where avoidant responses are few or weakly established, the child can take the first risky steps toward being a more adequate person.

At capacity each school has 40 children, ages 6 to 12, grouped in 5 groups of 8 children each. Each group is the responsibility of a team of two teacher-counselors, carefully selected young people, most of whom are graduates of a nine-month training program at Peabody. The two teacher-counselors, assisted by college students and by instructors in arts and crafts and physical education, are responsible for the children around the clock. Each school has a principal and an assistant principal, both educators, a liaison department staffed by social workers and liaison teachers, and a secretarial and house-keeping staff, who are full partners in the reeducation effort. The principal of a Re-ED school has an exacting job of management, training, interpretation, and public relations. The two schools have developed under the leadership of four able men: John R. Ball and Neal C. Buchanan at Wright School and James W. Cleary and Charles W. McDonald at Cumberland House.[2]

Of course, the teacher-counselors are the heart of Re-ED. They are young people, representing a large manpower pool, who have had experience in elementary school teaching, camping, or other work that demonstrates a long-standing commitment to children. After careful screening, in which self-selection plays an important part, they are given 9 months of training in a graduate program leading to the Master of Arts degree. The program includes instruction in the characteristics of disturbed children, in specialized methods of teaching, including evaluation and remediation of deficits in reading, arithmetic, and other school subjects, in the use of consultants from mental health and educational fields, and in arts and crafts and games and other skills useful on the playing field, on a canoe trip, in the living units after dinner at night. They get a thorough introduction to child-serving agencies in the community and to the operation of a Re-ED school through an extensive practicum. Finally they are challenged with the task of helping invent what Re-ED will become.

But most of all a teacher-counselor is a decent adult; educated, well trained; able to give and receive affection, to live relaxed, and to be firm; a person with private resources for the nourishment and refreshment of his own life; not an itinerant worker but a professional through and through; a person with a sense of the significance of time, of the usefulness of today and the promise of tomorrow; a person of hope, quiet confidence, and joy; one who has committed himself to children and to the proposition that children who are emotionally disturbed can be helped by the process of reeducation.

The total school staff, and especially the teacher-counselors who work directly with the children, are backed by a group of consultants from psychiatry, pediatrics, social work, psychology, and education, an arrangement that makes available to the schools the best professional talent in the community and that has the further attractive feature of multiplying the effectiveness of scarce and expensive mental health and educational personnel.[3]

The Children

What kind of children do the teacher-counselors work with? It can be said, in general, that diagnostic classification has not been differentially related to a successful outcome; that the children are normal or superior in intelligence but are in serious trouble in school, often retarded two or three years in academic development; that they do not need continuing medical or nursing care, and that they can be managed in small groups in an open setting. Re-ED is not a substitute for a hospital. There are children too disturbed, too out of touch, too aggressive, too self-destructive to be worked with successfully in small groups in any open setting. However, Re-ED schools do take many children who would otherwise have to be hospitalized.

Susan was 11, with a diagnosis of childhood schizophrenia. She had attended school one day, the first day of the first grade, and had been in play therapy for four years. She was a pupil at Cumberland House for a year, staying longer than most children. She has been in a regular classroom for three years now, an odd child still but no longer a prospect for life-long institutionalization. Ron was a cruelly aggressive child, partly an expression of inner turmoil and partly an expression of class values and habits; he is much less destructive now, and is back in school. Danny was simply very immature, so that school was too much for him; his problem could be called school phobia if that would help. Dick was extremely effeminate, wearing mascara and painting his nails. Both boys responded to masculine activities guided by a trusted male counselor. Billy was a gasoline sniffer and an ingenious hypochondriac; he returned to a reunion recently much more mature though still having trouble with school work. Larry, age 12, was quite bright yet unable to read; nor were we able to teach him to read. So we failed with him. It is such children as these that we aspire to help. To call them all "emotionally disturbed" is clearly to use language to obscure rather than to clarify. Nonetheless, they are all children who are in serious trouble, for whom the Re-ED idea was developed.

During the summer of 1966, under the direction of William and Dianne Bricker and Charles McDonald, we worked at Cumberland House with six of the most severely disturbed children we could find, mostly custodial cases from state institutions. Regular Re-ED activities are supplemented by a 24-hour schedule of planned behaviors and contingent rewards, the staff being augmented to make such individualized programming possible, but still using inexpensive and available personnel, such as college students. While at this writing, Sept. 1966, it is too early to assess the effectiveness of this effort, we are pleased with the progress that most of the children are making, and we are certain we are giving them more of a chance than they had when their principal challenge was to learn how to live in an institution.

Ecological Concepts

Let us turn now to an examination of the theoretical assumptions and operational procedures involved in the process of reeducation. We do not, of course, make use of the principles involved in traditional psychotherapy; transference, regression, the promotion of insight through an exploration of inner dynamics and their origins are not a part of the picture. The teacher-counselor is not a psychotherapist, nor does he aspire to be one.

We have become increasingly convinced that a major barrier to effective national planning for emotionally disturbed children is the professional's enchantment with psychotherapy. Everything in most model institutions revolves around getting the child to his therapist one, two, or maybe three hours a week. A few superb treatment centers combine psychotherapy with a program of daily activities conducive to personal growth and integration. But these are rare indeed. It is not uncommon to find children locked 15 stories high in steel and glass, with a caged roof to play on, drugged to keep them from doing too much damage to the light fixtures and air conditioning, while they await their precious hour, guarded by attendants who think disturbed children must scream, fight, climb walls, cower in a corner. Most frequently, of course, therapy is not available; most hospitals hold children hoping somehow they will get better.

An overcommitment to individual psychotherapy seems to us to stem from an uncritical acceptance of "cure" as the goal in working with a child, a consequence of defining the problem initially as one of "illness." That some disturbed children are "ill" in the usual sense may be accepted, but to define them all as such leads, we think, to a host of unvalidated and unquestioned assumptions; to a preoccupation with the intrapsychic life of the child, with what goes on inside his skull; to an easy use of drugs without knowledge of their long-term effects on character development; to the extended isolation of children from their families the presumed source of contagion; to a limitation of professional roles; to the neglect of schools and of schooling; and so on. The preemptive character of a definition and the semantic sets that ensue are major barriers to innovation in working with disturbed children.

Of course we have our own ways of talking about the problem, and our metaphors are no less preemptive, making it all the more important for us to be explicit about definitions. We prefer to say that the children we work with have learned bad habits. They have acquired nonadaptive ways of relating to adults and to other children. They have learned to perceive themselves in limiting or destructive terms and to construe the world as an uncertain, rejecting, and hurtful place. We also recognize that the child lives in a real world that often falls short in giving him the affection, support, and guidance he needs. So we deal directly with social realities as well as with private perceptions.

This kind of thinking has led us gradually to a different way of defining our task, a definition of considerable heuristic merit (see Figure 17.1). For want of a more felicitous phrase, we have been calling it a systems approach

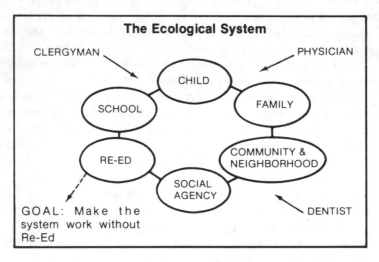

FIGURE 17.1   Chart of ecological system, the smallest unit in a systems approach to working with a disturbed child.

to the problem of working with a disturbed child. We assume that the child is an inseparable part of a small social system, of an ecological unit made up of the child, his family, his school, his neighborhood and community. A social agency is often a part of the picture when a child has been designated emotionally disturbed, and other people—a physician, a clergyman—may be brought in as needed. The system may become "go" as a result of marked improvement in any component (the father stops drinking and goes back to work, a superb teacher becomes available, the child improves dramatically), or it may work as a result of modest improvement in all components. The effort is to get each component of the system above threshold with respect to the requirements of the other components. The Re-ED school becomes a part of the ecological unit for as brief a period of time as possible, withdrawing when the probability that the system will function appears to exceed the probability that it will not. We used to speak of putting the child back into the system but we have come to recognize the erroneous assumptions involved; the child defines the system and all we can do is withdraw from it at a propitious moment.

Once we abandoned cure as a goal and defined our problem as doing what we can to make a small social system work in a reasonably satisfactory manner, there ensued a number of operational patterns that contrast sharply with the practices of existing residential treatment centers for children.

For one thing, parents are no longer viewed as sources of contagion but as responsible collaborators in making the system work. Parents are involved in discussion groups and are helped to get assistance from mental health centers. They actively participate in the ongoing program of the school. They organize an annual reunion, publish a parent's manual, sew for the children, and in many ways assume responsibility for reestablishing the child as quickly as possible in his own home, school, and community.

The children go home on weekends to keep families and children belonging to each other, to avoid the estrangement that can come from prolonged separation, and to give the child and his parents and brothers and sisters an opportunity to learn new and more effective ways of living together. Visitors ask "Aren't your Mondays awful?" They are, indeed, but we cherish their chaos as a source of new instruction; we try to keep in mind that our goal is not to run a tranquil school but to return the child as quickly as possible to his own home and regular school.

The ecological model requires new strategies to involve home, neighborhood, school, agency, and community in a contract with us to help a child. It requires new patterns for the deployment of personnel, and it has led to the development of a new kind of mental health worker: the liaison teacher. The liaison teacher is responsible for maintaining communication with the child's regular school, again to prevent alienation and to arrange optimum conditions for the child's early return to a regular classroom. For example a liaison teacher may personally accompany a child to a new school to which he has been transferred in order to increase the probability that that component of the ecological system will function effectively.

The social worker in Re-ED honors an early heritage of his profession, before the lamentable sit-behind-the-desk-and-do-psychotherapy era got established. He reaches out to the family, to community agencies, and to individuals—to any reasonable source of help for a child in trouble. Again, the goal is to make the system work, not simply to adjust something inside the head of the child.

Now, let us turn to the child himself, to our relationships with him, and to what is meant operationally by the process of reeducation. Here are an even dozen underlying concepts that have come to seem important to us as we try to talk about what goes on in a Re-ED school.

Item 1: Life is to be lived, now. We start with the assumption that each day, that every hour in every day, is of great importance to a child, and that when an hour is neglected, allowed to pass without reason and intent, teaching and learning go on nonetheless and the child may be the loser. In Re-ED, no one waits for a special hour. We try, as best we can, to make all hours special. We strive for immediate and sustained involvement in purposive and consequential living. We constantly test the optimistic hypothesis that if children are challenged to live constructively, that if they are given an opportunity for a constructive encounter with other children and with decent adults, they will come off well—and they do, most of the time.

Item 2: Time is an ally. We became convinced, in the early stages of planning the project, that children are kept too long in most traditional treatment programs. The reasons for this are many. The abstract goal of cure through psychotherapy leads to expectations of extensive personality reorganization, of the achievement of adequacy in a wide array of possible life roles. It thus takes a long time either to succeed in this ambitious endeavor or to become aware that one has failed. Staff and children become fond of each other, making separation difficult. The widespread practice of removing the child from his home for extended periods of time causes a sometimes irreparable estrangement; the family closes ranks against the absent member. While everyone recognizes the importance of school in the life of the child, mental health programs have neither operational concepts nor specialized personnel necessary to effect an easy transition for the child from the institution back to his own school. Furthermore, the expectation of a prolonged stay in a treatment center becomes a self-validating hypothesis. A newly admitted child asks "How long do kids stay here?" He is told "about two years," and he settles down to do what is expected of him, with full support of staff and parents who also "know" that it takes two years to help a disturbed child. Before we admitted the first child, we set six months as the expected, average period of stay, a goal we have now achieved.

Time is an issue of importance in the process of reeducation in yet another way. We work with children during years when life has a tremendous forward thrust. Several studies suggest that therapeutic intervention is not demonstrably superior to the passage of time without treatment in the subsequent adjustment of children diagnosed as emotionally disturbed (Lewis 1965). Treatment may simply speed up a process that would occur in an unknown percentage of children anyway. There is a real possibility that a long stay in a treatment center may actually slow down this process. Furthermore, in ecological perspective, it is clear that children tend to get ejected from families at low points in family organization and integrity. Most families get better after such periods; there is only one direction for them to go and that is up. The systems concept may entail simply observing when the family has regained sufficient stability to sustain a previously ejected child. The great tragedy is that children can get caught up in institutional arrangements that must inexorably run their course. In Re-ED we claim time is an ally and try to avoid getting in the way of the normal restorative processes of life.

Item 3: Trust is essential. The development of trust is the first step in reeducation of the emotionally disturbed child. The disturbed child is conspicuously impaired in his ability to learn from adults. The mediation process is blocked or distorted by the child's experience-based hypothesis that adults are deceptive, that they are an unpredictable source of hurt and help. He faces each adult with a predominant anticipation of punishment, rejection, derision, or withdrawal of love. He is acutely impaired in the very process by which more mature ways of living may be acquired. A first step, then, in the reeducation process, is the development of trust. Trust, coupled with understanding, is the beginning point of a new learning experience, an experience that helps a child know that he can use an adult to learn many things: how to read, how to be affectionate, how to be oneself without fear or guilt.

We are intrigued by the possibility, indeed are almost sure the thesis is true, that no amount of professional training can make an adult worthy of the trust of a child or capable of generating it. This ability is prior to technique, to theory, to technical knowledge. After seeing the difference that teacher-counselors in our two schools have made in the lives of children I am confident of the soundness of the idea that some adults know, without knowing how they know, the way to inspire trust in children and to teach them to begin to use adults as mediators of new learning.

Item 4: Competence makes a difference. The ability to do something well gives a child confidence and self-respect and gains for him acceptance by other children, by teachers, and, unnecessary as it might seem, even by his parents. In a society as achievement oriented as ours, a person's worth is established in substantial measure by his ability to produce or perform. Acceptance without productivity is a beginning point in the process of reeducation, but an early goal and a continuing challenge is to help the child get good at something.

What, then, in the process of reeducation, does the acquisition of competence mean? It means first and foremost the gaining of competence in school skills, in reading and arithmetic most frequently, and occasionally in other subjects as well. If a child feels that he is inadequate in school, inadequacy can become a pervasive theme in his life, leading to a consistent pattern of failure to work up to his level of ability. Underachievement in school is the single most common characteristic of emotionally disturbed children. We regard it as sound strategy to attack directly the problem of adequacy in school, for its intrinsic value as well as for its indirect effect on the child's perception of his worth and his acceptance by people who are important in his world. A direct attack on the problem of school skills does not mean a gross assault in some area of deficiency. On the contrary, it requires utmost skill and finesse on the part of the teacher-counselor to help a disturbed child move into an area where he has so often known defeat, where failure is a well-rooted expectancy, where a printed page can evoke flight or protest or crippling anxiety. The teacher-counselor need make no apologies to the psychotherapist with reference to the level of skill required to help a disturbed child learn.

So, in Re-ED, school keeps. It is not regarded, as it is in many mental health programs, as something that can wait until the child gets better, as though he were recovering from measles or a broken leg. School is the very stuff of a child's problems, and consequently, a primary source of instruction in living. Special therapy rooms are not needed; the classroom is a natural setting for a constructive relationship between a disturbed child and a competent, concerned adult.

Much of the teaching, incidentally, is through the unit or enterprise method. The residential character of the Re-ED school means that the acquisition of competence does not have to be limited to increased skill in school subjects. It may mean learning to swim, to draw, to sing; it may mean learning to cook on a Dakota Hole, to lash together a table, to handle a canoe, to build a shelter in the woods; it may mean learning to talk at council ring, to assert one's rights, to give of one's possessions, to risk friendship, to see parents as people and teachers as friends.

Item 5: Symptoms can and should be controlled. It is standard doctrine in psychotherapeutic practice that symptoms should not be treated, that the one symptom removed will simply be replaced by another, and that the task of the therapist is to uncover underlying conflicts against which the symptom is a defense, thus eliminating the need for any symptom at all. In Re-ED we contend, on the other hand, that symptoms are important in their own right and deserve direct attention. We are impressed that some symptoms are better to have than other symptoms. The bad symptoms are those that alienate the child from other children or from the adults he needs as a source of security or a source of learning. There is much to be gained then from identifying symptoms that are standing in the way of normal development and working out specific plans for removing or altering the symptoms if possible. The problem is to help the child make effective contact with normal sources of affection, support, instruction, and discipline. We also work on a principle of parsimony that instructs us to give first preference to explanations involving the assumption of minimum pathology, as contrasted to professional preference for deep explanations and the derogation of all else as superficial.

Item 6: Cognitive control can be taught. Though little emphasis is placed on the acquisition of insight as a source of therapeutic gain, there is a lot of talking in Re-ED about personal problems and how they can be managed better. The teacher-counselor relies primarily on immediate experience, on the day-by-day, hour-by-hour, moment-by-moment relationship between himself and the child; he relies on specific events that can be discussed to increase the child's ability to manage his own life. The emotionally disturbed child has fewer degrees of freedom in behavior than the normal child, yet he is not without the ability to shape his own behavior by self-administered verbal instruction. He can signal to himself if he can learn what the useful signals are. The teacher-counselor works constantly to help a child learn the right signals. The focus of this effort is on today and tomorrow, not on the past or the future, and on ways for the child to signal to himself to make each day a source of instruction for the living of the next. At the council ring at night, at a place set apart from the business of living, children in a group are helped to consider what was good about the day just past, what went wrong that might be handled better tomorrow, and what was learned, especially in successes and failures in relationships among themselves. Possibly more important than the solving of particular problems is the acquisition of the habit of talking things over for the purpose of getting better control over events, a habit that can frequently be carried over into the child's home and become a new source of strength for his family.

Item 7: Feelings should be nurtured. We are very interested in the nurturance and expression of feeling, to help a child own all of himself without guilt. Children have a way of showing up with animals and we are glad for this. A child who has known the rejection of adults may find it safest, at first, to express affection to a dog. And a pet can be a source of pride and of sense of responsibility. Anger, resentment, hostility are commonplace, of course, and their expression is used in various ways: to help some children learn to control their violent impulses and to help others give vent to feelings too long repressed. In Re-ED Schools one finds the familiar ratio of four or five boys to one girl, a consequence in part, we believe, of a lack of masculine challenge in school and community today. Thus we contrive situations of controlled danger in which children can test themselves, can know fear and become the master of it. The simple joy of companionship is encouraged. We are impressed by the meaningfulness of friendships and how long they endure. The annual homecoming is anticipated by many youngsters as an opportunity to walk arm-in-arm with an old friend associated with a period of special significance in their lives. And we respect the need to be alone, to work things through without intrusion, and to have a private purpose. Feelings also get expressed through many kinds of creative activities that are woven into the fabric of life in a Re-ED school. Throwing clay on a potter's wheel gives a child a first sense of his potential for shaping his world. A puppet show written by the children may permit freer expression than is ordinarily tolerable. Drawing and painting can be fun for a whole group. And an object to mold gives something to do to make it safe for an adult and child to be close together.

Item 8: The group is important to children.   Children are organized in groups of eight, with two teacher-counselors in charge. The group is kept intact for nearly all activities and becomes an important source of motivation, instruction, and control. When a group is functioning well, it is extremely difficult for an individual child to behave in a disturbed way. Even when the group is functioning poorly, the frictions and the failures can be used constructively. The council ring, or powwow, involving discussion of difficulties or planning of activities can be a most maturing experience. And the sharing of adventure, of vicissitudes, and of victories, provides an experience in human relatedness to which most of our children have been alien.

Item 9: Ceremony and ritual give order, stability, and confidence. Many Re-ED children have lived chaotic lives, even in their brief compass. They may come from homes where interpersonal disarray is endemic. We have stumbled upon and been impressed by the beneficence of ceremony, ritual, and metaphor for children and have come to plan for their inclusion in the program. The nightly backrub is an established institution with the Whippoorwills, a time of important confidences. Being a Bobcat brings a special sense of camaraderie and has its own metaphorical obligations. And a Christmas pageant can effect angelic transformation of boys whose ordinary conduct is far from seraphic.

Item 10: The body is the armature of the self.   We are intrigued by the idea that the physical self is the armature around which the psychological self is constructed and that a clearer experiencing of the potential and the boundaries of the body should lead to a clearer definition of the self, and thus to greater psychological fitness and more effective functioning. The Outward Bound schools in England, developed as an experience for young men to overcome the anomie that is the product of an industrial civilization, are built around the concept. Austin Des Lauriers' ideas about treatment of schizophrenia in children emphasize differentiating the body from the rest of the world. Programmatically, in Re-ED, the idea has been realized in such activities as swimming, climbing, dancing, tumbling, clay modeling, canoeing, building a tree house, and walking a monkey bridge.

Item 11: Communities are important. The systems concept in Re-ED leads to an examination of the relationship of the child to his home community. Many children who are referred to our schools come from families that are alienated or detached from community life or that are not sufficiently well organized or purposeful to help the child develop a sense of identity with his neighborhood, his town, or city. He has little opportunity to discover that communities exist for people and, while the goodness of fit between the two may often leave much to be desired, an important part of a child's education is to learn that community agencies and institutions exist for his welfare and that he has an obligation as a citizen to contribute to their effective functioning. This is especially true for many of the boys referred to Re-ED, whose energy, aggressiveness, lack of control, and resentment of authority will predispose them to delinquent behavior when they are a few years older and gain in independence and mobility. This idea has a number of implications for program planning. Field trips to the fire, police, and health departments are useful. Memberships in the YMCA, a children's museum, a playground group, or a community center may be worked out for a child. Church attendance may be encouraged and a clergyman persuaded to take special interest in a family, and a library card can be a proud possession and a tangible community tie.

Item 12: Finally, a child should know joy. We have often speculated about our lack of a psychology of well-being. There is an extensive literature on anxiety, guilt, and dread, but little that is well developed on joy. Most psychological experiments rely for motivation on avoidance of pain or hunger or some other aversive stimuli; positive motivations are limited to the pleasure that comes from minute, discrete rewards. This poverty with respect to the most richly human of motivations leads to anemic programming for children. We thus go beyond contemporary psychology to touch one of the most vital areas of human experiencing. We try to develop skill in developing joy in children.

Costs and Effectiveness

Now, let us turn to the practical questions of cost and of effectiveness.

A Re-ED school costs about $20 to $25 per child per day to operate. Thus the per-day cost is about one-third of the cost of the most widely accepted model and perhaps four times the cost of custodial care. Cost per day, however, is not the best index to use, for the purpose of a mental health program is not to keep children cheaply but to restore them to home, school, and community as economically as possible. In terms of cost per child served, the cost of a Re-ED program is equivalent to or less than the cost of custodial care. The cost per child served is approximately $4,000. If Re-ED can prevent longer periods of institutionalization, this is a modest investment indeed.

Appropriate to the systems analysis of the problem, most of our studies of effectiveness of Re-ED schools have employed ratings by concerned observers: mother, father, teacher, our own staff, and agency staffs, all important persons in the ecological space of the child. However, Laura Weinstein (1965) has been interested in the way normal and disturbed children construct interpersonal space, as illustrated by the accompanying representations of felt board figures. She used two techniques. In the first (the replacement technique), each of two figure pairs—a pair of human figures and a pair of rectangles—is present on a different board and equally far apart (Figures 17.2 and 17.3). The child is asked to replace the felt figures "exactly as far apart as they are now." Normal and disturbed children make systematic errors, but in opposite directions: normal children replace human figures closer together while Re-ED children replace human figures farther apart (Figure 17.4). In the second technique (the free placement technique), human figures are used, representing mothers, fathers, and children. The children are asked to place the figures on the board "any way you like." Again systematic differences occur. Normal children place the child very close to the mother. Re-ED children place greater distance between the mother and the child than between any other human pair (Figure 17.5).

FIGURE 17.2 Geometric felt figures used in replacement technique (after Weinstein 1965).

FIGURE 17.3 Human felt figures used in replacement technique (after Wein-stein 1965).

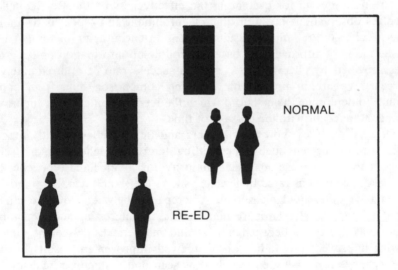

FIGURE 17.4 Placement of geometric and human felt figures by normal and disturbed children (after Weinstein 1965).

The mother-child relationship is clearly crucial in the life space of the 6- to 12-year-old children with whom we work. It is gratifying to report that children after the Re-ED experience put the child figure closer to the mother than they did before; that is, they structure interpersonal space as normal children do.

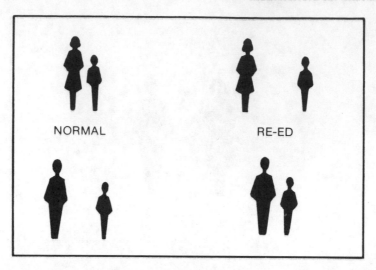

NORMAL   RE-ED

FIGURE 17.5   Mother, father, and child felt figures as placed by normal and disturbed children (after Weinstein 1965).

The basic design for evaluating the effectiveness of the Re-ED schools involves observations taken at time of enrollment and repeated six months after discharge. Preliminary results present an encouraging picture. A composite rating of improvement, based on follow-up information on 93 graduates provided by all evaluators, gives a success rate of approximately 80 percent. We are in process of obtaining comparison data from control groups to determine the extent to which the reeducation effort is superior to changes that occur with the passage of time.

Detailed analyses show that mothers and fathers independently report a decrease in symptoms such as bedwetting, tantrums, nightmares, and school fears, and an increase in social maturity on a Vineland-type checklist. School adjustment as rated by teachers shows the same favorable trends. On a semantic differential measure of discrepancy between how the child is seen and parental standards for him, there is an interesting and dynamically significant difference between fathers and mothers. Both see the child as having improved. For fathers the perceived improvement results in lower discrepancy scores between the child as seen and a standard held for him. For some mothers, however, improvement results in a raising of standards so that discrepancy scores frequently remain high. This is not true of all mothers but it is more frequently true of mothers than of fathers.

But *T* tests seldom determine the fate of institutions; public and professional acceptance is crucial.

To obtain an informed and mature professional appraisal of Re-ED, we have established a panel of visitors composed of men whose judgment is held in high esteem: Eli M. Bower, psychologist; Reginald S. Lourie, psychiatrist; Charles R. Strother, psychologist; and Robert L. Sutherland, sociologist. Members of the panel have been visiting the schools regularly since their inception and will make public their final appraisal at the end of the project period. It is enough to say now that they are all strong supporters of the Re-ED idea.[4]

Our aspiration and our growing confidence are that the Re-ED model will be replicated in many states, that it will have its influence on the character of more traditional treatment programs, and that the beneficiaries will be the disturbed children of America.

NOTES

1. The work here reported was made possible by Grant No. MH 929 of the United States Public Health Service, and by funds provided by Peabody College, the State of Tennessee, and the State of North Carolina. We are grateful for the support and wise counsel of Commissioner Joseph J. Baker and Commissioner Nat T. Winston, Jr., of Tennessee, Commissioner Eugene A. Hargrove and Sam O. Cornwell of North Carolina, Leonard J. Duhl and Raymond J. Balester of NIMH, and Paul W. Penningroth and Harold L. McPheeters of the Southern Regional Education Board. (The first four paragraphs have been omitted. M. W.)

2. So many people have worked to make Re-ED a reality it is impossible even to record their names. They will have received recompense from seeing children flourish in their care. Yet Alma B. McLain and Letha B. Rowley deserve special recognition for long service and uncommon skill and grace in managing many problems.

3. The consultants have meant much more to Project Re-ED than can be recorded in this brief account. We here inadequately recognize the invaluable contribution of our colleagues: Jenny L. Adams, MSW, Gus K. Bell, PhD, Lloyd J. Borstelmann, PhD, Eric M. Chazen, MD, Julius H. Corpening, BD, Jane Ann Eppinger, MSW, John A. Fowler, MD, Ihla H. Gehman, EdD, W. Scott Gehman, PhD, Maurice Hyman MD, J. David Jones, MD, and Bailey Webb, MD.

4. The evaluation has been completed and published. Information is available from the author of this chapter.

18

The Treatment Group Technique

REUVEN FEUERSTEIN
AND DAVID KRASILOWSKY

A major objection to environments composed largely or entirely of deviant populations is their great capacity to socialize to their prevailing behavior and norms. Jails and prisons commonly are more adept at teaching delinquency than law observance, and bizarre behavior of hospital inmates has a contagious quality. In short, the jail is no place for the delinquent, and the residential treatment center is no place for the emotionally disturbed child if modeling and rewards for generally (i.e., outside the institution) acceptable behavior are posited as the major determinants of change. Instead we must search out tolerant yet powerful, healthy environments. The foster family is often employed to this end. In principle this should work. Homer Folks (1896) and many others after him have reasoned why it should. Families, even foster families, unlike institutions, are in and of the community; so troubled children who live in them are constantly exposed to normal behavior and the expectations that they will conform. Given understanding, support, and professional help, they should improve. Unfortunately the wish and hope did not father reality as many families proved neither tolerant enough to live with marked deviance nor powerful enough to contain it. As DeFries et al. (1964) in one of the very few serious studies of this issue have shown, the arrangement tends to fail.

The present chapter is a modified and up-dated version of a paper which originally appeared in *The Israel Annals of Psychiatry and Related Disciplines* 5, 1 (Spring 1967): 61–90. (The first section of the paper has been omitted. M. W.) Reuven Feuerstein and David Krasilowsky. "The Treatment Group Ttechnique." In *Group Care: An Israeli Approach,* eds. Martin Wolins and Meir Gottesmann. New York: Gordon and Breach, 1971. Reproduced by permission.

The choice, then, with the disturbed child seems to lie between two undesirable alternatives: the institution, which confirms his illness and enhances it with its own expectations, or the family, which can neither accept difficult behavior nor control it. Like Hobbs (Chap. 17), Feuerstein and Krasilowsky attempt to cope with this dilemma, but they come up with a different solution. Since in Israel group care of normal, healthy adolescents is commonplace, the environment of youth villages, boarding schools, and similar facilities can be used to treat disturbed children on the basis of maximal osmosis from the healthy to the ill.

The Treatment Group Technique

Since 1958 we have established six treatment groups in an attempt to create the combination of simultaneously providing protection and preserving contact with the normal peer group. The model on which the educative and therapeutic approach was built is somewhat reminiscent of osmosis in that we have created an interaction between two environments by means of a controlled and regulated permeability between them. The factors determining the activation of the interactional process, its intensity, its quality, and its timing, are related to the modifications occurring in the child and the specific needs and forces developed as a result of these changes.

In practice this was done in the following way. We placed 25 deeply disturbed children as a group unit into a youth village where 5 or 6 group units of so-called normal children are living. The disturbed group was put under a regimen specially adapted to their very low and regressive level of functioning and to their disruptive patterns of behavior.

Some basic principles were considered essential in dealing with these groups. The situations that will be described arose from our experience with one particular group established in 1960 in Neve Hadassah (a youth village located in the central part of Israel near Natanya). This was the second group of its kind we had established. From the outset it was designed as an experiment, and the experience acquired in the previously established group played a role both in the development of concepts and in the choice of techniques we applied with this group.

UNCONDITIONED ACCEPTANCE

One of the major and most effective elements we used in dealing with these particular children we call the principle of *unconditioned acceptance*. The vicious circle of disturbance and rejection, the basis of his deep frustration, cannot be arrested by the child himself. If it is not dealt with by the adult or the environment at large, it will perpetuate its tragic effects. In order to interrupt the rejecting experience, unconditioned acceptance is a first and vital condition. This will allow the youngster to perceive the environment as willing to accept him on his own terms. This is the relationship between the child and his mother in the earliest stage of development, before the environment becomes involved in the process of socialization. Many of these children had suffered repetitive rejecting experiences from these earliest stages until the time of their referral to our treatment group.

As a result, their behavior was dominated by the compulsive need to repeat their long-lasting traumatic experience endlessly by provoking it over and over again (Blos 1965). Many of them went through three or four placements without being able to adjust to any one of them. At this age, however, unconditioned acceptance runs counter to the compelling need to adapt oneself to the age-specific requirements of society. Any overt attempt to use it will be resisted not only by the environment but also by the adolescent himself. On the other hand the "symbolic realization" of regressive needs offered in therapy (Alpert 1957; Sechehaye 1951) is not considered effective in adolescence, and its effect on the youth's integration into life seems very limited (Fraiberg 1955). The use of unconditioned acceptance in a relatively open environment, therefore, requires the involved adults to make very fine and continuous adaptations in the educational environment to the specific level of functioning of the disturbed individual (Fenichel et al. 1960). In many ways it can be compared to walking a tightrope. A state of equilibrium had to be maintained between two antagonistic needs: on the one hand to help the individual become socialized; on the other to accept him despite his disruptive and regressive behavior. That these children had to be accepted by an environment in which they were living 24 hours a day was both a help and a problem. Numerous areas for support and for clash arose from the total situation.

In practical terms this meant that no child accepted within the treatment group was ever rejected because of behavioral problems, signs of misadaptation, or other reasons for being viewed as unsuitable, although justification for such measures presented itself frequently. Even if the child was considered dangerous to his immediate environment, everything was done in order to avoid rejection. This is the major way in which unconditioned acceptance was expressed.

R. was a 12½-year-old psychotic girl with florid symptomatology. She had always been very passive and erratic and suddenly became very aggressive toward the group. It was the group itself which asked to have her removed. This request was expressed by them in a very ambivalent way. R. was given an enforced trial leave, giving the group time to reconsider their decision. A short time after her departure, we received a letter from the group asking imperiously for her reinstatement.

This illustrates and confirms our own hypothesis that the danger of rejection of one of the group members is not only (and not always) damaging to the rejected one but is a threat to the security of the entire group. The very fact that the adults responsible for the group—psychotherapists, psychologists, teachers, leaders, etc.—may be ready to give up one of them for no matter what reason is likely to be interpreted as a looming threat of rejection to every single group member. This, in turn, would immediately block any real redevelopment and remediation, both of which rely on unconditioned acceptance. It is not difficult to imagine the magnitude of the efforts required to create the necessary level of tolerance to preserve this principle. Out of a group of 43, we succeeded in avoiding rejection in every case but one.

This does not mean that children were not removed from the group. The group was an open one and, after the first year, children who could be integrated into normal groups in the same village or in other places were transferred. Even these separations, although they could be interpreted as "hope" for each member, were not easily accepted by the children and often threw the group into states of disequilibrium. Such transfers were not effected until the initial stages of adaptation had been mastered. By that time many of the children were already able to perceive that leaving for "better groups" was an avenue open even to themselves. It should be made clear at this point, however, that unconditioned acceptance does not mean total tolerance or passive acceptance of deviant behavior.

Unconditioned acceptance also meant that any provocation of the children toward the environment at large or, specifically, toward responsible adults involved with their treatment was not allowed to evoke a generalized reaction and to become a basis for rejection. If one of the adults had to use disciplinary action or rejecting behavior toward a certain child at a given time, his approach was not shared in by all the members of the staff, as is very often the case. On the contrary, another group leader was encouraged to work with the child and to help him out of his stressful situation, not so much by undoing the punishment as by helping the youngster accept it and by reducing the anxiety connected with it. Where the child had succeeded in destroying all his links to the environment, one last door still remained open to him: the child guidance clinic in the person of the counselor responsible for the group.

A great deal of work had to be done with staff in order to help them overcome their own feelings of frustration; in the face of manipulation we were often faced with great difficulties in this area.

REDUCTION OF ANXIETY

The second principle was the *reduction of anxiety*. Anxiety was common to all the children in this group, and it arose from a great variety of overlapping factors. Besides the anxiety inherent in their disturbance per se, a major increase in anxiety had to be expected as a direct outcome of living with normal children. The negative, damaged self-image that came from previous experiences of rejection and the intense feelings of inferiority connected with their current low level of functioning were inevitably increased by their direct contact with children functioning at a normal level, at school, at work, and in group life. The constant unfavorable comparison with other children evoked or exaggerated a great deal of defensiveness. It was therefore important to try to reduce these states of anxiety by selecting out of the children's environment only those stimuli to which they were able to respond in a relaxed and tension-free way.

If we consider that the overwhelming majority of these children were completely illiterate or almost so, had very poor language skills, and were low in the performance of day-to-day tasks, it is clear why one had to protect them as much as possible from confrontation with more successful youngsters, and more important still from allowing them to compete with the normal peer group. On the other hand, it was this very confrontation which we felt should be made available to them in order to enable them to become aware of new goals and horizons and gradually to develop motivation to move toward them.

The major source of frustration and anxiety for these children lay in the area of learning. It was therefore vital that schooling be presented to them in such a way as to render it less highly valued or, to put it differently, that they would not perceive themselves measured or valued only by the criterion of their academic achievement.

Accordingly, the children were placed in two special classes organized around a great variety of nonacademic activities. The high level of tolerance displayed by the teachers allowed for a great deal of spontaneous expressive behavior in class. The therapeutic value in this was not easily recognized either by the teachers or by others in the immediate surroundings (Blom et al. 1966). On the surface it looked like a wanton explosion of aggressive and disruptive behavior. In this way the children openly expressed their need to depreciate the area of performance, which was the cause of their greatest distress, frustration, and sense of failure. Although they all objected to their own behavior, which prevented the teacher from carrying out the normal teaching activity, they could not really help acting in this way. Much of the early time at school was spent outside the classroom on long and instructive walks and excursions or in activities heavily tainted by regressive, childlike behavior such as drawing and paper-cutting. At the same time, major steps were taken toward developing ego functions and school skills through individualized tutoring given by their group workers. Every child was assigned to one particular group worker with whom it was hoped the child would have a more intensive relationship (Fenichel et al. 1960). The hours of private tutoring were used for ego strengthening and supportive measures as well as for life-space interviews (Redl and Wineman 1951). It was only after the children were able to perceive learning as less essential than they had previously regarded it—i.e., only after there was some reduction in the anxiety about learning as the sole criterion for being valued as a human being— were they able to learn (Minuchin et al. 1966).

INDUCED REGRESSION

We have already touched on our third guiding principle which we call *induced regression* (Alpert 1957, 1959). Many of these children had learned to control their behavior in the wake of their frequent clashes with social reality. Unfortunately, this control was achieved only by means of a total blockage of their intellectual and social capacities. There was no ability to discriminate between areas of desirable activity and that leading to rejection and punishment. In many cases this became a pattern of total withdrawal or a hypersubmissive type of conforming behavior, alternating with outbursts of extreme aggression and disruptive acting-out behavior. It was clear to us that as long as these patterns prevailed many of the unfulfilled needs could not be met and would create foci of resistance to any attempt to modify them. Even in those who made some tentative steps toward social adaptation it was always in a fragmentary idiosyncratic manner according to the makeup of that particular individual.

"E. was a fat little boy who was referred to us by his former educators because of his total incapacity to function in school or in the group. He was very passive, untalkative, and morose. In his former institution he was viewed as mentally retarded and could not be reached or activated by any stimuli. Regardless of what was tried, he showed complete disinterest. Within our group at the outset he functioned much like he did in his former institution. After a short period, however he became more adapted. This manifested itself only by an enormous need to conform to each individual, adult and child, with whom he came in contact. As part of this exaggerated servility, he played the role of the "butler" not only for the group but also for his teachers whom he insistently wanted to help in their various administrative and technical tasks. At the same time, no progress was noted in his school achievement. It was only after he went through a very severe regression manifested by childish clinging, demanding behavior, and temper tantrums, with marked incapacity to delay gratification, that he became more self-assertive and developed the motivation and capacity to progress in a variety of fields." This phenomenon, called by Alpert (1957, 1959) and by us induced regression, appeared in as many as 60–70 percent of our children. In retrospect its impact on the redevelopment of the individual seems to us to be decisive.

Regression was induced in many ways. The major vectors were, of course, unconditioned acceptance and the reduction of anxiety, but they included as well planned manipulations to bring about meaningful relationships with staff members who were carefully responsive to the emerging regressive needs of the individual adolescent. Another device involved keeping the group at a low pace of development by periodically introducing new children. These newcomers were inevitably considerably less well adapted than the original group and were thus perceived as deviant. In this way we not only demonstrated to the group that the educators accept children who function on even a lower level than they did but we were also able to counteract a very strong tendency among the educators themselves who were inclined to respond prematurely to positive changes occurring in the individual or the group by reducing the amount of acceptance and tolerance toward them. The fact that the group was open at both ends, with children being promoted and moving upward on the one hand and children coming in with lower levels of functioning on the other, played a role in avoiding deterioration of the self-concept of the group as well as allowing them to indulge in regression.

Since their low level of functioning and the unavoidable confrontation with children of other groups evoked feelings of inadequacy and inferiority, we had to endow the group with a variety of compensatory experiences (Bower 1966), which would be at once pleasant, gratifying, and enriching. This made it possible for the children to express their attachment to the group openly even after they became aware of its true nature. The children in the normal groups knew that to belong to the treatment group meant to be à "school failure" and/or "disturbed." Nevertheless, many of them were rather jealous of the advantages associated with the treatment group. Stimulated and given many possibilities for creative and sublimative activities, this group very soon became a successful competitor in many areas of performance such as carpentry, sports, drama, and pottery—activities highly valued as status-granting by the entire population of the village.

In many instances the children of other groups became furious at the repeated victories of the treatment group against their own groups in sports competitions. On such occasions some children would say: "You have in your legs what we have in our heads," but these remarks were met with good humored reactions of "So what?" The treatment group felt protected, and they accepted this "protection" as their "Good Right." For a long time they saw nothing derogatory in this. They looked for strong, omnipotent figures as their auxiliary egos in order to compensate for their own weakness and feelings of impotence. By intimate association with a high-status counselor, with whom they identified, they were able to improve their self-image much sooner than they would have accomplished this through their own achievements. It was only gradually that they were able to give up their need to cling to and to be helped by the omnipotent supportive figure and to reach out for more objective, self-realizing accomplishments.

NORMAL PEER GROUP AS A SOCIALIZING FACTOR

Social learning and imitation (Bandura and Huston 1961) are the major avenues for shaping and modifying behavior, attitudes, and motivations. They can be regarded as vital to the whole therapeutic technique. Hence, in our view, the most essential principle of the treatment group technique is the *planned and controlled relationship with a normal peer group.*

If the three principles mentioned above are found to be operative in a great variety of settings and used by many therapists and educators involved with the disturbed adolescent, this fourth principle lends its predecessors a specific quality. The major theoretical concepts underlying this principle are the following. The adolescent is most resistant to influences from the adult world (Ausubel 1954; Blos 1962; Erikson 1959; Jacobson 1961). It is probably at this age that the human being finds himself most removed from his previous attachments (Freud 1958). At the same time, there is a great need "to belong." This stems from the shattering of the previously established rudimentary ego and self-identity brought about by the youngster's detachment from his primary objects. This loss of auxiliary ego figures comes at a time when other changes are occurring in almost all sectors of his life, biological, psychological, and social.

The two antagonistic tendencies—namely, the need to detach oneself and sever strong ties on the one hand, and the great need to "belong" as the only way to secure inner continuity on the other—make the peer group the most important medium for creating new identifications. The peers then become a vital source of social learning and imitation. This is true for the great majority of normal adolescents, and it is even more so for the disturbed ones. The disturbed adolescent tends to use the peer group as a carrier for his antisocial attitudes and aggressiveness. This in turn powerfully affects his peer choices and results in gang formation (Frankenstein 1947).

Thus, as part of the several strategies for modifying the inner structure of the disturbed individual, it is essential to make available to him identification objects from the normal adolescent peer culture. Since the adult's ability to socialize the adolescent is limited in terms of transmitting to him attitudes, values, and motivations, it is essential to use the peer group as the main transmitter of values and the principal means of modifying and shaping his behavior (Bettelheim and Sylvester 1947; Bronfenbrenner 1962; Lebovici 1966; Makarenko 1955).

If properly and successfully applied, the above-mentioned principles may enable the disturbed youngster to perceive goals and behavior patterns other than those characteristic of his own makeup and that of his group. Until then, however, he has to be protected from these goals, which he cannot achieve because of his problems. It is here that our model of osmotic-like interaction becomes meaningful. The penetrability of the group was secured. With the normal children an ego-directed educational approach was effective. The treatment children lived in close relationship with normal children. In this way a permeable situation was achieved. Both groups met on the grounds, in the dining room, at general activities, and were able to associate as individuals. They could make friends or come into conflict with one another. This close contact could have become either a source of beneficial social learning or a highly noxious experience, depending on how it was planned and controlled by the staff members.

In order to control behavior in an open environment where all the activities of life occur in a geographically small and functionally undifferentiated area, a relatively large number of intervening adult figures was necessary. Along with their own functions, these adults would be with the children continuously so that they could intervene at the right moment, help out with the inevitable distress situations, or mediate the social meaning of the event to their charges. The group was therefore provided with a relatively high number of workers (averaging 4 group care workers to 23–27 children).

Another important factor was the choice of the youth village. The proper human environment for the treatment group was one with an optimal but not a maximal gap between the level of functioning of the treatment group and the level characteristic of the total village population. It made no sense to try to integrate our group into a population whose standards were too high. In order for a model to become an effective object of imitation, an optimum balance of distance and proximity is vital. If the object is too far removed from the imitator he will not become sensitive to and perceptive of it. If too closely related it would lose its enticive quality, or even worse it would be altogether ineffective in remodeling existing behavior.

We had to choose a youth village whose population consisted of children of average level, and would even include many disturbed children (whose level of disturbance did not block them from functioning in a normal group). The selected village also had to have an educational and technical staff who could accept the disturbed group and cooperate with us in our endeavor to raise the threshold of tolerance of the environment. In addition, we had to inventory the capacities and ego strengths of the group as a whole and of each child in particular in order to ascertain his stage of development and his capacity to respond adequately to requirements. On this basis we were able to plan and organize the whole life curriculum. The following example may illustrate this.

As previously mentioned, work is a basic requirement for every child in the village. The treatment group children were confronted with this universal requirement; they, too, had to assume responsibilities, be persistent and stable in their work, and cooperate with normal children and untrained adult workers in fulfilling their tasks. This exposed them to enormous danger of rejection and failure. We therefore had to avoid this confrontation at the outset and postpone it until their developing ego strengths would allow us to involve them in regular work routine of the village. At the same time we had to be very careful that this "privilege" would not be interpreted derogatorily by the other children. We therefore created a variety of pleasant work tasks for the treatment group where they could function at their own rhythm under the benevolent and encouraging supervision of their own well-informed group care workers. This was planned to continue for the first year, but it lasted only eight months. During this interval the children became aware that their work did not have the same meaning, usefulness, and status-granting quality typical for that youth village. During a group session they organized themselves and imperiously demanded to be integrated into the regular work program.

Here a word must be added about the underlying meaning of this demand. During the first stage of regressive childlike activities the children were not even aware that other children of the same age functioned differently. With the passage of time, however, the maturational process hand-in-hand with the immediate presence of models from the other peer groups acted to modify their needs for achieving social status (Bettelheim and Sylvester 1947). A very important incentive was the fact that even when we did allow them to indulge in childlike activity the difference between their activities and those of the other children was symbolized by the existing system of rewards given to children in the regular program, which were not granted to them. When they asked to be allowed to work like the others, they were aiming at being rewarded like the others. The mere fact of becoming aware of and motivated by rewards of a symbolic nature, like being acknowledged, must be considered a great step toward maturation and socialization. Small wonder, then, that the field of work very soon became the site for their move into responsible productive activities. Work has enormous meaning for the development of ego strengths and for freeing energy to master other skills (Erikson 1959). We had to act in this same way in various other areas of activity such as school and group work, etc., and at the same time to be very alert—through constant reevaluation of the children's level of functioning—to changes occurring in them in order to adapt the curriculum and the requirements made on them. Occasionally certain group members became prematurely drawn toward goals that they could not attain at that time; so we had to cope with this to prevent inevitable failures. When we were unable to discourage a child from attempting such tasks and he did actually fail, we had to impress him with the temporary quality of his failure in order to undo its ill-effects.

The environment had to be carefully prepared to be able to accept not only the group but all its implications for their general program. For example, they had to change the daily routine of some of the other children in order to fit in with the program required for the treatment group.

It is not feasible to describe here all the steps that were needed to make planning and control possible. In fact, we were not always successful. At times we had to fight the natural tendency of the institution to push the children prematurely toward duties, but in the long run it was possible to work things out; and, in many instances, it was even beneficial to the other groups living in the youth village.

In setting up the treatment groups the major problem and the chief basis for resistance was the fear of contagion implicit in mixing normal and disturbed children. This danger is in many ways the reason why disturbed children are isolated from their normal peers. In our situation this feared development did not materialize. Throughout our experience with the six treatment groups we received no complaint that children belonging to normal groups were being "contaminated" by contact with the disturbed ones. This suggests the impact and the efficacy of the norms created by a "majority" on a "minority" group living within it. Unhappily, we have no real experimental data bearing on this point in the same sense that we were able to evaluate our other theoretical considerations presented in this paper. However, the very fact that this was not a source of complaint from staff, educators, and parents speaks strongly against the stereotype of social contagiousness in such a guided setting and its damaging consequences. Major evidence of this and perhaps the most gratifying outcomes of the treatment group was the fact that both the director of the youth village and his staff were ready to accept deeply disturbed children into the village. Indeed, they established special classes for them whose functioning is based very largely on the principles used with the treatment group.

It is not within the scope of this paper to give a full account of all the strategies employed with the treatment group. In addition to presenting the basic principles we will briefly report a number of other technical devices employed.

1. In terms of its relationship to the clinic, the status of the treatment group was not the usual one[1] where the educational supervision held overall responsibility and the child guidance clinic had merely consultative power. Here the relationship was reversed, with the clinic assuming complete responsibility and holding the final power of decision over the group as a whole and the individual in particular.

2. The clinic was represented by two counselors, each of whom worked at the village one day per week. The work consisted mainly of a weekly staff meeting where children were reviewed at regular intervals or discussed specifically for particular problems. In addition, each counselor met regularly with children for life-space interviews (Caplan 1959) stemming from events reported at the staff meetings or at the request of the child himself.

3. A major device used to restrain educators from acting impulsively in the face of dramatic situations was the freedom they had of calling on these counselors at any time. It is important to understand how crucial this was in preventing youth leaders and other responsible adults from allowing situations to develop whose only solution could be rejection. To do this a deliberately induced state of dependency was created; however, if one considers the

seriousness of some of the situations they were faced with they could not be left with a responsibility that would have made it impossible for them to carry out their task. Of course, this state of dependency was gradually reduced, and responsibilities were progressively shifted back to them as the children's status changed and more ego-directed demands could be made on them.

4. One-third of the children were treated by individual psychotherapy of various degrees of intensity and duration with the sessions held outside the village at the clinic. Referral involved not only the need for individual psychotherapy but also the problem of accessibility. Obviously not every adolescent could use it.

Follow-up

We carried out a follow-up study on the group and evaluated the development of each individual belonging to it. This included data on social and familial adaptation six years after admission to the group (which was three years after it disbanded). In addition, the subjects were reexamined with a variety of psychological tests, and the results were compared to those obtained at the time of admission.

The following is a brief description of the diagnostic and sociofamilial status of the group at admission and after they left the treatment group.

During the 3½ years of the existence of the project, a total of 43 adolescents (28M, 15F) were treated. They came from 15 countries and 4 continents; 23 came from Oriental-Sefardic and 20 from Ashkenazi ethnic backgrounds. Thirty-five percent of the children belonged to either divorced or broken families, including 12 percent born out of wedlock. Sixteen percent of the children were full orphans, 23 percent had lost their mothers, and 7 percent were orphaned of fathers—a total of 46 percent full or partial orphans. One girl did not know her parents at all, others had unknown fathers, 2 children had been adopted; 12 percent had stepmothers, 21 percent stepfathers. Five children were of mixed Christian-Jewish marriages. Almost half of the parents of the European subjects were victims of the Holocaust and had remarried after losing previous families.

The socioeconomic level of the families was in general very low. Only 25 percent could be considered as living on a relatively satisfactory level, the remainder were economically dependent, impaired, or very low.

Considering their poor economic level, the educational level of the parents was not so low as one would expect (only 25 percent of them were illiterate, 58 percent had completed an elementary school education, and 16 percent even had attended high school and college). This emphasizes that psycho- and sociopathology were responsible for their status rather than cultural differences or educational deprivation. Actually, this is clearly evident in our data on manifest pathology among parents: 9 of the mothers (or 20 percent) were known to suffer from mental illnesses and so were 3 (7 percent) of the fathers. Nine other fathers and 6 mothers suffered from chronic physical diseases, and in 3 of the subjects both parents were afflicted with chronic physical conditions.

Sociopathology, such as alcoholism (21 percent), delinquency (14 percent), and promiscuity (33 percent), was found in many families and had profoundly affected the childrearing patterns of the family and the character formation of the child. One father was condemned for the attempted murder of his mistress.

The treatment group included 12 percent who were only child, 26 percent first born, 40 percent middle child, and 23 percent last born. Separation from parents before the first birthday occurred in 16 percent of the cases, but by age 5 a total of 30 percent of the children were separated. Several of the subjects had had severe illnesses that involved separation by hospitalization (Bowlby 1950, 1952 ed.). Six out of 25 boys (25 percent) underwent circumcision after the age of 10. Both the social histories and our direct observations indicate that 25 out of 43 children were subjected to overt and repetitive rejection by their families. Even the absence of rejection, which we observed in only 7 cases, cannot be defined as genuinely accepting behavior on the part of the parents (Frankenstein 1947).

We found no obvious deficiencies in the children's educational opportunities. Half of them entered kindergarten at the normal age, and 84 percent were reported to have begun school at the required age. Hence, illiteracy and failure to acquire good school habits cannot be explained simplistically by a lack of adequate facilities or as a result of cultural background. One has to look for the explanation of this phenomenon in the pathological states of these children (Blanchard 1946). Thirteen (30 percent) of the children had emigrated to Israel without their parents; 26 (60 percent) were received on their arrival in Israel by Youth Aliyah[1] and placed within its regular framework. The other 17 children attended public schools in Israel for some time after immigration and were not referred to Youth Aliyah until later.

The age distribution of the children on entrance into the group was rather wide. In the overwhelming majority of cases (91 percent) referral to the group followed an unsuccessful attempt to place the child in regular Youth Aliyah educational settings. Several were tried out in and rejected by 2–4 placements. In 26 (60 percent) of the cases the declared reasons for failure and subsequent referral to the treatment group as the only remaining resource were emotional disturbance and behavior disorder. In 13 (30 percent) the emphasis was on persistent school failure. Four (9 percent) were identified as unable to function in a normal setting after their referral to Youth Aliyah.

At the time of their entrance the children were at a very low level in a

TABLE 18.1.   *Age distribution on entrance*

Age (years)	11–12	13–14	15–16
No. (percent)	17 (40)	20 (46)	6 (14)

The following diagnoses were based on psychodiagnostic and psychiatric evaluation prior to entrance as well as direct observation during the stay of these children in the group. The majority came to us after having been examined by other clinics or agencies.

Psychological status

Psychotic regressed	7 (3M, 4F)
Borderline	4 (M)
Schizoid	5 (M)
Neurotic	8 (3M, 5F)
Severe behavior disorders	5 (4M, 1F)
Brain damage	1 (M)
Socially abandoned with neurotic or paranoid symptoms	10 (7M, 3F)
Not sufficient data	3 (1M, 2F)

Manifest "level of cognitive functioning"[2]

Severe retardation (pseudo-imbecility)	9 (5M, 4F)
Mildly retarded or borderline	19 (12M, 7F)
Relatively normal level of functioning	14 (10M, 4F)
Above average	1 (M)

number of basic skills. Only one child could read fluently (although limited to beginning Hebrew texts with vowels). The level of the rest of the group involved illiteracy, severe dyslexia, or otherwise slow and impaired reading, which made comprehension limited or impossible (see Table 18.2). The level of writing (Table 18.3) was even lower, with only six children achieving a relatively satisfactory level of spelling easy texts. In arithmetic (Table 18.4) almost 62 percent of the children did not know at all, knew one or at most two of the four arithmetic operations, 33 percent had command of three, and only one child had some proficiency in basic exercises of division.

TABLE 18.2.   *Reading level at admission and subsequently*

Level of Reading when Entering Group	Number of Subjects	Mean Age when Entering Group (Yrs:Mos)	Mean Stay in Group (Yrs:Mos)	Mean Grade when Leaving Group	Mean Grade at Date of Follow-up
Full illiteracy	9	13:1	2:8	5.8	7.6
Semiilliteracy	13	12:8	2:5	6.5	8.4
Severe dyslexia	7	12:11	2:0	7.0	8.9
Impaired reading	13	13:7	1:2	7.6	9.6
Fluent reading	1	14:0	1:2	7.0	10.0
Total/mean	43	13:1	2:1	6.8	8.7

TABLE 18.3.   *Writing level at admission and subsequently*

Level of Writing when Entering Group	Number of Subjects	Mean Age when Entering Group (Yrs:Mos)	Mean Stay in Group (Yrs:Mos)	Mean Grade when Leaving Group	Mean Grade at Date of Follow-up
No writing	8	13:2	2:6	5.6	7.0
Writing letters	8	12:6	2:9	6.7	9.2
Severe dysgraphia	10	12:10	2:2	6.9	8.6
Moderate dysgraphia	11	13:5	1:2	7.1	8.9
Relatively satisfactory writing	6	13:8	1:5	7.7	10.0

TABLE 18.4.   *Arithmetic level at admission and subsequently*

Level of Arithmetic when Entering Group	Number of Subjects	Mean Age when Entering Group (Yrs:Mos)	Mean Stay in Group (Yrs:Mos)	Mean Grade when Leaving Group	Mean Grade at Date of Follow-up
No knowledge	6	13:1	2:4	5.2	6.6
Addition	7	12:2	3:1	7.1	9.0
Subtraction	14	13:1	1:9	6.7	8.9
Multiplication	14	13:6	1:8	7.4	9.2
Division	2	14.0	1:10	7.0	8.5

During their stay in the program children generally moved ahead. However, one must carefully weigh the meaning of these achievements. It should be noted that even though certain children achieved 10th grade level they did not always perform evenly and displayed gaps in certain areas of functioning. This was largely because these areas were not dealt with in the treatment group for understandable reasons (e.g., English, history) or because of the level of the school in which the children were placed after their treatment group.

In an attempt to sum up briefly and to interpret the data on our population as derived from our follow-up studies and our most recent contacts with the youngsters, we may point out the following.

1. A modest but dramatic result found in our population is the absolute lack of delinquent behavior. Up to this point we are aware of only one graduate of the group who was involved in a minor legal offense. If we consider the extreme delinquency proneness of our group (Glueck and Glueck 1950) and compare this with the numerous delinquent acts and major involvement in legal procedures usually observed in youngsters educated in

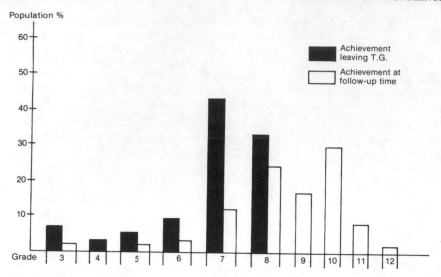

Fig. 18.1.

special residential settings for the disturbed, the difference is striking. Antisocial behavior can be considered a major product of being isolated in a disturbed peer-group culture (Polsky 1962), but it was not so in our population.

2. Following their stay in the village almost all of our age-eligible boys were accepted by and actually entered the army either through the kibbutz movement or individually. Again, up to the present we have received no particular complaint from the military authorities concerning their behavior or adaptation. According to our experience, this, too, is very different in the case of youngsters from special residential settings.

3. The achievement of our children in academic, social, and professional areas compared to their initial level of functioning clearly points to the enormous degree of reversibility one may expect, even in adolescence, so long as the above outlined conditions for such modification are available (Freedman and Bender 1957).

4. This paper provides insufficient space to try to encompass a full presentation of the changes that occurred in the personality structure of the children. However, comparative work, both on projective tests and with data derived from direct observation, interviews, and social histories, clearly points to the significant favorable changes in emotional structure and ego-functioning that occurred in a great percentage of our children. These cannot be explained simply by age, change of environment, or other incidental factors. The capacity of the great majority of the children to function in a way very close to normal was evidenced by the fact that they were accepted into social situations that had previously rejected them, such as normal peer

groups and their own families, and that they have adapted themselves to society at large.

5. Another phenomenon that must be emphasized is the strong feeling of belongingness which still exists among the great majority of the members of the group. Not only do they write to each other but when writing to the counselors they always request information about each other, ask for meetings to be arranged, and are ready to provide help to their former colleagues.

Life within the treatment group is described by many of them as a joyful and significant experience whose painful and pleasant memories are recalled with good humor. We would say with Alpert (1957) that life within the group can be viewed as the basis of a "corrective emotional experience" whose effects are felt both in the adaptational capacities and in the emotional makeup of the children.

NOTES

1. Youth Aliyah has in placement 8,000–10,000 children. Most can be described as either new immigrants or academically and culturally deficient. The emphasis in their care is largely on education and the development of culture-appropriate values.

2. This does not take into account the "hidden potential" disclosed by our examination (Learning Potential Assessment Device), which proved to be much higher than the manifest level of functioning (Feuerstein and Shalom 1967; Schwebel 1965).

ADDITIONAL READING FOR PART V

De Fries, Zera; Jenkins, Shirley; and Williams, Ethelyn S. "Foster family care for disturbed children—a nonsentimental view." *Child Welfare* 14, 2 (February 1965): 73–84.

Hylton, Lydia F. *The Residential Treatment Center: Children, Programs, and Costs.* New York: Child Welfare League of America, 1964.

King, Roy D.; Raynes, Norma V., and Tizard, Jack. *Patterns of Residential Care: Sociological Studies in Institutions for Handicapped Children.* London: Routledge and Kegan Paul, 1971.

Levitt, Eugene E. "The results of psychotherapy in children: An evaluation." *Journal of Consulting Psychology* 21, 3 (1957): 189–96.

———. "Psychotherapy with children: A further evaluation." *Behavioral Research and Therapy* 1 (1963): 45–51.

Morris, Pauline. *Put Away: A Sociological Study of Institutions for the Mentally Retarded.* New York: Atherton Press, 1969.

Polsky, Howard W., and Claster, Daniel S., with Carl Goldberg. *The Dynamics of Residential Treatment: A Social System Analysis.* Chapel Hill: University of North Carolina Press, 1968.

Street, David; Vinter, Robert D.; and Perrow, Charles. *Organization for Treatment: A Comparative Study of Institutions for Delinquents.* New York: The Free Press, 1966.

VI

Two Challenging Proposals

19

Behavior Modification in Total Institutions

RILEY PRICE, SCOTT BRIAR,
AND TROVA HUTCHINS

Until quite recently behavior modification had been much concerned with developing appropriate contingency situations for individuals. While in some instances such persons resided in group settings, the environment was merely a convenience. As in any medical or educational environment, the aggregation of clients, patients, students, or other recipients and the concentration of technical and professional resources was a way of economizing on or facilitating services; it was not in itself an instrument of change. To be sure, as long as a decade ago some reports (see Bronfenbrenner 1962, for example) described Russian uses of group contingencies, modeling, and other collective-oriented behavioral approaches. However, the impact of these reports was limited because the populations at issue were generally not found in American total institutions.

Lately the situation has undergone considerable change. The work described in this chapter and the implications developed for the use of total settings as instruments and not merely as convenient containers deserves special attention. Here is an excellent example of recognition that the settings themselves represent a powerful environment (Bloom 1964) that can and should be aimed at producing desired and eliminating unacceptable behavior. The specific requirements for developing such an environment are a guide and a challenge. They will direct attempts at environmental change, but not without continuously challenging the innovator to justify any new arrangements in terms of their behavioral consequences.

Introduction

TOTAL INSTITUTIONS

Total institutions are residential facilities that provide 24-hour care and treatment for individuals who for various reasons have demonstrated an inability to function adequately in society. An ultimate goal of most total institutions (e.g., mental hospitals, prisons, juvenile correctional facilities) is the rehabilitation and resocialization of residents for return to life in the community (Goffman 1961). Institutional treatment programs tend to vary, depending on the particular problems of the resident population and on the biases and specialties of professional staff; however, the majority of rehabilitation programs are characterized by *(a)* eclecticism—i.e., a variety of methods and approaches are used—with a preponderance of techniques being predicated on the traditional medical model; and *(b)* a disconcerting lack of success.

The vexations of accurately assessing outcome and treatment success are well known. But despite the limitations inherent in evaluative and outcome research, it is clear that traditional therapeutic approaches are notably imperfect. Recidivist rates alone offer convincing evidence that institutions are not fulfilling their commitment to permanent rehabilitation. In fact, it has been suggested that it would be more realistic to "focus on the problem of whether (and how) failure rates have been reduced—not whether an institution can claim success [Lerman 1968, p. 55]."

The inadequacy of institutional programs specifically—and of all therapeutic endeavors generally—gives impetus to the drive for change and improvement. Obviously, if something is not working it is warranted to consider trying something else. It has been argued that a large proportion of the current failures can be traced to the widespread use of methods that stem from a medical model.[1] In particular, two main shortcomings of this model have been noted.

First, the medically based approaches tend to view aberrant behaviors not primarily as problems per se but as symptoms of *underlying,* and perhaps unconscious pathology. Whether this general assumption is true or not, it still remains that *the problem*—that is, the object of treatment—must always be inferred and can never, by definition, be confirmed through direct observation. Therefore, the potential for errors of inference is constantly present. Stuart (1970) has summarized assessment based on the medical model.

> In short, assignment of an individual to a clinical diagnostic category indicates (at least in principle) that he shares certain behaviors with other individuals so diagnosed, but it does not shed light upon other socially productive aspects of his behavior, the etiology of his problems or potential strategies for the solution of his problems [p. 170].

The second limitation, an outgrowth of the first, concerns the rudimentary state of the conceptualization of techniques (Thomas 1968). Specific interventive strategies and tools cannot be explicated or translated into definitive therapist behaviors. Actual implementation becomes heavily dependent on the individual therapist's interpretation and personality. Some research has shown that one of the most influential variables in some treatment situations is therapist personality rather than method, field or auspice (Truax and Carkhuff 1967).

It is well beyond the scope of this paper to consider challenging the fundamental tenets and premises of the so-called medical or other traditional approaches. But it is important to note that these methods frequently tend to be associated with high rates of failure and that the specific sources of failure appear to relate to the wide margin for error by the therapist in identifying problems and selecting appropriate methods.

THE BEHAVIORAL APPROACH

Methodologies derived from a behavioral model have recently emerged as one possible alternative to traditional therapeutic approaches. The behavioral perspective offers many different techniques that are all broadly related to the general field of experimental work in learning and operant conditioning, which was first developed in the animal laboratory. Some, but not all, of the laboratory principles have been extrapolated for use in natural environments. Differences between the laboratory model and the behavioral technologies applied from operant conditioning have been delineated by Baer, Wolf, and Risley (1968).

> Analytic behavioral application is the process of applying sometimes tentative principles of behavior to the improvement of specific behaviors, and simultaneously evaluating whether or not any changes noted are indeed attributable to the process. . . . In short, analytic behavioral application is a self-examining, self-evaluating, discovery-oriented research procedure for studying behavior. . . . The differences between applied and basic research are not differences between that which "discovers" and that which merely "applies" what is already known. Both endeavors ask what controls the behavior under study. Non-applied research is likely to look at any behavior, and at any variable which may conceivably relate to it. Applied research is constrained to look at variables which can be effective in improving the behavior under study [p. 9].

Behavioral approaches to the treatment of human beings always involve: *(a)* a focus on observable actions and behaviors, rather than on inferred or underlying conditions; and *(b)* detailed specification of interventive techniques. The overall goal is to facilitate, effectively and efficiently, a decrease in undesirable behavior and an increase in desirable behavior. Most behavioral changes are effected through rearrangement of the environment.

Environment is a multifaceted concept that encompasses both the physical and the social. The *physical environment* includes the tangible surroundings and may or may not be amenable to modification. Within the treatment setting every effort should be made to provide surroundings that are convenient, pleasant, and conducive to optimal attention and functioning. The *social environment* can be defined by three levels of interaction: the interaction between individuals, between an individual and a group, and between groups. Since people do not live and function in isolation, it is neither desirable nor possible to consider altering the behavior of a single individual without regard for his social environment(s). Rather, it is postulated that the relationship between behavior and environment is reciprocal and ongoing; a change in one will produce a change in the other (Stuart 1970; Patterson and Reid 1970). Therefore, an important target of behavioral technology is *interaction patterns*. Minimally the goal would include modification of the interaction between two individuals; usually the focus encompasses *many* of the dyads and groups with which an individual interacts.

The behavioral engineer attempts to modify the environment through the management and control of contingencies and stimuli. *Contingency management* is concerned with the specification and control of the *consequences* of behavior. Consequences may be positive or negative, desirable or undesirable, rewarding or punishing. *Stimulus control* involves the selection and arrangement of stimuli that elicit the performance of desired behavior. "Stimulus control exists to the extent that the presence or absence of a stimulus controls the probability of a response [Homme et al., 1970, p. 19]." Contingency management requires no knowledge of stimulus control to be effective; however, success of stimulus control does depend on the proper management of contingencies.

The success of techniques derived from the behavioral model is well documented.[2] Behaviorists have long been successful with many specific problems, especially among traditionally hard-to-treat groups such as children, the autistic, and the retarded. As a result of this apparent effectiveness, applications of behavioral techniques have gradually expanded to include other, more general and complex problems and populations. Methodologies have been refined and clarified and technologies have been elaborated (Ulrich, Stachnik, and Mabry 1970). The potential for the behavioral design of entire treatment systems has been recognized.

PURPOSE

The purpose of this paper is to suggest the value and expediency of utilizing behavioral principles and techniques in total-care institutional settings. More specifically, the paper suggests that the behavioral perspective can be applied to the *entire* design of the system—rather than being restricted to one institutional segment or unit, and rather than being accompanied or supplemented by other, more traditional perspectives.

To date apparently no total institutions are designed and run wholly on the basis of behavioral principles. However, many institutions have introduced partial or experimental behavioral programs on one ward or unit, often with impressive results. These partial applications deserve consideration and review. Their success, coupled with the encouraging evidence concerning the use of behavioral methods generally, suggests the feasibility of attempting a total, behaviorally based program design.

The remainder of this paper presents a review and discussion of recent experiments involving the use of behavioral techniques in institutional settings. The possibility of generalizing these specific findings for broader application is emphasized. In addition, seven requirements for the design of institutions according to behavioral principles are suggested and explained.

Introduction of Behavior Modification into Institutions

EARLIEST EXPERIMENTS

One of the first studies was Fuller's (1949) utilization of operant conditioning with an 18-year-old inmate who was classified as "feeble-minded" and whose behavior was that of a "vegetative idiot." Using a warm, sugar-milk solution as the reinforcing stimulus, Fuller was able to condition arm movement responses in only four sessions.

In the late 1950s and early 1960s, Lindsley (1957, 1963) employed the free operant conditioning paradigm to study psychotic behavior. Isaacs, Thomas, and Goldiamond (1960) reported the application of operant conditioning to reinstate verbal behavior in two institutionalized "psychotics, classified as schizophrenics, who had been mute for 19 and 14 years [p. 202]." Wolf, Risley, and Mees (1964) used operant conditioning techniques to modify the behavioral problems of an institutionalized autistic child.

> By manipulating the consequences of the behaviours, we concurrently developed techniques for dealing with Dicky's tantrums, sleeping and eating problems, for establishing the wearing of glasses, and appropriate verbal and social behaviour. . . . According to a report from the mother six months after the child's return home, Dicky continues to wear his glasses, does not have tantrums, has no sleeping problems, is becoming increasingly verbal, and is a new source of joy to the members of his family [pp. 188–93].

Since the time of Fuller's experiment, many other empirical studies in institutions have provided evidence of effectiveness of behavioral techniques for modifying a variety of behaviors (Davidson 1969; Paul 1969; Sherman and Baer 1969). The work of Ayllon et al. has been particularly important for demonstrating the utility of behavioral technology in mental hospitals (Ayllon 1963, 1965; Ayllon and Haughton 1962; Ayllon and Michael 1959; and Haughton and Ayllon 1965). By the use of contingent reinforcement, extinction, and stimulus satiation, the investigators were able to modify several chronic problems, such as stealing, hoarding, excessive dressing (Ayllon 1963), entering the nurses' office, psychotic talk, and refusal to eat (Ayllon and Michael 1959).

TOKEN ECONOMIES

Another significant advance is seen in the development of systematic programs of behavioral change at a small-unit level. Called "token economies" (Paul 1969), these unitwide technologies have been instigated in a variety of settings, including the classroom (O'Leary and Becker 1967; Bushell, Wrobel, and Michaelis 1968; Wolf, Giles, and Hall 1968; O'Leary et al. 1969; Zimmerman, Zimmerman, and Russell 1969; Miller and Schneider 1970), institutions for the mentally retarded (Lent, Le Blanc, and Spradlin 1970), institutions for delinquents (Cohen, Filipczak, and Bis 1967; Cohen 1968; Phillips 1968; Bailey, Wolf, and Phillips 1970; Findman 1968; Burchard 1969), and mental hospitals (Ayllon and Azrin 1965, 1968; Schaefer and Martin 1966, 1969; Atthowe and Krasner 1968).

A token economy utilizes symbolic objects (for example, coupons, chips, points), which can be accumulated and exchanged for items of real value. Tokens serve as conditioned secondary reinforcers "much in the way money does in a natural economy [Paul 1969, p. 88]."

Krasner (1970b) has suggested that establishment of an effective token economy requires at least three conditions. First, the behaviors that will be reinforced and will earn a token must be clearly designated. "This involves clear value determination on the part of the behavior modifier as to what are desirable behaviors." Second, the token itself must be an object that has an obvious degree of value. It should openly "stand for" something else and have strong, backup reinforcers. Examples of tokens include ". . . small cards shaped like credit cards . . . small metallic coins, marks on a piece of paper or even green stamps." Finally, the tokens should lead to privileges and rewards that are desirable to a given individual. Backup reinforcers can ". . . range from food to being able to sit peacefully in a chair [p. 95; see also Krasner 1970a]."

Ayllon and Azrin (1964, 1965, 1968) established a token economy on a closed ward in a state mental hospital and were able to foster considerable behavior change among chronic psychotic patients. Schaefer and Martin (1966) used a token economy with hospitalized female schizophrenic patients who were judged to show varying degrees of apathy. The experiment compared a treatment group and control group, both of which were required to use tokens to fulfill their daily wants and needs. The control patients received tokens on a noncontingent basis; each patient was given each morning "a sufficient number of tokens to see her through that day [p. 85]." The treatment group could obtain tokens only for the emission of positive behaviors relating to personal hygiene, social interaction, and adequate work performance. Baseline measures indicated no initial differences between the two groups. A significant decrease in apathy for the treatment group was reported. No significant changes occurred for the control patients. It was also found that patients in the experimental treatment group had a lower rate of rehospitalization, which suggests that token economy procedures can have effects that are long range and lasting.

Atthowe and Krasner (1968) instigated a systematic contingency program for chronic psychiatric patients who were exhibiting many signs of "institutional behavior"; i.e., they rarely left the ward and spent most of their time sleeping. The goal of the program was to change these habitual patterns and to "foster more responsible, active, and interested individuals who would be able to perform the routine duties associated with self-care, to make responsible decisions, and to delay immediate reinforcement in order to plan for the future [p. 90]." It was concluded that the introduction of the token economy brought about "a significant increase in those behaviors indicating responsibility and activity [p. 92]." There was improvement in self-care activities such as showering, shaving, and appearing neatly dressed, and many of the "ward problems" that had previously required the presence of extra aides (for example, refusal to get out of bed) decreased in frequency. There were also significant increases in social interaction, communication, and attendance at group activities. A special program was developed for the 12 bedwetters on the ward and "at the end of the experimental period no one was wetting regularly [p. 93]." The most dramatic outcome was revealed in the number of patients who were able to earn passes and hospital discharges.

> Of the core sample of sixty patients, 80 percent had never been off the hospital grounds on their own for a period of eight hours since their hospitalization. During the experimental period, 19 percent went on overnight or longer passes, 17 percent went on day passes, and 12 percent went out on accompanied passes for the first time. . . . Twenty-four patients were discharged and eight were transferred to more active and discharge-oriented ward programs as compared to eleven discharges and no such transfers in the preceding 11-month period [p. 93].

These studies are representative of the growing number that have demonstrated the effectiveness of contingent reinforcement in token economies to bring about significant behavioral change in the direction of institutional goals. They were successful largely because they were able to "incorporate every phase of ward and hospital life within a systematic contingency program [Atthowe and Krasner, p. 90]." But all of these social engineering efforts have been limited to one unit or ward. A logical next step is to speculate on how the behavioral perspective might be applied to the institution as a whole.

TOTAL INSTITUTIONAL PLANNING

The objective of rehabilitative institutions is to foster in residents the prosocial behaviors required for successful functioning in society. This socializa-
ton task has two basic components: (1) the acquisition or strengthening of
behaviors necessary for successful social performance; and (2) the elimination or reduction of behaviors that interfere with social functioning; of particular concern are aversive behaviors—i.e., behaviors that evoke social
sanctions such as institutionalization or negative social evaluations. It is not
uncommon for institutions to neglect one of these tasks in favor of the other.
Psychiatric institutions, for example, often attend most to elimination of
"sick" behavior and give less systematic effort to the acquisition of prosocial
behaviors. Schools, on the other hand, tend to concentrate on instilling positive behaviors and can only minimally cope with antisocial activity.

The behavioral approach to institutional planning stresses analysis of both
desirable and undesirable behaviors. The goals, therefore, focus on systematically influencing not only the elimination of undesirable behaviors but
also the acquiring and strengthening of prosocial behavior repertoires. Clarification of specific goals is essential to the design of the system. Careless
planning can lead to inadvertent reinforcement of behavior that is counter to
institutional goals. For example, Madsen et al. (1968) found that in classroom situations the teachers' attending to disruptive behavior increased the
frequency of that behavior.

Other studies also have demonstrated the adverse consequences of institutional planning that is not systematic and fails to account for all contingencies. Many correctional facilities, for example, have been unable to supersede the powerful influence of resident peer groups and subcultures. In
three pilot studies that "identified and measured social reinforcers occurring
among inmates and staff in institutions for delinquent children," it was
found that the peer group tended to reinforce delinquent behavior and punish socially conforming behavior, while the staff tended to indiscriminately
reinforce and punish delinquent behavior (Buehler, Patterson, and Furniss
1966, p. 324). It was hypothesized "that the inmate behavioral system not
only shapes and controls its own members but also shapes and controls the
behavior of the staff [p. 323]." The peer group was more influential than
the staff in arranging the conditions leading to the acquisition, performance,
and maintenance of behavior. It was concluded that a major problem for institutions is "to identify and to establish controls over the behavior occurring
in peer groups which keep the group resistant to institutional treatment
objectives [p. 332]."

A study of the interaction patterns of six chronic psychotic patients is indicative of the inconsistency of the reinforcements and reactions offered by
staff members. The patients' inappropriate behavior was frequently reward-

ed by nurses and nursing assistants; prosocial behavior was inadquately rewarded and psychotic activity was reinforced on an intermittent basis (Gelfand, Gelfand and Dobson 1967). Patients are confused by such inconsistency. They are unable to distinguish the desirable from the undesirable and cannot acquire the incentive to modify their actions.

Institutional planning that does not facilitate staff consistency and peer group control can lead to the establishment of multiple and competing reinforcement contingencies for residents. Behavior change either does not occur or occurs in a direction counter to institutional goals.

The experimental evidence indicates that behavior modification principles, when carefully applied, can enable the systematic structuring of institutional arrangements so that significant and favorable behavioral change will be fostered. Although major alterations in structure are required for the introduction of behavioral technologies, total institutions offer an ideal environment for the instigation and direction of a treatment regime that will influence all of the features of the residents' inadequate functioning. This paper posits seven guidelines, extrapolated from the behavior modification research and literature, which could be used for the design of treatment programs on an institutionwide basis. The guidelines are interrelated and overlapping and, when combined, propose a strategy composed of the following principles.

1. Institutional goals should be specific and behavioral.

2. Institutional arrangements must provide an opportunity for the acquisition and strengthening of prosocial behaviors.

3. Institutional arrangements must provide means for the reduction or elimination of undesirable behavior.

4. Control of consequences should be delegated to staff who have the greatest contact with the residents.

5. Staff behavior should be managed by behavioral principles.

6. Institutional planning should allow for steps or levels that increasingly approximate the desired behavioral outcome.

7. Institutional care systems should develop means to assure generalization of behavior change on return to the community.

Each of these principles is discussed and elaborated below.

Institutional goals should be specific and behavioral. Goal setting should be undertaken from the time of the residents' admission to the institution and should be an integral part of the initial problem assessment. One of the most common shortcomings of traditional treatment is a failure to establish goals directly related to the assessment process used in intervention planning. Moreover, if goals are conceptualized only in broad, general terms, and if they refer primarily to unobservable, inferred pathology, they will be relatively useless for directing the course of treatment.

The behavioral approach requires the specification of objective goals that point to distinctive, observable units of behavior. The substance of target behaviors will, of course, vary depending on the type of institution and the composition of the resident population;[3] however, the *specificity* of goals is always essential.

Ross (1967) suggests that neglecting to delineate specific criteria can lead to program failure.

> . . . attempts to make reinforcement contingent on behavior which is assessed other than by specific responses is unlikely to meet with success. We frequently found evidence . . . that the more global or general the behavioral criteria used on rating scales or other devices, the less control and modification of behavior was achieved. Employing categorizations of responses into broad classes (e.g., personal hygiene, intimacy) was much less effective than employing specific responses (e.g., bathing, physical contact) [p. 19].

Goals are both long range and short term. Long-range goals refer to the desired *terminal* behavioral repertoires and can be conceptualized in fairly broad categories (for example, acquiring adequate communication skills, ability to maintain self-care and personal hygiene, elimination of hallucinatory or psychotic production). The terminal repertoires, however, are the product of complex modes of behavior and require the learning of many different responses.

Short-term objectives refer to *instrumental* goals that specify the intervening tasks necessary to the acquisition of terminal behaviors. The desired end state can usually be reached only through a sequential series of intermediate steps or levels. These subgoals, which are also important ends in themselves, will eventually be accumulated and combined into increasingly complex behavioral patterns. Thus, for example, the acquiring of "personal hygiene skills" might represent the learning of a composite of discrete behaviors such as showering, dressing, and shaving.

Both terminal and incremental goals can be addressed to the acquisition of positive behaviors or to the elimination of negative behaviors. The tasks of behavior removal and behavior acquisition are wholly separate and must be dealt with individually. It is erroneous to assume that the elimination of an undesirable behavior will automatically lead to the performance of a positive behavior. For example, if the aim is to instill eating etiquette it may be necessary to discourage activities such as eating with the hands, food throwing, and spilling (behavior removal), and to encourage such behaviors as proper use of utensils (behavior acquisition). Many treatment programs are so preoccupied with the elimination of pathology that they neglect to stimulate and maintain normal behavior (Stuart 1970); consequently, residents may be unable to acquire many positive behaviors and, even worse, may fail to maintain some of the desirable functioning they exhibited at the time of their admission. Such "institutional degeneration" can be prevented only through the specification and fulfillment of goals that consider both the abnormal and the normal.

Careful goal setting can offer an additional advantage to the institution by providing a built-in mechanism for evaluating and monitoring the effectiveness of the program. The degree to which goals are attained can be easily measured and assessed empirically if the rules of goal specificity have been followed. Such data provide important feedback and suggestions for making improvements in the program.

Institutional arrangements must provide the opportunity for acquisition and strengthening of prosocial behavior. At the time they are admitted to institutions, most residents display marked deficits in the scope of their functioning. These gaps in the behavioral repertoire point to specific skills that must be acquired in order to function adequately. Behavior acquisition requires the identification and learning of behaviors that for the most part are entirely new to the resident.

Behavior Acquisition. Three major paradigms can direct the acquisition of behavior. The *respondent conditioning paradigm* suggests that learning will occur when a neutral stimulus (for example, a bell) is paired with an unconditioned stimulus (food). All unconditioned stimuli elicit automatic (unconditioned) responses (food promotes the response of salivation). The neutral stimulus, when consistently paired with the unconditioned stimulus, will eventually produce a similar response.

| Unconditioned stimulus (food) | → | Unconditioned response (salivation) |
| Neutral stimulus (bell) | → | Conditioned response (salivation) |

The respondent conditioning paradigm demands considerable technical control for implementation at a complex level. It is perhaps best used for the induction of simple responses in a single individual.

The *operant conditioning paradigm* is also somewhat impractical for widespread institutional use because it requires extensive individual time and attention. The paradigm dictates a series of shaping and differential reinforcement procedures through selective reinforcement of behaviors that increasingly approximate the final behavior desired. Complex chains and patterns of behavior can be built or new behaviors can be developed from simple elements. More specifically, the operant conditioning paradigm offers two techniques that can be applied to a range of behavioral deficits: priming and nonsocial cuing procedures.

Priming can be either verbal or nonverbal. Nonverbal priming refers to the use of physical guidance in the making of a response. A reward is given as soon as the response is completed. The physical assistance is combined with verbal instructions and can be gradually faded as the response comes under verbal control. Physical priming is particularly helpful with children and with such problems as mental retardation and autism (Lovass 1966). Verbal priming concerns the use of verbal instructions to explain the consequences that behaviors will produce (Baer and Wolf 1970a, 1970b) and is an integral feature of token economies (see, e.g., Phillips 1968; Ross 1967; Martin et al. 1968).

Verbal priming will be effective only if the consequences are carefully clarified and consistently applied. One study compared the effects of positive reinforcement, verbal priming, and priming-plus-reinforcement on mental patients' picking up eating utensils. It was found that verbal instructions alone are more effective than reinforcement alone; however, instructions-plus-reinforcement were the most effective with all patients (Ayllon and Azrin 1964). Verbal prompting requires that the necessary response exist somewhere in the patient's repertoire, if only in a rudimentary form; otherwise, the verbal instructions are likely to be meaningless.

Nonsocial cuing procedures offer another path to response evocation (Bandura 1969a). A nonsocial stimulus that can exert strong control over a desired response is initially used (for example, light or sound). This discriminative stimulus is paired with more natural stimuli (verbal instructions), and the response is rewarded. The nonsocial stimulus is gradually diminished as the response becomes linked to the social cue. Nonsocial cuing can be especially beneficial for socially unresponsive individuals who need to develop behaviors that are requisites for social learning.

The *observational learning paradigm* appears to have the greatest utility for institutional settings because it allows for group interaction. It is concerned with *modeling* and *vicarious* procedures—one of the most fundamental means of response acquisition and transmission (Bandura 1969a, 1969b). Within the institution, the staff and the residents may serve as models that a patient will emulate. Through his observations of others, the resident may be able to *(a)* identify and adopt entirely new or novel behaviors; *(b)* inhibit or modify behaviors by noting the consequences of the model's actions; and *(c)* make finer discriminations among responses already learned in a rudimentary form (Bandura 1969a).

Exposure to modeling stimuli can result in a shortened and accelerated response acquisition process, especially when the incentives for response acquisition are high. This is central to institutional design since

> virtually all learning phenomena resulting from direct experiences can occur on a vicarious basis through observation of other persons' behavior and its consequences for them. . . . Modeling procedures are, therefore, ideally

suited for effecting diverse outcomes including elimination of behavioral deficits, reduction of excessive fears and inhibitions, transmission of self-regulat-
ing systems, and social facilitation of behavioral patterns on a group-wide
scale [Bandura 1969*a*, p. 118].

Behavior Maintenance. Acquisition of behavior does not guarantee
continued performance (Bandura 1965*b*). Once acquired, behaviors must
be maintained and strengthened through procedures that serve to supplement and reinforce the acquisition techniques. Most maintenance procedures involve an ongoing management of environmental consequences.
Highly positive consequences are required in order to sufficiently strengthen
a newly learned response. The impact of positive reinforcement is dependent
on *(a)* the temporal sequence; and *(b)* the reinforcement schedule.

Temporal aspects refer to the timing of the presentation of the consequence. Most behaviorists agree that performance is best strengthened if the
reward is presented *after* the successful completion of the response (Baer
and Wolf 1970*b*; Burchard 1967; Ayllon and Azrin 1965). One study noted
a severe decrement in job performance when patients in a mental hospital
were reinforced in advance of their work rather than on the basis of work
completion. Therefore, consequences should be clearly contingent on response completion.

Temporality also pertains to the amount of delay between the completion
of the desired response and the presentation of the consequence. Experimental research has shown that as the time interval between response emission and consequence delivery increases, behavior control decreases. A time
lag allows the relationship between the response and the consequence to become ambiguous. Time delays also increase the risk of mistakenly reinforcing an untoward intervening behavior. Therefore, most responses should be
immediately reinforced; however, Bandura (1969*a*) has suggested that *verbal instructions* can sometimes be applied to mediate a delay in the presentation of consequences.

> Although relevant experimental evidence is lacking, there is every reason to
> expect from informal observation that, in the case of humans, symbolic activi-
> ties can effectively mediate a delayed reinforcement contingency without any
> appreciable loss of behavior control. Therefore, if contingencies are explicitly
> defined for an individual, he is able to link eventual consequences with partic-
> ular performances. Verbal mediation will, in all probability, eliminate irrele-
> vant responses even though a considerable time may elapse between perform-
> ance of the requisite behavior and its consequences [p. 231].

Since time delays are an inevitable feature of the environment outside the
institution and must eventually be somewhat tolerated if adequate functioning is to be restored, it is worthwhile to apply verbal mediation wherever
possible. But it is likely to be successful only when there is a past learning
history of delayed reinforcement—an assumption that is only slightly tena-

ble with most institutional residents. In particular, verbal mediation should not be attempted with "young children, grossly deviant adults whose behavior is under weak stimulus control, and individuals whose efforts extinguish rapidly under delayed reinforcement contingencies [p. 232]."

In addition to temporal considerations, the *reinforcement schedule* is also crucial to the management of consequences. Experimental work with animals has indicated that the schedule of consequence delivery can dramatically affect the rate of behavior occurence and the degree of future maintenance. The most influential scheduling effects are continuous reinforcement and intermittent reinforcement.

Continuous reinforcement involves rewarding a behavior every time it occurs and is generally effective in producing and maintaining high response rates. Continuous schedules are especially useful for building complex behavioral repertoires because each element can be maintained while others are gradually added. The satiation that sometimes results from continuous reinforcement can usually be prevented if secondary reinforcers (such as tokens, or points) are used to gain access to other rewards.

If the continuous schedule is stopped, most responses will rapidly cease. However, the danger of extinction can be overcome if the continuous reinforcement is slowly reduced until the behavior can be maintained by *intermittent reinforcement*. Intermittent schedules can improve on continuous schedules because they "produce greater resistance to extinction, are more efficient in terms of reinforcement cost per response, and reduce the likelihood of satiation during training [Kanfer and Phillips 1970, p. 269]." Another advantage is that intermittent schedules are more like those found outside the institution and will reduce difficulties in the transition from institutional settings to community life. Kanfer and Phillips (1970) have stressed the importance of scheduling effects in treatment planning by the behavior therapist.

> . . . schedule effects have important clinical implications. The behavior therapist must look for schedule changes as possible precipitating factors for his client's problems. In training new behaviors and in providing for transition from clinic or hospital to the client's usual daily world, the therapist must engineer appropriate schedule effects. He may elect to use changes in schedule as 's' treatment *method*, or he may develop in the client an ability to operate on new schedules as 's' treatment *target* [p. 272].

Incentives.   Techniques of behavior acquisition and behavior maintenance are extremely dependent on the establishment of a powerful incentive system. Reinforcers must be sufficiently influential and durable "to maintain responsiveness over long periods while complex patterns of behavior are being established and strengthened [Bandura 1969a, p. 225]." It has been demonstrated, for example, that appropriate incentive systems will allow young children to maintain responsiveness while engaged in complex learning activities (Staats 1965) and will enable hyperactive children to concentrate on task-oriented projects (Levin and Simmons 1962).

Examples of typically high incentive systems are token economies and Premack's (1965) differential probability design. Used as conditioned reinforcers, tokens tend to maintain their incentive potential because they can always be used to purchase other valued items. Premack's differential probability hypothesis states that a behavior that has a high probability of occurrence will serve as a reinforcer for a behavior that has a low probability of occurrence. In other words, a behavior can be reinforced (increased in frequency) if it is followed immediately by another behavior that occurs more frequently in the individual's repertoire.

Such extrinsic incentives are vital to the initial establishment and maintenance of behaviors. However, if the institution is to succeed in rehabilitation it must be able to transmit many behaviors that will not be maintained by extrinsic rewards outside the care system. Therefore, planning must include the gradual reduction of extrinsic reinforcement and an introduction of social rewards and self-monitoring reinforcement systems; only then can generalization of behavior change be somewhat assured.

Organizational Features. The contingency system of an institution must be organized to effect the behavior modification of a large number of people. Of necessity, the system needs to be efficient and pragmatic as well as effective in meeting the individual and group needs of the residents. The institution must be able to offer a balance of programs that attend to the individual and to the group as a whole.

The development and use of conditioned reinforcers with fairly uniform terminal repertoires allows implementation on an institutionwide basis. The structure and goals are uniform, but the residents are reinforced on an individual basis for emitting desirable behaviors. This is no more than an extension of the token economy throughout the facility. Within the broad organizational structure it is also possible to establish special contingency programs for individual patients.

Other programs can be addressed to groups and subgroups within the setting. These have the obvious advantage of efficiency but can also be remarkably effective. Cross-cultural studies have indicated the powerful influence that groups can exert on individual behavior (Bronfenbrenner 1970) and have suggested the use of group contingencies—i.e., reinforcement for all group members being dependent on group performance. One study (Wodarski et al. 1971) used an experimental design to compare the effects of individual contingencies, group contingencies, and two reinforcement contingencies (composed of different proportions of individual and group reinforcement) on arithmetic performance, studying, disruptive behavior, and helping behavior. As the proportion of group reinforcement increased, a learning situation was created "in which the better pupils in a group helped the slower pupils, where the students generally studied more and where the acquisition rates of most benefited as a result [p. 10]." There is other beginning evidence that group contingencies—or some modified form of group contingencies—can be a planned part of the organizational structure of the institutional program and can effect significant behavior change (Patterson et al. 1969; Brown and Tyler 1968).

Institutional arrangements must provide means for the reduction or elimination of undesirable behavior. In addition to having marked behavioral deficits and gaps, institutional residents also tend to exhibit a wide variety of deviant and pathological actions. Hopefully, these deviances can be replaced and superseded by desirable functioning. But even if positive behaviors cannot be immediately instilled, a necessary fundamental goal is to work for the reduction and elimination of the undesirable behavior. Extinction and punishment are the primary mechanisms that can be used.

Extinction.   Extinction—the gradual elimination of a response—is fostered by withholding reinforcement. Repeated nonreinforcement tends to result in a decrease of the undesired response. The decrease in response rate is governed by factors such as the irregularity with which the behavior was reinforced in the past, the amount of effort required to perform it, the level of deprivation present during extinction, the ease with which changes in conditions of reinforcement can be discerned, and the availability of alternative modes of response (Bandura 1969a).

Behavioral theory assumes that an undesired behavior is being maintained because it is being reinforced; therefore, extinction first requires that these sources of reinforcement be identified and removed. If the behavior is being fostered by several sources, each must be removed in order to eliminate the response; otherwise, some form of the response is likely to continue whenever a reinforcement is available (Bandura 1969a). This is particularly difficult to do in institutional settings because reinforcement can emerge from many different staff members and from other residents.[4] Extinction also can be rendered ineffective if the sources of reinforcement are more potent than the sources of nonreinforcement.

Extinction already has been applied in a variety of institutional facilities with encouraging results. Ayllon and Michael (1959) used extinction to reduce psychotic verbal behavior in one female patient whose persistent psychotic verbalizations had resulted in considerable verbal and physical abuse from other patients. Extinction, combined with positive reinforcement for sensible talk, resulted in a significant decrease in psychotic behavior as well as a marked reduction in abusive attacks from other patients. Ayllon and Haughton (1964) used extinction combined with positive reinforcement to alter significantly the incidence of psychotic talk and somatic complaints in three hospitalized schizophrenic patients.

It is difficult to evaluate the contribution of extinction in behavior change because, as in the above studies, extinction is usually combined with positive reinforcement for incompatible response. Extinction results in a decrease of previously rewarded behavior, with an eventual emergence of alternative patterns of behavior, including responses for which the individual has been reinforced in similar situations in the past. Extinction alone should provide no difficulties for the change agent if the alternative forms of behavior are desirable. However, if the alternative behaviors are not desired, a situation in which many successive responses must be extinguished will occur.

Punishment. The use of punishment immediately raises ethical questions that cannot be ignored. Although the question is considerably clouded by misunderstanding and the emergence of pseudoissues, a number of strong objections have been made. Some of the objections are rooted in ethical guidelines (personal or professional) that state, in some form or other, that punishment is wrong because any infliction of discomfort is wrong. Punishment, it is argued, runs counter to the rights of any human being to maintain dignity, worth, and freedom. At this level the ethical dilemmas remain, by definition, unresolvable because the exact meaning and priority of cherished values are a matter of debatable interpretation. However, at another level the ethical questions can be viewed in terms of the extent to which the means are able to justify the ends.

Many behaviorists would argue that the long-range benefits of punishment far outweigh the possibilities—which are as yet unspecified anyway— of harm accompanying the method. On the other hand, it has been pointed out that the untoward effects of punishment should be constantly kept in mind precisely because the concept has so many negative connotations in a society where "survival of the human organism appears to be so completely dependent upon the maintenance of harmonious social relations [Azrin and Holz 1966, p. 441]." It is important to remember that behaviorists, as human beings and as professionals, are responsible to the same humanitarian tenets that guide all therapeutic endeavors. Punishment, like any method, can be used and misused in ways that go far beyond the intent of the theory.

In addition to ethical considerations, doubts have also been raised about the efficacy of the method. While there is no question that punishment can effectively eliminate a target behavior, there is some evidence that, at the same time, punishment may produce *side effects*. Side effects refer to unintended consequences, and the fact that they occur at all is indicative of the current lack of total understanding and control. However, it should be emphasized that punishment side effects are not necessarily undesirable. Many of the predictions about negative side effects and the inevitability of a neurotic outcome have not been borne out.[5]

Research has only begun to explicate the parameters of punishment and to explore side effects. However, at least two types of side effects have been noted. The first concerns the degree of generalization of the punishment-produced response suppression. Desired response suppression may occur with one stimulus condition but not with others because the patient is able to make discriminations among the stimuli. The extent to which discriminations can occur is evident from Risley's (1968) study on the use of punishment to reduce climbing behavior of an autistic child.

> The original direct effect of the punishment was restriction to the specific stimulus conditions of the presence of the experimenter in the laboratory room. After punishment, climbing occurred in the laboratory when the experimenter was absent, at home when he was present, but not in the laboratory in his presence, even when the shock device was absent [p. 32].

Risley countered this problem in the home by having the child's mother utilize punishment to reduce the climbing behavior to tolerable limits.

Lovaas and Simmons (1969) and Birnbrauer (1968) also found the effects of presenting aversive stimuli to be highly discriminative. To be effective, punishment must "guard against the formulation of discriminations—between responses, between a response at one time from the same response at other times, between situations, and between people [Birnbrauer 1968, p. 209]. Such discriminations can be countered through the utilization of punishment by differing people, in various physical locations and with various examples of the response class.

The second and most significant side effect is that punishment sometimes facilitates the acquisition of new behaviors—which often may be highly desirable.

> In summary, this study showed that when punishment was used to eliminate a child's deviant behavior . . . (the) side effects were primarily desirable. Some deviant behaviors, maintained by unknown variables, interfered with the establishment of new behaviors. . . . This interference, which might be termed "functional incompatibility," suggests that the elimination of such deviant behaviors may be a necessary prerequisite to the establishment of new behaviors [Risley 1968, p. 34].

Lovaas and Simmons (1969) also report desirable side effects resulting from the use of punishment (shock) to eliminate severe self-destructive behavior in three retarded children. Elimination of the behavior resulted in an "immediate increase in socially directed behavior, such as eye-to-eye contact and physical contact, as well as the simultaneous decrease in a large variety of inappropriate behaviors such as whining, fussing and facial grimacing [p. 156]."

It has been suggested that many of the potential side effects can be eliminated or minimized by careful planning and constant program monitoring.[6] However, the range of applicability of punishment in institutional settings should be influenced by the outcome of future research on effects and side effects. In the meantime, punishment has been cautiously but effectively used in a number of ways. Results have been especially encouraging because punishment tends to be most often applied to those individuals and problems that have proved highly resistant to other techniques but eventually responded well to punishment methodology.

Punishment can be achieved through the presentation of aversive stimuli and by the removal of positive reinforcers. *Aversive conditioning* involves the presentation of a negative stimulus immediately following the performance of an undesired behavior. Most of the clinical-experimental studies of the use of aversive stimuli have employed shock as the punishment and have dealt with subjects who had resisted all other treatment efforts, such as severely self-destructive children (Lovaas and Simmons 1969). Risley (1968) used shouting and shaking as the aversive stimuli to eliminate autistic rocking in a six-year-old girl. An advantage of aversive conditioning is that behaviors tend to be eliminated totally and very rapidly; a disadvantage is that a high degree of technical control is needed to achieve significant results.

Punishment by *removal of positive reinforcers* can be implemented either by removing the patient from a reinforcing situation (time-out) or by removing conditioned reinforcers contingent on performance of undesired behavior (response cost). *Time-out* will serve as punishment only if the environment is reinforcing. If the surroundings are aversive, physical separation will simply offer escape from a noxious environment and will serve to increase the response rate. This is frequently the result when schools attempt to punish truants through suspension or expulsion. In addition, the effects of time-out will tend to be temporary if the undesired behavior is self-reinforcing (Baer 1962).

Time-out has already proved worthwhile in institutions. It has helped reduce negative mealtime behaviors with mentally retarded children (Barton et al. 1970) and to control loud and abusive verbal behavior in a 58-year-old wheelchair patient in a state hospital (Bostow and Bailey 1969).

Bostow and Bailey (1969) report another clinical-experimental study in which time-out was used to control extremely aggressive behavior in a 7-year-old retarded boy who had been institutionalized for 18 months. His behavior had led to his being separated from the other children and tied to a doorway. The behavior-change program applied two-minute time-out periods, which were contingent on any aggressive behavior, and reinforcement for each two-minute period when no aggressive behavior occurred. A significant reduction in aggressive responses and a concurrent increase in prosocial behavior were facilitated. After the end of the experimental study, which encompassed only 30 minutes a day, the attendants were trained to use time-out and reinforcement. The attendants left the child untied for increasingly longer periods of time until after a week the child was no longer tied up at all. All the side effects of this mild punishment were desirable. The most significant change was improvement in interaction; the boy was occasionally observed approaching other children to hug and embrace them —behavior markedly in contrast to his previous aggressive behavior toward others.

Response cost is another way to facilitate the removal of positive reinforcers by setting a cost to the resident's engaging in undesired behavior. Response cost techniques are commonly used in token economies and can be readily adapted to any program of conditional reinforcement. Research has indicated that response cost can have a greater suppressive effect than time-out (Weiner 1962). Phillips (1968) reports several experiments on the use of response cost with predelinquent boys at a home-style community-based treatment facility. It was found that the charging of fines was much more effective than verbal reprimands in preventing such behaviors as aggressive verbalizations, tardiness, and refusal to go to bed. In a token economy for antisocial retardates, Burchard (1967) applied a combination of time-out and response cost to control a variety of antisocial responses, including stealing, lying, cheating, and fighting.

The institutional environment is readily amenable to the incorporation of punishment techniques. It is essential, however, that punishment be arranged as an integral part of the organization and that it be directed particularly toward those behaviors that led to institutional placement, rather than only to foster conformity to the setting. There is every reason to believe that careful planning and consistent monitoring can minimize—or even completely remove—the negative side effects that otherwise may emerge.

Control of consequences should be delegated to staff who have the greatest contact with residents. Staff functions and roles are central variables of institutional design. They need to be clearly designated and assigned, with attention to maximizing the use of staff abilities and skills. Contingency management and program monitoring are two of the most important staff functions.

Contingency management—that is, the dispensing of reinforcement and punishment according to the program design—will often be most productive if it is delegated to paraprofessional staff (e.g., psychiatric technicians, house parents) and even to nonprofessional staff (e.g., cooks, janitors). It is these individuals who tend to have the most frequent contact with residents and who carry the day-to-day responsibility of program implementation. While professionals must be used for general supervision and for applying techniques that require specialized training (e.g., desensitization), paraprofessionals can easily be instructed to apply the basic techniques. Expanding the use of personnel in this way not only improves the operation and consistency of the treatment program but also frees professional staff from routine tasks and contributes to a greater sense of involvement for both employees and residents. One token economy in a mental hospital has even demonstrated the feasibility of designating selected patients to serve as contingency managers (Kale, Zlutnick, and Hopkins 1970).

Monitoring of the program requires a continuous, systematic assessment of institutional effects and effectiveness and is essential to program improvement. Monitoring mechanisms can be incorporated into the overall design (e.g., measures that tap the degree to which the stated goals are reached). Monitoring is primarily a professional staff responsibility but should allow for the contributions and feedback of other staff and of residents.

Staff behavior should be managed by behavioral principles. It has been emphasized that a behavioral treatment program will be effective only to the extent that it is *consistently* and *totally* applied. Gaps and exceptions in implementation will weaken the impact and will lengthen and complicate the tasks of behavior change. Consistency requires the full cooperation and involvement of all staff members, particularly those staff who have the most frequent contact with residents. Maximal staff involvement can be facilitated—even at very large institutions—if the necessary mechanisms are built in from the outset as an integral part of the overall program design and of staff training procedures. Effective staff-oriented mechanisms can be developed according to the same basic behavioral principles that direct the treatment program.

Behavioral principles and technologies need not be restricted to the study and treatment of deviancy but can apply as well to the behavior of "normal" individuals. In particular, there is evidence to support the use of behavioral theory in designing institutional contingencies for maintenance of desired staff behavior (Ayllon and Azrin 1968). Bandura suggests that reinforcement helps direct normal behavior through informational feedback and incentive functions.

The sources for *staff incentives* are an obvious and natural part of any employment situation and can be readily adapted to a behavioral regime. Benefits such as salary increases, vacations and holidays, work-shift preferences, etc., can be offered in relation to job performance. The idea that effective job performance will be rewarded is an accepted expectation of most employment situations, instigation of behavioral methods allows for nothing more than a consistent and systematic application of this norm. A staff contingency system should ideally include all of the personnel levels and positions; even the administrators and program designers can be evaluated on the basis of the success of the program. Incentives for high-level personnel might include salary increases or paid attendance at professional meetings.

While the use of extrinsic incentives will inevitably optimize job performance, attention should also be given to the provision of opportunities for social and self-reinforcement. Job satisfaction and accomplishment will be fostered in an environment that enables the development of staff rapport and
communication. A contingency system that is completely extrinsic and applied without consideration of social factors entails a danger of inhibiting incentives for improvement and innovation; for if the risks associated with loss
of reinforcement are too great, incentives for changing the status quo will be
reduced. Therefore, it is important that opportunities for intrinsic reward be
fostered.

Informational feedback regarding job performance can be instrumental to
the maintenance of both staff consistency and staff improvement. Personnel
should know exactly what is expected of them, particularly in their role as
contingency managers for the treatment program (Ayllon and Azrin 1968).
Adequate feedback mechanisms are essential to the facilitation of ongoing
monitoring and evaluation of the staff and the program. Panyan, Boozer,
and Morris (1970) found that feedback helped nonprofessional hall personnel (in an institution for the mentally retarded) to improve their understanding and use of behavioral treatment techniques. Another study
emphasized the need for effective monitoring mechanisms, particularly when
residents are used as staff aides (Kale, Zlutnick and Hopkins 1970).

*The institutional care system should be designed according to categorical
steps or levels that increasingly approximate desired behavioral outcomes.*
Optimal behavioral learning involves the acquisition of complex behavior
patterns that tend to be a cumulative expression of simpler responses. Most
behaviors must be learned through a series of stages that represent successively closer approximations to the desired terminal repertoires. An institution can permit the gradual acquisition of repertoires if it is designed in
terms of hierarchical levels or phases. A higher level—defined by the greater complexity of behaviors it requires—will demand more responsibility
from the resident but will also provide more sources of reinforcement.

Each step must contain clear and specific behavioral goals. Movement
from one level to another is contingent on the quality and consistency of
performance at the prior level. Each phase should provide more opportunities for reinforcement in line with the greater responsibilities required of the
residents. This might include, for example, not only the privilege to earn
more tokens but also an increase in what can be purchased with the tokens.

Eventually the levels should begin to provide for movement from external
means of control based on tokens and extrinsic rewards to social reinforcement and self-regulation (Ross 1967; Martin et al. 1968). Kanfer (1970)
has summarized the importance of developing self-regulation and control.

Even during the early stages of the development of behavioral engineering techniques, it has become apparent that principles of modification based on the use of continuous environment control are insufficient for the treatment of most psychiatric problems, for long-range modification of social attitudes, or for improvement of educational techniques . . . the behavioral engineer . . . [is forced eventually] to rely on the actions of his subjects to maintain behavior changes, even when they have been initially obtained by direct environmental manipulation [p. 179].

Self-regulation is an ultimate goal because it is required for successful functioning outside the institution. It can eventually be fostered, along with other complex, prosocial behaviors, by providing in the advanced phases an environment that is as similar as possible to the external milieu. For example, at higher levels residents could be allowed to go into town shopping or to hold a job outside the institution.

Phase programs tend to encourage learning by means of modeling. The motivation to attend to peer behavior is high because it becomes obvious to the resident that improved behavior and learning will gain access to more sources of reinforcement. It has been suggested that phase programs serve a symbolic modeling function by describing appropriate behaviors for a given stimulus situation (Martin et al. 1968).

A use of phases has accompanied many token economies. Atthowe and Krasner (1968) instigated a carte blanche system for residents who were able to function independent of the token system. The residents were given the privileges of the token economy along with added benefits and greater status. Kale, Zlutnick, and Hopkins (1970) placed residents in project staff positions that required varying degrees of ability. Reinforcement was commensurate with the responsibilities required, and movement to more responsible positions was dependent on prior performance. Martin et al. (1968) found that with adolescents displaying extreme behavioral problems a phase system with sequential goals produced more significant behavioral change than an individualized token system.

Institutional care systems should develop means to assure generalization of behavior change on return to the community. A fundamental task of total-care institutions is to ensure the generalization of behavior change to the community situation. The problems associated with "bridging the gap" between the institution and the community are well known (Fairweather et al 1969; Paul 1969; and Stuart 1969, 1970). The acquisition of behavior in one stimulus situation will not guarantee its generalization to another stimulus situation; however, generalization will be more likely if: (1) the institutional environment is as similar as possible to the natural milieu; and (2) the transition from the institution to the community is made gradually.

Unfortunately, the specific stimuli that render complex situations similar or different are still relatively unknown to behavioral scientists. However, one variable that appears to be important is the *form* of the reinforcement. Token economies, for example, have shown considerable promise partly because of their similarity to the use of money in outside society; however, a behavior that the institution maintains by use of tokens will not be assured of generalization if it tends to be rewarded only by social reinforcement in the community. Hyperactive children can be taught to attend to schoolwork tasks if the incentives are powerful, but this attending behavior would not be maintained if there were an abrupt shift to a usual classroom environment where the primary reinforcements are social. Use of a step system involving a gradual transition from tokens to social or self-reinforcement would be more effective in producing permanent behavior change.

The influence of the differences between the institutional environment and the community also can be minimized if the institution maintains contact after the resident is discharged. The institution's involvement can be progressively decreased when adequate social functioning is demonstrated. Halfway houses, for example, permit residents to try out their newly acquired behaviors in the community environment while also receiving the support of professional staff and other residents. As soon as the new behaviors are found to be reinforcing, the need for maintenance activities will markedly decrease.

Other supportive living arrangements within the community are also possible. One study, conducted with newly released chronic mental patients, supports the potential for teaching ex-residents to live together compatibly in the community and to adjust to the declining contact of the institution. The sudy compared release to a "community lodge" with release to usual sites of after-care. The lodge plan provided for a decreasing amount of professional supervision until the patients were functioning autonomously. The lodge group was significantly higher in regard to length of stay in the community and maintenance of employment (Fairweather et al. 1969).

Most residents eventually return to the same milieu they knew prior to their institutionalization. Generalization of behavior change can be increased by training significant others in maintenance techniques. Wolf, Risley, and Mees (1964), for example, taught the mother of an autistic child how to maintain behavior changes in the home. Foster homes and other supportive living arrangements, where the community caretaker is taught how to maintain and strengthen desirable behaviors, also are feasible.

Conclusion

Many "unscientific legends" have persistently accompanied the development and growth of behavior modification (Solomon 1964). These myths usually suggest that behaviorism is somehow antihuman, a conclusion that tends to be made hastily and on the basis of remarkably insufficient information.

People are repelled, for example, by much of the behavioral terminology, by techniques like punishment, and by the fact that the field emerged originally from the study of animals. It is erroneously and irrationally assumed that the goals of scientific precision and technical control run counter to the values of human independence and freedom. In rebuttal it should be emphasized that behaviorists are subject to exactly the same ethical dilemmas and constraints that confront *any* therapists, including the problem of defining and separating the desirable and the undesirable, the need to determine treatment priorities, the decision to abandon one treatment mode and attempt something new, and so on. And there is always the danger, as with *any* method of influence, that behavioral techniques will be irresponsibly or inappropriately applied. When properly utilized, however, there is little doubt that behavioral principles serve a clearly humanizing rather than dehumanizing function.

First and most important, behavioral modification is eminently human because it is *effective* for the promotion, restoration, and maintenance of prosocial functioning; moreover, most evidence suggests that behavioral techniques work more rapidly and more lastingly than other treatment modalities. It should be noted that this encouraging success has been possible primarily because of the behavioral perspective's insistence on precision, specificity, and control.

The method is also humanizing because it completely avoids the need for diagnostic categorization, which tends to be an inevitable result of the use of traditional psychiatric nosology. Psychiatric labeling stamps people—often for the rest of their lives—with brands that are notably insufficient and impersonal. In addition, the labeling categorizes an individual on the basis of only a small fraction of his total behavior repertoire (Stuart 1970) and often tends to set the stage for attention to and reinforcement of these few behaviors (Bandura 1969a). The result is a perpetuation of the very problems that initially prompted the treatment.

More specifically, the application of behavior modification in institutional settings is pointedly geared to the restitution of functioning that will allow for productive life in the community. The aim is to break up the usual pattern of constant reentry to the institution. Enabling an individual to function adequately, comfortably, and independently is surely a worthwhile way to meet the needs for human freedom and dignity.

In calling for the total design of institutional systems according to behavior modification principles, the limitations in the level and scope of current knowledge are recognized.[7] Although the behavioral perspective has led to significant advances in the understanding and treatment of human problems, it does not claim to have all the answers. Contributions from experimental research and clinical work will undoubtedly offer modifications and supplements to the beginning guidelines suggested here.

NOTES

1. See, for example, Stuart (1969, 1970).

2. See, for example, Bandura (1969a), Kanfer and Phillips (1970), and Krasner (1971).

3. For example, different goals will be required for children, for adults, for the mentally retarded, for geriatric patients, and so on.

4. See Buehler, Patterson, and Furniss (1966), and Gelfand, Gelfand, and Dobson (1967).

5. See, for example, Azrin and Holz (1966).

6. See, for example, Bandura (1969a), Kanfer and Phillips (1970).

7. See, for example, Browning and Stover (1971).

20

On the Making of New Men: Some Extrapolations from Research

URIE BRONFENBRENNER

The group program is a people-changing instrument of the first order. Evidence is abundant, and we are even beginning to understand why it is and, in a limited way, how the forces impinging on the child in group care may be orchestrated to his advantage. In this chapter Bronfenbrenner explores the theoretical causes and practical implications of these powerful environments, beginning with a succinct review of the state of pertinent knowledge, then discussing the elements necessary for successful and positive impact, and ending with some ideas on how these may be achieved. While Bronfenbrenner does not address himself to total institutions per se, his requirements for the "making of the new men" explicate the elements necessary for successful group care. These include:

1. Powerful models (e.g. the kibbutz members in Chap. 15).
2. Social reinforcement (e.g. the attitude toward education in the Polish institution, Chap. 14).
3. Intensive relationships (e.g. the child-staff patterns of Re-Ed, Chap. 17).
4. Group forces (e.g. the impact of the healthy on the disturbed in the Feuerstein and Krasllowsky treatment in Chap. 18).
5. Superordinate goals (e.g. the kibbutz youth movement in Chap. 15).

Urie Bronfenbrenner. "On the Making of New Men: Some Extrapolations from Research." *Canadian Journal of Behavioral Science* 1: 4–24. This paper represents a condensed and revised version of the Blatz Memorial Lecture presented on 27 May 1968 under the joint sponsorship of the Institute of Child Study at the University of Toronto and the Department of Psychology of York University.

All of the successful settings described in the preceding chapters have these attributes although, to be sure, the point of emphasis varies, as it must, with the condition of the child and the capabilities of the environment. Clearly the operating social structures within which these conditions can be developed may vary widely. Among them, along with the capable family in an endowed milieu, is the competent group care program.

This paper deals with some results of research and their social implications. The research is concerned with a phenomenon which students of human behavior call *socialization*—the process through which the human biological organism becomes a social being, a member of a particular society, be it a slave in ancient Rome, a Canadian pioneer, a devout Soviet Communist, a poor white in the American South, a successful business executive, or that very special product of the socialization process—a child brought up in accordance with Blatzian principles.

In short, socialization is the process of becoming what society makes us —for better or for worse. Being socialized is not necessarily the same as being civilized. Nazi youths were also the products of a socialization process. The example is an instructive one, for it reminds us that the family is not the only possible agent of upbringing in a society. Groups of children and young people can serve as very powerful influences on the values and behavior of their members. The reminder is especially appropriate for the American scene, for studies of socialization in the United States (which comprise the great bulk of research on the topic) have, until recently, focused almost exclusively on the family as the agent of upbringing. In our own investigations, we decided to take into consideration not only the family but also the *peer group*—the other children with whom a youngster spends his time, both in school and out. The general research question we are investigating can be stated as follows: How do parents and peers influence the development of socially responsible behavior in childhood and adolescence?

In pursuing answers to this question, we decided to take advantage of an experiment of nature. Specifically, contemporary societies differ from one another in respect to the role of the family *versus* the peer group in the socialization of the child. In some, the family is an almost exclusive agent of upbringing, especially in early years. In others, both family and peer group play important but rather different roles. In others still, the peer group is given priority over the family as the major force for character development. Accordingly, we selected for study those societies which provided the sharpest contrasts in these respects in order to observe what differences, if any, appeared among the children growing up under these divergent arrangements. To reflect contemporary trends and ensure some homogeneity in the sample, we limited ourselves to modern urbanized cultures.

As an example of a relatively family-centred society, we chose West Germany; to represent the opposite extreme of heavy involvement of the peer group in the process of socialization, we picked two societies reflecting contrast patterns: England and the U.S.S.R. The former provided our closest approximation to what we called *autonomous peer groups;* that is, peer groups who were relatively independent of the adult society and who developed and enforced their own norms for the behavior of members. In contrast, the Soviet Union was selected as a society in which the peer group (or, in Soviet terms, the "children's collective") was deliberately formed, under adult guidance, to inculcate values and patterns of behavior regarded as socially desirable. Finally there are the familiar patterns of childrearing found in contemporary America.

In each of the nations in which we have worked it has been possible, with the collaboration of native colleagues, to conduct interviews, observations, and systematic experiments. In the case of the Soviet Union, we have been able to establish an exchange relationship between Cornell and the Institute of Psychology in Moscow with a scientist from each country visiting for periods of time in the other.

Making the New Soviet Man

To turn to some of the results of our studies, let us begin with the U.S.S.R. As already noted, the Soviet Union gives high priority to collective upbringing carried out in nurseries, boarding schools, and so-called "schools of the prolonged day," which offer essentially the same program as the boarding schools, but with pupils going home at about six in the evening. In all of these institutions, emphasis is placed on training in collective living and productive activity. Upon entry, at three months of age, infants are placed in group playpens with six to eight children in each. In the younger groups, there is one "upbringer" for every four charges. In addition to providing routine care, the upbringer carries out daily, with every child, special exercises designed to foster sensory, motor, mental, and social development. Particular stress is placed on teaching children to share and to engage in cooperative activity. Frequent reference is made to common ownership, "mine is ours, ours is mine." By 18 months the infants are said to be toilet-trained and are being taught to care for themselves (dressing, washing, feeding). As soon as the children are able to talk, they are given training in evaluating and criticizing each other's behavior from the point of view of the group. It becomes the upbringer's task to develop each "collective" into a self-reliant unit in which the members both help and discipline each other. At the kindergarten level, children engage in role playing of real-life social situations (store, doctor's office), and the collectives are assigned modest communal responsibilities (e.g., gardening, care of animals).

In the boarding schools and schools of the prolonged day, major emphasis is placed on vocational education, group competitiveness, and collective discipline. The principles and methods employed are those developed by the outstanding Soviet educator and social psychologist, A. S. Makarenko (1949), who in the 1920s and 1930s established dramatically successful programs for the psychological and social rehabilitation of juvenile delinquents. Specifically, each school offers an assortment of three or four types of vocational training (e.g., automotive mechanics, dressmaking, radio repair, computer programming) from which the student is required to choose a specialty in which he will receive daily instruction, first in the school shops and later on the job in an affiliated factory, institute, or farm. An equally prominent role is played by "socialist competition" between successive levels of collectives, first between the individual rows or "links," then between classes and schools, and finally between cities and local regions. The competition involves all phases of activity and behavior: academic work, sports, shop work, service projects, housekeeping, personal grooming, moral conduct. The overall status of each pupil is evaluated weekly by his peers, following standards and procedures taught by the upbringers. Since each child's status depends in part on the standing of the collective of which he is a member, it is to each pupil's enlightened self-interest to watch over his neighbor, encourage the other's good performance and behavior, and help him when he is in difficulty. In this system the children's collective becomes the agent of adult society and the principal source of reward and punishment. The latter typically takes the form of group sanctions expressed through public criticism and, ultimately, the threat of excommunication. The individual is taught to set the judgment of the group above his own and to subordinate his interests to that of the collective. In Makarenko's words, ironically expressed in a familiar cadence, the child is to be brought up "in the collective, by the collective, and for the collective."

An especially prominent feature of collective upbringing is the emphasis on altruistic behavior at both the individual and the social level. Not only are the members of the collective taught to help each other but, through a system of what might be called "group adoption," each class takes on responsibility for the upbringing of a group of children at an earlier grade level. For example, a seventh-grade class "adopts" a third-grade class in the same school; the older children escort the younger ones to school, play with them in the schoolyard, teach them new games, read to them, help them with schoolwork—in general act as older brothers and sisters. Moreover, the manner in which they fulfill this civic responsibility enters into the evaluation of their total school performance as a regular part of the curriculum. Finally, the system of "adoption" embraces adult collectives outside the school so that each classroom may also be a "ward" of a shop in a factory or a bureau of a municipal agency with the workers devoting their spare time to activities with or in behalf of "our class" at the neighborhood school. Such arrangements reflect the far wider involvement of the segments of the adult society in the lives of children than is common in our own country. Indeed, it is not an exaggeration to say that in the Soviet Union upbringing is a national hobby.

The Unmaking of the American Child

How do current trends in childrearing in America compare with Soviet developments? One obvious difference would appear to be our far heavier reliance on the family as the principal agent of childrearing. Specifically, given the prevalence of institutional upbringing in the U.S.S.R., one might conclude that American parents are closer to their children than their Russian counterparts. Paradoxically, our observations fail to support such a conclusion. Collective upbringing notwithstanding, emotional ties between Russian parents and children are exceptionally strong. Maternal overprotection, overt display of physical affection, and simple companionship between parents and children appear more pronounced in Soviet society than in our own. Although, because of longer working hours and time lost in shopping and commuting, Soviet parents may spend less time at home, more of that time appears to be spent in conversation, play, and companionship than in American families.

Nor is it only in comparison with Russians that American parents pay less attention to their children. In a comparative study of parental behavior in the United States and West Germany (Devereux, Bronfenbrenner, and Suci 1962) we found, somewhat to our surprise, that German parents not only disciplined their children more but were also more affectionate, offered more help, and engaged in more joint activities. The differences were especially marked in the case of fathers with "Dad" perceived as appreciably less of a "pal" to his kids than "Vati" to his "Kinder."

Still another difference between German and American upbringing appears when we look beyond the family to the peer group. One of the reasons that German parents are more salient in the lives of their children is that they have less competition from other sources of influence. The German child spends much of his leisure time in the company of his family, the American child in the company of his age-mates. Moreover, as has been indicated elsewhere (Bronfenbrenner 1967b), there is evidence that the latter tendency has increased markedly over recent decades. We live today in a society segregated not only by race and class but also by age. The children's hour has become the cocktail hour. Urbanization, child labor laws, the abolition of the apprentice system, commuting, centralized schools, zoning ordinances, the working mother, the delegation and professionalization of child care—all of these manifestations of progress have operated to decrease opportunity for contact between children and parents or, for that matter, adults in general.

Moreover segregation operates not only between children and adults; it characterizes relations between all the age groups. With the passing of the neighborhood school in favor of "educational advantages" made possible by consolidation, homogeneous grouping by age—and more recently by ability —has set the pattern for other activities so that from preschool onward a child's contacts with other children in school, camp, and neighborhood tend to be limited to youngsters of his own age and social background.

If we now compare current trends in childrearing in the United States with those taking place in the Soviet Union, we note both a major similarity and a striking difference. In both societies the peer group has gained increased importance as the context of socialization, but in the Soviet Union the peer group is systematically developed and guided by the adult society, whereas in the United States it is relatively independent of adult influences and standards.

What is the effect of this difference on the behavior and development of children in the two countries? Some light is shed on this question by an experiment which my Cornell colleagues and I recently carried out with school children in the United States and in the Soviet Union (Bronfenbrenner 1967a). Working with a sample of over 150 sixth-graders (six classrooms) in each country, we placed the children in situations in which we could test their readiness to engage in morally disapproved behavior such as cheating on a test or denying responsibility for property damage. The results indicate that American children were far more ready to take part in such actions. In addition, the effect of the peer group (one's friends in school) was quite different in the two societies. When told that their friends would know of their actions, American children were even more willing to engage in misconduct. Soviet youngsters showed just the opposite tendency. In their case, the peer group operated to support the values of the adult society, at least at this age level.[1]

Soviet children are of course not without their problems. To the Western observer they often appear unduly submissive and uncritical. But whatever these problems are, they belong to Soviet society and not our own, for our difficulties appear to lie in the opposite quarter. As we read the evidence, both from our own research and that of others, we cannot escape the conclusion that, if the current trend persists, if segregation by age remains unchanged, if the institutions of our society continue to remove parents, other adults, and older youth from active participation in the lives of children, and if the resulting vacuum is filled by the peer group, *we can anticipate increased alienation, indifference, antagonism, and violence on the part of the younger generation in all segments of our society—including the middle class as well as the disadvantaged*. The signs of this development are already seen in the sharp rise in rates of juvenile delinquency in recent years, with a substantial number of the offenders now coming from "good families." In short, the empirical evidence points to trouble ahead for American society, unless some changes are made to insure greater effectiveness in the process of socialization.

What kind of changes would be effective and feasible? What are the forces that shape human behavior and development, and how can these be utilized for constructive ends?

Principles and Possibilities

A review of the available research evidence in child development, social psychology, and related fields points to several general forms of environmental intervention which appear to be especially effective in influencing the behavior and development of children. These forms are conveniently discussed under five general headings: *(a)* the potency of models; *(b)* social reinforcement; *(c)* intensive relationships; *(d)* group forces; and *(e)* superordinate goals.

THE POTENCY OF MODELS

The implications of contemporary research in this area can be summarized in five general statements.

1. Behavior change can be facilitated by placing the child in an environment in which he is exposed to models exhibiting the desired pattern at a level which the child can emulate with some degree of success (Bandura and Walters 1963).

2. The potency of the model to induce behavior is considerably enhanced when the persons exhibiting the behavior are people with whom the child feels a strong emotional involvement, in particular his parents, playmates, and older children or adults who play a prominent role in his everyday life (Sears, Rau, and Alpert 1965; Bandura and Walters 1959; Clausen 1966).

3. Although mere exposure to the model exhibiting a new pattern of behavior can lead to the induction of that behavior in the child, the optimal condition for learning from a model is one in which the child is engaged in increasingly more complex patterns of reciprocal interaction with the model —for example, conversation that gradually invokes wider vocabulary and complexity of structure, or games involving progressive development of basic skills (Bronfenbrenner 1967c).

4. The inductive power of the model increases with the extent to which the model is perceived as having high status and control over resources. For example, experiments have shown that children are more likely to emulate a person who can grant presents or privileges than one who is the recipient of such benefits (Bandura, Ross, and Ross 1963).

5. The inductive effect increases markedly when the behavior in question is exhibited not merely by a single individual but represents a salient feature in the actions of a group of which the child already is or aspires to be a member. Thus the child will tend to adopt patterns of behavior that are prominently engaged in by his family, by his classmates, the neighborhood gang, older children whom he admires, and similar groups (Bronfenbrenner 1962).

SOCIAL REINFORCEMENT

The second strategy we consider does not require the presence of an external model although it can use such models to great advantage when they are available. In effect, this strategy uses the child's own behavior as a model to be improved upon through intensification and further development of that behavior. Specifically, by giving affection or approval, or by providing some other gratifying experience when the child exhibits the desired behavior (even if only in crude form), it is possible to increase the frequency and precision of that behavior on the part of the child.

As in the case of modeling, the potency of reinforcement is increased as a function of the child's emotional attachment to the person giving the reinforcement, so that once again the child's parents, friends, and intimate associates emerge, at least potentially, as the most important agents for motivating the child's behavior and development. And again, as in the case of modeling, the potency of the reinforcing agent increases with the extent to which he is perceived as having high status and control over resources.

But it is where reinforcement can be combined with modeling that it can have its maximal impact. One way of exploiting this joint effect is to employ reinforcing stimuli which simultaneously serve as models of the behavior to be learned. Thus one of the most efficient procedures for developing the young child's capacity for communication is to respond to his spontaneous utterances with ordinary conversation at gradually increasing levels of complexity. In the preceding example, the model and the reinforcer are the same person. But once a child becomes conscious of his social world, still another advantageous mix of these two strategies becomes possible. This is the technique of so-called *vicarious reinforcement* in which the person reinforced is not the learner (i.e., the child) but the model. Researchers have demonstrated, for example, that rewarding the model for exhibiting a particular behavior pattern increases the frequency of that behavior in a child observing the model (Bandura and Walters 1963). In addition, the reinforcing power of the model is also enhanced. In other words, if we wish to maximize the development of a particular skill or behavior in the child we do well to reinforce not only the child himself but also the models manifesting the desired behavior, who in turn would also reinforce the child. Note that such an optimal arrangement requires the involvement of at least three persons

—the child himself, a model, and a reinforcer. It is of course precisely this kind of triad that is found in the human family.

The foregoing comment calls attention to the importance of social context for the effective operation of such processes as modeling and reinforcement. In the following section we begin our consideration of this problem.

INTENSIVE RELATIONSHIPS

In our discussion both of modeling and reinforcement we noted that the most potent agents for each of these processes were persons with whom the child has developed intensive and enduring relationships—typically his parents, relatives, and other persons, both children and adults, with whom he becomes closely involved on a day-to-day basis. We consider next some evidence bearing on this issue and its implications for educational practice.

There is a substantial body of data demonstrating the powerful effect of parents as models in shaping the behavior and psychological development of the child (Sears, Rau, and Alpert 1965; Bandura and Walters 1959, 1963; Clausen 1966). The evidence is as eloquent in negative as in positive instances. Thus the difficulties of the disadvantaged child on entry into school have been traced by a number of investigators to lack of stimulation, both cognitive and motivational, in his home environment. But, at the same time, other studies show that where conditions permit forming and maintaining an intensive relationship with the child, even a presumably inadequate mother can do a great deal for the development of a seriously deprived child. The most dramatic evidence on this score comes from Skeels' (1966) remarkable follow-up study.[2]

This example carries a number of provocative implications for educational and social programs. To begin with, it suggests that insuring a high level of expertise in the persons dealing directly with the child may not be so critical for furthering the child's psychological development as creating possibilities for those who are potentially the most powerful influences in the child's life—his parents, friends, and immediate associates—to realize that potential.

Putting the issue in this way points up a serious problem. Some level of "expertise" on the part of the "teacher" is obviously essential if the child is to learn the skills, behaviors, and motives necessary to cope successfully with his environment. It is precisely these skills, behaviors, and motives that must be exhibited in the behavior of the persons surrounding the child and be reinforced by them. And the research ordinance indicates that this is precisely what *does not happen* in the day-to-day world of the disadvantaged child. His parents and other intimate associates typically do not exhibit an adequately high level of the behaviors and motives which the child most needs to learn. Nor do they sufficiently often reinforce such behaviors when they are exhibited by the child or by others in his environment. It is not only that the disadvantaged child may receive insufficient attention from his parents and other adults but that this attention is not appropriately discriminating. Often it is so generalized and diffuse as to have no impact in selective reinforcement; on other occasions it is differentially responsive not to the expressions of the child's constructive capacities (e.g., exploratory behavior, vocal expressiveness, curiosity) but to his passive reactions (praising him when he is quiet or inactive) or disruptive behavior (e.g., paying attention to the child principally when he is "making trouble").

This brings us to an important question. Is the problem that persons in the day-to-day environment of the disadvantaged child *cannot* engage in behavior appropriate to his needs because they lack the requisite ability or skill? Or are they capable of such behaviors but simply do not engage in them because they are not motivated to do so? Undoubtedly both considerations are operative to some degree, but the available evidence suggests that the second factor is much more important than the first. For example, we read in Skeels' account that the mentally retarded "mothers" in the institution "spent a great deal of time with 'their children,' playing, talking, and training them in every way. The children received constant attention and were the recipients of gifts; they were taken on excursions and were exposed to special opportunities of all kinds." Nor were the mothers themselves without models and reinforcers, for the ward attendants also spent "a great deal of time" with the children, and the matron in charge introduced "new play materials, additional language stimulation," and other special experiences.

In other words, given motivation, opportunity, and exposure to the kinds of activities that are enjoyable and instructive for young children, parents and other close associates of children from disadvantaged backgrounds can do a great deal to further the psychological development of the child in their midst.

There is a second and even more compelling reason for actively involving parents and other persons close to the child in educational programs. We have noted that models are influential not only in instigating new behavior patterns but also in determining which patterns already in the child's repertoire are activated and maintained and which are allowed to become extinguished. As the most powerful models for the child, parents and other intimate associates thus become not only the most important potential agents for bringing about change in the child's behavior but also the principal figures who maintain established patterns of activity (whether adaptive or nonadaptive) and who, in so far as they fail to expose the child to constructive experiences, prevent him from realizing his full potential. In short, it is the parents and other close companions of the child who are the primary determiners not only of what the child learns but what he fails to learn.

It follows that *any appreciable, enduring improvement in the child's de-*

velopment can be effected only through an appreciable enduring change in
the behavior of the persons intimately associated with the child on a day-to-
day basis.

How can such a radical change be brought about? For answers to this
question we turn to a second kind of social context in which the processes of
modeling and reinforcement can thrive—namely, a structure extending beyond an intensive relationship between two people to include groups of persons sharing a common identity.

GROUP FORCES

Recent research indicates that a child's classmates have far greater consequence for his development—intellectual, emotional, and social—than we
have hitherto recognized. For example, the Coleman (1966) report concluded that how well a child did in school depended less on the educational
facilities or the qualifications of the teacher than on the characteristics of the
child's schoolmates—that is, their abilities, interests, and aspirations. Subsequently, a further analysis of national survey data, cited in the 1967 report
of the United States Commission on Civil Rights, showed that the beneficial
effect for a disadvantaged child of being in a class with nondisadvantaged
pupils increased substantially with the proportion that such nondisadvantaged children represent of the class as a whole. Thus those disadvantaged
children who were gaining the most academically were attending classes in
which the majority of pupils came from white middle class families. Moreover, these gains were substantially greater than any attributable to teacher
characteristics or quality of instruction, a findng which led the authors of the
report to conclude that "changes in the social class or racial composition of
schools would have a greater effect on student achievement and attitude
than changes in school quality [p. 100]."

This conclusion provides but one illustration of the power of a group to
modify the behavior of its members. The result comes about not only because other class members serve as models and reinforcers of good performance but also because the child's dependence on the group, his desire to belong, serves as an additional motivating factor to behave like the others.

But what if the others are not performing or behaving very well? The
processes of modeling, reinforcement, and group pressure for conformity are
no less efficient. Nonadaptive or antisocial behavior is as readily communicated as competence or constructive action. For example, contrary to the
great conclusion reached by Coleman, Pettigrew (1967), in a special reana-
lysis of some of Coleman's data, showed that white children in predominantly Negro schools performed on the average below comparable white children in predominantly white schools; furthermore, "those white children in
predominantly Negro schools with close Negro friends" scored significantly
lower on tests of verbal achievement than white pupils in the same school

without "close Negro friends." Analogous effects are being found in the sphere of social behavior as well. In a study still in progress involving 40 sixth-grade classrooms in a large city, my colleagues and I at Cornell find that the willingness of the rest of the class to engage in antisocial behavior (such as cheating on a test) is significantly increased by the presence of a small lower class minority (in this instance all white).

In other words, a strategy that relies principally on introducing into the world of the disadvantaged child middle class models from whom he can learn runs the risk that these models themselves may be adversely affected by the experience, not only in terms of lowered academic but also of increased antisocial behavior. In short, social contagion is a two-way street.

The consequences of this proposition turn out to be equally troublesome as we return to a consideration of the already established social environment of the disadvantaged child—his family, friends, older companions. The amount of assimilable, competent, or constructive behavior which they typically exhibit may be far too small and heavily outweighed by nonconstructive or even negative elements.

Fortunately, what is typical is not thereby inevitable. In the case of older children and adults, where some competence and capacity for constructive action already exist within the behavioral repertoire, it is possible to increase substantially the amount of such behavior that is actually exhibited by structuring the social situation so that it invites and demands such behavior. Contemporary research suggests that such a change can be accomplished by utilizing the motivating power of what Muzafer Sherif (1958) has called "superordinate goals."

SUPERORDINATE GOALS

In the robbers' cave experiment Sherif and his colleagues (1956, 1961) demonstrated that it was possible to take groups of normal, middle class, 12-year-old boys and, within the space of a few weeks, bring about a series of contrasting changes in their behavior. First he transformed them into hostile, destructive, antisocial gangs. Then, within a few days, they were changed into cooperative, constructive workers concerned with and ready to make sacrifices for other members of the community. Sherif's principle for bringing about this second, constructive change was involvement in what he called a superordinate goal—an overriding problem extending outside the individual himself and requiring coordinated effort for its solution. For instance, shortly after hostile and destructive activities had reached their peak, Sherif announced to the boys, who were at a camp, that there was a leak somewhere in the water line and there could be no fresh water until the leak was found and repaired. Hatreds and hostilities were forgotten as the entire camp population cooperated to solve the problem.

An example more relevant to our concerns comes from a Head Start program operating in an urban slum. The problem was getting children to and from the center in a "tough" neighborhood. Since not enough parents were available at the needed hours, the staff turned for help to the local gang— the Golden Bombers. The resulting operation was a sight to behold as twice every day the Bombers in "snap formation" proudly conducted their charges through heavy traffic with "complete protection." What is more, after seeing what was going on at the center, they volunteered to help by reading to the children, taking them on outings, and other activities.

In our discussion up to this point we have repeatedly been confronted with the same problem: how to "turn off" the predominantly negative and counterproductive behaviors often exhibited by the most significant persons in the life of the disadvantaged child and to evoke, in their place, constructive behaviors of which these persons are actually capable. We now see that superordinate goals have the power of effecting exactly this kind of behavior change. Specifically, involving persons actually or potentially important to the child in pursuit of a superordinate goal can have the effect of maximizing the incidence and inductive power of constructive behaviors and motives while reducing disruptive and negative influences.

But is it possible to find a concrete superordinate goal that would have appeal for persons in the child's own environment and at the same time cut across such demonstrably divisive barriers as age, class, and color? We believe that such a common, potentially strongly motivating concern exists. That focus is the young child, especially the young child of poverty, whose need for help speaks out eloquently to all who see him. In other words we are proposing that if we turn to any existing or potential segment of this child's world—be it his immediate family, his actual or possible classmates, older children or adults from his own neighborhood or from the other side of the tracks—and ask their cooperation in activities in behalf of the child, the requested help will be given generously, competently, and conscientiously, provided the nature of the requisite activity is clear and lies within the capability of the individual or group of whom it is asked.

Concrete Proposals

We have now come to the point where we can suggest concrete proposals consistent with the principles outlined above.

Proposals are described under five headings representing the major contexts in which the child lives: *(a)* classroom, *(b)* school, *(c)* family, *(d)* neighborhood, *(e)* larger community. The order is not one of priority but simply of convenience for discussion.

THE CLASSROOM

The classroom contains two major sources for influencing behavior and development—the teacher and the children themselves.

1. Potentialities in the teacher's role.   Our discussion implies a broadened conception of the teacher's role. Not only must she herself function as a motivating model but *it becomes her responsibility to seek out, organize, develop, and coordinate the activities of other appropriate models and reinforcing agents both within the classroom and outside.* How this might be done will become apparent as we proceed.

2. The sociomotivational structure of the classroom.   Although modifications in classroom composition in terms of social class and race can be expected to make a significant contribution to the development of the disadvantaged child, they by no means represent the most powerful resources at our disposal. Indeed, their potential is realized only to the extent that they facilitate development of the motivating processes (modeling, reinforcement, group commitment, involvement in superordinate goals, and so on) outlined above. Such development need not be left to chance. It can be directly fostered through setting up within the classroom the kinds of social and situational structures in which these processes thrive: such devices as teams, group competition, and organized mutual help patterns, including the incorporation into such social units of different mixes of race, social class, sex, achievement level, and the like. In short, we must learn to make more effective use of group forces in fostering human development. The power of the group, including the children's group, in motivating goal-directed activity in its members is well established in American social research, but the practical implications of this principle for education have thus far remained unexploited in this country. Where practical applications have been made on a broad scale, as in the Soviet Union, the effects have been impressive (see Bronfenbrenner 1962, 1967*a*), but unfortunately they continue to be justified primarily on an ideological rather than an objective, empirical basis. It therefore remains for American educators and social scientists to reap the fruit of systematic application and evaluation of such promising innovations.

The potential of motivational structures will remain unplumbed and probably seriously underestimated, however, so long as the participants in such structures are limited to the members of the conventional classroom with its homogeneous age grouping. Full exploitation of the possibilities of motivational structures can occur only when one can move beyond the classroom into the larger contexts of school and neighborhood.

THE SCHOOL

Perhaps the most promising possibility which the total school offers in furthering the development of the child is the active involvement of older and, subsequently, younger children in the process. For the preschooler or primary-grader, an older child, particularly of the same sex, can be a very influential figure, especially if he is willing to spend time with his younger companion. Except for the occasional remaining one-room school, this potential resource remains wholly unexploited in American education and, for that matter, in the process of general socialization as it usually takes place in our country. Opportunities for experimentation are therefore legion. One might begin with an Americanized adaptation of the Soviet system of "adoption" in which every preschool or primary class is "adopted" by an older class. This example illustrates how an enduring social situation can be created which simultaneously exploits all of the motivating processes and social structures outlined earlier, for here the effects of modeling and reinforcement are enhanced in the context of intensive relationships, group membership, and common commitment to a superordinate goal.

An extension of this same principle points to a potential contribution of the school as a whole to the development of the individual child. Within the formal educational context, the school is the social unit with which the child, and those concerned for his welfare, can most readily identify. If the school as a total community becomes visibly involved in activities focused on the child and his needs, if older children, school organizations, other teachers, school administrators, PTAs, if all these persons and groups in some way participate in the program and publicly support those most actively engaged in the effort, the reinforcing effect increases by geometric proportions. Conversely, if a special program is confined to an isolated classroom, it is not only deprived of powerful reinforcing influences but risks the danger that the rest of the school, especially children in other classes, will perceive the "special class" in invidious terms (e.g., "dummies," "queers") and treat its members accordingly. When this occurs the powerful influences of modeling, negative reinforcement, and group pressure serve only to undermine the already unfavorable self-image of a "problem child."

Similar considerations dictate the necessity of involving the child's family in the school's total educational effort.

THE FAMILY

Although some educational programs (e.g., Head Start) profess strong commitment to the principle of family involvement, in practice implementation is limited to two rather restricted forms: the first is the inclusion of some parents on the program's advisory board; the second involves meetings for parents at which staff members make presentations about some aspect of the program. Both of these measures have the effect of bypassing the most important aspect of family involvement—engaging parents and older children in new and more mutually rewarding patterns of interaction with their children.

An essential first step in bringing about such changed patterns of interaction is exposure of the parent and other family members to them. This can be done at one of two places—at the educational center or in the home. The basic approach is one of demonstration, of showing the family the kinds of things that are done at the center which also happen to be things that family members can themselves do with the child—for example, games to play, books to read, pictures to look at and talk about. Particularly valuable in this connection are activities that involve and require more than one person in patterns of interaction with the child—that is, not just the teacher (i.e., mother) but also other adults and older children (i.e., father, grandmother, brother, sister). A useful technique is to ask the visiting or visited family members to help in carrying out particular activities with the child. It is important that the activity not be seen as a "lesson" with its ever-present threat of failure, but rather as an engaging activity in which learning is incidental to a total gratifying experience.

The involvement of family members in the educational program of course poses a difficult dilemma to professional staff. On the one hand, there is the need to expose parents and other family members to new or different ways of dealing with their children. On the other hand, this must be done in such a way as to enhance rather than lower the power and prestige of these persons in the eyes of the child. The second requirement arises from the evidence that the inductive and reinforcing capacity of a model varies directly with the model's status, command over resources, and control of the social environment. An ingenious demonstration of how this dilemma may be resolved was observed at an all-Negro Head Start and Follow Through program in the rural South. Since the local white-dominated school administration refused to have anything to do with the program, it was organized by Negro church groups under the leadership of an 86-year-old minister. Several days before the official opening of the program, this man invited all the parents and teen-agers to an orientation meeting—a pass-the-dish picnic in a nearby forest area (a forest which he himself had "planted" years ago with seeds obtained free from the United States Department of Agriculture). After the picnic, the minister offered to take the whole group on a tour of the forest. During the walk he would ask adults and teen-agers alike to show him interesting plants and animal life which they observed, give names of flowers, trees, and birds, explain how plants grow, what animals feed on, and so forth. While drawing out much information from the group, he also added considerable material from his own experience. At the end of the walk, he turned to the group with a request: "On Saturday we start our Head Start program. In the afternoon the children need some recreation and the teachers need a rest. Could you folks bring the children here and tell them all the things you know that they don't know about the forest?"

The turnout on Saturday was impressive, and so was the performance of the "instant experts."

NEIGHBORHOOD

The foregoing example also illustrates the reinforcing potential of the other people with whom the child frequently associates and identifies—his neighbors. These persons, particularly the adults and older children who are looked up to and admired by the young, probably stand second only to parents in terms of their power to influence the child's behavior. For this reason it would be important for educational programs to try to exploit this potential in a systematic way. The most direct approach would be to discover from the families and neighborhoods themselves who are the popular and admired individuals and groups and then to involve them as aides in the program. The activities must be constructive in nature and reinforce other aspects of the program. They may take a variety of forms: supervising and playing games, exhibiting or teaching a hobby or skill (whittling, playing a musical instrument, magic tricks). The significant factor is the activity be seen by the child as part of and supporting all of the things the child is doing "in school."

A second important use of neighborhood resources involves exposing the child to successful models in his own locality—persons coming from his own background who are productive members of society—skilled or semiskilled workers, teachers, government employees. Providing opportunities for such persons to associate with the children (e.g., as escorts, recreation supervisors, part-time aides, tutors), tell something about their work, and perhaps have the children visit the person at work can help provide a repertoire of possible occupational goals unknown to many children of poverty today.[3]

As the foregoing examples clearly indicate, many desirable activities cannot be carried out effectively if they are conducted only during school hours or solely in a school classroom. Accordingly, some kind of *neighborhood center* becomes a highly desirable feature of any comprehensive educational program. Such a center would have to be open after school, on weekends, and during vacations and would require staff members on duty at all times. The center should be represented to the community not merely as a place where children go but rather as one where all members of the community go in the joint interest of themselves and their children. The neighborhood center might be housed in a school building, but, if so, facilities available should include something other than traditional classrooms with fixed seats.

THE LARGER COMMUNITY

The contribution of the total community of educational programs is analogous to that of the neighborhood but now with representatives and resources drawn from the larger context. Use can be made of both older children and adults from middle class backgrounds provided they are not the only "competent" models on the scene, for without the example and support of "his own people" the child's receptivity to what may then be seen as an alien influence is much reduced. It follows that activities by persons or in settings from outside the child's subculture must be heavily interlaced with representatives from his own world who manifestly cooperate in the total effect. This in turn implies close working relationships of mutual respect between workers from within and outside the child's own milieu. Mutual respect is essential in these relationships not merely for the purpose of maintaining a viable learning atmosphere but more importantly to further the constructive development of the child's own sense of identity and worth as a person and as a member of society.

Finally, especially for the disadvantaged child, the greatest significance of the total community lies in the fact that many of the problems he faces and the possibilities for their solution are rooted in the community as a whole and are, therefore, beyond the reach of segmental efforts at the level of the neighborhood, the school, or the home. We have in mind such problems as housing, welfare services, medical care, sanitation, police protection, community recreation programs, and the like. Given this state of affairs, it is a sobering fact that neither in our communities nor in the nation as a whole is there a single agency that is charged with the responsibility of assessing and improving the situation of the child in his total environment. As it stands, the needs of children are parceled out among a hopeless confusion of agencies with diverse objectives, conflicting jurisdictions, and imperfect channels of communication. The school, the health department, the churches, welfare services, youth organizations, the police, recreation programs, all of these see the children of the community at one time or another, but no one of them is concerned with the total pattern of life for children in the community—where, how, and with whom they spend their waking hours and what may be the impact of these experiences on the development of the child as an individual and as a member of society. An inquiry of this nature would, we believe, reveal some sobering facts which in themselves would suffice to generate concerted action. Accordingly, an important aspect of the educational program at the level of the total community would be the establishment of a commission on children, which would have as its initial charge finding out how, where, and with whom the children in the community spend their time. The commission should include among its members representatives of the major institutions in the community that deal with children, but should also draw in businessmen and parents from all class levels as well as the young themselves, teenagers from diverse segments of the community who could speak from recent experience, for example. The commission would be expected to report its findings and recommendations to appropriate executive bodies and to the public at large.

We thus conclude our inquiry into models of socialization present and projected. In doing so, we must take cognizance of a new and as yet unfamiliar role for the scientist dealing with problems of human development. As his colleagues in the physical sciences have learned to do long ago, he must go beyond natural history to recognize and probe as yet unexploited theoretical possibilities and their practical applications. The present essay represents a modest effort to move toward this broader objective.

NOTES

1. See Chapter 13 for more details.
2. See Chapter 10.
3. In view of the frequency of father absence among disadvantaged families and the predominance of female personnel in educational programs generally, the involvement of male adults and teenagers is highly desirable, especially in the case of boys.

ADDITIONAL READING FOR PART VI

Ayllon, Teodoro, and Azrin, Nathan. *The Token Economy: A Motivational System for Therapy and Rehabilitation.* New York: Appleton-Century-Crofts, 1968.

Bandura, Albert. *Principles of Behavior Modification.* New York: Holt, Rinehart & Winston, 1969.

Baumrind, Diana. "Socialization and instrumental competence in young children." *Young Children* 26, 2 (December, 1970).

Caudill, William. *The Psychiatric Hospital as a Small Society.* Cambridge, Mass.: Harvard University Press, 1958.

Erikson, Erik H. "Youth: Fidelity and diversity." *Daedalus* 91, 1 (Winter 1962): 5–27.

Gewirtz, Hava B., and Gewirtz, Jacob L. "Visiting and caretaking patterns for kibbutz infants: Age and sex trends." *American Journal of Orthopsychiatry* 38, 3 (April 1968): 427–43.

Goffman, Erving. *Asylums: Essays on the Social Situation of Mental Patients and other Inmates.* New York: Doubleday, 1961.

Sherif, Muzafer, et al. *Intergroup Conflict and Cooperation: The Robber's Cave Experiment,* Norman University of Oklahoma Press, 1961.

Wheeler, Stanton. "The structure of formally organized socialization settings," in O. G. Brim, Jr. and S. Wheeler, *Socialization After Childhood: Two Essays.* New York: John Wiley & Sons, 1966.

Bibliography

Adler, A. 1964. *Social interest: A challenge to mankind.* Rev. ed. New York: Harcourt.

Adler, H. 1965. *Youth in the Morasha quarter of Jerusalem.* Report of the Committee for the Examination of the Problem of Youth in the Morasha Quarter of Jerusalem. (Hebrew)

Adorno, T. W. et al. 1950. *The authoritarian personality.* New York: Harper.

Afanasenko, E. I. and Kairov, I. A., eds. 1961. *Five years of boarding schools.* Moscow: RSFSR Academy of Pedagogical Sciences Press. (Russian)

Ainsworth, M. D. Reversible and irreversible effects of maternal deprivation on intellectual development. In *Maternal deprivation.* pp. 42–62. New York: Child Welfare League of America.

Ainsworth, M. D. and Bowlby, J. 1954. Research strategy in the study of mother-child separation. *Courrier* 4: 105–31.

Ainsworth, M. D. et al. 1962. *Deprivation of maternal care: A reassessment of its effects.* Geneva: World Health Organization, Public health papers 14.

Allerhand, M. E.; Weber, R. E.; and Haug, M. 1966. *Adaptation and adaptability.* New York: Child Welfare League of America.

Allport, G. W. 1953. The trend in motivational theory. *Am. J. Orthopsychiatry* 23: 107–19.

Alon, M. 1961. "Education for values," from a series of lectures in memory of Shmuel Golan. *Ofakim.* no. 1-2: 11–27. (Hebrew)

Alpert, A. 1957. A special therapeutic technique for certain developmental disorders in prelatency children. *Am. J. Orthopsychiatry* 27: 256–69.

———— 1959. The reversibility of pathological fixations associated with maternal deprivation in infancy. *The Psychoanalytic Study of the Child* 14: 169–84.

———— 1965. Institute on programs for children without families. *J. Acad. Child Psychiatry* 4 (2): 163–67.

Alt, H. 1960. *Residential treatment for the disturbed child.* New York: International Universities Press.

411

Alt, H., and Alt, E. 1964. *The New Soviet man.* New York: Bookman Associates.

Alterman, C. et al. 1966. *Adolescents in kibbutz care: Selected issues.* Master's thesis, University of California, Berkeley, School of Social Welfare.

Ambler, E. 1961. The Soviet boarding school. *The American Slavic and East European Review* 20: 237–52.

Amir, Y. 1967. Adjustment and promotion of soldiers from kibbutzim (communal settlements). *Megamot* 15: 250–58. (Hebrew)

Anderson, J. W. 1965. A special hell for children in Washington. *Harper's* 2 (31): 51–56.

Andrews, R. G. 1968. Permanent placement of negro children through quasi-adoption. *Child Welfare* 47: (10) 583–86, 613.

Anthony, E. J. 1966. Les réactions des adultes aux adolescents et à leur comportement. *Psychiatric approaches to adolescence.* Sixth International Congress of the International Association for Child Psychiatry and Allied Professions.

Arnold, M. B. 1962. *Story sequence analysis.* New York: Columbia University Press.

Arthur, G. A. 1952. *The Arthur adaptation of the Leiter International Performance Scale.* Washington: Psychological Service Center Press.

Asch, S. E. 1952. *Social psychology.* New York: Prentice-Hall.

Asperger, H. 1964. Biologische Grundlagen der Kinderdorfidee (Biological foundations of the children's village concept). *Blätter der Wohlfahrtspflege* 1: 21–25. Stuttgart.

Atkinson, J. W. 1964. *An introduction to motivation.* Princeton, N. J.: Van Nostrand.

Atthowe, J. M., Jr., and Krasner, L. 1968. A preliminary report on the application of contingent reinforcement procedures (token economy) on a "chronic" psychiatric ward. *J. Abnorm. Psychol.* 73: 37–43.

Ausubel, D. P. 1954. *Theory and problems of adolescent development.* New York: Grune and Stratton.

Ayllon, T. 1963. Intensive treatment of psychotic behavior by stimulus satiation and food reinforcement. *Behaviour Research and Therapy* 1: 53–61.

——— 1965. Some behavioral problems associated with eating in chronic schizophrenic patients. In L. P. Ullmann and L. Krasner, *Case studies in behavior modification,* pp. 73–77. New York: Holt, Rinehart & Winston.

Ayllon, T., and Azrin, N. H. 1964. Reinforcement and instructions with mental patients. *J. Experimental Analysis of Behavior* 7: 327–31.

——— 1965. The measurement and reinforcement of behavior of psychotics. *J. Experimental Analysis of Behavior* 8: 357–83.

——— 1968. *The token economy: A motivational system for therapy and rehabilitation.* New York: Appleton-Century-Crofts.

Ayllon, T., and Haughton, E. 1962. Control of the behavior of schizophrenic patients by food. *J. Experimental Analysis of Behavior* 5: 343–52.

——— 1964. Modification of symptomatic verbal behavior of mental patients. *Behaviour Research and Therapy* 2: 87–97.

Ayllon, T., and Michael, J. 1959. The psychiatric nurse as a behavioral engineer. *J. Experimental Analysis of Behavior* 2: 323–34.

Azrin, N. H., and Holz, W. C. 1966. A Punishment. In W. K. Honig (ed.), *Operant behavior: Areas of research and application,* pp. 380–447. New York: Appleton-Century-Crofts.

Baer, D. M. 1962. Laboratory control of thumbsucking by withdrawal and re-presentation of reinforcement. *J. Experimental Analysis of Behavior* 5: 525–28.

Baer, D. M., and Wolf, M. M. 1970a. The entry into natural communities of reinforcement. In R. Ulrich, T. Stachnik, and J. Mabry (eds.), *Control of human behavior II: From cure to prevention,* pp. 319–24. Glenview, Ill.: Scott, Foresman.

————— 1970b. Recent examples of behavior modification in preschool settings. In C. Neuringer and J. L. Michael (eds.), *Behavior modification in clinical psychology,* pp. 10–25. New York: Appleton-Century-Crofts.

Baer, D. M.; Wolf, M. M.; and Risley, T. R. 1968. Some current dimensions of applied behavior analysis. *J. Applied Behavior Analysis* 1: 91–97.

Bailey, J. S.; Wolf, M. M.; and Phillips, E. L. 1970. Home-based reinforcement and the modification of pre-delinquents' classroom behavior. *J. Applied Behavior Analysis* 3: 223–33.

Bakwin, H. 1942. Loneliness in infants. *Am. J. Diseases of Children* 63: 30–40.

Bandura, A. 1965a. Vicarious processes: a case of no-trial learning. In L. Berkowitz (ed.), *Advances in experimental social psychology, Vol. II,* pp. 1–55. New York: Academic Press.

————— 1965b. Influence of models' reinforcement contingencies on the acquisition of imitative responses. *J. Personality and Social Psychology* 1: 589–95.

————— 1969a. *Principles of behavior modification.* New York: Holt, Rinehart & Winston.

————— 1969b. Social-learning theory of identificatory processes. In D. A. Goslin (ed.), *Handbook of socialization theory and research.* Chicago: Rand McNally.

Bandura, A., and Huston, A. C. 1961. Identification as a process of incidental learning. *J. Abnormal and Social Psychology* 63: 311–18.

Bandura, A., and McDonald, A. J. 1963. The influence of social reinforcement and the behavior of models in shaping children's moral judgments. *J. Abnormal and Social Psychology* 67: 274–81.

Bandura, A.; Ross, D.; and Ross, S. A. 1961. Transmission of aggression through imitation of aggressive models. *J. Abnormal and Social Psychology* 63 (3): 575–82.

————— 1963. A comparative test of the status envy, social power, and secondary reinforcement theories of identificatory learning. *J. Abnormal and Social Psychology* 67 (6): 527–34.

Bandura, A., and Walters, R. H. 1959. *Adolescent aggression.* New York: Ronald Press.

————— 1963. *Social learning and personality development.* New York: Holt, Rinehart & Winston.

Bar-Netzer, H. 1963. *Sociometry: Studying group relations.* Jerusalem: Rubin Mass.

Barron, F. 1953. An ego-strength scale which predicts response to psychotherapy. *J. Consulting Psychology* 17: 327–33.

————— 1963. *Creativity and psychological health.* Princeton, N. J.: Van Nostrand.

Barton, E. S.; Guess, D.; Garcia, E.; and Baer, D. M. 1970. Improvement of retardates' mealtime behaviors by timeout procedures using multiple baseline techniques. *J. Applied Behavior Analysis* 2: 77–84.

Bar-Yosef, R. 1960. Patterns of socialization in the kibbutz and their relationship to the structure of kibbutz society. *Megamot* 11: 23–32. (Hebrew)

Baumrind, D. 1966. Effects of authoritative parental control on child behavior. *Child Development* 37 (4): 887–907.

———— 1968. Authoritarian vs. authoritative parental control. *Adolescence* 3: 255–72.

———— 1970. Socialization and instrumental competence in young children. *Young children* 26.

Bayley, N. 1949. Consistency and variability in the growth of intelligence from birth to eighteen years. *J. Genet. Psychol.* 75: 165–96.

———— 1961. *Manual of directions for infant scales of development (Temporary standardization).* Bethesda, Md.; National Institute of Neurological Diseases and Blindness, Collaborative Research Project. Mimeographed.

Bel'gus, V. 1959. Education in labor in the Shkola-Internat. In A. Tolmachev (ed.), *Party organizations and the school: Collected articles,* pp. 158–68. Moscow: State Publishers of Political Literature. (Russian).

Bell, W. 1965. *Aid to dependent children.* New York: Columbia University Press.

Bender, L., and Yarnell, H. 1941. An observation nursery: A study of 250 children on the psychiatric division of Bellevue Hospital. *Am. J. Psychiatry* 97: 1158–74.

Benjamin, A., and Weatherly, H. E. 1947. Hospital ward treatment of emotionally disturbed children. *Am. J. Orthopsychiatry* 17: 665–74.

Bentwich, N. (n.d.) *Ben-Shemen: A children's village.* Israel: Etudes Pédagogiques, Fédération Internationale des Communautes d'Enfants F.I.C.E.

Ben-Yosef, A. C. 1963. *The purest democracy in the world.* New York: Herzl Press and Thomas Yoseloff.

Berelson, B., and Steiner, G. A. 1964. *Human Behavior: An inventory of scientific findings.* New York: Harcourt, Brace & World.

Berenda, R. W. 1950. *The influence of the group on the judgments of children.* New York: King's Crown Press.

Beres, D. 1965. Ego disturbances associated with early deprivation. *J. Am. Acad. Child Psychiatry* 4: 188–201.

Beres, D., and Obers, S. J. 1950. The effects of extreme deprivation in infancy on psychic structure in adolescence: A study in ego development. *The Psychoanalytic Study of the Child* 5: 214–15.

Berg, I. A.; Hunt, W. A.; and Barnes, E. H. 1949. *Perceptual reaction test.* Evanston, Ill.: Irwin A. Berg.

Bettelheim, B. 1960. *The informed heart.* Glencoe, Ill.: The Free Press.

———— 1962. Does communal education work? The case of the kibbutz. *Commentary* 33 (2): 117–25.

———— 1969. *Children of the dream.* New York: Macmillan.

Bettelheim, B., and Sylvester, E. 1947. Therapeutic influence of the group on the individual. *Am. J. Orthopsychiatry* 17: 684–92.

Bingham, W. C.; Burke, H. R.; and Murray, S. 1966. Raven's progressive matrices: construct validity. *J. Psychology* 62: 205–9.

Birnbrauer, J. S. 1968. Generalization of punishment effect—a case study. *J. Applied Behavior Analysis* 1: 201–11.

Birnbrauer, J. S.; Bijou, S.; Wolf, M.; and Kidder, J. 1965. Programmed instruction in the classroom. In L. P. Ullman and L. Krasner (eds.), *Case studies in behavior modification,* pp. 364–66. New York: Holt, Rinehart & Winston.

Blanchard, P. 1946. Psychoanalytic contributions to the problems of reading disabilities. *The Psychoanalytic Study of the Child* 2: 163–87.

Blatt, M. 1969. *The effects of classroom discussion programs upon children's level of moral judgment.* Doctoral dissertation, University of Chicago.

Bloch, Z. 1955. Fathers and sons in the kibbutz. *Ofakim* 3: 288–91. (Hebrew).

Block, J. H.; Haan, N.; and Smith, M. B. 1971. Activism and apathy in contemporary adolescents. In F. Adams (ed.), *Contributions to the understanding of adolescence.* New York: Allyn and Bacon.

Blom, G. E.; Rudnick, M.; and Searles, J. 1966. Some principles and practices in the psychoeducational treatment of emotionally disturbed children. *Psychology in the Schools* 3 (1): 30–38.

Bloom, B. S. 1964. *Stability and change in human characteristics.* New York: Wiley.

Blos, P. 1962. *On adolescence.* New York: Free Press of Glencoe.

———— 1965. The initial stage of male adolescence. *The Psychoanalytic Study of the Child* 20: 145–64.

Board of State Commissioners. 1871. The Congregate System. *First biennial report of the Board of State Commissioners of Public Charities of the State of Illinois, 1870.* Springfield Ill.: Illinois Journal Printing Office.

Bodman, F. et al. 1950. The social adaptation of institution children. *Lancet* 258: 173–76.

Boehm, B. 1958. *Deterrents to adoption of children in foster care.* New York: Child Welfare League of America.

Boguslawski, D. B. 1966. *Guide for establishing and operating day care centers for young children.* New York: Child Welfare League of America.

Borgatta, E. F., and Fanshel, D. 1965. *Behavioral characteristics of children known to psychiatric outpatient clinics.* New York: Child Welfare League of America.

Borow, H. 1966. Development of occupational motives and roles. In M. L. Hoffman and L. W. Hoffman (eds.), *Review of child development research, Vol. II.* New York: Russell Sage Foundation.

Bossard, J. H. S., and Boll, E. S. 1955. Personality roles in the large family. *Child Development* 26: 71–78.

Bostow, D. E., and Bailey, J. B. 1969. Modification of severe disruptive and aggressive behavior using brief timeout and reinforcement procedures. *J. Applied Behavior Analysis* 2: 31–37.

Bower, E. M. 1966. The achievement of competency, learning, and mental health in the school. *ASCD Yearbook:* 23–45. Washington, D.C.

Bowlby, J. 1946. *Forty-four juvenile thieves: Their characters and home life.* London: Bailliere, Tindall & Cox.

———— 1950. *Maternal care and mental health.* Monograph series 2. Also 1951 and 1952 eds. New York: World Health Organization.

———— 1958. Separation of mother and child. Letter to the editor. *Lancet* 272 (7029): 1070–71.

———— 1969. Attachment and loss. Manuscript, 1967. Subsequently published as *Attachment and loss: Vol. I—Attachment.* New York: Basic Books.

Bowlby, J.; Ainsworth, M.; and Rosenbluth, D. 1956. The effects of mother-child separation: A follow-up study. *The British J. Medical Psychology* 29, parts 3 and 4.

Brace, C. L. 1872. The dangerous classes of New York and twenty years' work among them. New York: Wynkoop and Hallenbeck.

———— 1880. What is the best method for the care of poor and vicious children? *J. Social Sciences* 11: 93–98.

Brackbill, Y. 1958. Extinction of the smiling response in infants as a function of reinforcement schedule. *Child Development* 29: 115–25.

Braun, S. J., and Caldwell, B. M. 1973. Emotional adjustment of children in day care who enrolled prior to or after the age of three. *Early Child Development and Care* 2 (1): 13–21.

Briar, S. 1969. Why children's allowances? *Social Work* 14 (1): 5–12.

Brim, O. G. Jr. 1959. *Education for child rearing*. New York: Russell Sage Foundation.

———— 1966. Socialization through the life cycle. In O. G. Brim and S. Wheeler, *Socialization after childhood*. New York: Wiley.

Bronfenbrenner, U. 1943. A constant frame of reference for sociometric research. *Sociometry* 6: 363–97.

———— 1944. A constant frame of reference for sociometric research: Part II—experiment and inference. *Sociometry* 7: 40-75.

———— 1958. The study of identification through interpersonal perception. In R. Tagiuri and L. Petrullo (eds.), *Person, perception and interpersonal behavior*. Stanford, Calif.: Stanford University Press.

———— 1961. Toward a theoretical model for the analysis of parent-child relationships in a social context. In J. D. Glidewell (ed.), *Parental attitudes and child behavior*, pp. 90–109. Springfield, Ill.: Charles C. Thomas.

———— 1962. Soviet methods of character education: Some implications for research. *Am. Psychologist* 17 (8): 550–64.

———— 1963. "Upbringing in collective settings in Switzerland and the USSR." Paper presented at the 17th International Congress in Psychology, Washington.

———— 1967a. Response to pressure from peers versus adults among Soviet and American school children. *International J. Psychology* 2 (3): 199–207.

———— 1967b. The split-level American family. *Saturday Review* 7 October: 60–66.

———— 1967c. The psychological costs of quality and equality in education. *Child Development* 38: 909–25.

———— 1968. On the making of new men: Some extrapolations from research. *Canadian J. of Behavioral Science* 1: 4–24.

———— 1969. "Reaction to social pressure from adults versus peers among Soviet day school and boarding school pupils in the perspective of an American sample." Paper presented at the 19th International Congress of Psychology, London.

———— 1970. *Two worlds of childhood: US and USSR*. New York: Russell Sage Foundation.

Brown, G. D., and Tyler, V. O. Jr. 1968. Time out from reinforcement: A technique for dethroning the "duke" of an institutionalized delinquent group. *J. Child Psychology and Psychiatry* 9: 203–11.

Browning, R. M., and Stover, D. O. 1971. *Behavior modification in child treatment: An experimental and clinical approach*. Chicago: Aldine.

Bruner, J. S. 1966. *Toward a theory of instruction*. Cambridge, Mass.: Belknap Press of Harvard University.

Buehler, R. E.; Patterson, G. R.; and Furniss, J. 1966. The reinforcement of behavior in institutional settings. *Behavior Research and Therapy* 4: 157–67.

Bühler, Ch. 1931. *Kindheit und Jugend*. Leipzig: S. Hirzel.

Bühler, K. 1942. *Die geistige Entwicklung des Kindes* (4th ed.). Jena.

Burchard, J.D. 1967. Systematic socialization: A programmed environment for the rehabilitation of antisocial retardates. *The Psychological Record* 17: 13–21.

———— 1969. Systematic socialization: A programmed environment for the rehabilitation of antisocial retardates. In R. L. Burgess and D. Bushell, Jr. (eds.), *Behavioral sociology: The experimental analysis of social process.* New York: Columbia University Press.

Burchard, J. D., and Tyler, V. O. 1965. The modification of delinquent behavior through operant conditioning. *Behavior Research and Therapy* 2: 245–50.

Burgess, M. E., and Price, D. O. 1963. *An American dependency challenge.* Chicago: American Public Welfare Association.

Burke, H. R. 1958. Raven's progressive matrices: A review and critical evaluation. *J. Genet. Psychol.* 93: 199–228.

Burns, E. M. 1949. *The American social security system.* Boston: Houghton-Mifflin Co.

Burns, E. M. (ed.). 1968. *Children's allowances and the economic welfare of children.* New York: Citizen's Committee for Children.

Bushell, D. Jr.; Wrobel, P. A.; and Michaelis, M. R. 1968. Applying "group" contingencies to the classroom study behavior of preschool children. *J. Applied Behavior Analysis* 1: 55–61.

Caldwell, B. M. 1967a. On reformulating the concept of early childhood education. *Young Children* 22: 348–56.

———— 1967b. What is the optimal learning environment for the young child? *Am. J. Orthopsychiatry* 37 (1): 8–21.

———— 1967c. *The preschool inventory.* Princeton, N.J.: Educational Testing Service.

———— 1968. The fourth dimension in early childhood education. In R. D. Hess and R. M. Bear (eds.), *Early Education*, pp. 71–80. Chicago: Aldine.

———— 1969. "The supportive environment model of early enrichment." Paper presented at the meeting of the American Psychological Association, Washington, D.C., September, 1969.

Caldwell, B. M. et al. 1963. Mother-infant interaction in monomatric and polymatric families. *Am. J. Orthopsychiatry* 33 (4): 653–64.

Caldwell, B. M., and Richmond, J. B. 1964. Programmed day care for the very young child—a preliminary report. *J. Marriage and the Family* 26: 481–88.

Caldwell, B. M.; Wright, C. M.; Honig, A.; and Tannenbaum, J. 1970. Infant Day Care and Attachment. *Am. J. Orthopsychiatry* 40: 397:412.

Canziani, W. 1965. Die verschiedenen Formen der Fremdplazierung von Kindern. *Pro Juventute,* 7/8/9 II.

Caplan, G. 1954. Clinical observations on the emotional life of children in the communal settlements in Israel. In M. J. Senn (ed.), *Problems of infancy and childhood*, pp. 91–120. New York: Josiah Macy Foundation.

———— 1959. *Concepts of mental health and consultation.* Washington, D.C.: U.S. Children's Bureau.

Casler, L. 1961. Maternal deprivation: A critical review of the literature. *Monograph of the Society of Research in Child Development* 26 (2): 1–64.

———— 1965. The effects of extra tactile stimulation on a group of institutionalized infants. *Genetic Psychology Monographs* 71 (1): 137–75.

Castaneda, A.; McCandless, B.; and Palermo, D. S. 1956. The children's form of the manifest anxiety scale. *Child Development* 27: 317–26.

Caudill, W. 1958. *The psychiatric hospital as a small society.* Cambridge, Mass.: Harvard University Press.

Chapin, H. D. 1915a. Are institutions for infants necessary? *J. A. M. A.* January.

——— 1915b. A plea for accurate statistics in infants' institutions. *Archives of Pediatrics.* October.

Chauncey, H. (ed.) 1969. *Soviet preschool education.* New York: Holt, Rinehart & Winston.

Chazan, B. 1956. Problems of the institution in Mishmar Haemek. *Ofakim* 4.

Child Welfare League of America. 1959. *Standards for foster family care service.* New York.

——— 1960. *Standards for day care service.* New York.

Child and Youth Aliyah Public Relations Section. 1968. *Bulletin 43.* Jerusalem: The Jewish Agency.

Chilman, C. S. 1966. *Growing up poor.* Washington, D.C.: U.S. Department of Health, Education and Welfare (May).

Clark, B. R. 1956. Organizational adaptation and precarious values: A case study. *American Sociological Review* 21 (3): 327–36.

Clark, D. H. 1965. The therapeutic community—concept, practice and future. *British J. Psychology,* 111 (479): 947–54.

Clarke, A. D. B., and Clarke, A. M. 1954. Cognitive changes in the feeble-minded. *British J. Psychology* 45 (3): 173–79.

Clausen, J. A. 1966. Family structure, socialization, and personality. In M. L. Hoffman and L. W. Hoffman (eds.), *Review of child development research, Vol. 2.* New York: Russell Sage Foundation.

Clothier, F. 1950. The need of new facilities for the care of disturbed children. *Mental Hygiene* 34: 97–105.

Cohen, H. I.; Filipczak, J.; and Bis, J. S. 1967. *Case I: An initial study of contingencies applicable to special education.* Silver Spring, Md.: Institute of Behavioral Research.

Cohen, H. L. 1968. Educational therapy: The design of learning environments. In J. M. Shlien (ed.) *Research in psychotherapy, Vol. III,* pp. 21–53. Washington, D.C.: American Psychological Association.

Cohen, R. 1958. Instruction and education in the kibbutz. *Ofakim* 3/4: 444–48. (Hebrew).

Cohen-Raz, R. 1968. Mental and motor development of kibbutz, private home and institutionalized infants. *Megamot* 15 (4): 366–88. (Hebrew).

Coleman, J. C. and Hewett, F. M. 1962. Open-door therapy: A new approach to the treatment of under-achieving adolescent boys who resist needed psychotherapy. *J. Clinical Psychology* 18: 28–33.

Coleman, J. S. 1961. *The adolescent society.* New York: The Free Press of Glencoe.

Coleman, J. S. et al. 1966. *Equality of educational opportunity.* Washington, D. C.: U.S. Office of Education.

Collective authorship. 1948. Generation to generation: A record of the central school in Kibbutz Mishmar Haemek. Palestine: Sifriyat Hapoalim. (Hebrew).

Collective authorship. 1959. *The education of our children.* Tel-Aviv: Religious Kibbutz.

Collective authorship. 1962. *Collective education.* Collection of lectures from a conference organized by Department of Education of Hashomer Hatsair. Merhavia, Israel: Department of Education of Hakibbutz Haartzi, Hashomer Hatsair.

Compayré, G. 1893. *L'evolution intellectuelle et morale de l'enfant.* Paris.

Corti, W. 1966. Genese der Kinderdorfbewegung (The genesis of the children's villages movement). *Blätter der Wohlfahrtspflege* 2: 35–38.

Coser, L. A. 1965. The sociology of poverty. *Social Problems* 13 (2): 140–48.

Crandall, V. 1967. Achievement behavior in young children. In W. W. Hartup and N. L. Smothergill (eds.), *The young child,* pp. 165–85. Washington, D.C.: National Association for the Education of Young Children.

Crissey, O. L. 1937. Mental development as related to institutional residence and educational achievement. *University of Iowa Studies* 13 (1).

Cronbach, L. J. 1960. *Essentials of psychological testing* (2nd ed.). New York: Harper & Row.

Darin-Drabkin, H. 1961. *The Other Society.* Merhavia, Israel: Sifriyat Hapoalim. (Hebrew)

Davidson, G. C. 1969. Appraisal of behavior modification techniques with adults in institutional settings. In C. M. Franks (ed.), *Behavior Therapy: Appraisal and status.* New York: McGraw-Hill.

Dawe, H. C. 1942. A study of the effect of an educational program upon language development and related mental functions in young children. *J. Experimental Education* 11: 200–209.

DeCocq, G. A. 1962. The withdrawal of foster parent applicants. San Francisco: United Community Council. Mimeograph.

DeFrancis, V. 1955. *The fundamentals of child protection.* Denver: Children's Division, American Humane Association.

DeFries, Z.; Jenkins, S.; and Williams, E. C. 1964. Treatment of disturbed children in foster care. *Am. J. Orthopsychiatry* 34 (4).

Dennis, W. 1960. Causes of retardation among institutional children: Iran. *J. Genetic Psychology* 96: 47–59.

Dennis, W., and Najarian, P. 1957. Infant development under environmental handicaps. *Psychological Monographs* 71 (7). Whole No. 463.

Dennis, W., and Sayegh, Y. 1965. The effect of supplementary experiences upon the behavioral development of infants in institutions. *Child Development* 36: 81–90.

Deutsch, H. 1944. *Psychology of women.* New York: Grune and Stratton.

Deutsch, M. 1965. The role of social class in language development and cognition. *Am. J. Orthopsychiatry* 35: 78–88.

Devereux, E. C.; Bronfenbrenner, U.; and Suci, G. J. 1962. Patterns of present behavior in the United States of America and the Federal Republic of Germany—a cross-national comparison. *International Social Science Journal* 14 (3): 488–506.

Dewey, J. 1909. *Moral principles in education.* Boston: Houghton-Mifflin.

Dinnage, R., and Pringle, M. L. K. 1967a. *Foster home care—facts and fallacies.* London: Longmans.

—— 1967b. *Residential child care—facts and fallacies.* London: Longmans.

Dixon, W. J. (ed.). 1965. *General linear hypothesis (BMDOSV).* Biometrical computer program, U.C.L.A. Los Angeles: Health Services Computing Facilities.

Doherty, W. J. 1915. A study of the results of institutional care. *Proceedings of the National Conference of Charities and Correction,* 1915, pp. 175–93. Chicago: Hildeman Printing Co.

Dornbusch, S. M. 1955. The military academy as an assimilating institution. *Social Forces* 33: 316–21.

Douvan, E. 1956. Social status and success strivings. *J. Abnormal and Social Psychology* 52: 219–23.

Douvan, E., and Adelson, J. 1966. *The adolescent experience*. New York: Wiley.

Douvan, E., and Gold, M. 1966. Model patterns in American adolescence. In M. L. Hoffman and L. W. Hoffman (eds.), *Review of child development research*, Vol. 2. New York: Russell Sage Foundation.

Dunn, L. M. 1959. *Peabody picture vocabulary test manual*. Minneapolis: American Guidance Service.

Dunsdon, M. I. 1947. Notes on the intellectual and social capacities of a group of young delinquents. *British J. Psychology* 38: 62–66.

Durfee, H., and Wolf, K. 1933. Anstaltspflege und Entwicklung im 1. Lebensjahr (Institutional care and development in the first year of life). *Zeitschrift für Kinderforschung* 42 (3): 273–320.

Edmiston, R. W., and Baird, F. 1949. Adjustment of orphanage children. *J. Educational Psychology* 40 (8): 482–88.

Eisenberg, L. 1962. The sins of the fathers: Urban decay and social pathology. *Am. J. Orthopsychiatry* 32 (1): 5–17.

———— 1965. Deprivation and foster care. *J. Am. Academy of Child Psychiatry* 4 (2): 243–48.

Eisenberg, L., and Neubauer, P. B. 1965. Mental health issues in Israeli collectives—kibbutzim. *J. Am. Academy of Child Psychiatry* 4: 426–42.

Eisenstadt, S. N. 1956. *From generation to generation: Age groups and social structure*. Glencoe, Ill.: Free Press.

Elkin, R. 1965. *Analyzing time, costs, and operations in a voluntary children's institution and agency*. Washington, D. C.: U. S. Children's Bureau.

Emerson, W. R. P. 1922. *Nutrition and growth in children*. New York: Appleton & Co.

Engel, M.; Marsden, G.; and Woodaman, S. 1966. "Saturday's children: Further studies in the psychology of working boys." Paper presented at the annual convention of the American Psychological Association, New York.

Epperson, D. C. 1964. A reassessment of indices of parental influence in "Adolescent society." *Am. Sociological Review* 29: 93–96.

Erikson, E. H. 1950. *Childhood and society*. New York: W. W. Norton.

———— 1959. Identity and the life cycle. *Psychological Issues* 1 (1): 1–171.

———— 1962. Youth: Fidelity and diversity. *Daedalus* 91 (1): 5–27.

Ettinger, A. 1958. Education of the individual within the group. In *The individual and the group in Youth Aliyah education*, pp. 14–21. Jerusalem: Youth Aliyah.

Etzel, B. C., and Gewirtz, J. L. 1967. Experimental modification of caretaker-maintained high-rate operant crying in a 6- and 20-week-old infant (Infans tyrannotearus): Extinction of crying with reinforcement of eye contact and smiling. *J. Experimental Child Psychology* 5 (3): 303–17.

Ey, H.; Berard, P.; and Brisset, Ch. 1960. *Manuel de psychiatrie*. Paris: Masson.

Fairweather, G. W. (ed.). 1964. *Social psychology in treating mental illness: An experimental approach*. New York: Wiley.

Fairweather, G. W.; Sanders, D. H.; Maynard, H.; and Cressler, D. L.; with Bleck, D. S. 1969. *Community life for the mentally ill: An alternative to institutional care*. Chicago: Aldine.

Fanshel, D. 1966. *Foster parenthood: A role analysis*. Minneapolis: University of Minnesota Press.

Fanshel, D., and Maas, H. S. 1962. Factorial dimensions of the characteristics of children in placement and their families. *Child Development* 33 (1): 123–44.

Fenichel, C.; Freedman, A. M.; and Klapper, Z. 1960. A day school for schizophrenic children. *Am. J. Orthopsychiatry* 30 (1): 130–43.

Ferguson, D. H. 1946. Maryland evaluates licensing of agencies and institutions. *Public Welfare* 4 (10): 227–30.

Ferguson, S. M., and Fitzgerald, H. 1954. *Studies in the Social Services*. London: Her Majesty's Stationery Office.

Festinger, L. 1962. *The theory of cognitive dissonance*. Stanford, Calif.: Stanford University Press.

Feuerstein, R. 1968. "The role of social institutions and subsystems in the causation, prevention and alleviation of retarded performance: A contribution to a dynamic approach." Paper presented at the Peabody-NIMH Conference on Social-Cultural Aspects of Mental Retardation, Nashville, Tenn., Mimeographed.

———— 1971. The development of the socio-culturally disadvantaged adolescent in group care. In M. Wolins and M. Gottesmann (eds.), *Group Care: An Israeli approach—Educational paths of Youth Aliyah*. New York: Gordon and Breach.

Feuerstein, R. et al. 1967. "Problems of assessment and evaluation of the mentally retarded and the culturally deprived." Paper presented at the First International Congress for the Scientific Study of Mental Deficiency, Montpellier, Vt.

Feuerstein, R., and Hamburger, M. 1965. "A proposal to study the process of re-development in several groups of deprived early adolescents in both residential and non-residential settings." Report for the Research Unit of the Hadassah-WIZO Canada Child Guidance Clinic. Jerusalem: The Youth Aliyah Department of the Jewish Agency.

Feuerstein, R., and Krasilowsky, D. 1967. The treatment group technique. *The Israel Annals of Psychiatry and Related Disciplines* 5 (1): 61–90.

Feuerstein, R., and Shalom, H. 1967. Learning potential assessment of culturally and socially disadvantaged children. *Megamot* 15 (2–3): 174–87. (Hebrew).

Fichter, J. *Religion as an occupation*. 1961. South Bend, Ind.: University of Notre Dame Press.

Findman, K. R. 1968. An operant conditioning program in a juvenile detention facility. *Psychological Reports* 22: 1119–20.

Fischer, G. 1965. Untersuchungen über die Schulleistungen in einem SOS-Kinderdorf (Study of school achievement in one SOS-Children's Village). *Neue Wege, Band II*, Heft 3: 63–96. Innsbruck: SOS-Kinderdorf-Verlag.

Flavell, J. H. 1963. *The developmental psychology of Jean Piaget*. Princeton, N.J.: Van Nostrand.

Flitner, A.; Bittner, G.; and Vollert, M. 1965–66. Pädagogische Probleme des Kinderdorfs (Educational problems of the Children's Village). *Zeitschrift für Pädagogik*. Special printing.

Folks, H. 1891. The care of delinquent children. In *Proceedings of the National Conference of Charities and Correction*, pp. 136–44. Boston: Press of George H. Ellis.

———— 1896. Why should dependent children be reared in families rather than in institutions? *Charities Review* 5: 140–45.

———— 1902. *The care of destitute, neglected, and delinquent children*. New York: Macmillan.

Fradkin, H. (ed.). 1965. *Organization of services that will best meet needs of children*. New York: Columbia University School of Social Work.

Fraiberg, S. 1955. Introduction to therapy in puberty. *The Psychoanalytic Study of the Child* 10: 264–86.

Frankenstein, C. 1947. *Youth abandoned.* Jerusalem: The Szold Institute. (Hebrew).

Franklin, D. S., and Massarik, F. 1969. The adoption of children with medical conditions. *Child Welfare* 48 (8): Part I, Process and outcome, 459–67; Part II, The families today, 533–39; Part III, Discussions and conclusions, 595–601.

Fraser, G. G. 1937. *Licensing of boarding homes, maternity homes, and child welfare agencies.* Chicago: University of Chicago Press.

Freedman, A. M., and Bender, L. 1957. When the childhood schizophrenic grows up. *Am. J. Orthopsychiatry* 27 (3): 553–62.

Freud, A. 1946. *The ego and the mechanisms of defense.* New York: International Universities Press.

——— 1958. Adolescence. *The Psychoanalytic Study of the Child* 13: 254–78.

——— 1967. Comments on first day's reports. In H. Witmer, (ed.), *On rearing infants and young children in institutions,* pp. 47–55. Washington, D.C.: Children's Bureau Research Reports, No. 1.

Freud, A., and Burlingham, D. T. 1942. *Young children in war time.* London: George Allen and Unwin.

——— 1965. *Infants without families.* New York: International Universities Press. 2d ed. London: Allen and Unwin.

Freud, A., and Dann, S. 1951. An experiment in group upbringing. *The Psychoanalytic Study of the Child* 6: 127–68.

Friedan, B. 1963. *The feminine mystique.* New York: W. W. Norton.

Frostig, M. 1963. Implications of developmental diagnosis of children with learning difficulties and applications in the normal classroom. *J. Humanistic Psychology* 3: 10–19.

Frostig, M., et al. 1961. A developmental test of visual perception for evaluating normal and neurologically handicapped children. *Perceptual Motor Skills* 12: 383–94.

Fuller, P. R. 1949. Operant conditioning of a vegetative human organism. *Am. J. Psychology* 62: 587–90.

Gambrill, E. D.; Thomas, E. J.; and Carter, R. D. 1971. Procedure for socio-behavioral practice in open settings. *Social Work* 16 (1): 51–62.

Gans, H. J. 1964. *The urban villagers.* New York: Free Press of Glencoe.

——— 1967. Income grants and dirty work. *The Public Interest* 6: 110–13.

Gardner, D. B.; Hawkes, G. R.; and Burchinal, L. G. 1961. Non-continuous mothering in infancy and development in later childhood. *Child Development* 32: 225–35.

Gardner, D. B.; Pease, D.; and Hawkes, G. R. 1961. Responses of two-year-old children to controlled stress situations. *J. Genetic Psychology* 98: 29–35.

Gardner, D. B., and Swiger, M. K. 1958. Developmental status of two groups of infants released for adoption. *Child Development* 29: 521–30.

Garfinkel, H. 1956. Conditions of successful degradation ceremonies. *Am. J. Sociology* 61: 420–24.

Garvin, J. A. 1960. "A Thematic Apperception Test study of non-intellective factors related to academic success on the college level." Doctoral dissertation, Loyola University, Chicago.

Gavrin, J. B., and Sacks, L. S. 1963. Growth potential of pre-school aged children in institutional care: A positive approach to a negative condition. *Am. J. Orthopsychiatry* 33: 399–408.

Geiger, H. K. 1964. "Change, values and national integration in the U.S.S.R." Paper presented before the American Association for the Advancement of Slavic Studies, April 1–4.

Gelfand, D.; Gelfand, S.; and Dobson, W. R. 1967. Unprogrammed reinforcement of patients' behavior in a mental hospital. *Behaviour Research and Therapy* 5: 201–7.

Gerson, M. 1957. Relations between daughters and parents in the period of adolescence. *Ofakim* 4: 469–84. (Hebrew).

Gesell, A. 1940. *The first five years of life*. New York: Harper.

Gesell, A., and Ilg, F. 1937. *Feeding behavior of infants*. Philadelphia: J. P. Lippincott.

Gesell, A., and Thompson, H. 1934. *Infant behavior: Its genesis and growth*. New York: McGraw-Hill.

Gewirtz, H. B., and Gewirtz, J. L. 1965. Caretaking settings, background events and behavior differences in four Israeli child-rearing environments: Some preliminary trends. In B. M. Foss (ed.) *Determinants of Infant Behaviour IV*, pp. 229–95. London: Methuen.

———— 1968. Visiting and caretaking patterns for kibbutz infants: Age and sex trends. *Am. J. Orthopsychiatry* 38 (3): 427–43.

Gewirtz, J. L. 1965. The course of infant smiling in four childrearing environments in Israel. In B. M. Foss (ed.), *Determinants of Infant Behaviour III*. London: Methuen.

———— 1968. On designing the functional environment of the child to facilitate behavioral development. In L. L. Dittmann (ed.), *Early child care: The new perspective,* pp. 169–213. New York: Atherton Press.

Gewirtz, J. L., and Baer, D. M. 1958. The effect of brief social deprivation on behaviors for a social reinforcer. *J. Abnormal and Social Psychology* 56: 49–56.

Gewirtz, J. L., and Etzel, B. C. 1967. "Contingent caretaking as a solution for some childrearing paradoxes." Paper read at biannual meeting of the Society for Research in Child Development. New York.

Gil, D. G. 1964. Developing routine followup procedures for child welfare services. *Child Welfare* 43 (5): 229–40.

———— 1967. Nationwide survey of legally reported physical abuse of children. *Brandeis University Papers in Social Welfare* 15.

———— 1968. "Physical abuse of children: One manifestation of violence in American society." Confidential Research Report, *Brandeis University Papers in Social Welfare.*

Gil, D. G., and Noble, J. H. 1967. *Public knowledge, attitudes, and opinions about physical child abuse in the United States*. Waltham, Mass.: Brandeis University. Photo-offset.

Gilbert, A. 1965. Adolescents in state hospitals: Expensive experience. *Am. J. Orthopsychiatry* 35 (4): 825–27.

Gittelman, M. 1965. Behavior rehearsal as a technique in child treatment. *J. Child Psychology and Psychiatry* 6: 251–55.

Glidewell, J. C. et al. 1966. Socialization and social structure in the classroom. In M. L. Hoffman and L. W. Hoffman (eds.), *Review of child development research, Vol 2*. New York: Russell Sage Foundation.

Glueck, S., and Glueck, E. 1950. *Unravelling juvenile delinquency*. New York: The Commonwealth Fund.

Gmeiner, H. 1960a. Das SOS-Kinderdorf als Verwahrlosungsprophylaxe (The SOS-Children's Village as prophylactic against neglect). *Neue Wege, Band I,* Heft 2, pp. 13–17. Innsbruck: SOS-Kinderdorf-Verlag.

———— 1960b. *Die SOS-Kinderdörfer: Moderne Erziehungsstäten für verlassene Kinder* (The SOS-Children's Village: Modern development facilities for neglected children). Innsbruck: SOS-Kinderdorf Verlag.

———— 1964. *SOS-Children's Villages.* Innsbruck: International Office, The Hermann Gmeiner Fund. Letter by Hermann Gmeiner asking for funds, accompanying pamphlet, *Grains of Rice.*

Goffman, E. 1961. *Asylums.* Garden City, N. Y.: Doubleday Anchor Books.

Golan, S. 1961. *Collective education.* Merhavia, Israel: Sifriyat Hapoalim. (Hebrew).

Goldfarb, W. 1943a. Infant rearing and problem behavior. *Am. J. Orthopsychiatry* 13 (2): 249–66.

———— 1943b. The effects of early institutional care on adolescent personality. *J. Experimental Education* 12: 106–29.

———— 1944a. Infant rearing as a factor in foster home replacement. *Am. J. Orthopsychiatry* 14: 162–67.

———— 1944b. Effects on early institutional care on adolescent personality: Rorschach data. *Am. J. Orthopsychiatry* 14: 441–47.

———— 1945. Psychological privation in infancy and subsequent adjustment. *Am. J. Orthopsychiatry* 15 (2): 247–55.

———— 1947. Variations in adolescent adjustment of institutionally-reared children. *Am. J. Orthopsychiatry* 17: 449–57.

———— 1949. Rorschach test differences between family-reared, institutionally-reared, and schizophrenic children. *Am. J. Orthopsychiatry* 19: 624–33.

Goldfarb, W., and Klopfer, B. 1944. Rorschach characteristics of 'institutional' children. *Rorschach Research Exchange* 8: 92–100.

Goodman, E. M. 1968. Habilitation of the unwed teenage mother: An interdisciplinary and community responsibility. *Child Welfare* 47 (5): 274–80, 301.

Goodman, J. D.; Silberstein, R. M.; and Mandell, W. 1963. Adopted children brought to the Child Guidance Clinic. *AMA Archives of General Psychiatry* 9 (5): 451–56.

Gorshkova, A. I. 1961. Along with the nation. In E. I. Afanasenko and I. A. Kairov (eds.), *Five Years of Boarding Schools,* pp. 256–68. Moscow: Academy of Pedagogical Sciences Press. (Russian).

Gough, H. G. 1949. A short social status inventory. *J. Educational Psychology* 40: 52–56.

Gray, S. W., and Klaus, R. A. 1965. An experimental preschool program for culturally deprived children. *Child Development* 36 (4): 887–98.

Gray, S., and Miller, J. O. 1967. *The vertical diffusion effect in preschool enrichment programs.* Manuscript.

Greenleigh Associates. 1960. Facts, fallacies and future: A study of the Aid to Dependent Children program in Cook County, Illinois. New York. Minneographed.

Gritsch, D. 1960. Die Mutter im SOS-Kinderdorf (The mother in the SOS-Children's Village). *Neue Wege, Band I,* Heft 1, pp. 3–11. Innsbruck: SOS-Kinderdorf-Verlag.

Gula, M. 1964. *Agency operated group homes: A special resource for serving children and youth.* Washington, D.C.: U.S. Department of Health, Education and Welfare, Children's Bureau.

Haider, F. 1960. Die SOS-Kinderdörfer Idee und Verwirklichung (The SOS-Children's Villages: Idea and realization). *Neue Wege, Band I,* Heft 4, pp. 31–45. Innsbruck: SOS-Kinderdorf-Verlag.

Haider, F.; Hegel, E.; Lange, U.; and Schroder, E. 1964. Die Beziehungen der Kinder in den SOS-Kinderdörfern zui hren leiblichen Eltern (Relationship between children in the SOS-Children's Villages and their natural parents). *Neue Wege, Band II,* Heft 2, pp. 21–58. Innsbruck: SOS-Kinderdorf-Verlag.

Hall, E. A. 1900. Comments. *Proceedings of the National Conference of Charities and Correction,* 1899, pp. 181–84. Boston: George H. Ellis.

Hall, J. C. 1957. Correlation of a modified form of Raven's Progressive Matrices (1938) with the Wechsler Adult Intelligence Scale. *J. Consulting Psychology* 21: 23–26.

Harlow, H. F. 1953. Mice, monkeys, men, and motives. *Psychological Review* 60: 23–32.

Harlow, H. F., and Harlow, M. K. 1962. Social deprivation in monkeys. *Scientific American* 207 (5): 136–46.

Harris, D. B. 1963. *Measuring the psychological maturity of children: A revision and extension of the Goodenough Draw-a-Man Test.* New York: Harcourt, Brace & World.

Harris, F. R.; Wolf, M. M.; and Baer, D. M. 1967. Effects of adult social reinforcement on child behavior. In W. W. Hartup and N. L. Smothergill (eds.), *The young child,* pp. 13–41. Washington, D.C.: National Association for the Education of Young Children.

Hartshorne, H., and May, M. A. 1928–30. *Studies in the nature of character.* 3 vols. New York: Macmillan.

Hasenclever, C. 1964. Kinderdorf statt Kinderheim? Zum Problem der SOS-Kinderdörfer (Children's village in place of children's home? On the problem of the SOS-Children's Villages). *Neues Beginnen* 10: 150–52.

Haughton, E., and Ayllon, T. 1965. Production and elimination of symptomatic behavior. In L. P. Ullmann and L. Krasner (eds.), *Case studies in behavior modification,* pp. 94–98. New York: Holt, Rinehart & Winston.

Hegel, E. (n.d.) *Das SOS-Kinderdorf—Ruf und Antwort* (The SOS-Children's Village—Call and Response). Innsbruck.

Heinicke, C. M. 1956. Some effects of separating two-year-old children from their parents: A comparative study. *Human Relations* 9 (2): 106–76.

Heinicke, C. M., and Westheimer, I. J. 1965. *Brief separations.* New York: International Universities Press.

Held, R., and Hein, A. 1963. Movement-produced stimulation in the development of visually-guided behavior. *J. Comparative and Physiological Psychology* 56 (5): 872–76.

Heller, E. 1966. Applications by married parents for adoptive placement of their in-wedlock children. *Child Welfare* 45 (7): 404–9.

Hersher, L. et al. 1968. *Consistency in maternal behavior during the first year of life.* Manuscript.

Hess, R. D. 1965. Educability and rehabilitation: the future of the welfare class. *J. Marriage and the Family* 26 (4): 422–29.

Hess, R. D., and Shipman, V. C. 1965. Early experience and the socialization of cognitive modes in children. *Child Development* 36 (4): 869–86.

Hesterly, S. O. 1963. Deviant response patterns as a function of chronological age. *J. Consulting Psychology* 27 (3): 210–14.

Hetzer, H., and Wolf, K. 1928. Babytests. *Zeitschrift für Psychologie* 107: 62–104.

Hewett, F. 1968. *The emotionally disturbed child in the classroom.* New York: Allyn and Bacon.

Hilgard, J. R.; Newman, M. F.; and Fisk, F. 1960. Strength of adult ego following childhood bereavement. *Am. J. Orthopsychiatry* 30: 788–98.

Hirschback, E. 1963. A group foster home. *Canadian Welfare* 39 (1): 12–16.

Hobbs, N. 1964. Mental health's third revolution. *Am. J. Orthopsychiatry, 34* (5): 822–33.

———1965. How the Re-ED plan developed. In N.J. Long, W. C. Morse, and R. G. Newman (eds.), *Conflict in the classroom,* pp. 286–96. Belmont, Calif.: Wadsworth Publishing Co., Inc.

———1966. Helping disturbed children: Psychological and ecological strategies. *Am. Psychologist,* 21 (12): 1105–15.

Hollander, L. 1965. Foster care services in a child placement agency. *J. Am. Academy of Child Psychiatry,* 4 (2): 206–25.

Hollingshead, A.B., and Redlich, F. C. 1958. *Social class and mental illness: A community study.* New York: Wiley.

Holstein, C. 1968. *Parental determinants of the development of moral judgment.* Doctoral dissertation, University of California, Berkeley.

Homme, L., et al. 1969. *How to use contingency contracting in the classroom.* New York: Research Press.

Homme, L.; de Baca, P. C.; Cottingham, L.; and Homme, A. 1970. What behavioral engineering is. In R. Ulrich, T. Stachnik, and J. Mabry (eds.), *Control of human behavior II: From cure to prevention.* Glenview, Ill.: Scott, Foresman.

Hoopes, J. L., et al. 1969. *A followup study of adoptions: Post-placement functioning of adopted children.* Vol. II. New York: Child Welfare League of America.

Hopkins, B. L. 1970. The first twenty years are the hardest. In R. Ulrich, T. Stachnik and J. Mabry (eds.), *Control of human behavior II: From cure to prevention,* pp. 358–65. Glenview, Ill.: Scott, Foresman.

Horowitz, A. 1958. Isolated youths in youth groups. *Megamot,* 9 (2): 103–23 (Hebrew).

Howe, G. E. 1880. The family system. *Proceedings of the Seventh Annual Conference of Charities and Correction, 1880.* Boston: A. Williams.

Hunt, J. McV. 1961. *Intelligence and experience.* New York: Ronald Press.

———1964. The psychological basis for using preschool enrichment as an antidote for cultural deprivation. *Merrill-Palmer Quarterly of Behavior and Development,* 10: 209–48.

Hunt, J. McV., and Uzgiris, I. 1967. *An ordinal scale of infant development.* Manuscript. Urbana: University of Illinois.

Hylton, L. F. 1964. *The residential treatment center.* New York: Child Welfare League of America.

———1965. Trends in adoption, 1958–1962. *Child Welfare,* 44 (7): 377–86.

Inglis, D., and Marsh, E. J. 1958. Use of state mental hospitals for children. *Am. J. Orthopsychiatry,* 28 (4): 689–98.

Isaacs, S. (ed.) 1941. *Cambridge evacuation survey: A wartime study in social welfare and education.* London: Methuen.

Isaacs, W.; Thomas, J.; and Goldiamond, I. 1960. Application of operant conditioning to reinstate verbal behavior in psychotics. *J. Speech and Hearing Disorders,* 25: 8–12.

Itel'son, L. B. 1960. Studying the individual peculiarities of pupils in Shkoly-Internaty. *Sovetskaya Pedagogika* (Soviet Education), 24 (8): 84–92 (Russian).

Izvestia, 1964. Work passport—the face of the Soviet citizen. February 26. (Russian).

Jacobson, E. 1961. Adolescent moods. *The Psychoanalytic Study of the Child* 16: 164–83.

Jaffe, E. 1967. Correlates of differential placement outcome for dependent children in Israel. *The Social Service Review,* 41 (4): 390–400.

————1969. Effects of institutionalization on adolescent, dependent children. *Child Welfare,* 48 (2): 64–71, 111.

Jahoda, M. 1958. *Current concepts of positive mental health.* New York: Basic Books.

Jencks, C. 1966. Is the public school obsolete? *Public Interest,* 2: 18–27.

Jenkins, S., and Sauber, M. 1966. *Paths to child placement.* New York: New York City Department of Welfare and The Community Council of Greater New York.

Jennings, H. H. 1950. *Leadership and isolation.* 2d ed. New York: Longmans Green.

Jeter, H. R. 1963. *Children, problems and services in child welfare programs.* Washington, D.C.: Government Printing Office, 1963.

Jones, H. E. 1940. Personal reactions of the yearbook committee. *39th Yearbook, National Society for the Study of Education* I: 454–56.

Jones, K. 1967. The development of institutional care. In *New thinking about institutional care.* London: Association of Social Workers.

Jones, M. 1963. The treatment of character disorders. *British J. Criminology* 3 (3): 276–82.

Josselyn, I. M. 1950. Treatment of the emotionally immature child in an institutional framework. *Am. J. Orthopsychiatry,* 20 (2): 397–409.

Kadushin, A. 1967. *Child welfare services.* New York: Macmillan.

Kagan, J., and Moss, H. A. 1962. *Birth to maturity: A study in psychological development.* New York: Wiley.

Kahn, A. 1963. *Planning community services for children in trouble.* New York: Columbia University Press.

Kairov, I. A. 1959. Some questions on establishing Shkoly-Internaty. *Uchitel'skaya Gazeta* (Teacher's Newspaper), 27 June p. 2. (Russian).

Kale, R. J.; Zlutnick, S.; and Hopkins, B. L. 1968. "Patient contribution to a therapeutic environment." Michigan Department of Mental Health, *Michigan Mental Health Research Bulletin,* 2 (2): 33–38.

————1970. Patient contributions to a therapeutic environment. In R. Ulrich, T. Stachnik, and J. Mabry (eds.), *Control of human behavior II: From cure to prevention,* pp. 96–99. Glenview, Ill.: Scott, Foresman.

Kaneti-Baruch, M. 1960. A Youth Aliyah group in a kibbutz. *Megamot,* 11 (2): 124–41 (Hebrew).

Kanfer, F. H. 1970. Self-regulation: Research, issues and speculations. In C. Neuringer and J. L. Michael (eds.), *Behavior modification in clinical psychology,* pp. 178–220. New York: Appleton-Century-Crofts.

Kanfer, F. H., and Phillips, J. S. 1970. *Learning foundations of behavior therapy.* New York: Wiley.

Kanner, L. 1943. Autistic disturbances of affective content. *Nervous Child,* 2 (3): 217–50.

Karaseva, N. 1963. Mixed age groups. *Shkola-Internat,* 2: 37–39 (Russian).

Kardiner, A. 1961. When the state brings up the child. *Saturday Review,* 26 August pp. 9–11, 47.

Kasiuk, M. 1962. Is there a crisis in institutional rearing? *Problemy Opiekuńczo-Wychowawcze* (Problems of Upbringing) (July): 23–24 (Polish).

Keefe, J. 1965. "A study of two seminary and two non-seminary high school groups on selected aspects of maturity." Doctoral dissertation, Fordham University.

Kelman, H. C. 1961. Process of opinion change. *Public Opinion Quarterly,* 25: 57–78.

Kephart, N. C. 1960. *The slow learner in the classroom.* Columbus, Ohio: Charles E. Merrill.

Khrushchev, N. S. 1958. Control figures for development of the U.S.S.R. national economy in 1959–65. *Pravda,* (November) (Russian).

King, R. D.; Raynes, N. V.; and Tizard, J. 1971. *Patterns of Residential Care: Sociological Studies in Institutions for Handicapped Children.* London: Routledge and Kegan Paul.

Kinkead, E. 1957. A reporter at large: The study of something new in history. *The New Yorker,* 26 October, 114–69.

————1959. *In every war but one.* New York: Norton.

Kirk, S. A. 1958. *Early education of the mentally retarded.* Urbana: University of Illinois Press.

Knizheva, L. (ed.) 1960. *Fundamentals of communist upbringing.* Moscow: Politizdat (Russian).

Knox, J. H. M. 1915. Discussion: Infant mortality. *Proceedings of the National Conference of Charities and Corrections, 1915,* pp. 133–34. Chicago: Hildeman Printing Co.

Kochetov, A. I. 1958. Productive work in the Shkola-Internat. In *Sovetskaya Pedagogika* (Soviet Education) 22: 48–59 (Russian).

Kohlberg, L. 1958. *The development of modes of moral thinking and choice in the years ten to sixteen.* Doctoral dissertation, University of Chicago.

————1963. Moral and religious education and the public schools: A developmental view. In H. Stevenson (ed.), *Child Psychology.* Chicago: University of Chicago Press.

————1964. Development of moral character and moral ideology. In M. L. Hoffman and L. W. Hoffman (eds.), *Review of child development research,* Vol. I. New York: Russell Sage Foundation.

————1966. Moral education in the schools: A developmental view. *The School Review,* 74 (1): 1–30.

————1969. Stage and sequence: The cognitive-developmental approach to socialization. In D. Goslin (ed.), *Handbook of socialization theory and research.* Chicago: Rand McNally.

Kolbanovski, V. N. 1961. Readers' comments: Working life and communism. *Novyi Mir* (New World) 37 (2): 276–82. (Russian).

Kol'makova, M. N. 1961. School for the rounded development of the individual. In *Nachal'naya Shkola* (Elementary School), (10) 12–18 (Russian).

Kommunist. 1964. Communism is being built for the people. January: 3–13 (Russian).

Korczak, J. 1967. *Selected works of Janusz Korczak.* Warsaw, Poland: Scientific Publications Foreign Cooperation Center of the Central Institute for Scientific, Technical, and Economic Information.

Kramer, R. 1968. *Moral development in young adults.* Doctoral dissertation, University of Chicago.

Krasner, L. 1970a. Token economy as an illustration of operant conditioning procedure with the aged, with youth, and with society. In D. J. Levis (ed.), *Learning approaches to therapeutic behavior change*, pp. 74–101. Chicago: Aldine.

————1970b. Behavior modification, token economies and training in clinical psychology. In C. Neuringer and J. L. Michael (eds.), *Behavior Modification in clinical psychology*, pp. 86–104. New York: Appleton-Century Crofts.

————1971. Behavior therapy. *Annual Review of Psychology*, 22: 483–532. Palo Alto, Calif.: Annual Reviews.

Krush, T. P., et al. 1966. Some thoughts on the formation of personality disorder: Study of an Indian boarding school population. *Am. Psychiatry*, 122 (8): 868–76.

Kubie, L. 1954. The fundamental nature of the distinction between normality and neurosis. *Psychoanalytic Quarterly*, 23: 167–204.

Kugel, R. B. 1963. Familial mental retardation: Some possible neurophysiological and psychosocial interrelationships. In A. J. Solnit and S. Provence (eds.), *Modern perspectives in child development*, pp. 206–16. New York: International Universities Press.

Kunkel, J. H. 1970. *Society and economic growth*. New York: Oxford University Press.

Lambert, R., et al. 1970. *A manual to the sociology of the school*. London: Weidenfeld and Nicolson.

Lange, U. 1965a. Das alleinstehende Kind und seine Versorgung (The abandoned child and his care). *Psychologische Praxis*, Heft 38, Basel.

————1965b. Die Aufgaben der SOS-Kinderdörfer im Rahmen der modernen Jugendhilfe (The functions of the SOS-Children's Villages in the framework of modern child welfare). *Neue Wege, Band II*, Heft 4, pp. 103–23. Innsbruch: SOS-Kinderdorf-Verlag.

Lawton, R. W., and Murphy, J. P. 1915. A study of results of a child-placing society. *Proceedings of the National Conference of Charities and Correction, 1915*, pp. 164–74. Chicago: Hildeman Printing Co.

Leary, T. 1957. *The interpersonal diagnosis of personality*. New York: Ronald.

Leay, B.; Hansen, E.; and Harlow, H. F. 1962. Mother-infant separation in monkeys. *J. Child Psychology and Psychiatry*, 3 (3–4): 123–32.

Lebovici, S. 1966. Les modes d'adaptation des adolescents. *Psychiatric Approaches to Adolescence*. Sixth International Congress of the International Association for Child Psychiatry and Allied Professions.

Lee, P. 1929. Social work, cause and function. *Proceedings of the National Conference of Social Work, 1929*. Chicago: University of Chicago Press.

————1937. *Social work as cause and function*. New York: Columbia University Press.

Lent, J. R.; LeBlanc, J.; and Spradlin, J. E. 1970. Designing a rehabilitative culture for moderately retarded, adolescent girls., In R. Ulrich, T. Stachnik, and J. Mabry (eds.) *Control of human behavior II: From cure to prevention*, pp. 121–35. Glenview, Ill.: Scott, Foresman.

Lerea, L. 1958. Assessing language development. *J. Speech and Hearing Research*, 1: 75–85.

Lerman, P. 1968. Evaluative studies of institutions for delinquents: Implications for research and social policy. *Social Work*, 3: 55–64.

Levin, G. 1960. What is maternal nearness? *Ofakim*, 1: 93–97 (Hebrew).

Levin, G. R., and Simmons, J. J. 1962. Response to food and praise by emotionally disturbed boys. *Psychological Reports,* 11: 539–46.

Levitt, E. E. 1963. Psychotherapy with children: A further evaluation. *Behavior Research and Therapy,* 1 (1): 45–51.

Levshin, A. 1963. Thoughts about the educator. *Shkola-Internat,* 1 (Russian).

Levy, D. M. 1943. *Maternal overprotection.* New York: Columbia University Press.

Lewin, A. 1960. Some problems of group rearing in an internat. *Problemy Opiekuńczo Wychowawcze* (Problems of Upbringing), February: 16–19 (Polish).

Lewin, D. S. 1953. Prediction of the adjustment of children in guardianship care: An application of statistical methodology to social work data. *Dissertation Abstracts,* 13: 1294–95.

Lewin, K. 1935. *A dynamic theory of personality.* New York: McGraw-Hill.

———1936. *Principles of topological psychology.* New York: McGraw-Hill.

———1948. *Resolving social conflicts.* New York: Harper.

Lewis, W. W. 1965. Continuity and intervention in emotional disturbance: A review. *Exceptional Children,* 31 (9): 465–75.

———1966. Project Re-Education—a new program for the emotionally disturbed child. *The High School Journal,* 49: 279–86.

———1967. Project Re-ED: Educational intervention in discordant child rearing systems. In E. L. Cowen, E. A. Gardner, and M. Zax (eds.), *Emergent approaches to mental health problems.* New York: Appleton-Century-Crofts.

Lindsley, O. R. 1957. Operant conditioning methods applied to research in chronic schizophrenia. *Psychiatric Research Reports,* 5: 118–39.

———1963. Free operant conditioning and psychotherapy. In J. Masserman (ed.), *Current psychiatric therapies,* pp. 47–56. New York: Grune and Stratton.

Lindzey, G. 1961. *Projective techniques and cross-cultural research.* New York: Appleton-Century-Crofts.

Lippitt, R.; Polansky, N.; Redl, F.; and Rosen, S. 1958. The dynamics of power: A field study of social influence in groups of children. In E. Maccoby, et al. (eds.), *Reading in Social Psychology,* pp. 251–64. New York: Holt.

Lippitt, R., and White, R. K. 1943. "Social climate" of children's groups. In R. G. Barker, J. S. Kounin, and H. F. Wright (eds.), *Child behavior and development,* pp. 485–508. New York: McGraw-Hill.

Loevinger, J. 1966. The meaning and measurement of ego development. *Am. Psychologist,* 21 (3): 195–206.

London, J. et al. 1963. *Adult education and social class.* Berkeley, Calif.: Survey Research Center, University of California.

Lovaas, O. I. 1966. A program for the establishment of speech in psychotic children. In J. K. Wing (ed.) *Early childhood autism,* pp. 115–44. Oxford: Pergamon.

Lovaas, O. I.; Berberich, J. P.; Perloff, B. F.; and Schaeffer, B. 1966. Acquisition of imitative speech in schizophrenic children. *Science,* 151: 705–07.

Lovaas, O. I.; Frietag, G.; Gold, V. J.; and Kassorla, I. C. 1965. Experimental studies in childhood schizophrenia: Analysis of self-destructive behavior. *J. Experimental Child Psychology,* 2: 67–84.

Lovaas, O. I.; Schaeffer, B.; and Simmons, J. Q. 1965. Experimental studies in childhood schizophrenia: Building social behaviors using electric shock. *J. Experimental Research in Personality,* 1: 99–109.

Lovass, O. I., and Simmons, J. Q. 1969. Manipulation of self-destruction in three retarded children. *J. Applied Behavior Analysis*, 2: 143–57.

Low, S. 1965. *America's children and youth in institutions, 1950–1960–1964.* Washington, D.C.: U.S. DHEW Pub. 435.

———1966. *Foster care of children: Major national trends and prospects.* Washington, D.C.: U.S. DHEW.

Lowrey, L. G. 1940. Personality distortion and early institutional care. *American J. Orthopsychiatry*, 10 (3): 576–86.

Luria, Z.; Goldwasser, A.; and Goldwasser, M. 1963. Response to transgression in stories by Israel children. *Child Development*, 34 (2): 271–80.

Lystad, M. H. 1958. Day hospital care and changing family attitudes toward the mentally ill. *J. Nervous Mental Diseases*, 127: 145–52.

Maas, H. S. 1963*a*. Long term effects of early childhood separation and group care. *Vita Humana*, 6 (1–2): 34–56.

———1963b. The young adult adjustment of twenty wartime residential nursery children. *Child Welfare*, 42 (2): 57–72.

Maas, H. S., and Engler, R. E. 1959. *Children in need of parents.* New York: Columbia University Press.

McCarthy, D. 1954. Language development in children. In L. Carmichael (ed.), *Manual of child psychology*, pp. 492–630. New York: Wiley.

McCarthy, J. J., and Kirk, S. A. 1961. *Illinois Test of Psycholinguistic Abilities* (Exp. ed.). Urbana: University of Illinois, Institute of Research on Exceptional Children.

McClelland, D. C. 1961. *The achieving society.* Princeton, N.J.: Van Nostrand.

———1965. Toward a theory of motive acquisition. *Am. Psychologist*, 20 (5): 321–33.

McDougall, W. 1908. *An introduction to social psychology.* London: Methuen.

McGinnies, E. 1970. *Social behavior: A functional analysis.* Boston: Houghton Mifflin.

McKenna, C. F. 1907. Orphans and orphanages. *Catholic encyclopedia.* Vol. II, pp. 322–25. New York: Robert Appleton.

Madsen, C. H., Jr.; Becker, W. C.; Thomas, D. R.; Koser, L.; and Plager, E. 1968. An analysis of the reinforcing function of "sit down" commands. In R. K. Parker (ed.), *Readings in educational psychology*, pp. 265–78. Boston: Allyn and Bacon.

Maenchen, A. 1953. Notes on early ego disturbances. *The Psychoanalytic Study of the Child* 8: 262–70.

Maier, N. R. F. 1949. *Frustration: A study of behavior without a goal.* New York: McGraw-Hill.

Maisels, J. F., and Loeb, M. B. 1956. Unanswered questions about foster care. *Social Service Review*, 30 (1): 239–46.

Makarenko, A. S. 1949. *A pedagogical poem.* Leningrad: Leningradskoye gazetozhurnalnoye i knizhnoye izdatelstvo (Leningrad newspaper periodical and book publishing house) (Russian).

———1953. *Learning to live.* Moscow: Foreign Languages Publishing House.

———1955. *The road to life: An epic of education.* 3 vols. Moscow: Foreign Languages Publishing House.

Maksimova, E. K. 1961. Bring up ideologically convinced people. In E. I. Afanasenko and I. A. Kairov (eds.), *Five years of boarding schools.* Moscow: RSFSR Academy of Pedagogical Sciences Press (Russian).

Maksimovski, M. N. 1961. Pioneers and Komsomols—our support. In E. I.

Afanasenko and I. A. Kairov (eds.), *Five years of boarding schools*. Moscow: RSFSR Academy of Pedagogical Sciences Press (Russian).

Malone, C. A. 1966. Safety first: Comments on the influence of external danger in the lives of children of disorganized families. *American J. Orthopsychiatry*, 36 (1): 3–12.

Malzberg, B. 1959. Important statistical data about mental illness. In S. Arieti (ed.), *American handbook of psychiatry*. New York: Basic Books.

Mannheim, K. 1936. *Ideology and utopia*. New York: Harcourt, Brace.

Manvelian, G. 1961. Thoughts on child rearing. *Shkola-Internat*, 6: 17–23. (Russian).

Martin, D. 1962. *Adventure in psychiatry*. London: Cassirer.

Martin, M.; Burkholdre, R.; Rosenthal, T. L.; Tharp, R. G.; and Thorne, G. L. 1968. Programming behavior change and reintegration into school milieux of extreme adolescent deviates. *Behaviour Research and Therapy*, 6: 371–84.

Maslow, A. H. 1954. *Motivation and personality*. New York: Harper.

Matejcek, Z., and Langmeier, J. 1965. New observations on psychological deprivation in institutional children in Czechoslovakia. *Slow Learning Child*, 12 (1): 20–36.

Mayakova, A. 1956. Comments of a worker in the "Red October" chocolate factory. *Uchitelskaya Gazeta* (Teacher's Newspaper), 18 April (Russian).

Mead, M. 1947. The implications of cultural change for personality development. *American J. Orthopsychiatry*, 17 (4): 633–46.

———— 1954. Some theoretical considerations on the problem of mother–child separation. *American J. Orthopsychiatry*, 24 (3): 471–83.

Merton, R. 1957. *Social theory and social structure*. Glencoe, Ill.: Free Press.

Meyer, H. J., and Borgatta, E. F. 1959. *An experiment in mental patient rehabilitation*. New York: Russell Sage Foundation.

Meyer, H. J.; Borgatta, E. F.; and Jones, W. C. 1965. *Girls at vocational high: An experiment in social work intervention*. New York: Russell Sage Foundation.

Miller, D. R., and Swanson, G. E. 1958. *The changing American parent*. New York: Wiley.

Miller, L. K., and Schneider, R. 1970. The use of a token system in Project Head Start. *J. Applied Behavior Analysis*, 3: 213–20.

Minuchin, S.; Chamberlain, P.; and Graubard, P. 1966. *A project to teach learning skills to disturbed delinquent children*. Unpublished report to the Wiltwyck School for Boys, New York (April).

Mirkhaidarova, R. 1963. Boarding school and society. *Shkola-Internat*, 1: 32–36 (Russian).

Moore, O. K., and Anderson, A. R. 1969. Some principles for the design of clarifying educational environments. In D. A. Goslin (ed.), *Handbook of socialization theory and research*. Chicago: Rand McNally.

Morris, T., and Morris, P. 1963. *Pentonville*. London: Routledge and Kegan Paul.

Moyles, E. W., and Wolins, M. 1971. Group care and intellectual development. *Developmental Psychology* 4 (1): 370–80.

Moynihan, D. P., and Barton, P. 1965. *The Negro family: The case for national action*. Washington, D.C.: Office of Policy Planning and Research, U. S. Department of Labor.

Murdock, G. P. 1949. *Social structure*. New York: Macmillan.

Nadad, A., and Achiram, E. 1962. *Wards of Youth Aliyah in independent life*. Jerusalem: The Jewish Agency (Hebrew).

National Center for Health Statistics. 1966. Changing trends in illegitimacy. *Vital Statistics*, 15 (13).

National Institute of Child Health and Human Development. 1968 *Perspectives on human deprivation: Biological, psychological and sociological*. Washington, D.C.: U.S. Department of Health, Education and Welfare.

Nedeljković, Y. 1960. *Wards of children's homes in residence and upon entering independent life*. Belgrade: Department of Social Problems of the People's Republic of Serbia (Serbo-Croatian).

Neubauer, V. 1959 Die sozialen Aufgaben der SOS-Kinderdörfer (The social functions of the SOS-Children's-Villages). *Neue Wege, Band I*, Heft, 3 pp. 19–29. Innsbruck: SOS-Kinderdorf-Verlag.

———— 1962. Grundzüge einer Kinderdorf-Pädagogik (Basic principles of children's village upbringing). *Neue Wege, Band I*, Heft, 6 pp. 53–58. Innsbruck: SOS-Kinderdorf-Verlag.

Neubauer, V. (ed.) 1964. *Die Beziehungen der Kinder in den SOS-Kinderdörfern zu ihren leiblichen Eltern* (Contacts between children in the SOS-Villages and their natural parents). *Neue Wege, Band II*, Heft 2. Innsbruck: SOS-Kinderdorf-Verlag.

Neugarten, B. L. 1963. Personality changes during the adult years. In R. G. Kuhlen (ed.), *Psychological background of adult education*. Chicago: Center for the Study of Liberal Education for Adults.

New Educational Institutions. 1956. *Trud* (27 July): 1 (Russian).

Newcomb, T. M. 1943. *Personality and social change*. New York: Dryden Press.

Newman, R. 1960. The way back: Extramural schooling as a transitional phase of residential therapy. *Am. J. Orthopsychiatry*, 30: 588–98.

New York Times. 1964. Soviet studies tighter curbs to reduce worker turnover. 28 February.

Norman, R. D. 1966. Interpersonal values of parents of achieving and nonachieving gifted children. *J. Psychology*, 64 (1): 49–57.

North, C. C., and Hatt, P. K. 1947. North-Hatt scale to determine relative occupational prestige. *Opinion News*, 9: 3–13.

Northway, M. L. 1952. *A primer of sociometry*. Toronto: University of Toronto Press.

Oettinger, K. B. 1966. A Spectrum of services for children: In *Spotlight on Day Care*. Proceedings of the National Conference on Day Care Services. Children's Bureau Publication No. 438, pp. 121–34. Washington, D.C.

O'Leary, K. D., and Becker, W. 1967. Behavior modification of an adjustment class: A token reinforcement program. *Exceptional Children*, 33: 637–42.

O'Leary, K. D.; Becker, W. C.; Evans, M. B.; and Saudargas, R. A. 1969. A token reinforcement program in a public school: A replication and systematic analysis. *J. Applied Behavior Analysis*, 2: 3–13.

Ourth, L. and Brown, K. 1961. Inadequate mothering and disturbance in the neonatal period. *Child Development*, 32: 287–95.

Packard, R. G. 1970. The control of "classroom attention:" A group contingency for complex behavior. *J. Applied Behavior Analysis*, 3: 13–28.

Palmer, F. H. 1961. Critical periods of development: Report on a conference. *Items*, 15 (2).

Panyan, M.; Boozer, H.; and Morris, N. 1970. Feedback to attendants as a reinforcer for applying operant techniques. *J. Applied Behavior Analysis*, 3: 1–4.

Papanek, E. 1956. Das Kinderheim: Seine Theorie und Praxis im Lichte der Individualpsychologie (The children's home: Its theory and practice in the light of individual psychology). *Acta Psychotherapeutica et Psychosomatica Ortho-paedagogica*, 2: 53–72.

Parnass-Honig, T. 1958. The significance of Youth Aliyah education for the social integration of immigrant youth from rural settlements. *Megamot*, 9 (2): 124–33 (Hebrew).

———— 1959. *A follow up on graduates of an agricultural institution for children from new immigrants' settlements*. Jerusalem: Szold Institution (Hebrew).

Parsons, T., Bales, R. F. et al. 1955. *Family socialization and interaction process*. Glencoe, Ill.: Free Press.

Patterson, G. R., and Reid, J. B. 1970. Reciprocity and coercion: Two facets of social systems. In C. Neuringer and J. L. Michael (eds.), *Behavior modification in clinical psychology*. New York: Appleton-Century-Crofts.

Patterson, G. R.; Shaw, D. A.; and Ebner, M. J. 1969. Teachers, peers and parents as agents of change in the classroom. In F. A. Benson (ed.), *Modifying deviant social behaviors in various classroom settings*. Monograph No. 1. Department of Special Education, College of Education, University of Oregon, Eugene, Oregon (February): 13–47.

Patton, R. G., and Gardner, L. I. 1962. Influence of family environment on growth: The syndrome of "maternal deprivation." *Pediatrics*, 30 (6): 957–62.

Paul, G. L. 1966. *Insight vs. desensitization in psychotherapy*. Stanford, Calif.: Stanford University Press.

———— 1969. Chronic mental patients: Current status—future directions. *Psychological Bulletin*, 71: 81–94.

Paul VI. 1963. *Summi Dei verbum* (N.C.W.C. trans.) Boston: St. Paul editions.

Pavenstedt, E. 1965. A comparison of the child-rearing environment of upper-lower and very low-lower class families. *Am. J. Orthopsychiatry*, 35 (1): 89–98.

Pavenstedt, E. (ed.) 1967. *The drifters: Children of disorganized lower-class families*. Boston: Little, Brown.

Pearson, J. W., and Palmer, T. B. 1967. *The group home project: First year progress report*. Research Report No. 1. California Youth Authority.

Pease, D., and Gardner, D. B. 1958. Research on the effects of non-continuous mothering. *Child Development*, 29 (1): 141–48.

Peck, R. F., Havighurst, R. J. et al. 1960. *The psychology of character development*. New York: Wiley.

Peller, L. E. 1943. Institutions must be good. *Survey*, 79 (11).

Peshkin, M. M. 1930. Asthma in children. *J. Diseases of Children*, 39 (4): 774–81.

———— 1959. Intractable asthma of childhood. *International Archives of Allergy*, 15 (1–3): 91–112.

Petrikeev, D., and Dubkovski, E. 1956. What must the Shkola-Internat be like? *Uchitel'skaya Gazeta* (Teacher's Newspaper), 18 April (Russian).

Petrov, A. A. 1961. *The future belongs to the boarding schools*. Moscow: All Union Society for the Dissemination of Political and Scientific Knowledge (Russian).

Pettigrew, T. F. 1967. *Race and equal educational opportunity*. Paper presented at the Symposium on the Implications of the Coleman Report on Equality of Educational Opportunity at the annual convention of the American Psychological Association.

Phillips, E. L. 1968. Achievement place: Token reinforcement procedures in a home-style rehabilitation setting for 'pre-delinquent' boys. *J. Applied Behavior Analysis,* 1: 213–21.

Piaget, J. 1952. *The origins of intelligence in children.* New York: International Universities Press.

———— 1967. *Six psychological studies.* Translated and edited by A. Tenzer and D. Elkind. New York: Random House.

Piliavin, I. 1963. Conflict between cottage parents and caseworkers. *Social Service Review,* 37 (1): 17–25.

Pinneau, S. R. 1955. The infantile disorders of hospitalism and anaclitic depressions. *Psychological Bulletin,* 52: 429–52.

Pius XII. 1958. Menti nostrae. In P. Veuillot (ed.) *The Catholic priesthood according to the teachings of the church: Papal documents from Pius X to Pius XII,* pp. 155–204. Westminster, Md.: Newman.

Polier, J. W. 1958. *Parental rights.* New York: Child Welfare League of America.

Polsky, H. W. 1962. *Cottage six: The social system of delinquent boys in residential treatment.* New York: Russell Sage Foundation. Republished, Wiley, 1967.

Polsky, H. W.; and Claster, D. S.; with Goldberg, C. 1968. *The dynamics of residential treatment.* Chapel Hill: University of North Carolina Press.

Polsky, H. W.; Karp, I.; Beman, I.; and Gordon, T. 1961. *Toward a general theory of residential research and treatment conceptualization and observing individual, social, and cultural processes.* Paper read at Eastern Regional Conference, Child Welfare League of America, New York.

Pratt, C. 1966. Foster parents as agency employees. *Children,* 13 (1): 14–15.

Pravda. 1964. Work passport, 27 February.

Premack, D. 1965. Reinforcement theory. In D. Levine (ed.), *Nebraska symposium on motivation,* pp. 123–80. Lincoln: University of Nebraska Press.

Pringle, M. L. K. 1951. Social maturity and social competence. *Educational Research,* 3: Part I, 113–28; Part II, 183–95.

———— 1965. *Deprivation and education.* London: Longmans.

Pringle, M. L. K.; and Bossio, V. 1965. Intellectual, emotional and social development of deprived children. In M. L. K. Pringle, *Deprivation and education.* London: Longmans. First appeared in *Vita Humana,* 1 (2), 1958, 65–92.

———— 1960. Early prolonged separation and emotional maladjustment. *J. Child Psychology and Psychiatry,* 1: 37–48.

Provence, S. 1967. *Guide for the care of infants in groups.* New York: Child Welfare League of America.

Prugh, D. G., and Harlow, R. 1962. *Deprivation of maternal care.* Public Health Papers No. 14. Geneva: World Health Organization.

Przetacznikowa, M. 1960. Mental development in the first year of life in three kinds of educational environments. *Psychologia Wychowawcza,* 3 (17): 32–46 (Polish).

Pyzhko, E. 1963. The moral code is the center of attention. *Shkola-Internat,* 1 (Russian).

Rabin, A. I. 1957. Personality maturity of kibbutz and non-kibbutz children as reflected in the Rorschach. *J. Projective Techniques,* 21: 152.

———— 1965. *Growing up in the kibbutz.* New York: Springer.

Rapaport, Ch., and Arad, R. 1969. *Evaluation of the educational process in the Mechinot* (Preparatory classes for disadvantaged children). Research Report No. 136. Jerusalem: Szold Institute.

Rasmussen, J. E. 1961. *An experimental approach to the concept of ego identity as related to character disorders.* Doctoral dissertation. Washington, D.C.: American University.

Rat'kova, S. I. 1961. The upbringer and upper classmen in the internat. In E. I. Afanasenko and A. I. Kairov (eds.), *Five years of boarding schools.* pp. 61–195. Moscow: RSFSR Academy of Pedagogical Sciences Press (Russian).

Raven, J. C. 1960. *Guide to the standard progressive matrices, sets A, B, C, D, and E.* London: H. K. Lewis Ltd.

Redfield, R. 1941. *The folk culture of Yucatan.* Chicago: University of Chicago Press.

Redl, F., and Wineman, D. 1951. *Children who hate.* Glencoe, Ill.: Free Press.

Reeder, R. R. 1925. Our orphaned asylums. *Survey,* 54: 283–87, 313.

Rettig, S. 1966. Relation of social systems to intergenerational changes in moral attitudes. *J. Personality and Social Psychology,* 4 (4): 409–14.

Rheingold, H. L. 1956. The modification of social responsiveness in institutional babies. *Monographs of the Society for Research in Child Development,* 21 (63).

———— 1960. The measurement of maternal care. *Child Development,* 31: 565–75.

Rheingold, H. L.; Gewirtz, J. L.; and Ross, H. W. 1959. Social conditioning of vocalizations in the infant. *J. Comparative and Physiological Psychology,* 52: 68–73.

Riecken, H. W. 1952. *The volunteer work camp: A psychological evaluation.* Reading, Mass.: Addison-Wesley.

Riecken, H. W., and Homans, G. C. 1954. Psychological aspects of social structure. In G. Lindzey (ed.), *Handbook of social psychology, Vol. II.* Cambridge, Mass.: Addison-Wesley.

Ripin, R. 1930. A study of the infant's feeding reactions during the first six months of life. *Archives of Psychology,* 18 (116): 5–44.

Risley, T. R. 1968. The effects and side effects of punishing the autistic behaviors of a deviant child. *J. Applied Behavior Analysis,* 1: 21–34.

Robinson, H. B. 1969. From infancy through school. *Children,* 16: 61–62.

Rodgers, R. R.; Bronfenbrenner, U.; and Devereaux, E. C., Jr. 1968. Standards of social behavior among school children in four cultures. *International J. Psychology* 3 (1): 31–41.

Rokeach, M. 1961. Authority, authoritarianism, and conformity. In I. A. Berg and B. M. Bass (eds.), *Conformity and deviation,* pp. 230–57. New York: Harper.

Rokeach, M., and Eglash, A. 1956. A scale for measuring intellectual conviction. *J. Social Psychology,* 44: 135–41.

Rosen, B. C. 1955. The reference group approach to the parental factor in attitude and behavior formation. *Social Forces,* 34: 137–144.

Rosenzweig, S.; Fleming, E.; and Rosenzweig, L. 1948. The children's form of the Rosenzweig picture-frustration study. *J. Psychology,* 26: 141–91.

Ross, R. R. 1967. "Application of operant conditioning procedures to the behavioral modification of institutionalized adolescent offenders." University of Waterloo (September).

Schachter, S. 1959. *The psychology of affiliation.* Stanford, Calif.: Stanford University Press.

Schaefer, H. H., and Martin, P. L. 1966. Behavioral therapy for "apathy" of hospitalized schizophrenics. *Psychological Reports,* 19: 1147–58.

———— 1969. *Behavioral therapy.* New York: McGraw-Hill.

Schaffer, H. R., and Emerson, P. E. 1964. The development of social attachments in infancy. *Monographs of the Society for Research in Child Development,* 29 (Whole No. 94) : 1–77.

Schlossman, A. 1920. Zur Frage der Säuglingssterblichkeit (On the issue of infant mortality). *Münchner Med. Wochenschrift,* 67.

Schmidt, G. W., and Ulrich, R. E. 1969. Effects of group contingent events upon classroom noise. *J. Applied Behavior Analysis,* 2: 171–79.

Schorr, A. L. 1965. Mirror, mirror on the wall. . . . Review of *Girls at Vocational High. Social Work,* 10 (3) : 112–13.

——— 1966. *Poor kids.* New York: Basic Books.

Schwebel, M. 1965. *Who is educable?* New York University Bulletin V. New York: New York University.

Sears, R. R.; Maccoby, E. E.; and Levin, H. 1957. *Patterns of child rearing.* Evanston, Ill.: Row, Peterson.

Sears, R. S.; Rau, L.; and Alpert R. 1965. *Identification and child rearing.* Stanford, Calif.: Stanford University Press.

Sechehaye, M. A. 1951. *Symbolic realization.* New York: International Universities Press.

Segal, J. 1957. Correlates of Collaboration and resistance behavior among U. S. Army POWs in Korea. *J. Social Issues,* 8 (3) : 31–40.

Seibert, U. 1964. Die Fremdplazierung von Kindern und das Kinderdorf (The placement of foster children and the Children's Village). *Unsere Jugend,* 16 (1) : 8–13. A report of an international seminar held in Salzburg, September, 1963.

Seiden, R. 1965. Salutary effects of maternal separation. *Social Work,* 10 (4) : 25–29.

Sherif, M. 1936. *The psychology of social norms.* New York: Harper & Bros.

——— 1956. Experiments in group conflict. *Scientific American,* 195: 54–58.

——— 1958. Superordinate goals in the reduction of intergroup tensions. *American J. Sociology,* 63: 349–56.

Sherif, M.; Harvey, O. J.; White, B. J.; Hood, W. R.; and Sherif, C. W. 1961. *Intergroup conflict and cooperation: The Robber's Cave experiment.* Norman: University of Oklahoma Press.

Sherif, M., and Sherif, C. W. 1964. *Reference groups: Exploration into conformity and deviation of adolescents.* New York: Harper & Row.

Sherif, M., and Sherif, C. W. (eds.) 1965. *Problems of youth: Transition to adulthood in a changing world.* Chicago: Aldine.

Sherman, J. A., and Baer, D. M. 1969. Appraisal of operant therapy techniques with children and adults. In C. M. Franks (ed.), *Behavior therapy: Appraisal and status,* pp. 192–219. New York: McGraw-Hill.

Shirvindt, B. E., et al. 1961. Bring up people with great spirit and high ideals. In E. I. Afanasenko and A. I. Kairov (eds.), *Five years of boarding schools,* pp. 77–105. Moscow: RSFSR Academy of Pedagogical Sciences Press (Russian).

Shoben, E. J. 1956. Anxiety versus immaturity in neurosis and its treatment. *Am. J. Orthopsychiatry,* 25: 71–80.

——— 1957. Toward a concept of the normal personality. *American Psychologist,* 12: 183–89.

Simonsen, K. M. 1947. *Examination of children from children's homes and day nurseries.* Copenhagen: Busck.

Simpson, B. R. 1939. The wandering I. Q. *J. Psychology,* 7: 351–67.

Skeels, H. M. 1936. Mental development of children in foster homes. *Pedagogical Seminar and J. Genetic Psychology,* 49: 91–106.

———— 1938. Mental development of children in foster homes. *J. Consulting Psychology*, 2: 33–43.

———— 1940. Some Iowa studies of the mental growth of children in relation to differentials of the environment: A summary. *39th Yearbook, National Society for the Study of Education*, 39 (II): 281–308.

———— 1942. A study of the effects of differential stimulation on mentally retarded children: A followup report. *Am. J. Mental Deficiency*, 46: 340–50.

———— 1966. Adult status of children with contrasting early life experiences. *Monographs of the Society for Research in Child Development*, 31 (3): 1–65.

Skeels, H. M., and Dye, H. B. 1939. A study of the effects of differential stimulation on mentally retarded children. *Proceedings and Addresses of the American Association on Mental Deficiency*, 44 (1): 114–36.

Skeels, H. M. and Fillmore, E. A. 1937. The mental development of children from underprivileged homes. *J. Genetic Psychology*, 50: 427–39.

Skeels, H. M. and Skodak, M. 1965. Techniques for a high-yield follow-up study in the field. *Public Health Reports*, 80: 249–57.

Skeels, H. M.; Updegraff, R.; Wellman, B. L.; and Williams, H. M. 1938. A study of environmental stimulation: An orphanage preschool project. *University of Iowa Studies in Child Welfare*, 14 (4): 7–191.

Skinner, B. F. 1960. *Walden II*. New York: Macmillan.

Skodak, M. 1939. Children in foster homes: A study of mental development. *University of Iowa Studies in Child Welfare*, 16 (1).

Skodak, M., and Skeels, H. M. 1945. A follow-up study of children in adoptive homes. *J. Genetic Psychology*, 66: 21–58.

———— 1949. A final follow-up study of one hundred adopted children. *J. Genetic Psychology*, 75: 85–125.

Slingerland, W. H. 1919. *Child placing in families*. New York: Russell Sage Foundation.

Smilansky, M.; Nevo, D.; and Marbach, S. 1966. *Identification and intellectual advancement of gifted culturally disadvantaged youth in post-elementary education*. Technical Report I. Jerusalem: Szold Institute (October).

Solberg, S. 1961. *Research on the study achievements of mechina class pupils at Ramat Hadassah*. Mimeographed.

———— 1970. *Psychological and social aspects of intelligence and school adjustment in oriental immigrant children in Israel*. Asses, The Netherlands: Van Gorcum, (Dutch).

Solomon, R. L. 1964. Punishment. *Am. Psychologist*, 19: 239–53.

Solzhenitsyn, A. 1963. *One day in the life of Ivan Denisovich*. New York: Frederick A. Praeger.

SOS Messenger. No. 2, 3 (1963), 4, 5, 6 (1964) and 7 (1965). Innsbruck: International Office, The Hermann Gmeiner Fund.

Spiro, M. E. 1956. *Kibbutz: Venture in utopia*. Cambridge, Mass.: Harvard University Press.

———— 1958. *Children of the kibbutz*. Cambridge, Mass.: Harvard University Press.

———— 1960. Is the family universal?—The Israeli case. In N. W. Bell and E. R. Vogel (eds.), *A modern introduction to the family*, pp. 64–75. Glencoe, Ill. Free Press.

Spitz, R. A. 1945–46. Hospitalism: An inquiry into the genesis of psychiatric conditions in early childhood. *The Psychoanalytic Study of the Child* 1: 53–74; 2: 113–77.

———— 1965. *The first year of life.* New York: Norton.

Spitz, R. A., and Wolf, C. M. 1946. Anaclitic depression: An inquiry into the genesis of psychotic conditions in early childhood. *The Psychoanalytic Study of the Child* 2: 313–42.

Staats, A. W. 1965. A case in and a strategy for the extension of learning principles to problems of human behavior. In L. Krasner and L. P. Ullman (eds.), *Research in behavior modification,* pp. 27–55. New York: Holt, Rinehart & Winston.

Stanton, A. A., and Schwartz, M. S. 1954. *The mental hospital.* New York: Basic Books.

Steele, B. F., and Pollock, C. B. 1968. A psychiatric study of parents who abuse infants and small children. In R. E. Helfer and C. H. Kempe (eds.), *The battered child.* Chicago: University of Chicago Press.

Stern, W. 1930. *Psychology of early childhood.* London.

Stock, P., and Theler, H. A. 1958. *Emotional dynamics and group culture.* New York: New York University Press.

Stoddard, G. D. 1940. Intellectual development of the child: An answer to the critics of the Iowa studies. *School and Society,* 51: 529–36.

Stolz, L. M. 1960. Effects of maternal employment on children: Evidence from research. *Child Development,* 31 (4): 749–82.

Stone, C. L. 1960. Some family characteristics of socially active and inactive teenagers. *Coordinator,* 8: 53–57.

Stone, H. B. 1969. *Reflections on foster care.* New York: Child Welfare League of America.

Stouffer, S. A., et al. 1949. *The American soldier: Adjustment during army life: Studies in social psychology in World War II.* 4 vol. Princeton, N.J: Princeton University Press.

Street, D.; Vinter, R. D.; and Perrow, C. 1966. *Organization for treatment.* New York: Free Press.

Strumilin, S. G. 1960. Working life and communism. *Novyi Mir* (New World), 36 (7): 203–20 (Russian).

Strunk, O., Jr. 1958. Relationship between self-reports and adolescent religiosity. *Psychological Reports,* 4: 683–86.

Stuart, R. B. 1969. Critical reappraisal and reformulation of selected "mental health" programs. In L. A. Hamerlynck, P. O. Davidson, and L. E. Acker (eds.), *Behavior modification and ideal health services.* pp. 5–100. Alberta, Canada: The University of Calgary.

———— 1970. *Trick or treatment: How and when psychotherapy fails.* Champaign, Ill.: Research Press.

Sulla, P. 1957. The year's work in Shkoly-Internaty. In *Sovetskaya Moldavia,* 10 May, p. 2. Translated in *Current Digest of the Soviet Press,* 9 (21): 40–41.

Sulzbacher, S. I., and Houser, J. E. 1970. A tactic to eliminate disruptive behaviors in the classroom: Group contingent consequences. In R. Ulrich, T. Stachnik and J. Mabry (eds.), *Control of human behavior II: From cure to prevention,* pp. 187–89. Glenview, Ill.: Scott, Foresman.

Super, A. S. 1956. *Alonei Yitzhak, A Youth Village in Israel.* Jerusalem: Jerusalem Post Press.

Swift, J. W. 1964. Effects of early group experience: The nursery school and day nursery. In M. L. Hoffman and L. W. Hoffman (eds.), *Review of child development research, Vol I.* New York: Russell Sage Foundation.

Sykes, G. M. 1958. *The society of captives.* Princeton: Princeton University Press.

Szczurzewski, A. 1962. *Social Insurances in Poland*. Warsaw: Wydawnictwo Zwiazkowe (Polish).

Talks with warriors. 1967. Tel-Aviv, Israel: Achdut Press (Hebrew).

Talmon-Garber, Y. 1962. Social change and family structure. *International Social Science Journal*, 14 (3): 468–87.

Tamar. 1958. The diary of Tamar. Extracts of the diary and letters written between the ages of 15 and 19 by a kibbutz girl who died of leukemia at the age of 21. *Ofakim*, 3–4: 327–412 (Hebrew).

Tamari, M. 1960. *Youth Aliyah in a religious kibbutz*. Jerusalem: Youth Aliyah.

Tate, B. G. 1968. An automated system of reinforcing and recording retardate work behavior. *J. Applied Behavioral Analysis*, 1: 347.

Taylor, D. A., and Starr, P. 1967. Foster parenting: An integrative review of the literature. *Child Welfare*, 46 (7): 371–85.

Templin, M. C., and Darley, F. L. 1960. *The Templin-Darley tests of articulation*. Iowa City: University of Iowa Bureau of Education Research and Service.

Terman, L. M. 1916. *The measurement of intelligence*. Boston: Houghton Mifflin.

Terman, L. M. and Merrill, M. A. 1937. *Measuring intelligence*. Cambridge, Mass.: Houghton Mifflin.

———— 1960. *Stanford-Binet Intelligence Scale*. Boston: Houghton Mifflin.

Tesarek, A. 1966. Das Kinderdorf im gesellschaftlichen Spannungsfeld (The children's village in social context). *Blätter der Wohlfahrtspflege*, 2. Stuttgart: (February): 39–40.

Tharp, R. G,, and Wetzel, R. J. 1969. *Behavior modification in the natural environment*. New York: Academic Press.

Theis, S. V. 1924. *How foster children turn out*. New York: State Charities Aid Association.

Thibaut, J. W., and Kelley, H. H. 1959. *The social psychology of groups*. New York: Wiley.

Thomas, E. J. 1968. Selected sociobehavioral techniques and principles: An approach to interpersonal helping. *Social Work*, 13: 12–26.

Tierney, L. 1963. *Children who need help: A study of child welfare policy and administration in Victoria (Australia)*. Melbourne University Press.

Tillich, P. 1962. The philosophy of social work. *Social Service Review*, 36 (1): 13–16.

Timasheff, N. S. 1960. The attempt to abolish the family in Russia. In N. W. Bell and E. R. Vogel (eds.), *A modern introduction to the family*, pp. 55–63. Glencoe, Ill.: Free Press.

Titmuss, R. M. 1950. *Problems of social policy*. London: His Majesty's Stationery Office and Longmans, Green.

Tolman, E. C. 1932. *Purposive behavior in animals and men*. New York: Century.

Townsend, P. 1962. *The last refuge*. London: Routledge and Kegan Paul.

Trasler, G. 1960. *In place of parents: A study of foster care*. London: Routledge and Kegan Paul.

Trotzkey, E. 1930. *Institutional care and placing-out*. Chicago: Marks Nathan Jewish Orphan Home.

Traux, C. B., and Carkhuff, R. R. 1967. *Toward effective counseling and psychotherapy: Training and practice*. Chicago: Aldine.

Turiel, E. 1966. An experimental test of the sequentiality of developmental stages in the child's moral judgment. *J. Personality and Social Psychology,* 3: 611–18.

Tyler, L. E. 1964. The antecedents of two varieties of vocational interests. *Genetic Psychology Monographs,* 70: 177–227.

Tyler, V. O., and Brown, G. D. 1967. The use of swift, brief isolation as a group control device for institutionalized delinquents. *Behavior Research and Therapy,* 5: 1–9.

Ulhorn, G. 1883. *Christian charity in the ancient church.* New York: Charles Scribner's Sons.

Ullman, L. P., and Krasner, L. 1963. *Case studies in behavior modification.* New York: Holt, Rinehart & Winston.

——— 1969. *A Psychological approach to abnormal behavior.* Englewood Cliffs, N.J.: Prentice-Hall.

Ulrich, R.; Stachnik, T.; and Mabry, J. 1970. *Control of human behavior II: From cure to prevention.* Glenview, Ill.: Scott, Foresman.

UNESCO. 1948. *Care of homeless children.* New York: United Nations.

U.S. Bureau of the Census, 1960. 1963a *Methodology and scores of socio-economic status.* Working Paper 15. Washington, D.C.: Government Printing Office.

——— 1963b. *U.S. census population, 1960. Vol. I. Characteristics of the population.* Part 17, Iowa. Washington, D.C.: U.S. Government Printing Office

——— 1963c. *U.S. census population, 1960. Detailed characteristics, United States summary. Final report.* PC(L)–1D. Washington, D.C.: Government Printing Office.

U.S. Children's Bureau. 1927. *Handbook for the use of boards of directors, superintendents, and staffs of institutions for dependent children.* Washington, D.C.: Government Printing Office.

——— 1929. *Foster home care for dependent children.* Washington, D.C.: Government Printing Office.

——— 1964. *Child welfare statistics.* Statistical series. 82. Washington, D.C.: Government Printing Office.

——— 1965. *Child welfare statistics—1965.* Washington, D.C.: Department of Health, Education and Welfare.

——— 1966. *Foster care of children: Major national trends and prospects.* Washington, D.C.: Government Printing Office.

U.S. Congress, Committee on Government Operations. 1966. *Hearings before the subcommittee on executive reorganization, federal role in urban affairs.* 89th Cong., 2d sess., August 29–30, Part 5.

U.S. Senate. 1909. *Proceedings of the conference on the care of dependent children, 1909.* Senate Document 721.Washington, D.C.: Government Printing Office.

Updegraff, R. 1932. The determination of a reliable intelligence quotient for the young child. *J. Genetic Psychology,* 41: 152–66.

Van Ingen, P. 1915. Infant mortality in institutions. *Proceedings of the National Conference of Charities and Correction.* Chicago: The National Conference of Charities and Correction.

Vardi, D. (ed.) 1956. "What young people say about their education in the kibbutz." Writings of students of the graduating class of institutions of the Hakibbutz Haartzi. *Ofakim* 2–3 (August): 268–75.

Vincent, C. E. 1961. *Unmarried mothers.* New York: Free Press.

Vinter, R. D. 1963. Analysis of treatment organizations. *Social Work,* 8 (3):
3–15.

Viteles, H. 1967. *The history of the co-operative movement in Israel. Book two:
The evolution of the kibbutz movement.* London: Vallentine-Mitchell.

Wachstein, S. 1963. An Austrian solution to the problem of child placement.
Child Welfare, 42 (2): 82–85.

Walski, W. 1962. "Language development of normal children, four, five and six
years of age as measured by the Michigan Picture Language Inventory." Doctoral dissertation, University of Michigan.

Warner, W. L.; Meeker, M.; and Eells, H. 1960. *Social class in America: The
evaluation of status.* New York: Harper.

Weber, M. 1947. *The theory of social and economic organization.* Translated by
A. M. Henderson and T. Parsons. Glencoe, Ill.: Free Press.

Webster, R. L. 1970. Stuttering: A way to eliminate it and a way to explain it.
In R. Ulrich, T. Stachnik and J. Mabry (eds.), *Control of human behavior, II:
From cure to prevention,* pp. 157–60. Glenview, Ill.: Scott, Foresman.

Wechsberg, J. 1957. They learn to smile again. *Saturday Evening Post,* 5 January: 30–31, 74–75.

———— 1962. Profiles: A house called peace. *New Yorker.* 22 December:
39–65.

Wechsler, D. 1967. *A manual for the Wechsler preschool and primary scale of
intelligence.* New York: Psychological Corporation.

Weeks, A. L., 1965. The boarding school. *Survey,* 56: 81–94.

———— 1968. *The first Bolshevik: A political biography of Peter Tkachev.* New
York: New York University Press.

Weiner, H. 1962. Some effects of response cost upon human operant behavior. *J.
Experimental Analysis and Behavior,* 5: 201–08.

Weiner, O. D. 1961. Found: A home for Suzie. *Child Welfare,* 40 (7): 19–20,
23.

Weinstein, E. A. 1960. *The self-image of the foster child.* New York: Russell
Sage Foundation.

Weinstein, L. 1965. Social schemata of emotionally disturbed boys. *J. Abnormal
Psychology,* 70 (6): 457–61.

———— 1969. Project Re-Ed schools for emotionally disturbed children: Effectiveness as viewed by referring agencies, parents and teachers. *Exceptional
Children,* 35: 703–711.

Weisberg, P. 1963. Social and non-social conditioning of infant vocalizations.
Child Development, 34 (2): 377–88.

Weisen, A. E.; Hartley, G.; Richardson, C.; and Roske, A. 1967. The retarded
child as a reinforcing agent. *J. Experimental Child Psychology,* 5: 109–113.

Wellman, B. L. 1938. Our changing concept of intelligence. *J. Consulting Psychology,* 2: 97–107.

Werner, H. 1948. *Comparative psychology of mental development.* New York:
International Universities Press.

Werth, A. 1962. *Russia under Khrushchev.* New York: Crest Books.

"What must the Shkola-Internat be like?" 1956 discussion, *Uchitel's Gazeta*
(Teacher's Newspaper) (18 April): 3.

Wheeler, S. 1966. The structure of formally organized socialization settings. In
O. G. Brim, Jr. and S. Wheeler, *Socialization after childhood: Two essays.*
New York: Wiley.

White, B. L., and Held, R. 1966. Plasticity of sensorimotor development in the
human infant. In J. F. Rosenblith and W. Allinsmith (eds.), *The causes of be-*

havior II—Readings in child development and educational psychology, pp. 60–70. Boston: Allyn and Bacon.

White House Conference on Child Health and Protection. 1931. *Addresses and Abstracts of Committee Reports, 1930*. New York: Appleton-Century.

White, R. K., and Lippitt, R. 1960. *Autocracy and democracy*. New York: Harper & Row.

Whiting, J. W. M.; Kluckhohn, R.; and Anthony, A. 1958. The function of male initiation ceremonies at puberty. In E. E. Maccoby et al. (eds.), *Readings in social psychology*, 3d ed. pp. 358–70. New York: Henry Holt.

Wilson, A. B. 1959. Residential segregation of social classes and aspirations of high school boys. *American Sociological Review*, 24: 836–45.

Witkin, H. A. 1969. Social influences in the development of cognitive style. In D. A. Goslin (ed.), *Handbook of socialization theory and research*. Chicago: Rand McNally.

Witmer, H. L. 1965. National facts and figures about children without families. *J. Am. Academy of Child Psychiatry*, 4 (2): 249–53.

Witmer, H. L. (ed.) 1967. *On rearing infants and young children in institutions*. Washington, D.C.: U.S. DHEW, Children's Bureau.

Witmer, H. L. et al. 1963. *Independent adoptions: A follow-up study*. New York: Russell Sage Foundation.

Wodarski, J. S.; Hamblin, R. L.; Buckholdt, D. R.; and Ferritor, D. E. 1971. Group reinforcement contingencies and helping behaviors in inner-city classrooms. St. Louis: Washington University.

Wolf, M. M.; Giles, D. K.; and Hall, R. V. 1968. Experiments with token reinforcement in a remedial classroom. *Behaviour Research and Therapy*, 6: 51–64.

Wolf, M. M.; Risley, T.; and Mees, H. L. 1964. Application of operant conditioning to the behavior problems of an autistic child. *Behaviour Research and Therapy*, 1: 305–12.

Wolff, D. 1964. Die unkritische Einstellung der Oeffentlichkeit zu pädagogischen Fragen—und das SOS-Kinderdorf. (The uncritical attitude toward educational issues and the SOS-Children's Villages). *Unsere Jugend*, 16 (10): 457–59.

Wolins, M. 1958. Cost of care in a children's institution. In E. E. Schwartz and M. Wolins, *Cost analysis in child welfare services*. Washington, D.C.: Government Printing Office.

——— 1962. *A manual for cost analysis in institutions for children*. Parts I and II. New York: Child Welfare League of America.

——— 1963a. Some theory and practice in child care: A cross-cultural view. *Child Welfare*, 42 (8): 369–77, 399.

——— 1963b. *Selecting foster parents*. New York: Columbia University Press.

——— 1964. Political orientation, social reality, and child welfare. *Social Service Review*, 38 (4): 429–42.

——— 1965a. Group care of children: The problem of legitimacy. In H. Fradkin (ed.), *Organization of services that will best meet needs of children*. New York: Columbia University School of Social Work.

——— 1965b. Another view of group care. *Child Welfare*, 44 (1): 10–18.

——— 1969. Group care: Friend or foe? *Social Work*, 14 (1): 35–53.

Wolins, M., and Piliavin, I. 1964. *Institution or foster family: A century of debate*. New York: Child Welfare League of America.

Woodworth, R. S. 1941. *Heredity and environment: A critical survey of recently published material on twins and foster children*. Bulletin 47. Social Science Research Council.

Worling, R. V. 1966. Maternal deprivation—a reexamination. *Canada's Mental Health,* 14 (4): 3–11.

Wortis, H., et al. 1963. Child-rearing practices in a low socioeconomic group. *Pediatrics,* 32: 298–307.

Yabolokov, L. A., and Kustkov, S. I. 1959. Means of forming a student collective in the Shkola-Internat, on the basis of experience. *Sovetskaya Pedagogika* (Soviet Education), 23 (10): 93–101 (Russian).

Yarrow, L. J. 1961. Maternal deprivation: Toward an empirical and conceptual re-evaluation. *Psychological Bulletin,* 58 (6): 459–90.

———— 1964. Separation from parents during early childhood. In M. L. Hoffman and L. W. Hoffman (eds.), *Review of child development research, Vol. I,* pp. 89–130. New York: Russell Sage Foundation.

Yitshaki, F. 1968. *Open Gates.* Bulletin 43. Jerusalem: The Jewish Agency, Child and Youth Aliyah Public Relations Section (May).

Yitshaki, S. 1956. Our educational way. *Ofakim,* 4 (36): 379–84 (Hebrew).

Yonemura, M., and Jones, R. 1962. Nursery school in an institutional setting. *Child Welfare,* 41 (6): 256–60, 269.

Youmans, E. G. 1956. Occupational expectations of twelfth grade Michigan boys. *J. Experimental Education,* 24: 259–71.

Young, L. 1964. *Wednesday's child.* New York: McGraw-Hill.

Yugoslav National Board of Social Work. 1956. *Social Welfare in Yugoslavia.* Belgrade.

Zaporozhets, A. V. 1960. *The development of voluntary movements.* Moscow: Academia Pedagogicheskich Nauk (Academy of Pedagogical Sciences) (Russian).

Zax, M.; Gardiner, D. H.; and Lowy, D. G. 1964. Extreme response tendency as a function of emotional adjustment. *J. Abnormal and Social Psychology,* 69 (6): 654–57.

Zimmerman, E. H.; Zimmerman, J.; and Russell, C. D. 1969. Differential effects of token reinforcement on instruction-following behavior in retarded students instructed as a group. *J. Applied Behavior Analysis,* 2: 101–12.

Name Index

Subject Index

455